English Medieval Nar
the Thirteenth and Fourtee.

English Medieval Narrative in the Thirteenth and Fourteenth Centuries

Piero Boitani

translated by Joan Krakover Hall

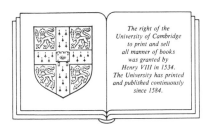

The right of the
University of Cambridge
to print and sell
all manner of books
was granted by
Henry VIII in 1534.
The University has printed
and published continuously
since 1584.

CAMBRIDGE UNIVERSITY PRESS

Cambridge

London   New York   New Rochelle

Melbourne   Sydney

Published by the Press Syndicate of the University of Cambridge
The Pitt Building, Trumpington Street, Cambridge CB2 1RP
32 East 57th Street, New York, NY 10022, USA
10 Stamford Road, Oakleigh, Melbourne 3166, Australia

First published 1982
First paperback edition 1986

Printed in Great Britain at
the University Press, Cambridge

Library of Congress catalogue card number 81–17081

British Library cataloguing in publication data
Boitani, Piero
English medieval narrative in the
thirteenth and fourteenth centuries.
1. English literature – Middle English,
1100–1500 – History and criticism
I. Title   II. La narrativa del medioevo
Inglese. *English*
820.9'0001   PR255
ISBN 0 521 23562 6 hard covers
ISBN 0 521 31149 7 paperback

Contents

To Joan

Preface to the English edition

In this book I have tried to trace the growth of medieval English narrative in the thirteenth and fourteenth centuries. This might seem an ambitious undertaking if I proposed to offer a single consistent and absolutely original thesis. My aim, however, is much more modest: it is to attempt a broad reconstruction of this development, within the framework of certain trends that I consider important, illustrating it as clearly as possible and adding my own interpretations where I can usefully do so.

Nothing of this nature has previously been attempted for medieval English narrative, by either Italian or continental or, as far as I can discover, English critics. My first task, therefore, was to organise the material. I have done this according to a mixed set of criteria: the chapters are divided according to literary 'genres' in the traditional way, but within these the historical categories tend to overlap. Certain parts of the book are devoted to types of narrative setting, such as the dream and the vision, which do not belong to any genre; others deal with structural systems, like the story collection, which include various genres. Finally almost half the book is concerned with a single author, Chaucer, in whose work all genres and all structures come together.

My aim has been to follow the development of medieval English narrative from what seem to be its primary, almost unconscious elements, pieces of writing meant to be employed in specific ways (such as the *exempla* contained in sermons), to the use made of these elements by authors for deliberately artistic ends (for example the poet of *Patience* and *Cleanness* in the same religious sphere) and to the organisation of these elements into collections – at first mechanical or imitative (like the *Early South English Legendary* and *Handlyng Synne* on the one hand, and the various collections of 'secular' stories on the other), then more and more individual and aesthetically conscious (the great collections of Gower and Chaucer). In other words, I have tried to trace the emergence of an increasingly strong artistic, ideological and even national self-consciousness. Of course this progress was not predetermined, nor was it without parentheses: in some cases an apparently simple and naive text reveals a high degree of technical elaboration and structural and stylistic ambiguity.

Three aspects have been singled out for particular attention: structure, mimesis and style. The ways in which a narrator organises his plot, using certain devices rather than others and bringing out correspondences, parallelisms, contrasts and implications, are phenomena that must be observed if we wish to understand the nature of a narrative work. While largely avoiding generalisations, I have made use of certain indispensable modern critical concepts, such as those of Russian formalist criticism (especially Viktor Shklovsky) and studies by medievalists such as Eugene Vinaver and W. W. Ryding. Where necessary, I have given bibliographical references and summary explanations of terms and concepts appearing in the text. With regard to the question of structure, my book follows a fairly precise scheme, though not a rigid one: the movement is from simple structures and devices towards increasingly complex mechanisms that are less directly traceable to earlier models – thus, for example, from *The Fox and the Wolf* in the second chapter to *The Nun's Priest's Tale* in the last, or from *Handlyng Synne* to the *Confessio Amantis* and *The Canterbury Tales*. But structural complexity, narrative and compositional artifice, while they develop with the passing of time, can be seen even in the earliest compositions.

I use the word 'mimesis' in the sense intended by Erich Auerbach: it is the representation of reality. And I apply this concept on Auerbach's lines, by a detailed study of representation of time and space and the objects and persons that fill them, and the creation of inner, psychological dimensions with the emergence of characterisation and dialogue. As indications of the path of development of narrative art, these elements cannot be overlooked. And medieval English narrative reveals interesting features in this area, from Robert Mannyng's minute realism through the great mimetic achievement of the poet of *Sir Gawain*, to Chaucer's subtle and complex realism – and, on the other hand, in the representation in *Sir Orfeo*, *Pearl* and *Piers Plowman* of an ideal, enchanted or metaphysical world. Here too, we find no water-tight categories; mimesis can coexist with a generic mode of narration, often within the same genre or even the same text.

Structure and mimesis are but particular aspects of the general style of a work. Together with these, I have considered others: the presence or absence of the author and/or narrator; monologue, dialogue and polyphony; figures of thought and speech; *topoi* and types; forms and genres and their 'contamination'; unity or plurality of styles and registers. It would be impossible and out of place here to mention all those to whom I am indebted for the theoretical and practical approaches that have gone into this treatment; these are acknowledged in the notes where appropriate. Together with the works of Auerbach, the reader will find that this book refers to those of

M. Bakhtin, G. Contini, E. R. Curtius and N. Frye, in connection with problems of style applied to specific works or to literary genres. My debt to the theoretical ideas and the poetic practice of Dante is more than obvious: his works represent a model and a paradigm for the whole of the Middle Ages. Dante, the Italian writers of the fourteenth century and other medieval European works are often referred to in the pages that follow. These references are necessary in order to place English narrative in the broader perspective of the continental literary scene, with which it has many points of contact as well as many differences.

In dealing with the texts I have made free use of secondary material where I found it useful. Classical texts, where not otherwise specified, are those of the Loeb editions. The Latin Bible is the text of the *Biblia Vulgata* (Madrid, 1965). All other editions are indicated in the notes. Further-reading lists are provided for each chapter and for the first two sections of chapter 6; in the third section the notes themselves contain all the references that are necessary to an understanding of my argument.

This book is a translation of the Italian *La Narrativa del Medioevo Inglese*, published by Adriatica, Bari, in 1980. I wish to thank Dr Macinagrossa and Professor Lombardo for accepting the proposal to publish an English translation made by the Cambridge University Press. The text has been modified to adapt it to the needs of the English reader, but without radical alterations.

Both text and author owe much to the translator, Joan Hall. Valuable suggestions and criticisms have come from Sarah Stanton and Richard Beadle. And a fundamental contribution in all stages of the work's composition and translation has been made by my wife, to whom this English edition is dedicated. I should like to record my great indebtedness to the late J. A. W. Bennett, who patiently followed this work and gave me his friendship and his teaching. To my friends in Rome, Dublin and Cambridge, where I have worked on the project, I am indebted for many suggestions and for their unfailing readiness to listen. I wish to mention with particular gratitude Patrick Boyde, Paolo Chiarini, Joseph Cremona, Peter Dronke, John Fanagan, Kenelm Foster, Uberto Limentani, Vanda Perretta, Carlo Serra, Jonathan Steinberg and George Watson. Obviously none of these persons is responsible for the errors contained in the book. My thanks to the Master and Fellows of St John's College, Cambridge, for the Visiting Fellowship that, in the Michaelmas Term, 1979, allowed me to bring this work to conclusion. Finally, I wish to dedicate a special note of appreciation to the memory of Piero Mattei-Gentili and of Gwyneth Bennett.

Rome, 1980   P.B.

I

The Religious Tradition

Among the various genres into which we can classify Middle English narrative, religious narrative (that is, the kind of writing that is linked to religion by its subject, its ends, or its background) is not only among the oldest but, in its historical and sociological interest, also one of the richest. It purposely ignores any aesthetic functions or intention; its aims are those proper to ecclesiastical teaching – conversion and edification. Religious narrative was born to fulfil two needs – that of providing good examples to follow and bad ones to avoid, and that of entertaining a public that would not have taken to indoctrination pure and simple. A large number of these narratives were therefore composed to be heard, especially in sermons, and what has come down to us in manuscripts is a formalisation (due to the writing-down of what was spoken) of a kind of narrative that was originally different.

This body of literature was produced almost exclusively by churchmen. Its audience differed according to time and circumstance. Since we are here dealing with works written in English, it is obvious that this kind of literature tended to reach a wider audience as the English language spread upwards throughout the social classes. Thus, in the thirteenth century, religious literature aimed almost exclusively at priests and nuns, at the lower or middle classes and later at the heterogeneous public of the universities; in the fourteenth, and to an even greater extent in the fifteenth, its audience included the aristocracy, which until that time had had its own religious narrative, but written in French. For example, whereas the stories of the so-called 'Katherine Group' in the thirteenth century were probably written for anchorites, the *Golden Legend*, printed by Caxton in 1483, was aimed at the noble patrons who had always encouraged his work. Thus, with the passing of time, the writer himself changed: from the thirteenth-century monk or friar he became the translator-cum-entrepreneur of the fifteenth century. The figure of the intellectual, whilst remaining that of both a teacher and a moralist, little by little drifted away from ecclesiastical institutions. In adapting himself to a different public, he placed more weight on entertainment. His work, though it was still highly formalised, lost its rigidity; it now tended to be written in prose and also to become prosaic.

The changes that took place between the *Early South English Legendary* and Caxton's *Golden Legend* are self-evident.

There are three kinds of composition from which a study of these narratives must start: sermons, biblical paraphrases and hagiography. Each of these has its own history, rooted in over a thousand years of Christian civilisation, but it is impossible to reconstruct this history here, nor shall I attempt to do so. I shall rather select what seem to me the most relevant English examples of each tradition and discuss them whenever possible in chronological order. The emphasis will, however, fall on the development of different structures and modes of presentation, and on the growth of artistic aims within each genre. Swift leaps of a hundred years from one section to another are thus inevitable.

Beginning with the thirteenth century, the sermon is at the centre of the religious tradition, and in particular the sermon as it developed in the hands of the new mendicant orders – Dominicans and Franciscans – zealous in their evangelical work. From these friars come those homilies – often preached in Latin and then translated into the vernacular by monks or anchorites, or gathered by the friars themselves into collections and hand-books – which, like the *Summa Praedicandi* of the Dominican John Bromyard, attempt to organise liturgical themes into a coherent system. As Owst has pointed out,[1] it is in sermons that we find many of the elements that go into narratives: descriptions of everyday scenes, proverbs and aphorisms, all the 'bitter realism' and 'sad lament' that the preacher used to incite the faithful to repent. It is in sermons that we find (along with traditional exegesis) scenes and characters from the Bible and the lives of saints, imaginatively reworked and humanised. And, finally, it is in sermons that we find the *exemplum*, which is both the typical medieval form of perception of reality and a literary genre. Taking in history, humour, personal reminiscence, impressions of foreign people and places, classical myths and marvels, stories of animals and men, the *exemplum*, as Salvatore Battaglia says, 'created a perspective of the psychological universe, which offered its audience, time and again, an understanding of human types and the dialectic of instincts. It was, in a certain sense, the anti-Bible, or, to put it more cautiously, the Bible of everyday life, of the common man.' Precisely because it has an ethical value, the *exemplum* represents the existence of the world and of man in what Battaglia calls 'paradigmatic constancy': it becomes a form of 'historical knowledge' because history itself, in the Middle Ages, has an 'exemplary value'. At the same time, as a literary form, the *exemplum* 'gathers together, from everywhere, narrative episodes or fragments, which it reduces to their starkest outline; and in their turn these series of *exempla* come to constitute a prodigiously fertile seedbed

of themes for story-telling'. The *exemplum* uses material that 'official literature' – that of the Court and of the schools – would never dream of using:
it 'represents a sort of "sub-literature": the only one which amid the official
literary "genres" (all intent on overcoming reality and on transferring it to
the realm of the ideal), is able to deal with the facts of daily life and of
practical experience'.[2] This, as Chaucer's Pardoner points out, was what the
public wanted:

> Thanne telle I hem ensamples many oon
> Of olde stories longe tyme agoon.
> For lewed peple loven tales olde;
> Swiche thynges kan they wel reporte and holde.[3]

Collections of sermons are full of *exempla*, especially from the fourteenth
century on, as, for example, John Mirk's *Festial* (early fifteenth century), or
Jacob's Well (c. 1440), or the collection of *Middle English Sermons* in MS
Royal 18 b xxiii in the British Library, which were composed between the
end of the fourteenth century and the first decades of the fifteenth.

Perhaps one or two illustrations can best serve to clarify what I have said
up to now about *exempla*. John Mirk's *Festial* is a collection of seventy-four
sermons, each of which is dedicated to a particular day in the liturgical year.
Numbers 45 and 46 concentrate on a particular historical period, that of
Rome during Nero's reign – the period that includes the martyrdom of
St Peter and St Paul. The first of these sermons is, in fact, called 'De Festo
Apostolorum Petri et Pauli et Eorum Solempnitate'.[4] In the space of about
five modern printed pages, this text manages to concentrate many of the
events handed down by the Gospels and the Acts of the Apostles, adding
two episodes on Simon Magus that are clearly apocryphal inventions,[5] and
concluding with a story in which St Peter visits London. The occasion is
the night before the consecration of the churches of St Peter and St Paul in
London, in the times of King Aethelbert. Here, the saint performs a series
of small marvels and miracles that are very appropriate to the coming feast.
The story is, of course, edifying. But the two episodes concerning Simon
Magus, ultimately just as edifying, are written in a different register.
Simon turns a devil into a dog and throws him against Peter, but Peter
blesses the animal. The dog then turns on Simon, who is forced to abandon
the fight after most of his clothes are torn to shreds. In the second episode,
Simon decides to ascend to Heaven from the towers of the Capitol and
invokes the help of two devils to lift him up. But Peter and Paul arrive on
the scene. Peter orders the devils to let go of Simon, who falls to the ground,
smashed to smithereens. In this way the comic register enters the sermon.

Sermon no. 46 is, beginning with its title, even more interesting.
It is dedicated not to a liturgical occasion but to the death of Nero, which is

a tangible proof that 'a curset lyfnyng schewythe a fowle ende' and therefore an *exemplum* in itself.[6] The story consists of various episodes in the life of Nero, all chosen to show him as the mad and murderous emperor. The last one, which was common currency in the Middle Ages, concerns his artificial pregnancy. This story contains both marvellous and comic elements, with an etymological finale. Nero wanted to bear a child and called his doctors in to do what they could to bring this about. They made him swallow a frog and let it grow in his stomach. Nero began to feel ill and ordered the doctors to let him give birth. Accordingly, the medical men gave the emperor a potion and he vomited up the frog. When he saw this 'abominable child' of his, Nero decided to keep it out of his sight but to treat it with honour. The frog was therefore given a house, on the site of which was later built the church of St John Lateran, 'Þat ys yn Lateyne, Latens, and yn Englysch, a daring [or, variant, "drawyng"] frogge'. After this episode, the narrator recounts the story of Nero's death. As I have said, the story as a whole is an *exemplum*, within which we find, as in a set of Chinese boxes, other *exempla*. To take an obvious case, at the beginning of the sermon, when the preacher is railing against obscene language, in particular in the mouths of priests, an 'ensampul', as he himself declares, is inserted. It is the story of an Irish priest who talked 'of rybawdy and iapys þat turnyd men to lechery'. Another 'ensampul', again aimed at bettering the behaviour of priests, is placed towards the end of the story of Nero.

This great variety of *exempla* and brief narratives can be found throughout the *Festial* and the collection of *Middle English Sermons*.[7] Whether they belong to the 'old' type of sermon, which is aimed at lay people and has no formal structure, or the 'modern' type, where the sermon is organised formally according to a precise *ars praedicandi*[8] and meant to be heard by a university audience and by cultured men, nearly all the sermons that have come down to us contain tales of all types and registers, both stories new coined and those of which the roots extend far back into the past. The sermon is indeed the first 'seedbed of themes for story-telling'.

If the *exemplum* is a microcosm of human existence seen in its 'paradigmatic constancy' and a sort of anti-Bible, biblical narrative, on the other hand, is a macrocosm that has been inserted into time. But its temporal dimension moves in one direction only, and we already know its beginning and end – Creation and the Last Judgement. Within this 'official' time-scheme, divided into 'official' stages (the birth and death of Christ, for example), we find characters and events consecrated by tradition but now recreated on the common level. A biblical paraphrase is not the Bible, the immutable text of which is fixed by the authorities and is read in Latin to those who can understand it; it is, on the contrary, a vernacular creation for people with no learning. Like the *exemplum* it may be described as 'sub-literature', even if in this case the subject is an 'official' one. It is noteworthy that the author of the *Cursor Mundi*,[9] the vast biblical narrative written at the end of the thirteenth century, should open his prologue with a list of romances of the various 'matters', which, he says, the public likes to listen to. He proposes, instead, to write a book in honour of the Blessed Virgin, and he will call it 'cursor o werld' because it will cover the entire course of the world. The book will be in English, because there are many books in French, but they are of no use to those who cannot understand them: his work will be in English and will aim at a public of uncultured Englishmen.[10] What the *Cursor Mundi* sets out to do is therefore clear; against the romances and verses written in French, English and Latin, purely to please the public, it sets a sacred story, popularised and written in the vernacular, which attempts to make the readers reform their lives. Thus sacred history is transposed to a level that is even more 'popular' than that which romances aim at, and this is done with an explicit rejection of French, which is seen as the language of another nation.

The history of the world is divided into seven ages, from the Creation to the Day of Judgement, and the author says that his work is solidly based on the Trinity. A 'shepherd of God's flock' who came from the North of England, he devoted about 30,000 verses to his subject, summing up 'the entire literature, religious and lay, of the thirteenth century'.[11] Such an undertaking seems enormous to us, yet it was not abnormal in the Middle Ages. And in this case it does not lack ideological meaning or poetic value. A writer such as this, a cleric, whose culture was wide if not deep, was performing a task not unlike that of the mendicant preachers. He performed it without effort. He transmits to his public the rich store of legendary and doctrinal material that had been built up in more than a thousand years, and he does so skilfully. When, for example, he wants to expound a point of doctrine, he outlines it in a few lines using simple words, so it will not be too heavy for his audience, which is curious but not scholarly. He describes the composition of man, made up of the four elements, with seven holes in his head like the seven planets in the heavens: the air gives him sight and hearing, the wind breath, the earth taste and touch; rocks give him bones. His soul is a spiritual light, made by God in His own image, 'als prient of scel in wax es thrist' ('as the print of a seal is thrust in wax'); it possesses the 'trinity' of perception, understanding and wisdom; unseen, it sees all; together with the body, it keeps man whole.[12] But once doctrine is embodied in an image and can therefore capture the attention of his audience, the

5

writer does not stint himself: this happens in the story of the King and his four daughters (Mercy, Truth, Justice and Peace), a parable of sin and salvation, which takes over 300 lines;[13] it also happens in the parable of the Castle of Love and Grace, where the image of the castle, a tangible reality for the contemporary audience, is overlaid with a description of its magnificent construction and precious ornaments, which places it in a different world altogether but also conceals an allegorical meaning.[14] The two parables are taken from Robert Grosseteste's *Chasteau d'Amour*: thus the culture of the schools and of French-speaking aristocratic circles is translated into the vernacular. In another example, allegorical definitions are given to the four evangelists: they are the four wheels of a cart; their style is like water, wine, milk and honey; their scent is of wax, myrrh, flowers and spices. We can find the whole allegorical imagery of the Middle Ages in the *Cursor Mundi*.

The same kind of imagination, though working in another direction altogether, creates stories of another type – those involving scriptural characters. Isaac, for example, is seen from a very human angle: he becomes old, his day becomes night, his blood begins to turn cold and dry, 'til vnwelth windes al his wald'. Isaac is but a poor old man.[15] Judas, 'Sir Iudas', after his betrayal of Christ, tells his mother what he has done. Their conversation is that of a mother and son. She foresees Judas's end and Christ's Resurrection, but the traitor scoffs: 'Yes, he will rise like the cock you boiled last night.' At this point the cock flies away and crows; it is the same cock that crowed for Peter. Judas begins to feel afraid.[16] The real world in which the audience lives is transposed into the world of Scripture, with the usual touch of the marvellous. At times this is done with a pathos that can affect the audience, as, for example, when Adam is about to die. He sends his son Seth to Paradise to talk to a cherub: Adam is tired of such a long life spent in 'striif and soruuing' and asks when he will be allowed to leave the world. The author, who then begins to recount the story of the Holy Rood tree, has a moment to spare for the feelings of the dying Adam. When Seth comes back from Paradise and tells him that he may die, Adam laughs and, turning to God, exclaims: 'Lord, now I have lived long enough, take my soul from my body and do with it what you will.' The author comments:

> Quat of þis werld he was ful sad
> Þat neuer a dai þarin was glad! –
> Þat lived nine hundret yeir and mare,
> And al his liue in site and care,   *sorrow*
> And leuer was siþen to lenge in hell   *later it was better*
> Þan langer in þis liue to dwell.
>
> (1407–12)

Thus Adam, seen as a frail, tired human being, dies and is buried where the seeds of the tree of the Cross will remain intact for thousands of years. In this way, the *Cursor Mundi* ties humanity and divinity together in a single, exemplary knot and, in the narrative technique that it takes from the Bible (emphasising and enlarging it) prefigures the psychological and mimetic tendencies that will be fully developed in the late thirteenth century.

The *Cursor* is an 'organic' work, which covers all of sacred history, but single episodes or parts of this story are used elsewhere to construct self-contained works, which are often later inserted into manuscripts made up of miscellaneous religious material. The *Life of Adam and Eve*, a prose version that is included in the Vernon MS of 1370–80 is a case in point.[17] It deals with 'hou the word was wrought and Adam and Eve, and the wo that Adam and Eve in heore lyve hedden',[18] to the death of Adam. Here the pathos that the author of the *Cursor* wrote into his corresponding episode is lacking, but the addition of geographical details, dialogues between the various characters and other apocryphal matter amply rewards the audience's curiosity and confirms that this is the line that biblical paraphrase has by now taken.

A more important example is that of the so-called *Northern Passion*, written around the end of the thirteenth or the beginning of the fourteenth century in northern England, with the explicit intention of teaching religion to lay people, and translated for this purpose from French into English octosyllables.[19] The author treats the central episode of the Gospel story as if he were looking at it through a magnifying-glass. It becomes even more dramatic, and between the lines it reveals acute observations of daily life. The two directions of the narrative – dramatic and mimetic – become evident when we reach the Crucifixion. The blacksmith who has to nail pieces of the Cross together tries to refuse; the way in which Christ is crucified is described in its minutest details, both to underline the physical torture of His martyrdom and to satisfy the curiosity of the audience. Jesus, naked, is laid 'wide open' on the Cross, which lies on the ground; His hands are pulled towards the holes for the nails but His arms are too short by a foot and cannot reach them. In order to avoid making new holes, the executioners tie ropes around His hands and by pulling on them, stretch His arms to the ends of the Cross. Christ's muscles and ligaments are torn in the process.[20] Pathos thus disappears, giving place to precise details, which are specified and then accumulated to create a reaction of horror.

The aim of the narratives that I have examined up to now is edification: they were written by churchmen and had no aesthetic pretensions. When the same subjects are treated by an artist, and for a different audience, biblical paraphrases become altogether different. They are still used to prove one or more moral points, but they are constructed according to a precise design. They are selected by more sophisticated authors, who are conversant with the philosophical discoveries of the schools, the techniques of thought and expression of the international *koinè* and the language of nobility. This is the case with *Cleanness* and *Patience*, two of the four short, alliterative poems usually attributed to the *Gawain*-poet in the second half of the fourteenth century, probably written for an aristocratic audience in north-western England.

Patience,[21] which is only little over 500 lines long, is a neat construction, as perfect as a Grecian urn. Its theme is announced at once, and inserted into the context of the Beatitudes:

> Pacience is a poynt, þaӡ hit displese ofte.
> When heuy herttes ben hurt wyth heþyng oþer elles, *scorn*
> Suffraunce may aswagen hem and þe swelme leþe, *lessen the bitterness*
> For ho quelles vche a qued and quenches malyce. *subdues every evil*
>
> Þay ar happen also þat con her hert stere, *blessed; govern their hearts*
> For hores is þe heuen-ryche, as I er sayde.
> (1–28)

At the end of the poem, the circle is closed: its 'point' has been proved:

> For-þy when pouerte me enpreceӡ and payneӡ in-noӡe
> Ful softly with suffraunce saӡttel me bihoueӡ; *make peace*
> For-þy penaunce and payne to-preue hit in syӡt
> Þat pacience is a nobel poynt, þaӡ hit displese ofte.
> (528–31)

As in a sermon, the *exemplum* is recounted between the statement of the theme and the conclusion. The *exemplum* is constituted not by the proverbial story of Job but by the more indirectly related one of Jonah.[22] At first glance, the biblical text seems to deal with themes that are slightly different from that of patience: disobedience to the divine command; rejection of the heavy burden of prophecy; the omnipresence of God, who sees and hears everything, everywhere; divine mercy and human pettiness. Medieval allegorical interpretation saw in the three days and nights that Jonah spends in the whale's belly a prefiguration of the three days that passed between the Crucifixion and the Resurrection. A nineteenth-century interpretation within a novel, in the sermon preached by Father Mapple in *Moby Dick*, uses the story of Jonah to condemn sin, to demonstrate the omnipresence of God and to show the road to salvation through penance, thus indicating, in moral terms, the deeper meaning of the adventure that will take place in the book.[23] But the author of *Patience*, driven perhaps by personal circumstances,[24] is more subtle:

The purpose of this poem is clear enough: to commend patience by an *exemplum* which first shows God's thwarting of impatience in a human being, and then expounds his own patience by contrast. The term 'patience', for which the poet's word is the same as ours, has a somewhat wider sense than it commonly possesses nowadays. It means both putting up with one's lot and being longsuffering towards folly and wickedness, rather than hasty to take vengeance on them. The first sense applies especially to man, the second especially to God.[25]

Patience moves from one meaning to the other: the first and longer part of the poem shows us God punishing Jonah's impatience; the second part, which is much briefer, shows us how God bears with the sins of Nineveh and how, as soon as its inhabitants repent, He spares the city. But the whole story can really be considered an ultimate test of divine patience. The Old Testament God, who normally punishes sinners pitilessly – who, as *Cleanness* will tell us, drowns the entire human race in the Flood and annihilates Sodom and Gomorrah – this God punishes Jonah, it is true, but He does so with great moderation. He saves him when the prophet invokes Him: He is a God who stops short of drastic action; He terrifies the sinner but, more than that, He humiliates him. He makes him pass three days and nights in the whale's stomach, dark, stifling, but, most of all, dirty and smelly. He ridicules him, teasing him almost, by making the shady bower for him and then destroying it – provoking Jonah's anger to then show up his pettiness, vanity and stupidity.

With regard to the biblical text, *Patience* is an *amplificatio*, following the rhetorical rules of the Middle Ages, but it is not merely a verbal *amplificatio*: it tends, like all homiletic literature,[26] towards a minute realism – that is, towards a description of details, of the objects that fill the story. But, more significantly, and beyond anything attempted in sermons, *Patience* shows a tendency towards a psychological characterisation of its protagonist. Whereas God remains the God of the Bible, the God who, according to Auerbach,[27] 'unexpected and mysterious, enters the scene from some unknown height or depth', Man takes his starting-point from moments of conflict and internal motivations, which Auerbach also finds in biblical characters but which are only hinted at in Scripture. And thus Man begins to become a character. To all this the author of *Patience* adds an extraordinary control of the technique he uses (that of alliteration) and of words.

Let me give a few examples of the processes I have just outlined. The first is of *amplificatio* pure and simple. The beginning of the *Prophetia Ionae* in the Vulgate is condensed and mysterious: 'Et factum est verbum Domini ad Ionam, filium Amathi, dicens: Surge, et vade in Niniven, civitatem grandem, et praedica in ea, quia ascendit malitia eius coram me'

('Now the word of the LORD came unto Jonah the son of Amittai, saying, Arise, go to Nineveh, that great city, and cry against it; for their wickedness is come up before me'). The author of *Patience* lengthens the text, he completes it rhetorically, with a clear homiletic and aesthetic intention:

Hit bi-tydde sum-tyme in þe termes of Jude,	
Jonas joyned watȝ þer-inne jentyle prophete;	*appointed; to the gentiles*
Goddes glam to hym glod þat hym vnglad made,	*speech; came*
With a roghlych rurd rowned in his ere:	
'Rys radly,' he says, 'and rayke forth euen;	
Nym þe way to Nynyue wyth-outen oþer speche,	
And in þat cete my saȝes soghe alle aboute,	*spread*
Þat in þat place, at þe poynt, I put in þi hert.	
For iwysse hit arn so wykke þat in þat won dowelleȝ,	*town*
And her malys is so much, I may not abide,	
Bot venge me on her vilanye and venym bilyue.	
Now sweȝe me þider swyftly and say me þis arende.'	*message*

(61–72)

Here the voice of God has become 'a roghlych rurd', and His command – which in the Bible had been reduced to the bare minimum necessary for its function – has been divided into two stanzas; in the first it is articulated by the use of the relative clause, and in the second it is emphasised by repetition. The last verse of the second stanza then repeats the command given in the first one. This type of *amplificatio* is a mechanism that we find throughout the poem and in particular in the storm scene, on which the author naturally dwells: each of the salient points of the original narrative is expanded, in the ways I have pointed out. The storm's rising is followed, step by step, in a crescendo of descriptions, in which Turneresque brush-strokes are mingled with nautical language, agitated talk and invocations of every kind of god – an effect that Father Mapple and Herman Melville would no doubt have appreciated. Having thus prepared the scenic background (lines 129–80), the author concentrates his attention on Jonah, who, having taken shelter in his cabin, 'slypped vpon a sloumbe-selepe, and sloberande he routes'. At this point the action begins. Jonah is dragged by his hair onto the deck; the sailors question him anxiously and the prophet tells the truth. The sailors are terrified but make every effort to save the ship, themselves and their passenger. Finally, they beg God not to be angry with them for casting His prophet to the mercy of the waves and they throw Jonah overboard. The biblical narrative, which contains the bare skeleton of this episode, is exploited to the utmost, and its background, which has been merely sketched, is transformed into a literally and metaphorically dramatic scene (lines 180–244).

The scene that follows enlarges ten times over the biblical text, which merely states: 'Et praeparavit Dominus piscem grandem ut deglutiret Ionam; et erat Ionas in ventre piscis tribus diebus et tribus noctibus' ('Now the LORD had prepared a great fish to swallow up Jonah. And Jonah was in the belly of the fish three days and three nights'). The poet, instead, follows Jonah's steps through the whale's teeth, down its throat, beyond its gills and down to what seems to be the end of the road, to a cavern 'as brod as a halle':

> And þer he festnes þe fete and fathmeȝ aboute,
> And stod vp in his stomak þat stank as þe deuel;
> Þer in saym and in sorȝe þat sauoured as helle,
> Þer watȝ bylded his bour þat wyl no bale suffer.* (273–6)
>
> * *There was built the bower of the man who would suffer
>   no hardship*

This is a stanza that shows the technique of the *Patience* poet in miniature: the whale's stomach is rapidly sketched; it is made concrete mainly by its stench; its space is taken up by the figure of Jonah who has stumbled to his feet and is groping around. His situation is defined by a doublet that is enhanced if not created by alliteration – a touch of genius: 'in saym and in sorȝe' ('in the grease and filth') – but with the ambiguity that characterises 'sorȝe', the primary meaning of which is 'pain'. The two colloquial similes 'as þe deuel' and 'as helle' give the scene a touch of vulgarity, and at the same time provide a religious correlative to Jonah's condition: having rejected God and His message, he now finds himself in Hell. Finally, the author's ironic comment completes the picture by making Jonah ridiculous, when he had already been miniaturised, eight lines earlier, in the comparison with a 'mote in at a munster dor'. This technique, in short, can compress allusion, realism, ambiguity and irony, all invented out of whole cloth on the basis of biblical text, into a very small space.

Jonah has been treated from the first with the ironic detachment that belongs not only to the preacher or moralist but, most of all, to the novelist, and from the very beginning he is given a psychological depth that is not to be found in the religious narratives I have discussed so far: in this, as we shall see, he is a character typical of the *Gawain*-poet. When Jonah in the Bible disobeys God, the text does not waste words: 'Et surrexit Ionas, ut fugeret in Tharsis a facie Domini' ('But Jonah rose up to flee unto Tharshish from the presence of the LORD'). The *Patience*-poet, on the other hand, searches out Jonah's motives, which are, naturally enough, dictated mainly by fear, but, as he does so, he points out the man's rebellious spirit and his bad-tempered irony, which makes Jonah profoundly human. It is the first time in English literature that a man, a prophet of God, talks to himself about his God with such bitterness – in an interior monologue.

> When þat steuen watȝ stynt þat stowned his mynde,
> Al he wrathed in his wyt, and wyþerly he þoȝt:
> 'If I bowe to his bode and bryng hem þis tale,
> And I be nummen in Nuniue, my nyes begynes. *troubles begin*
>
> He telles me þose traytoures arn typped schrewes;
> I com wyth þose tyþynges, þay ta me bylyue,
> Pyneȝ me in a prysoun, put me in stokkes,
> Wryþe me in a warlok, wrast out myn yȝen. *foot-shackle*
>
> Þis is a meruayl message a man for-to preche
> Amonge enmyes so mony and mansed fendes, *accursed*
> Bot if my gaynlych God such gref to me wolde, *gracious*
> For desert of sum sake, þat I slayn were.
>
> At alle peryles,' quoþ þe prophete, 'I aproche hit no nerre;
> I wyl me sum oþer waye þat he ne wayte after;
> I schal tee in-to Tarce and tary þere a whyle,
> And lyȝtly when I am lest he letes me alone.'
> . . .
> 'Oure syre syttes,' he says, 'on sege so hyȝe,
> In his glowande glorye, and gloumbes ful lyttel *worries*
> Þaȝ I be nummen in Nunniue and naked dispoyled,
> On rode rwly to-rent with rybaudes mony.'
>
> (77–96)

This is a man who is so terrified that he even doubts God's word; a man who imagines the most frightful punishments, a man who reasons (though in a way that seems perverse in the context of the Bible) like a rational being. Jonah the man is not at all a prophet of God: he is not even a patient servant of God. This can be taken as a synthesis of both the moral message and the artistic achievement of *Patience*.

Cleanness (or *Purity*)[28] is a much longer poem than *Patience* and undoubtedly has a much more complicated structure. Like *Patience*, it is a poem à thèse, which comes from the homiletic tradition and is constructed around a series of *exempla* taken from the Old Testament. The main difference between these two poems, attributed to the same author, is that whereas the former proceeds from the statement of the thesis to a single *exemplum*, to the conclusion that proves the thesis, in the latter the poet states his thesis and then illustrates it by means of a Gospel parable, which is the starting-point for a series of biblical stories. The first two of these have nothing at all to do with the chosen theme. The others, intermingled with transitions and comments, make up a chain in which each single link is an example that adds to the thesis an element slightly different from the preceding one. As in *Patience*, the thesis is announced in the first few lines of the poem:

> Clannesse who-so kyndly cowþe comende,
> And rekken vp alle þe resounȝ þat ho by riȝt askeȝ,
> Fayre formeȝ myȝt he fynde in forþering his speche,
> And in þe contrare kark and combraunce huge.   *trouble*
>
> For wonder wroth is þe wyȝ þat wroȝt alle þinges,
> Wyth þe freke þat in fylþe folȝes hym after. . .   *man*
> (1–6)

The poet's intention is to praise 'cleanness' or purity (we must remember that the word's connotations go beyond the sexual sphere). 'Cleanness' is also linked to the eighth Beatitude: 'Blessed are the pure in heart: for they shall see God.' But the statement of the theme also contains, indirectly, an indication of how it will be treated: purity will not only be praised in itself; it will, above all, be thrown into relief by contrast, through *exempla* of its 'contraré', its opposite, the 'fylþe' that provokes the wrath of God. A first reading of *Cleanness*, in fact, gives the impression of a series of biblical stories, in which the constant element is, on the one hand, the 'fylþe' of men and, on the other, the anger with which God deals out punishment. The poet himself seems to confirm the correctness of this impression when, at the end of the poem, he declares:

> Þus vpon þrynne wyses I haf yow þro schewed
> Þat vnclannes tocleues in corage dere   *belongs; heart; noble*
> Of þat wynnelych lorde þat wonyes in heuen,   *heart*
> Entyses hym to be tene, telled vp his wrake . . .   *incites Him to be angry*
> (1805–8)

The three 'ways' to which the poet here refers are the three major *exempla* of the poem: that is, the story of the Flood, of Sodom and Gomorrah, and of Belshazzar's Feast. In the most illuminating study of *Cleanness* yet to appear, Spearing has pointed out that the poem's structure is really much more subtle and complex. He has divided the poem into seven sections, of which the first, third, fifth and seventh constitute respectively the introduction, two transitions and the conclusion. Each of the remaining sections is made up of *exempla*, including the three major ones that I mentioned above. Another *exemplum*, the parable of the Royal Wedding, is included in the introduction.[29] It is worth noting that with the exception of the brief first transition and the conclusion, each section can be divided into two or three sub-sections. This seems to reveal that the poet wished to orchestrate the whole into proportionate parts.

13

This scheme is carried out according to the logic we have already seen at work in *Patience*, here elaborated and magnified: the parable of the Royal Wedding points out, in New Testament terms, the connection that exists between purity and the Kingdom of Heaven (as proclaimed in the eighth Beatitude), by showing its opposite. The King, noticing a man 'non vestitum veste nuptiali' ('which had not on a wedding garment') at his banquet, rebukes him and has him thrown, tied hand and foot, 'in tenebras exteriores' ('into outer darkness'), where there will be weeping and gnashing of teeth. The author of *Cleanness*, in describing the guest, adds that he was 'fyled with werkke3', that is, that he was wearing his dirty work-clothes. This detail shows that it is impurity that the poet wants to underline – and the punishment it deserves: the 'etterno dolore' of Dante's Hell. At the same time the King's anger is emphasised. Thus (as we shall find in *Pearl*) the theme of *Cleanness* acquires a specifically Christian dimension. At this point, the scope of the poem widens from divine punishment for impurity to punishment for sin itself. Lucifer and Adam are primeval examples. The poet now uses Genesis as a quarry for his *exemplum*, which shows impurity being punished. The theme is taken up at once in the story of the Flood, which destroyed the perverted human race. Following the narrative line of Genesis, *Cleanness* next takes up the story of Abraham: his meeting with the three angels is a sign of God's love towards righteous, pure human beings; the conversation between Abraham and God about the future of Sodom and Gomorrah and God's promise to save the two cities if in them ten just men can be found, shows God's wrath tempered by His mercy – a balance of perfect justice. This is followed by the destruction of the two cities and the episode of Lot and his wife. Having exhausted Genesis as a source for his negative *exempla*, the poet turns to the *positive* illustration of purity, the greatest example of which is God made man, Christ. The concept of 'cleanness' is thus broadened so as to become the emblem of all Christian life. In the final negative *exemplum*, it is no longer impurity seen as the perversion of the natural law that is stigmatised, but impurity as an offence against God. Zedekiah, King of Israel, who practises 'abominaciones of idolatrye' is defeated by Nebuchadnezzar; Jerusalem is vanquished, the Temple violated and the sacred vessels brought to Babylon. Nebuchadnezzar, a righteous king, does not dare to use them. After his death his son Belshazzar succeeds him and holds an orgy in the royal palace, during which he desecrates the sacred vessels of Jerusalem by drinking out of them. On the wall there appears the enormous shadow of a hand, which writes mysterious letters, 'runisch saue3' ('violent, strange words'). None of the king's sages is able to decipher the characters until Daniel is called. Belshazzar – and this is the message the prophet deciphers – has committed the ultimate sin, that of sacrilege. Because of this he will be punished by means of the Medes, whom God will allow to kill him and conquer Babylon. The prophecy comes true and *Cleanness* ends with a final example of divine punishment. The first punishment was that of the rebel angels, the second of the first man, the third of the entire human race, the fourth of the two cities, the fifth of Israel; the last is wrought by man on other men. God's might has thus been shown working both directly and indirectly.

As in *Patience*, the biblical text forms the basis of the poetic narrative of *Cleanness*, of that 'exemplary' plot, which, intermingled with transitions, introductions, comments and explanations, gives the poem its narrative character. Here, as in *Patience*, the technique of *amplificatio* is used, and it is used in the same way as in *Patience*: by verbal and rhetorical expansion, minute realism, mimetic and psychological depth, and ambiguity. To give examples or to enter into details would be superfluous: I refer the reader to Spearing's exhaustive analysis.[30] What I want to do here is to return to a subject I mentioned in dealing with *Patience* – that of the imaginative structure of these poems, which, though they arise from the homiletic tradition and that of biblical paraphrase, achieve an extraordinary dramatic individuality and narrative independence. We can see this more clearly in *Patience* because the text is short and only one story is narrated. In *Cleanness*, there are seven such narrative episodes, of which two are very short, one is of middling length (about 200 lines), the three most important ones are very long, and one (the parable of the Royal Wedding) is little more than a hundred lines long. It is through these narrative structures that I intend now to approach *Cleanness*. One must of course bear in mind that they belong in a homiletic context, that is, that they were written within the bounds of a completely medieval conception of 'religious' narrative. Nevertheless, I mean to evaluate them as narrative works to see whether, through this kind of analysis, they can reveal new facets.

It is obvious, in the first place, that the narrative scheme of these episodes is always the same – we can schematise it as follows: the creature violates the order of things as imposed by the Creator: this transgression provokes the anger of the Creator, who then punishes the creature. The scheme is thus divided into three separate moments; it is extremely simple and is repeated seven times, the only variable being the type of transgression and, to a certain extent, the kind of punishment. This repetition can already be found in the biblical text and it is, indeed, one of its messages. But in the Bible this formula is diluted, given the length of the text. In *Cleanness*, on the other hand, it is concentrated and is clearly hammered out by the poet with a definite intention. This repetition seems to the reader of *Cleanness* its salient characteristic: by the end of the third story he expects it and, having read the entire work, he feels quite oppressed by an accumulation of tragic episodes. In writing of the Bible, Northrop Frye says that

as a whole, it presents a gigantic cycle from creation to apocalypse, within which is the heroic quest of the Messiah from incarnation to apotheosis. Within this again are three other cyclical movements, expressed or implied: individual from birth to salvation; sexual from Adam and Eve to the apocalyptic wedding; social from the giving of the law to the established kingdom of the law, the rebuilt Zion of the Old Testament and the millennium of the New. These are all completed or dialectic cycles, where the movement is first down and then up to a permanently redeemed world. In addition there is the ironic or 'all too human' cycle, the *mere* cycle of human life without redemptive assistance, which goes recurrently through the 'same dull round,' in Blake's phrase, from birth to death. Here the final cadence is one of bondage, exile, continuing war, or destruction by fire (Sodom, Babylon) or water (the flood). These two forms of cyclical movement supply us with two epic frameworks: the epic of return and the epic of wrath.[31]

The repetition of the narrative scheme that we find in *Cleanness*, its application to the parable of the Royal Wedding, which has an eschatological dimension, and, on the other hand, its appearance immediately after the stories of Lucifer and Adam from Genesis – all this makes *Cleanness* tend towards Frye's 'epic of wrath'. In this sense the cyclical nature of the poem is more complete than may be thought at a first glance: the parable of the Royal Wedding at the beginning not only represents the narrative scheme typologically – it also constitutes the final point of the cycle, projecting the theme into the perspective of the Kingdom of Heaven and of judgement, both on the individual plane and on that of the Last Judgement for the whole of mankind. The poet adroitly places the central *exemplum* right at the beginning of the poem, tying the Old and New Testaments into a single knot.

There is, then, a tendency towards an epic structure in *Cleanness*. The language of the poem, in these narrative episodes, seems to move in the same direction, aided, perhaps, by the alliterative technique that lent itself so readily to the composition of epic poems in medieval England. A few examples will be useful. Let us begin with the Royal Wedding, the central scene of which takes place in a medieval 'halle', in the presence of the 'stewarde' and the 'marchal'. There all the guests are seated, according to their rank and their dress, at either the high or the low table, while the 'lorde' circulates among them to talk and make merry. This is a scene that elsewhere would lead us straight into an epic or a romance, as indeed happens in the alliterative *Morte Arthure* or *Sir Gawain and the Green Knight*. Here even a Gospel parable, given the *amplificatio* with which it is treated, is susceptible to epic tones – in fact to those of feudal epic. We see this in the Lord's words to his men, after he has discovered and interrogated the guest who arrived at the feast shabbily dressed:

> Þan þe lorde wonder loude laled and cryed,
> And talkeȝ to his tormenttoureȝ: 'Takeȝ hym', he biddeȝ,
> 'Byndeȝ byhynde at his bak boþe two his handeȝ,
> And felle fettereȝ to his fete festneȝ bylyue;
>
> Stik hym stifly in stokeȝ, and stekeȝ hym þerafter
> Depe in my dongoun þer doel euer dwelleȝ,
> Greuing and gretyng and gryspyng harde
> Of teþe tenfully togeder, to teche hym be quoynt.'   *well-dressed*
> (153–60)

The Gospel text is deliberately 'amplified' in order to describe the scene concretely in terms of feudal reality and of an epic setting. The lord who shouts, turning towards his 'tormenttoureȝ', replaces Matthew's 'tenebras exteriores' by his 'doungoun'.

Now let us turn to an example where the poet's imagination has a free rein – just after Lucifer has uttered his words of pride and rebellion. Divine punishment strikes at once:

> With þis worde þat he warp þe wrake on hym lyȝt,
> Dryȝtyn with his dere dom hym drof to þe abyme.   *Lord; stern judgement*
> In þe mesure of his mode his metȝ neuer þe lasse;   *blow*
> . . .
> As son as dryȝtyneȝ dome drof to hymseluen,
> Þikke þowsandeȝ þro þrwen þeroute;   *were flung*
>
> Fellen fro þe fyrmament fendeȝ ful blake,
> Sweued at þe fyrst swap as þe snaw þikke,   *fell; blow*
> Hurled into helle-hole as þe hyue swarmeȝ.   *tumbled*
> Fylter fenden folk forty dayeȝ lencþe,
>
> Er þat styngande storme stynt ne myȝt;   *venomous*
> Bot as smylt mele vnder smal siue smokes for þikke   *refined meal; sieve;*
> So fro heuen to helle þat hatel schor laste,   *thickly*
> On vche syde of þe worlde aywhere ilyche.
> (213–28)

Here, in one of its best moments, we can see the imaginative structure of *Cleanness*, which, by accumulating verbs and carefully chosen details (the 'fyrmament' contrasted with 'helle-hole', the 'blackness' of the demons, the forty days of the fall from Heaven) and by the use of three similes, which enlarge the scene visually to include the whole world, makes a Fall of the Angels that will not find its equal in English poetry until Milton.

If we turn to the words that God speaks to Himself before allowing the Flood to start, we can hear in them 'high' rhetoric and the weightiness of Milton's style:

> For I schal waken vp a water to wasch alle þe worlde,
> And quelle alle þat is quik with quauende flodeȝ.   *surging*
>
> Alle þat glydeȝ and gotȝ and gost of lyf habbeȝ,
> I schal wast with my wrath þat wons vpon vrþe.
>
> (323–6)

The epic of wrath, which we have seen exemplified in these two passages, is realised even more fully in the descriptions of the Flood, the destruction of Sodom and Gomorrah, the hand writing on the wall during Belshazzar's Feast and the assassination of Belshazzar himself. Here the Bible text is for the poet a point of departure from which he can create a scene comparable with the killing of the Burgundians in the *Nibelungenlied*. It would be impossible to quote all these examples: one will serve for all. When it comes to the destruction of Sodom and Gomorrah, the Vulgate simply says: 'Igitur Dominus pluit super Sodomam et Gomorrham sulphur et ignem a Domino de caelo: et subvertit civitates has, et omnem circa regionem, universos habitatores urbium, et cuncta terrae virentia' ('Then the LORD rained upon Sodom and upon Gomorrah brimstone and fire from the LORD out of heaven; and he overthrew those cities, and all the plain, and all the inhabitants of the cities, and that which grew upon the ground').[32] In *Cleanness* the description takes up twenty-four lines and rises to a climax of extraordinary intensity:

> For when þat þe helle herde þe houndeȝ ef heuen,
> He watȝ ferlyly fayn, vnfolded bylyue;   *utterly delighted;*
> Þe grete barreȝ of þe abyme he barst vp at oneȝ,   *opened quickly*
> Þat alle þe regioun torof in rifteȝ ful grete,
>
> And clouen alle in lyttel clouteȝ þe clyffeȝ aywhere,
> As lauce leueȝ of þe boke þat lepeȝ in twynne.   *leaves fly from*
> Þe brethe of þe brynston bi þat hit blende were,   *brimstone*
> Al þo citees and her sydes sunkken to helle.
>
> (961–8)

'Þe grete barreȝ of þe abyme he barst vp at oneȝ' – this, if no other, is a line that Milton could have written. In *Cleanness*, therefore, the Bible gives a new dimension to English poetry: while remaining both homily and paraphrase, the poem tends towards epic. The *sermo humilis* of the Scriptures[33] is transformed into a sublime style.

The third great branch of religious narrative is hagiography. The saint, the man of God, is the medieval hero. He is even more important than the knight, especially in that he can fulfil this role for a much wider audience than that of the knight – an international audience including all classes of society. By comparison with a biblical character, a saint often has the advantage of belonging to more recent times and of being a less imposing figure, which gives the writer a chance to describe things much closer to him. At the same time, a saint can form a point of contact between the popular imagination and 'official', ecclesiastical history: miracles appeal to all believers. Hagiography was therefore enormously popular and began to be written very early even in the vernacular. It is not by chance that the lives of the saints of the so-called 'Katherine Group', composed about the beginning of the thirteenth century, are among the earliest monuments of Middle English prose. Since the 'Katherine Group' contains a treatise in praise of chastity as well as the lives of three saints, Katherine, Juliana and Margaret, and since it is associated with *Ancrene Riwle*, the Rule written for three noble anchorites, we may conjecture that this was the kind of public at which hagiographical literature in the vernacular was most likely aimed at such an early date. The well-born anchorites probably knew neither French nor Latin, but they must have been rather exacting about English: the prose of the three Lives is, following the pattern of the ancient Anglo-Saxon tradition, alliterative and rhythmic, and direct speech, prayer and dialogue alternate regularly.

Seinte Marherete,[34] for example, is a sober work, with a linear structure, without deviations or excessive flights of fancy. We are told at the beginning that Teochimus was the one who learned the story, which is then recounted as follows: the mighty Olibrius desires Margaret and when she refuses him he puts her in prison and has her tortured. In prison, Margaret, who has taken a vow of chastity and devotion to God, has a long conversation with the Devil, who shows her how his temptations work and how they can be resisted. A dove appears, welcoming her to Paradise. Margaret is then brought before Olibrius and tortured: she prays and the dove reappears. Five thousand people are converted and martyred. Margaret is taken outside the city to be executed. Again she prays and again the dove appears. Margaret tells the onlookers to be of good cheer and is beheaded. Angels carry her soul to Heaven, singing the *Sanctus*; Teochimus brings her body to Antioch. The date of her martyrdom, 20 July, is noted, and the story ends with a brief exhortation to remember her in prayer. Within the frame provided by Teochimus's appearance both at the beginning and at the end of the story, the three-part structure of the narrative is obvious – three conversations with the devil, three apparitions of the dove. There are no superfluous details: the story is austere, written for devotion rather than for entertainment.

If we turn from *Seinte Masherete* to the earliest version of the *South English Legendary*, that is, the *Early South English Legendary*,[35] written in septenary-alexandrine couplets near the end of the thirteenth century, we can see how things have changed in hagiography. The *Early South English Legendary* is a collection of fifty-seven saints' legends, to which have been added two on the Cross, one on the eleven thousand virgins, one on All Saints' Day and one on All Souls'. The collection is one of those that have been rewritten and enlarged over a long period of time. In its complete form (which dates from about 1300), the *South English Legendary* consists not only of saints' lives but also of a *Temporale* for the feasts of Christ, a cycle for Advent and Christmas, the Passion and Easter: it is, as its editor, Horstman, recognised, a true *Liber Festivalis*, from which a preacher could take an enormous amount of material, already organised according to the liturgical calendar. Homiletics, hagiography and biblical paraphrases are thus mingled in a single work.

The saints whose lives are recounted in the *Legendary* are taken from all ages and countries. But those who interest us most are the English saints, Kenelm, Thomas à Becket, the Anglo-Saxon saints and the Irish saints. The story of the child, Kenelm, son of King Kenulf, hated by his sister Quendrith and killed in a wood by his tutor Askebert on her orders, is pure legend;[36] that is, there are no historical sources that the author could have consulted; it is a legend based on local tradition. But the author attempts to link it to historical fact, and this attempt (which had already been made in the Latin *Vita*, which is the source of this English version) is significant because it reveals a particular taste in the uncultured audience for which the work was intended. This story brings together all the elements that could capture the interest of a thirteenth-century public of country folk – the wicked sister and the treacherous tutor, the wet-nurse, the people, the cow, the Pope, the dove, the golden lettering, the English that the Pope cannot understand, the Archbishop of Canterbury, the spring, the quarrelling over the relics, the terrible punishment meted out to the Queen and the glorification of the child saint. Things marvellous and familiar, far away and near at hand, 'official' and rural, are mixed up together; what emerges is a structure that, within the narration of what is already known, introduces suspense and traces elementary correspondences and contrasts: Quendrith and Kenelm, the cow and the Pope, the Queen's body and that of the saint.

The story of Kenelm is, of course, a singular case, but the *Legendary* offers us several opportunities for interesting analyses. The legend of Thomas à Becket,[37] treated dramatically as befits the story of an 'official' person who represents England's religious and national identity, has a 'cap' in which the saint's parents, Gilbert and Alexandra, appear. The former, a crusader in the Holy Land, is taken prisoner by a Saracen admiral, whose daughter, Alexandra, falls in love with him. Gilbert escapes, but his lover follows him to London, where, with the consent of the bishops, the woman is christened and the couple are married. This is, as Wilson says,[38] 'a romance in miniature', clearly influenced by the romantic narrative of the Crusades.

The story of St Brendan,[39] is modelled on fantastic travel stories: it tells of marvellous islands, birds that sing prime and compline, whales, the dark and stinking land that is the hell of the far North, Judas Iscariot, Paul the Hermit, the Promised Land. These three are examples of the kind of stories that made up the most common and widespread reading of the age: we must remember that Chauntecleer in Chaucer's *Nun's Priest's Tale* has read 'the lyf of Seint Kenelm' with great attention.

In the fifteenth century, the *Legenda Aurea*, the brilliant compilation of saints' lives assembled in the middle of the thirteenth century by Iacopo da Varazze, the Dominican Archbishop of Genoa, began to circulate in English. Its audience, certainly wider than that of the earlier works, included people who till then could not have read English. It had been translated into French, and from French, with the addition of some national saints, it was translated into English by a friar in 1438. This is a sign that the *South English Legendary* did not lack an audience, for the friar took various legends from it. Finally, in 1483 the *Golden Legend* attained the dignity of 'History' in William Caxton's editorial programme, and after being re-translated and adapted by him from Latin, French and English, it circulated in print among the bourgeois, knights and nobles who made up Caxton's reading public.[40] Rewritten in English prose, the *Golden Legend* is a far cry from the 'Katherine Group', in both its style and the public at which it is aimed. Even so, hagiography reflects a continuity that was to be broken only by the Reformation; it represents a vital growing-point in the development of medieval narrative.

As we have found, *Patience* and *Cleanness*, produced within the homiletic and biblical traditions, outdistance these traditions by reason of their artistic maturity. In the same way, *St Erkenwald*, a short alliterative poem of the late fourteenth century – which may perhaps be attributed to the *Gawain*-poet himself – stands out among other hagiographic compositions because of its artistic merits.[41] Many legends had grown up around the figure of Erkenwald, fourth Bishop of London, who had been mentioned by Bede in his *Historia*. The *St Erkenwald*-poet chooses one of these legends and develops it in a fast-moving narrative about 350 lines long, managing to introduce some of the main themes of medieval Christianity into a carefully designed structure. To begin with, the opening takes us back to the time when London was called 'New Troy' and when pagan temples were being replaced by Christian churches. In digging the foundations of St Paul's, the workmen find a beautifully decorated sarcophagus; a crowd gathers round, and the general consensus is to open it. What the sarcophagus reveals is even more astonishing: a splendidly dressed body, uncorrupted, lies within, decorated with royal insignia. Books and chronicles are ransacked to discover who this person may be, but nothing can be found. The news reaches Erkenwald, who is visiting his diocese: he takes the situation in hand and proclaims that only God can reveal the mystery, as he, His minister, will prove at once. Erkenwald lifts the dead man's eyelids and commands him to speak. And then

> Þe bry3t body in þe burynes brayed a litelle,
> And wyt a drery dreme he dryues owte wordes,
> Þurghe sum Goste lant lyfe of hym þat al redes.   *help of; Him; rules*
>
> (190–2)

The body then tells its own story: he was a judge in pagan times and was honoured by all for his true justice. His body and vestments have been kept intact for centuries by the God who loves justice above all. But his soul is in Hell, in a part of Limbo. Erkenwald, moved by his story, promises to baptise him and thus release his soul, even though this will cause the body to decay. One of Erkenwald's tears falls on the judge's body, who thanks God with joy: the tear, and the saint's intention, have baptised him. At the same moment a light shines in the infernal abyss – the soul has been freed and rises to Heaven, where it is welcomed to the Heavenly Banquet. As soon as the judge has finished speaking,

> Bot sodenly his swete chere swyndid and faylide,
> And alle þe blee of his body wos blakke as þe moldes,   *beauty*
> As roten as þe rottok þat rises in powdere.   *fungus*
>
> (34–4)

Eternity wins over time: the soul has reached blessedness and so the body loses the little glory it had possessed. The people, laughing and weeping, celebrate the miracle, while all the bells in the city ring in unison.

The poet's eye is like a camera, which moves with great precision from the panorama of London in the past – the pagan New Troy – to the action that takes place in the story's present: the excavations, the crowd, the workmen, the nobles – until it focusses on the conversation between the saint and the judge (while the people listen, as if petrified, in total silence), and finally its visual field opens out once more to take in the crowd rejoicing over the miracle. As for time, the story begins in a remote, historical time, it moves to the present; then, with the judge's speech it goes even further back to the historical time in which he lived. It then moves beyond earthly time, to Limbo, and finally returns to the present. On the level of correspondences of meaning, we note that the body is suspended on earth, while its spirit is suspended in Limbo; the body's incorruption corresponds to the incorruption of the judge's justice; earthly justice is rewarded by heavenly justice; the marvellous mystery is made clear by means of an equally marvellous miracle. The saintly bishop stands before the pagan judge: Erkenwald's tear follows his promise of baptism by water, the tear is followed by light in the abyss, the Heavenly Banquet and the corruption of the body. The initial splendour of the sarcophagus and the judge's vestments finally dissolves into dust. The excited gathering of the crowd around the excavation gives way to its astonished and silent presence, and finally to its celebrations with joy and sorrow. The living word, 'aided by a heavenly spirit', conquers where the fruitless search for knowledge in human books fails. Doctrine is thus concealed in action and dialogue. The action itself is prepared, suspended, taken up again, once more suspended, and concluded. In *St Erkenwald* hagiography becomes an art.

We must now take another step forward, to show how religious narratives can be organised into a solid structure despite the cumbersome dimensions that nearly always characterise them. This is a half-way stage between compilations pure and simple – such as the collections of sermons, the biblical paraphrases and the *Libri Festivales* of saints' lives that I have examined in the foregoing pages – and works like the *Confessio Amantis* and the *Canterbury Tales*. Yet another religious tradition comes to bear on this intermediate phase – that of the *summae*, of the *specula*,[42] no longer aimed merely at preaching but at confession, which began to dominate the spiritual life of medieval Christendom with the coming of the mendicant orders and the Fourth Lateran Council of 1215. It is not my intention to recount this development, which would take up too much space, but to concentrate on one of the more significant and representative products of this intermediate stage.

The best example is, I think, *Handlyng Synne*, the handbook of sins that Robert Mannyng, a Gilbertine monk from Bourne in Lincolnshire, began to adapt from the French *Manuel des Pechiez* by William of Wadington in 1303. *Handlyng Synne*[43] is written in verse – about 13,000 octosyllabic iambic couplets – composed in English 'for lewde men', and in particular for the people of Bourne and for the monastic community at Sempringham to which the author – apart from a brief stay in Cambridge – belonged. The structure of *Handlyng Synne* is simple and solid: it consists of the discussion of the ten commandments, the seven deadly sins, sacrilege, the seven sacraments, and the twelve points and twelve graces of confession, in that order. Within this discussion, in the guise of *exempla*, are sixty-three narratives. The structure of *Handlyng Synne* is more austere than that of the *Manuel*, which begins with a discussion of the twelve articles of faith; the stories are more numerous, often longer, some of them different. *Handlyng Synne* is a free adaptation, not a translation, of the *Manuel*.

It is obvious that, both as a theoretical and practical instrument and in its own internal logic, *Handlyng Synne* aims at confession. The origin of this work can be found in manuals for confession, and as such it could be used by the monks of Sempringham. Yet the structure of *Handlyng Synne* follows a rising moral scale: from the discussion and illustration of the transgressions committed by man against the ten commandments, the seven deadly sins and sacrilege, we pass to the seven sacraments – the seven instruments with which to combat sin – and finally to the twelve points and twelve graces of confession – the victorious weapon against sin. It is not by chance that *Handlyng Synne* ends with the eighth grace of confession – 'joy without sorrow' – and with a repentant man, who has now become 'God's hostel'. The last story, moreover, tells of a devil who goes to confession because he has seen the blackest souls become 'bright as the sun in the sight of God' after confession and wants to be like them but, not having repented for his sins, he is condemned by his confessor to be 'blak and foule wyþ-outyn ende'. In confession, good and evil are thus finally divided by reward and punishment.

The framework of *Handlyng Synne* does not, however, determine the distribution of individual stories in an equally harmonious manner: they remain free illustrations of the themes that are developed. In other words, the narrative structure has a solid framework, but it is itself elastic, 'organic', spontaneous. In his choice of stories Robert Mannyng follows William of Wadington and his own inspiration: he is very far from the iron structures of Dante or Boccaccio. Practically speaking, therefore, *Handlyng Synne* is an open structure, such as is common to many medieval English narratives. The passage from discussion to narrative is still of the 'exemplary' type.

Most of the stories recounted by Robert are derived from material common in the Middle Ages:[44] the *Dialogues* of Gregory the Great, the *Vitas Patrum*, the Apocrypha, the Bible – as the author says, everything 'he finds written'. But it is precisely in this declaration of how he intends to write his book, that Robert reveals one of his most interesting tendencies:

> Talys shalt þou fynde þerynne,
> And chauncys þat haþ happed for synne,
> Meruelys, some as y fonde wrytyn,
> *And oþer þat have be seyn & wetyn*;
> None ben þare-yn, more ne lesse,
> But þat y founde wryte, *or had wytnesse*.
>
> (131–6)

He sees himself, then, as a witness, or as a collector from the life, of some of the tales he tells. This implies a special attention to contemporary reality and in particular to English reality. As a writer in English for 'lewd' Englishmen, Robert shows an interest in realism and a 'national' tendency, which represent a significant milestone in the development of England's literary identity. Among the stories that Robert added to the repertoire provided by the *Manuel* there are, in fact, several that take place in English surroundings, and three that seem to indicate a special interest in the eastern part of the country – Cambridgeshire, Norfolk and Suffolk. If these are the macroscopic cases of 'English realism' in *Handlyng Synne*, an infinite number of minor details create an atmosphere that must certainly be called 'realistic'. Not only are there generalisations – significant because they are presented as the *vox populi* (such as 'the French sin is lust, the English is envy') – but details of English life and customs in the thirteenth century fill the pages of *Handlyng Synne*. Reading it we learn that the English even then made Saturday a holiday, that people chattered during Mass, men swore on Christ's limbs 'below the belt'. A list of these details would be endless, for *Handlyng Synne* really is an enormous, if confused, fresco of English life in the Middle Ages.

There is, however, a fairly sharp limit to *Handlyng Synne*'s realism: it is as colloquial and detailed as one could wish, yet it belongs, in the history of Western mimesis, to a pre-individual, pre-psychological stage. Its characters are types, not, in fact, characters. They never go beyond those gestures that define them as examples of certain ways of behaving. They are frozen into sketches by the author's deliberate (and declared) refusal to violate individual 'pryvetee'. For example, Robert says that nowadays women have lovers as well as husbands, wives have become the mistresses of their houses and are beginning to become shrews, and then everything is 'veyes moy sy' ('look at me'). The French expression, precisely the right one for the occasion, reveals feminine coquetry. These undoubtedly clever colloquial words evoke an attitude that corresponds to the custom of the time, but they are merely a gesture – an allusion, in fact, that is not followed up. Another instance is when Robert says that there are ways of kissing that are 'foul', but, he adds, this often belongs to 'pryvetee' and so I will not describe it. In terms of literary freedom, we are miles away from Paolo's trembling kiss on Francesca's mouth, which Dante was describing more or less at the same time that Robert wrote *Handlyng Synne*.

This limited realism, the veto on entering the sphere of 'pryvetee', has its roots in the way in which Robert formulated his work: on the one hand, according to a strict, 'puritanical'[45] morality, on the other, an examination in social terms of this morality. Beyond advice and the injunction to go to confession, Robert gives the individual nothing:

Of pryuytes speke y ry3t nou3t;
Þe pryuytes wyl y nat name
For none þarefore shulde me blame.

(30–2)

The fourth commandment, 'Remember the sabbath day, to keep it holy', is interpreted by Robert on an exclusively social plane: on Sundays there must be no carolling, plays, fights or intercourse with women; one must not go to the tavern or gamble. This is a foretaste of the laws that will regulate Scottish and English Sundays after the Reformation. In the discussion of the eighth commandment, 'Thou shalt not steal', the social aspect is even more pointed: stealing includes kidnapping children, profaning churches, raping young girls or married women; servants can be robbed by their master; absenteeism is robbery, and so is the use of pawned goods, or usury. Tournaments, which were social occasions *par excellence*, give rise to all seven deadly sins; of the miracle plays, only those on the birth and resurrection of Christ are permitted. All 'lay' entertainment is dangerous and foolish. It was precisely to dissuade 'lewde' men from all this that Robert wrote *Handlyng Synne*.[46] His intention and his accomplishment are thus not unlike those of the author of *Cursor Mundi*. Mannyng conforms fully to ecclesiastical ideology – in this sense, as an intellectual, he is in perfect accord with the Church. So much so that, after the seven deadly sins, an entire chapter is devoted to sacrilege, a sin against the Church, which is for him an all-comprehending institution. But Robert's Church, we must remember, is undoubtedly the evangelical Church, as revived by the Franciscans in the thirteenth century. The entire moral message of *Handlyng Synne* moves in this direction. Gluttony, for example, is a sin committed by the rich, and the stories that illustrate it are all directed against the rich, beginning with Lazarus and Dives and ending with Bishop Troilus.

The world of Robert Mannyng's ideas, despite the social angles that I have pointed out, has only one dimension – that of religion. There are no secular worlds of love, courtesy and chivalry: the stories of *Handlyng Synne* are either negative or positive; that is, they show how sinners are inevitably punished and the righteous rewarded, or else they are stories of conversion. In other words, *Handlyng Synne* lacks *chiaroscuro*, narrative complexity, ambiguity. It is indicative that the Devil is often present to underline the 'black', negative pole. This rigid formulation deprives nearly all the tales in *Handlyng Synne* of a life of their own. Those invented by Robert himself are, indeed, more lively. This is true in the case of the 'Cambridgeshire Miser–Parson', the Norfolk servant who chides a knight for not showing respect for the churchyard, the Suffolk man who is able to leave Purgatory because of the masses his wife has had said for him. But most of the tales remain within the limits of the *exemplum*, and as such they are dogmatic works, in which stylistic freedom is restricted by the theme and the source.

As an 'intermediate' work, *Handlyng Synne* allows us to examine exemplary narrative at the very point where it is most consistent, both structurally and ideologically, where the limits of realism cannot be exceeded without breaking down the very structure (the ecclesiastical structure, in fact) of the handbook. That will happen later with Gower, who will insert the structure of the confession and the handbook of sins into the world of love and will open up to the *exemplum* the extraordinarily wide field of mythology. It will come about, most of all, in Chaucer, who will burst the formal structure of religious collections wide open with his artifice of a pilgrimage that is no longer a function of Christian life but an occasion for gathering tales. At the same time, the social 'puritanism' of *Handlyng Synne* is a sign of the growth of a new attitude in the intellectual and clerical life of the fourteenth century: by following this path we shall meet the vision of *Piers Plowman*. Robert Mannyng represents a truly significant moment in the development of medieval English narrative.

2

The Comic Tradition

At this point we leave the sphere of literature sanctioned by the authorities, and enter that of unofficial culture, which, as we have seen, was condemned as mad and dangerous in *Handlyng Synne*. Because of the oral character of its material, and because of the Church's domination over official culture, manuscripts were not widely produced and circulated until the second half of the fourteenth century. Hence very little of this literature has come down to us from the thirteenth and fourteenth centuries. This does not mean its production was scanty: the condemnations in *Handlyng Synne* show the contrary. But one fact is immediately clear: until this tradition was integrated into Court literature by Chaucer, in the second half of the fourteenth century, it remained on the fringe of official culture. Minstrels and goliardic clerics – priests, monks and university students who dropped out, travelled all over Europe and composed loose or satirical works – had been and continued to be the creators of *fabliaux* and interludes. Now these forms were taken up also by the Court intellectual, the refined bourgeois of international culture, Chaucer. By the fifteenth century the genre had already become widespread; with Caxton's 1481 translation of *Reynard the Fox*, which Margaret Schlauch has called 'anti-romance',[1] the printing-press took over a literature that had originated in the market place.

The public whose demand had made this diffusion possible was, from the start, a mixed audience: while works of this kind had been spreading in French among the upper classes, their counterpart in English, from the thirteenth century on, conquered everyone – the bourgeoisie, the popular public referred to in *Handlyng Synne* and the aristocratic public (as is shown by a passage in *Sir Gawain* concerning interludes). Written for entertainment and amusement, this literature has no ennobling elements or big romantic effects: indeed, as it aims primarily at satire and parody, it deflates and perverts such elements and effects. Not immoral but amoral, it observes the actions of men without making any conventional judgement. Its essential elements are earthly – carnal love, hunger, thirst: to these all men are subject, including clerics, and from them the stories invariably take their point of departure. That is to say, the story always begins with a need for something – carnal love, food, drink – and the action shows how some

28

particular character gains his object by means of wit. Thus the comic composition celebrates cunning, 'pretence', and at the same time verbal wit. All this is based on ambiguity and illusion; mimesis plays a very secondary part.

Let us take, for example, *Dame Sirith*,[2] a thirteenth-century *fabliau* probably meant to be performed by a single minstrel playing all the different parts. The story is simple: Willekin, a clerk, loves Margery, the wife of a merchant. As soon as her husband goes away on business Willekin presents himself, declares his love and demands satisfaction. Margery refuses. Willekin then goes to Dame Sirith, a procuress, and requests her help, promising payment and advancing twenty shillings. Sirith has a bitch, to which she feeds pepper and mustard. When the animal's eyes begin to water Sirith goes to see Margery, bringing the dog along. She complains to Margery about everything and in particular about the fate of her daughter, a married woman courted by a clerk in her husband's absence: when the girl rejected him, the clerk took his revenge by turning her into a bitch, which constantly weeps over her fate. Sirith shows her the animal. Margery is appalled, tells Sirith what has happened to her and begs her to find Willekin, promising payment. Dame Sirith soon returns with Willekin, who gets all he wants from Margery.

Thus cleverness overcomes reticence and honour. But the game is still more complex. Willekin, the worldly-wise clerk, must enlist the aid of Dame Sirith so as to appear, in Margery's eyes, as a clerk able to turn women into dogs! Sirith gets paid twice, for two opposite reasons, by Willekin and by Margery. But these two opposite reasons in the end lead to the same effect, the one Willekin originally desired. And in fact Margery, in her first interview with the clerk, had told him that if there was anything she could do to please him, she would. She had then refused his advances, but in doing so had specified, with more than necessary particularity, that she would not betray her husband 'either in bed or on the floor'; so that in the end Margery herself has become, metaphorically and morally, a bitch.

In short, ambiguity and allusion are everywhere. With its colloquial but elegantly controlled language, and probably enhanced by the mimicry of an actor, it must have been a sketch of irresistible comic verve. This same sketch must have formed the central part of the *Interludium de Clerico et Puella*,[3] a thirteenth-century composition, the plot of which is the same as that of *Dame Sirith*, although the characters have different names. The *Interludium*, again perhaps mimed by a single performer (a minstrel?) is, according to G. V. Smithers, 'the oldest secular play extant in English',[4] and what remains to us – only 84 lines – does not permit any structural comments. Yet the very existence of this interlude shows the *fabliau* in the process of becoming theatre.

Also from the thirteenth century comes the only surviving example of an animal fable in Middle English before the *Nun's Priest's Tale* of Chaucer. This is *The Fox and the Wolf*, which belongs to the great cycle of the *Roman de Renart* that originated in France and then spread all over Europe.[5] In this case the initial need that motivates the story is not sexual desire but hunger. The fox, the hero of the medieval animal epic, comes out of the forest hungry and approaches a house in which there are five hens and a cock, Chauntecler. Chauntecler asks the fox what he wants and shouts to him to go away. Reneuard, the fox, replies that he has always tried to help the hens, bleeding them when they were ill, and advises Chauntecler to submit to the same beneficial treatment. But this time the fox's clever words do not produce the desired effect, and Reneuard has to go away. He is thirsty, and when he comes across a well with two buckets he unthinkingly climbs into one of them. The bucket falls down the well, and the fox is trapped. As he cries and curses his own intemperance, Sigrim, the wolf, who is also hungry, passes by the well and hears the wailing. Recognising the fox's voice, the wolf stops and asks: 'Are you a Christian, or my friend?' Reneuard, at once seeing a chance of salvation, replies that he has been praying for the wolf to pass and join him. Sigrim is amazed and asks why on earth he should jump into the well; the fox replies that that was not a wise thing to say, because this well is Paradise, well provided with food and drink, with no worries and no hunger. The wolf asks if the fox has died and when: only three days ago Reneuard, with his wife and children, had dined with him! The fox replies that since then he has gone to his Creator and would not return to life for anything in the world. Sigrim then asks Reneuard to let him come down as well, but the fox says he can intercede for him only if he confesses and changes his life. The wolf then begs him to act as confessor, and after much urging Reneuard accepts, enjoining Sigrim to list his sins 'one by one, without leaving out even one'. The wolf joyfully begins his confession, saying he has killed more than a thousand sheep, then interrupts himself to ask if he must say more. 'Everything', Reneuard replies. 'My friend', says Sigrim then, 'pardon me, but I have often spoken ill of you. People were saying you sinned with my wife. In fact I once found you in bed together. So I hated you. My dear friend, don't be angry!' 'Wolf', replies the fox, 'for all the sins you have committed in thought, word, deed or any other way, I forgive you.' When the confession is ended, Sigrim wants to know how to join his friend. Reneuard indicates the second bucket, and the wolf jumps in. Half-way down, the wolf sees the fox on his way up in the other bucket and asks where he is going. 'Out!' replies the fox. 'Thank God! And you go down there, find your food! I am glad you have begun a new, clean life. I shall ring the passing bell for you, and sing a mass for your soul!' Thus the wolf, wretched and furious, remains in his turn trapped in the well. From the nearby monastery, a monk realises that something is wrong and begins to shout: 'There's a devil in the well!' The monks gather round, pull the wolf out and give him a holy drubbing. And so the tale ends, with Sigrim deceived, ridiculed and bedraggled.

The structure of the story is, as we see, more complex than that of *Dame Sirith*: there are four separate scenes: Reneuard with Chauntecler, Reneuard alone in the well, Reneuard and Sigrim, and finally Sigrim with the monks. The scene with Chauntecler prepares us for the others, giving us the measure of Reneuard's cleverness and his ability to falsify reality through the clever use of words. His failure reveals the futility of the game and prepares the ground for the following scene, in which Reneuard, despite his cleverness, falls down the well. The water sought by the thirsty fox turns out to be foul, his 'wisdom' is overcome by his appetite. So we have a double failure in the first two scenes – failure of words and failure of intelligence. At this point the wolf arrives, and the fox's failures are transformed into victory. With his words Reneuard transforms reality. The well becomes Paradise, a carnal Paradise where the belly is full. Reneuard, who would really die if he stayed in the well, pretends to be dead. The two terms on which the whole joke hinges, hunger and death, are now set up, and the ambiguity contained within them begins to work: the following scenes are completely based on the principle, invented by the fox and accepted by the wolf, of religion as a means of satisfying one's needs (Paradise = eating and drinking). The confession is a means of attaining this end, and the wolf submits to it without thinking twice: we note that the fox does not tell the wolf that he must die in order to reach Paradise but only that he must change to a 'klene lif'. When after his confession Sigrim, longing for Paradise, falls down the well in one bucket while Reneuard rises in the other (a precise image, suggesting a law of physics), reality again completely changes its aspect. The well, which he thought was Paradise, proves to be a Hell; the wolf finds there nothing but icy water and hunger; 'invited to a cold banquet, the frogs have kneaded his bread'. And at last for the monks, Sigrim himself becomes the Devil and is treated as such. The religious metaphor has reached its broadest distortion. Within this distorted image we can follow the various phases of Sigrim's fate: he is tricked by Reneuard with the triple false equivalence, well = Paradise = full belly, he is humiliated by the confession and, within it, betrayed and held up to ridicule by Reneuard who has gone to bed with his wife, and of whom he now begs pardon for thinking badly of him. Then he is ridiculed again by Reneuard who, once free, promises to ring the bells and have masses said for his soul (playing both on the notion of the well as death and on the trick of the confession and the 'klene lif', which is now quite pertinent since Sigrim is in danger of death). At last he is beaten by the monks as a devil. Sigrim finds, as the last two lines point out, neither the beatitude he looked for in Paradise nor the pardon he thought he had obtained by his confession. While Reneuard, defeated by Chauntecler and by his own appetite, rises from death to life, Sigrim, beaten by trickery and hunger, falls to Hell, from which he is extracted as a devil at the cost of a beating. In the image of the two buckets, one rising and the other falling, we measure the dynamic of cleverness and hungry stupidity, of life and death, of Paradise and Hell.

This same theme of Paradise as a place of satisfaction of the senses finds its purest comic expression in Middle English in a little poem written in Ireland, entitled *The Land of Cockayne*, which also goes back to the thirteenth century. Probably the work of a goliardic cleric, *The Land of Cockayne* is not a narrative but the description of a marvellous place where men, and in particular churchmen, monks and nuns, find everything that they lack on earth and will not find either in the 'earthly Paradise of the European literary tradition' nor in the 'spiritual Paradise of medieval Christianity'.[6] The poem is the celebration of a carefree world without negations. The Land of Cockayne lies in the west, beyond Spain, and it is better than Paradise: in Paradise there is nothing but grass, flowers and green plants, while in the Land of Cockayne there is plenty of food and drink to be had for the taking; it is always daytime, never night; there is no death but always life; human beings never get angry; there are no fierce beasts or domestic animals and no fleas, lice or flies, 'either in clothing, in the cities, or in the beds, or in the houses'; there is no dirt, there is no thunder, hail, rain, wind or storm; there are rivers of oil, milk, honey and wine; water is only for washing and to beautify the landscape. In other words, Cockayne is the Utopia of the thirteenth century: it is free of all the worst annoyances that surrounded man in that century – insects, dirt, domestic animals – things that are dirty and require work, that can become food only if they are tended. But it is not only a negative Utopia – it is also the land of abundance, the splendid and exotic land of wealth, of food, of the senses: in it is a beautiful abbey with walls made of meat and fish, pilasters of cakes and beams of puddings. Everything is held in common by young and old, strong and weak. The pillars of the cloister are made of crystal, with capitals of jasper and coral. In the meadow there is a tree that bears, in different parts, all the most exotic spices of the Orient. There are roses and lilies, which never wither; there are balms and perfumes, gold and all the most precious stones of the world, and birds that are always singing. Geese, already roasted and on the spit, fly into the abbey crying, 'Gees, al hote al hot!' When the monks go to Mass all the glass windows turn to crystal to let in more light for the readers. After Mass the young monks go out to play and fly about with their sleeves and hoods flapping. Then the abbot calls them to vespers, but they keep flying away. The abbot catches a young girl, lifts up her skirt and exposes her bottom: the monks come down at once, gather round the girl, touch her, 'work' and finally go home to dinner, 'a fine procession'. Nearby there is another abbey, a convent full of nuns. When it is summer and the weather is warm, the nuns take a boat and row on the river of milk that flows by the convent. When they get far enough away they strip naked, dive in and swim. As soon as the monks see them they fly over and grab a nun each, then carry them off to their own abbey and 'teach them a prayer with dancing up and down. The monk who proves to be the best stallion and manages to keep his hood up, can easily have twelve women a year.'

So this is a monastic paradise – the Land of Cockayne satisfies all the desires of a thirteenth-century monk and by implication pokes fun at the real world in which he must live, a world of penury, dirt and austerity; at the same time it sets on its head – quite intentionally – the common conception of the Earthly Paradise and the Celestial Paradise. Of the former, Cockayne is an exaggerated and distorted version, with rather too many precious stones, too many foods and spices, too many obliging nuns; it is, in short, a *locus* a bit too *amoenus*. As for the latter, Cockayne is an upside-down version, earthly and material: instead of angels it is the monks who fly about hither and thither, not to mention the roast geese; instead of pure virgins there are the girl on the street and the naked nuns. In *The Land of Cockayne* we see the culmination of a carefree and volatile form of humour, which is quite without force and satiric bitterness, but devastating all the same. When a composition of 190 lines manages, with delicacy and precision, to overturn one of the dearest and most sacred conventions of its world, and do it with originality (unlike its French analogue, *Le Fabliau de Coquaigne*), the literary tradition to which it belongs has reached maturity: for its full flowering it had only to wait for the touch of Chaucer, his cultural richness and his genius.

If we skip over almost a whole century, the fourteenth, in which the only noteworthy compositions in the comic vein are in fact those of Chaucer (who will be dealt with in another chapter), we can see that the concept of Paradise is not the only one to be turned upside-down by Middle-English literature. In the fifteenth century the great ideal of feudal courtly civilisation, chivalry, is ridiculed in two works totally different in origin, spirit and form: the short romance *The Tournament of Tottenham*, written at the beginning of the century, and Caxton's prose translation from Middle Dutch, published in 1481, of *Reynard the Fox*. The former is heir to a long tradition of romances, and this is certainly not the only work that could be cited in which that tradition is set on its head: apart from Chaucer's *Sir Thopas*, there is *The Wedding of Sir Gawain and Dame Ragnell* and *Sir Gawain and the Carl of Carlyle*. The second, Caxton's work, comes from the long tradition of the animal epic – it is a translation made by a man who was also publishing numerous chivalric romances.

In *The Tournament of Tottenham*,[7] the reversal is based on a simple social displacement of the chivalric situation: instead of the noble knights of the tradition we find country folk. The tournament that they fight to conquer the daughter of Tyb the bailiff, and her dowry of a hen and a cow, is an exaggeratedly crude version of the great knightly tournaments: clubs replace lances, sheepskins serve for armour. But the satire works two ways: it is aimed not only at the nobles but also at the peasants themselves, who often indulged in organised brawls on the village green. The scenario of the tournament – the form – is used to attack aristocratic chivalry, which is thus subjected to a sort of Quixotic deflation; the substance strikes at the peasants. The public for which the *Tournament* was written was clearly the urban middle and lower classes.

Also for an urban class, though of a higher social level, Caxton published his *Reynard the Fox*,[8] towards the end of which the wolf, weary of the fox's bullying and lies, challenges Reynard to single combat before the Court of King Lion. The traditional mechanism of the duel is set in motion: the wolf accuses Reynard of being a traitor and a murderer, and throws down the gauntlet; Reynard replies that the wolf is lying; seconds are assigned and the King fixes the meeting for the next morning. At this point the formal procedure changes: rather than the intervention of a magician or the presence of an invulnerable weapon, we have the advice given to Reynard by his aunt, a monkey, on how to deal with the wolf. Reynard has his whole body covered with grease and drinks a great deal, after which he receives an incomprehensible blessing from the monkey. The next day the wolf and the fox go into the field. Reynard at once uses the weapon recommended by his aunt: with his tail soaked in urine he strikes the wolf in the eyes and then blinds him completely by throwing sand at them. In vain the wolf tries to get hold of Reynard, who is greased all over and slips away easily. At last the wolf kicks the fox in the head, and before Reynard can get up he sits on him so as to suffocate him. The fox tears out one of the wolf's eyes, scratches his face and tries to trick him by promising eternal vassallage, but the wolf does not move. Finally Reynard grabs his genitals: and at this point the wolf loses all his strength, and Reynard has won the duel. A challenge that had opened in the most chivalric way ends in the most bestial. The 'romance' is completely inverted and becomes, in Schlauch's expression, an 'anti-romance'.[9] But it is not just a question of literary mutation. *Reynard the Fox* was one of Caxton's most popular publications: although the intention of the translator–publisher was mainly moral, it is clear that the public also enjoyed the satirical and parodic devices Caxton used for his purpose. But in 1481 the distance between the ideal and its reverse had undoubtedly lessened: in the England of the Two Roses, the reverse was in effect reality. The low blows of the fox are not only travesties of the honest strokes of the knights of 'antan' but also bitter reflections of the real world. When the world is turned upside-down, prose humour is mimesis.

3

The World of Romance

Preachers and writers of 'religious' narrative, such as Robert Mannyng, minced no words in condemning comic, amoral and dangerous compositions. With regard to the other great narrative current, that of romance, their attitude was slightly different: they fought it on its own ground, producing, as we have seen, works like the *Cursor Mundi*. Competition, therefore, rather than sanction: and this reveals some significant ideological and social facts. The fact that the Church did not condemn romances as 'dangerous and foolish' indicates that it was not too concerned about them from either a moral or a social point of view. Despite certain excesses and errors, such as the celebration of extramarital love and of violence (which were in fact censured by ecclesiastical authority), the genre was seen as fundamentally 'sound', and the Church felt that it could best be combated by a literature that was similar but better. Moreover, romantic literature upheld certain ideals, such as courtesy and chivalry, which could be useful to the Church and which in any case did not conflict with its teaching except on a few points. Finally, it celebrated a social order, feudalism, that had the blessing of the authorities.

Other considerations came into play: romantic literature was so widespread that it would have been impossible to ban it; above all, romances were extremely popular at all social levels, among the bourgeoisie, the aristocracy, the Court and even the masses. It would have been unrealistic to declare a crusade against a literature that enjoyed such support. This attitude explains why the surviving romance manuscripts are so much more numerous than the comic ones, though they are fewer than those of a religious nature. And this is particularly significant if we remember that the romance was the first great genre of secular narrative to become established in Europe, after the Anglo-Saxon and Carolingian epics.

England's familiarity with the romance went back to the beginnings of the genre, in the twelfth century: it was in the Anglo-Norman setting of the Court of Henry II and Eleanor that the romance first flourished. Thomas and Benoit de St Maure had connections with this milieu. And Arthurian literature, which was basically romance, had from the first been rooted in the British soil of Geoffrey of Monmouth and the Anglo-Norman Wace.

The romances produced in that environment for the Angevin Court were, however, written in French. Immediately after this period, while the Anglo-Norman production continued, France itself became the centre of European romance literature. Throughout the later Middle Ages, and especially from the second half of the twelfth century to the end of the thirteenth, the romance mode was French. The English Court and aristocracy formed an enthusiastic audience for the French romance. Thus the romance, which might otherwise have developed in English on the basis of Anglo-Saxon precedents (*Wonders of the East, Letter of Alexander to Aristotle*), re-entered England from France. The native tradition might perhaps have developed from the myth–chronicle of Layamon's *Brut* to produce something like the *Nibelungenlied*, half-way between romance and epic. But it did not have an autonomous development. Only 200 years later, at the end of the fourteenth century, can one catch a vague echo of Layamon's ideals and formal approach in the alliterative *Morte Arthure* – but in the meantime this theme had been treated in French. *King Horn* (*c.* 1240), which can in some ways be seen as an intermediate stage between Layamon and the romance, is undoubtedly based on the French type of couplet. In short, the indigenous tradition survived only at the cost of a compromise with French rhythms – a compromise already suggested, in fact, by Layamon.

Generally speaking, two tendencies can be seen in the development of English romantic narrative. On the one hand, stories of French origin were 'anglicised' – that is, adapted to the expectations of the English public. This is the case, for example, with *Ywain and Gawain*, where the original, *Yvain, le Chevalier au Lion* by Chrétien de Troyes, was shortened and rearranged to suit the requirements of an English baronial Court. As time went by, this tendency was accentuated: while the romantic mode always kept an international flavour, the romances themselves increasingly tended to describe characteristically English situations. *Sir Degrevant*, written at the beginning of the fifteenth century, does not even have a specific French source, and the fields and forests of its landscape are clearly English. On the other hand, from the very beginning indigenous legends survived, though in the literary sense they sometimes passed through French or Anglo-Norman intermediaries. All the romances of the so-called 'Matter of England' may come into this category; *Havelok* and *Athelston* certainly do.

It is important to note, however, that the English romances are later than the French ones. In the second half of the twelfth century Chrétien was already writing his works, which perhaps constitute the highest point reached by the medieval romance; it was not until the end of the thirteenth century that romances began to appear in the English language. By that time, in France, the great prose cycle of the Arthurian Vulgate had been constructed – that is, the romance that was read by Francesca da Rimini and by Dante. If we remember that the best English romances were composed in the second half of the fourteenth century, and that prose romances did not appear until the fiftenth century, it is clear that the English romance developed almost two centuries after the French. Moreover, while in France the romance mode changed in the course of time, passing from the *chanson de geste* to the *roman d'aventure*, to the *roman courtois* and the lay, in England the 'lyric' and 'epic' romances, as Derek Pearsall has called them, were simultaneous phenomena.[1] Nor did the 'interlace', a typical French romance form, ever take root in England. This was a pattern in which the plot consisted of interwoven strands, like the illuminated initials of Gothic manuscripts – a form that, in fact, is closely linked with prose and with the organisation of material into cycles such as the Arthurian Vulgate.

Of course one explanation for all this is the fact that England was on the periphery of French culture, but, more important, the characteristics of English romances derived from their dependence on the public for which they were intended: a public that, in most cases, belonged to the middle and lower classes, the small provincial nobility and the urban petty bourgeoisie. This audience required a narrative that was French in style and manner but stripped of the formal refinements, structural complications and subtleties of *sen* that were found in the best French romances.[2] When the public changed, so did the product: *Sir Gawain*, written for a large provincial Court, uses all the best techniques of the international romance, together with the English alliterative technique. Chaucer's romances, which were written for the great London public of the Court and mercantile circles, are certainly on a par with the French productions.

The very presence of Chaucer's romances, in all their complexity, serves to illuminate the overall historical development of the English romance and the nature of its formal problems. In the last decades of the fourteenth century, Chaucer wrote and circulated seven 'romances'. These were very different one from another, but they were all guided by the sure hand of a writer who had fully absorbed the French literary tradition, who had taken the measure of the Italian *avant-garde* (the great Trecento writers) and who had thoroughly mastered his own linguistic tools. With Chaucer a model of casual elegance and wit emerged from the Court and the great city: a model of style and language that no one could ignore. In a sense, Chaucer's romances are the watershed in the development of the genre: before Chaucer, in the thirteenth and fourteenth centuries, the prevalent form was what Pearsall calls the 'popular' romance,[3] intended for the middle classes, which developed on the basis of the 'four-stress couplet' and the 'tail-rhyme stanza'[4] – this is the romance mocked by Chaucer in his *Sir*

Thopas. In the second half of the fourteenth century public taste changed, largely thanks to Chaucer, who introduced a more sophisticated form. Since the new mode was centred in London and took longer to reach the provinces, the 'popular' romance continued in the north while it was beginning to disappear elsewhere. At the same time, independently, the alliterative romance was born (or reborn) in the west. This was meant for local consumption and was fed by an indigenous formal tradition but, as *Sir Gawain* shows, it was able to profit from all the refinements of the international mode. This type of romance remained essentially circumscribed and gradually became a blind alley; but in the fifteenth century the Chaucerian style, albeit simplified, was taken up by the new, refined, bourgeois public. Its influence can be seen in the verse romances and still more in the prose romance, which reached its culmination with Caxton and Malory. On the other hand, the rejection of the new models led to an almost total degeneration of the 'popular' romance: reduced to hackneyed plots and stock situations, it represented 'the regression of romance into oral tradition'.[5]

Part of the great formal lesson of Chaucer lies in the freedom with which he treated the traditional schemes and the way he often fitted them into wider contexts. The *Clerk's Tale*, for example, is a romance, but Chaucer, following Petrarch (and ultimately Boccaccio), turns it into a *roman à thèse*. The *Knight's Tale* is a romance, but Chaucer transforms it into a platform for discussion of problems of social order and disorder, Fortune, astral influences, nobility and death. *Troilus* is a romance, and it not only lays bare men's problems and torments with a breadth unprecedented in English literature but treats the characters themselves with such psychological depth and perspicuity that it seems to be moving from the 'romance' towards the 'novel'. Chaucer, in short, uses the genre but transfigures it: and the irony of *Sir Thopas* demonstrates that he himself was perfectly conscious of this.

If we try to measure the English romance against Chaucer's formal achievements, we find that it revolves around completely different poles – and for this reason it is difficult, if not impossible, to define the romance and catalogue its products in airtight categories. At one pole, for example, is the chronicle: mythical in the case of Layamon and epic–historical in the case of Barbour's *Bruce*. Another pole is the epic as such: Lydgate's *Troy-Book* belongs in this category, while the alliterative *Morte Arthure*, notwithstanding its romantic dimensions, moves towards the celebration of epic themes. These, then, are the limits – however approximate and arbitrary – within which the English medieval romance can be located.

In England, as in all Europe, the romance stories often tended to crystallise around a few centres of mythological interest. These were the so-called 'matters', which, following a convention that goes back to Jean Bodel, are divided into the matter of France, the matter of Rome, the matter of Brittany – and for the English romance critics have added the 'matter of England'. These categories, of course, are for the sake of convenience and often have to be accompanied by an appendix containing 'miscellaneous romances', in order to cover the remaining ground. Obviously the author of the *Cursor Mundi* did not know these classifications, and in his list of romances most favoured by the public he simply listed the stories of Julius Caesar, Greece and Troy, Alexander, Brut, King Arthur and the Round Table, Tristan and Iseult, Charlemagne and Roland, Ioneck and Ysambrase, and Ydoine and Amadasse, with the addition of 'various' other subjects – 'princes, prelates and kings'. This list does, however, confirm that in the contemporary mind the romance was associated with certain characters or certain historical periods: classical antiquity in its most heroic dimension, Carolingian Europe and the Arthurian world. There is no mention in the *Cursor* of any material that is specifically English, and this confirms the substantially international nature of the romance.

Half a century after the *Cursor*, in the period between 1330 and 1340, someone who would today be called an 'editor' put together one of the most important collections of English romances. This anthology, contained in the Auchinleck manuscript, undoubtedly reflects the tastes of its public. It includes more-or-less complete texts of seventeen romances and lays, among which are the 'classic' *Kyng Alisaunder*, the 'Arthurian' *Arthour and Merlin*, the 'French' *Roland and Vernagu*, the 'oriental' *Floris and Blanche-fleur*, the 'English' *Horn Childe* and other 'miscellaneous' works such as *Amis and Amiloun* and the pseudo-historic *Richard Coeur de Lion*. The Lincoln Cathedral Library Thornton manuscript contains romances as varied as *Octavian*, *Sir Ysymbras*, *The Erl of Toulous*, *Sir Degrevant*, *Sir Eglamour*, *The Awntyrs off Arthure*, *Sir Perceval of Galles* and the alliterative *Morte Arthure*. In this later collection only classical and Arthurian subjects are represented, the former by a story as peripheral as that of Octavian; in short, it consists mainly of independent romances, not linked to any cycle or 'matter'. This brings us back to the question of the 'essence of romance', which we have been skirting up to now. Since there are about seventy verse romances dating from the thirteenth and fourteenth centuries, not counting those of Chaucer, and it is impossible to deal with them all, I shall examine just a few of them in detail, so as to give a more precise idea of what medieval English romance was like before Caxton and Malory.

Let us begin with one of the poles of which we have spoken, the one at which romance merges with the epic. A considerable part of the alliterative tradition is made up of romances based on 'historical' and warlike subjects, in which the love episodes are set apart: such as, for example, the three *Alexanders* (A, B and c), the *Destruction of Troy* and the *Siege of Jerusalem*. To this tradition belongs the best epic of the English Middle Ages, the alliterative *Morte Arthure*, which I shall discuss presently. First, however, let us briefly examine the work that, with all due caution as to form and historical accuracy, may be considered the keystone of Middle-English heroic poetry. This is Layamon's *Brut*,[6] written by a provincial priest in the early thirteenth century. Modelled on the *Roman de Brut* by the Anglo-Norman Wace, it appears in many ways as a 'massive erratic' in the course of English poetry. Layamon's chronicle is dedicated to the Britannic past of England: from Brutus, great-grandson of Aeneas, who gave Britain its name, down to Cadwallader, the last 'Celtic' king of an England by then occupied by the Anglo-Saxons. It is a decidedly 'nationalistic' chronicle, celebrating the indigenous element, and it naturally culminates in the author's treatment of the story of Arthur:

> Hit com him on mode and on his mern þonke, *mind; lofty*
> þet he wolde of Engle þa æðelæn tellen. *the noble deeds*
> (6–7)
>
> Þe time com þe wes icoren. þa wes Arður iboren. *appointed*
> (9607)

From the vast field of a 'history' covering 1500 years, Layamon first selects certain matters for greater attention. He cuts out (or barely mentions) innumerable episodes of slight importance and concentrates on the major ones: Brutus, Belinus, Brennus and their conquest of Gaul and Rome; Caesar's invasion and the resistance of Cassivelaunus; the arrival of the Anglo-Saxons; King Lear; Arthur. The choice is heroic and tragic: the intention is to celebrate. This first, structural, choice leads Layamon to his second choice – of tone: it is 'aggressive, violent, heroic, ceremonial and ritualistic'.[7] The battles are hard, and all his drive and stylistic technique shine brilliantly in their description:

> Vp bræid Arður his sceld foren to his breosten,
> and he gon to rusien swa þe runie wulf. *frosty*
> þenne he cumeð of holte, bihonged mid snawe,
> and þencheð to-biten swulc deor swa him likeð. *animal*
> (10040–3)

Layamon's third choice is stranger, considering that his model was the gallicising Wace, but it is understandable and even brilliant in view of the preceding selections: his *Brut* deliberately harks back to ancient Anglo-Saxon poetry – if not the 'classical', the popular – and apart from Wace it ignores French precedents. Arthur becomes a Beowulfian 'hlaford', his companions become 'haleðes', his battles mass conflicts:

> Uppe þere Tambre heo tuhte to-somne,
> heuen here-marken halden togadere,   *lifted their banners*
> luken sweord longe, leiden o þe helmen.
> fur ut sprengen, speren brastlien,   *broke*
> sceldes gonnen scanen, scaftes to-breken;
> þer faht al to-somne folc vnimete.

(14244–9)

However, Layamon did not carry his archaism to the point of immersing himself in a language that, after all, was dead and was being revived by a purely intellectual, literary operation. In *Brut* the alliteration is not always present and, where it is, it is not perfectly coherent; rhyme and assonance are introduced into the text together with syllabic couplets; the kennings of classical Anglo-Saxon poetry have lost their vigour, and even the heroic terms have a vaguer meaning. And finally, Layamon uses the simile, which was almost unknown in Anglo-Saxon poetry: we have seen it in the image of Arthur throwing himself upon his enemies 'like the frosty wolf when he comes from the wood, covered with snow'. So Layamon works a compromise between the kenning and the simile, which can be seen as poles emblematic of two different styles and mentalities. He makes another compromise, of a different nature, between the repetition of formulae and their variations, which are the two other characteristics of Anglo-Saxon poetry. He often uses formulae as fillers, transitions, descriptive phrases or summaries: he applies the same formulae to the same circumstances, such as battles or journeys, but, as Dorothy Everett has pointed out, within a story he repeats one or more formulae and varies them, with a decidedly functional intent: to provide the 'sound-track' for an episode, such as that of Vortiger, or to link up the various parts of a narration, as in the case of Lear.

Layamon is, to be sure, a 'massive erratic' in English poetry, and he still remains a historical–stylistic enigma, but his appearance at the beginning of Middle-English literature, though isolated, throws a sort of shadow over the future development of the heroic genre. Perhaps the image that suits him best is the one with which he himself closes the story of Arthur, in which the end of the mortally wounded king is shrouded in mystery:

> Æfne þan worden þer com of se wenden.
> þat wes an sceort bat liðen, sceouen mid vðen,   *pushed by waves*
> and twa wimmen þerinne wunderliche idihte,
> and heo nomen Arður anan and aneouste hine uereden,   *lifted him*
> and softe hine adun leiden and forð gunnen hine liðen.

Þa wes hit iwurðen þat Merlin seide whilen:
þat weore unimete care of Arðures forðfare.
Bruttes ileueð 3ete þat he bon on liue   *Britons; yet*
and wunnien in Aualun mid fairest alre aluen,
and lokieð euere Bruttes 3ete whan Arður cvmen liðe.   *wait for*
Nis nauer þe mon iboren of nauer nane burde icoren,   *singled out by woman*
þe cunne of þan soðe of Arðure sugen mare.
Bute while wes an wite3e, Merlin ihate;
he bodede mið worde, his quiðes weoren soðe,   *sayings*
þat an Arður sculde 3ete cum Anglen to fulste.   *help*

(14283–97)

About two centuries later, around the end of the fourteenth or the beginning of the fifteenth century, in the full flower of the 'alliterative revival', the *Morte Arthure*[8] concentrated precisely on the final stages of the story of Arthur – his greatness, his fall, his death. But his end is not at all wrapped in mystery:

Thus endis kyng Arthure, as auctors alegges,
That was of Ectores blude, the kynge son of Troye,
And of sir Pryamous, the prynce, praysede in erthe;
Fro thythen broghte the Bretons alle his bolde eldyrs
Into Bretayne the brode, as the *Bruytte* tellys.

(4382–6)

A clearly epic–tragic ending, complete with the explicit reference to the dead hero's ancestors. The *Morte Arthure* has, in fact, some characteristics of the epic, of the *chanson de geste* – beginning with its four-part structure, which, as Finlayson has pointed out, resembles that of the *Chanson de Roland*. In this sense, for that matter, the story is typical: King Arthur receives an embassy from the Roman Emperor Lucius, ordering him to submit and pay tribute. Arthur refuses and goes off to war against Rome, leaving Guinevere and his realm entirely in the hands of Modred. The war in France is victorious: Lucius is defeated and killed. At this point, Arthur proclaims his intention to proceed to further conquests; he crosses the Gotthard and passes through Italy to march on Rome, where he means to have himself crowned by the Pope. But at the very gates of Rome a messenger arrives and tells him that Modred has taken possession of Britain and married Guinevere. Arthur returns home, defeats an enemy fleet, lands, conquers and kills Modred, but he too is mortally wounded. The skeleton of the plot is a parabola that traces the rise, the glory and the fall of the protagonist. This structure, which might seem very simple, is complicated and completed by a series of episodes that serve as supporting pillars; these correspond to a three-tiered scheme whereby they move the plot, provide variety and express an ethical vision. The crucial moment in Arthur's career comes right in the middle of the poem, when the King, who has defeated

Lucius and thus ended the war in defence of national honour and independence, and now remains as the undisputed champion, decides to go on to conquer other lands. He thereby yields to the 'imperialist' instinct, committing sins of prevarication, 'cirquytrie', and *hubris*. Before this decision Arthur is a hero without blemish and without fear; after it he is a hero who has sinned. Each of these two parts is heralded by a premonitory dream, which is followed by an explicit interpretation and the event itself. In the first part Arthur dreams of a fight between a bear and a dragon, in which the latter wins. The dragon, as is revealed by the 'philosophers' called in to interpret the dream, is Arthur himself; the bear represents the tyrants who torment his people, or else some giant whom the King will confront in single combat. And this is just what happens: shortly afterwards Arthur defeats a monstrous man-eating giant and then the Roman Emperor who wanted to impose his tyranny on the Round Table. In the second part, Arthur dreams of finding himself in a forest where fierce beasts lick the blood of his knights from their chops; then he dreams of flying to a beautiful meadow surrounded by mountains, where there are vines of silver and grapes of gold. Here a beautiful Lady appears to him, turning a strange wheel on which is a silver throne. Six kings have fallen from the throne and lament their misfortune, while two others try to climb up to the throne but cannot reach it. Arthur greets the Lady, who declares that the throne is reserved for him. Arthur is installed on it, the Lady pays homage to him, and all nature submits to him. But at noon everything changes: the Lady speaks to him harshly and turns her wheel until Arthur is smashed to pieces. This is the wheel of Fortune with its Nine Worthies – Alexander, Hector, Julius Caesar, Judas Maccabeus, Joshua, David, Charlemagne, Godfrey of Bouillon and, at last, Arthur. As the 'philosopher' immediately explains to the King, in the Lady, Fortune, he will find his enemy: he has reached his highest point; now he will be punished for his 'cirquytrie':

> Thow has schedde myche blode and schalkes distroyede,   *men*
> Sakeles, in cirquytrie, in sere kynges landis.   *innocent; many*
> (3398–9)

Immediately afterwards in fact, Arthur receives the news of Modred's betrayal, and his fall begins. Thus the two dreams build up the tension, prefiguring events that are to happen shortly afterwards: in this sense they are functional to the narrative. This is borne out by their symmetrical placement, one at the beginning and one at the end of the action. The second dream also serves as the keystone of the whole ethical system of the poem: Fortune punishes the hero's sin of *hubris*, so that his adventure becomes a tragedy.

The two dreams also enter, however, into the ornamental dimension of the romance: the violence of the first and the splendour of the second capture the listener's imagination and carry him into that far-away world, so strange and so varied, which he expects to find in a poem. Other episodes in the work also provide this necessary variety, while at the same time serving the needs of the plot and its moral message. In the first part, for instance, the man-eating giant fought by Arthur is described in all his horror as a deformed monster, with a frog's brow, a falcon's nose and skin as tough as a shark's. And in the second part we have the mysterious encounter between Gawain and the unknown knight Sir Pryamous – a battle from which they both emerge wounded and are both cured by a mysterious ointment. These are episodes typical of the *roman d'aventure*, and within the same fantastic dimension they open up to the *Morte Arthure* the thematic areas of horror and of 'courtesy'. At the same time, the first dream builds up the heroic figure of Arthur, who alone and gratuitously confronts the greatest peril a knight can meet; while the second shows the figure of Gawain in a characteristic moment.

The *Morte Arthure* certainly tends to an exuberant variety: in it we find land and sea battles, banquets and speeches, marvellous meadows, mountains and forests – in short everything required to assure its success with listeners who are of course interested in heroism and tragedy but not to the exclusion of all else. In the language, too, these are the characteristics that dominate the poem: a language of action, concentrated and vigorous, as in the following passage, in which Arthur's march from Italy to England presses on without respite:

> Nowe bownes the bolde kynge with [his] beste knyghtes,   *hurries*
> Gers trome and trusse, and trynes forth aftyre;*
> Turnys thorowe Tuskayne, taries bot littill,
> Lyghte noghte in Lumbarddye bot when the lyghte failede;
> Merkes ouer the mowntaynes fulle mervaylous wayes,
> Ayres thurghe Almaygne evyne at the gayneste;
> Ferkes evyne into Flawndresche with hys ferse knyghttes . . .
>
> $$(3591-7)$$
>
> * *prepares army and baggage*

Often the language is reinforced by the technique of accumulation: as in all alliterative poetry, this naturally occurs in battle scenes, where it reaches moments of extraordinary intensity. But it also appears in descriptions, where details are piled up one after the other and linked by an alliteration that is solid and brilliant at the same time·

> Than they roode by that ryuer, that rynnyd so swythe,
> Þare the ryndez ouerrechez whith realle bowghez;
> The roo and the raynedere reklesse thare ronnen,   *roebuck*

> In ranez and in rosers, to ryotte thame seluen;   *bushes; disport*
> The frithez ware floreschte with flourez full many,
> Wyth fawcouns and fesantez of ferlyche hewez . . .
>
> (920–5)

This description which goes on in the same splendid way for another nine lines, gives us an idea of the evocative power of this poetry. It reigns everywhere. In Arthur's dream, the bear prepares for his fight with the dragon:

> He baltyrde, he bleryde, he braundyschte þerafter;
> To bataile he bounnez hym with bustous clowez;
> He romede, he rarede, that roggede all þe erthe!
>
> (782–4)

It is in moments of tragedy that the poet of the *Morte Arthure* reaches his finest effects: for example, in Arthur's lament over the dead Gawain, in which the king, in his unbounded grief, has a premonition of his own destiny and recognises his sin of *hubris*:

> He is sakles supprysede for syn of myn one!
>
> (3986)

These are lines in which despair is hammered out:

> 'Dere kosyn o kynde, in kare am I leuede,
> For nowe my wirchipe es wente and my were endide;
> Here es þe hope of my hele, my happynge of armes –
> My herte and my hardynes hale one hym lengede,
> My concell, my comforthe, þat kepide myn herte! . . .'
>
> (3956–60)

Greatness returns shortly afterwards when the King himself dies:

> He saide *In manus** with mayne one molde where he ligges,   *force; earth*
> And thus passes his speryt, and spekes he no more.
>
> (4326–7)

* *Into thy hands*

Thus we see that the *Morte Arthure* brings to the epic romance a quite unusual imaginative capacity and power of visualisation of the real and the imaginary and that these are supported by an extraordinary, 'flamboyant', technical ability.

Much more austere is *Bruce*,[9] written around 1375 by the Archdeacon of Aberdeen, John Barbour, which has already been mentioned as the first monument of Scottish literature. In the present context it shows how vast, in the consciousness of the time, was the scope of the romance – because Barbour, who was probably the author of a lost *Brut* and of the *Stewartis Originalle* (a chronicle–genealogy of the Stuart family), calls *Bruce* a 'romanys' and intends to treat it as such. Significantly, it is constructed, like an epic romance, around the great figure of King Robert Bruce and his lieutenant Sir James Douglas and it is dominated by the national consciousness of Scotland, which in the name of liberty proudly resists English attempts at conquest. It hinges entirely on the ideal of 'freedom', which includes both 'liberty' and 'well-being':

> A! fredome is a noble thing!
> Fredome mayss man to haiff liking;
> Fredome all solace to man giffis,
> He levys at ess that frely levys!
> A noble hart may haiff nane ess,
> Na ellys nocht that may him pless,
> Gyff fredome failȝhe; for fre liking   *desired*
> Is ȝharnyt our all other thing.
> (1, 225–32)

It is significant, finally, that we find, at the centre of this poem of about 13,000 lines, the 800 or so that Barbour devotes to the battle of Bannockburn – that battle which, on Monday 24 June 1314, assured for the Scots 200 years of liberty and independence from England.

So this is epic, but it is treated as a dimension of history: in Barbour's poetics 'truth' is more delightful than 'fable':

> Storys to rede ar delitabill
> Suppos that thai be nocht bot fabill:
> Than suld storys that suthfast wer,
> And thai war said on gud maner,
> Hawe doubill plesance in heryng:
> The first plesance is the carpyng,
> And the tothir the suthfastnes,
> That schawys the thing rycht as it wes.
> (1–8)

The poem, then, is to be constructed like a simple chronicle of the Anglo-Scottish events between 1305 and 1332, until the death of the hero. In *Bruce* Barbour, faithful to these principles, ignores the 'fabulous' apparatus of romance – the monsters, the dreams, the fairies. He obviously enjoys the 'carpyng', the narration, which, however, he understands in the only way a cultured fourteenth-century man could understand it – full of those touches, some of them courtly and delicate, that belong to the chivalric ideal. Thus we have a description of spring; we see Bruce giving his horse to the ladies during a march, or reading the romance of Fierabras to his men while crossing Loch Lomond in a boat; the warrior here, in short, is a 'knycht'. On the other hand, 'suthfastnes' demands that the tale should be told 'on gud maner': and hence the description of battles, which is such a great part of this truth, calls for all the poet's energy. These battles, violent as they were in reality, and interpreted in an epic manner, form the heart of *Bruce*:

the duel between Bruce and De Bohun can serve as an example of them all. Nor does Barbour hide the ferocity that, despite chivalry, pervades this world: the great Douglas, for instance, first attacks, captures and loots a castle, then has his men put everything they cannot carry away into a cellar, together with grain, flour, barley and malt; then he kills the prisoners there and pours wine over the lot: this is 'Douglas's larder'. It is an image of the violence that gives *Bruce* a barbaric dimension reminiscent of the Nibelungs. Barbour's poem, constructed like a chronicle and intended as an epic romance, thus constitutes another pole of the medieval romance, that of the 'historical' romance. It is not surprising that Walter Scott loved it, or that it created in Scotland a tradition that found expression, towards the end of the fifteenth century, in *Wallace*, composed by that mysterious minstrel known by the name of 'Blind Harry'.

Having examined some of the poles between which the English medieval romance developed, I now come to those works whose characteristics are less eccentric, which can to some extent be considered typical of the genre. For the purpose of discussion these have been grouped in pairs in order to bring out the common features and the differences in their interest and stylistic solutions, even within limited periods of time.

The first pair to be examined is that of *King Horn* and *Havelok the Dane*: these have been so often linked that the combination is by now classic. Both these romances are classified as exponents of the matter of England; they appear in the same manuscript, and they go back to the same century (*Horn* around 1240, *Havelok* around 1280).

Horn is about 1,500 lines long,[10] but in that short space it manages to present almost all the typical motifs of the romance: it is the story of the son of a king who is killed by the pagans. The boy is exiled but is protected by King Aylmar and loved by his daughter. When he becomes a knight, Horn must prove himself and, after receiving from Rymenhild a golden ring with her portrait, he defeats a band of pagans as soon as they disembark. Rymenhild dreams of having a net, which is ripped open by a great fish. Fikenhild, on a hunt with Aylmar, convinces the King that Horn intends to kill him and marry Rymenhild. Horn is then exiled and leaves for Ireland, where, on behalf of the local King, he conquers the pagans (the same ones who killed his father). The King would like Horn to marry his daughter Reynhild and become his heir, but Horn refuses. Meanwhile Rymenhild is menaced by a suitor, a king, to whom Aylmar has consented to give her in marriage. Horn hears of this and returns, dressed as a pilgrim. He presents himself at Rymenhild's wedding feast, where he tests the girl's fidelity in various ways and then reveals his identity. Then, returning with followers, he kills his rival. At this point Horn decides to reconquer the realm that had been his father's; he returns to his homeland and as soon as he lands he makes himself known to a knight from his father's Court. The two fight the Saracens and defeat them. Meanwhile Fikenhild fortifies Aylmar's lands and pays court to Rymenhild. Horn dreams that Rymenhild is in a sinking boat and every time she tries to abandon it she is thrown back in by Fikenhild. Horn returns on the wedding day of Fikenhild and Rymenhild, disguises himself as a harpist and enters the castle, where, during the feast, he kills Fikenhild. The romance ends with several weddings between Horn's friends and the princesses of various countries where Horn has been, and with their crowning – not to mention, of course, the union of Horn and Rymenhild and their establishment as rulers of Horn's own country.

To tell this whole story in 1500 lines, the author must obviously limit himself to working out the plot, and it is, in fact, to the plot and its details that he gives all his attention. He manages to create a design that is on the whole simple and symmetrical: Horn is exiled twice, twice he wins the favour of the host king, twice he is betrayed, twice he returns to fight for Rymenhild (twice threatened), twice he disguises himself. All these elements – in this case structural – are in fact typical of the medieval romance. But there are others in *King Horn* that are added to suit the expectations of the listeners: for example, the two dreams (of course the second one also functions as a narrative mechanism), the golden ring that Rymenhild gives Horn, the recognition scene between Horn and Rymenhild, and that between Horn and his father's knight. Let us briefly examine the last but one: Horn, disguised as a poor pilgrim, presents himself at the wedding feast of Rymenhild, where the girl is entertaining and serving the guests. To start a conversation, Horn asks her for more beer. Rymenhild thinks he is a beggar, but Horn tells her he is a fisherman, come to fish at her feast:

> My net lith her by honde
> By a well fair stronde.
> Hit hath y-lege there
> Fulle seve yere.
> Ich am y-come to loke
> Ef eny fish hit toke.
> (1145–50)

Rymenhild, however, does not recognise Horn, who meanwhile invites her to drink his (Horn's) own health. Rymenhild then asks him if he has seen Horn: in reply, Horn throws the golden ring into the cup. Rymenhild finds it and thinks Horn is dead. She asks him where he has found the ring; he replies that Horn gave it to him when they were sailing together and Horn was dying. Rymenhild wants to kill herself, but Horn at last wipes his face clean and reveals himself.

The scene is clearly complicated. Horn makes four attempts to get Rymenhild to recognise him and at the same time to test her while hiding behind his disguise: he pretends to be a fisherman and alludes to Rymenhild's dream; he invites her to drink to Horn's health; he drops the ring in the cup; finally he concocts the story of his own death. The whole scene teases the listener's imagination and sense of suspense until the climax when Rymenhild wants to kill herself. Within the disguise of the pilgrim there is another, that of the fisherman, and behind this there is the allusion to the dream. It is, in short, a complete network of tricks and surprises.

The atmosphere of this world beyond space and time, in which the sea and the years function only as elements of the plot and the characters are only names – a world ruled absolutely by the *fabula* of dreams, disguises and rings – this is the atmosphere in which *King Horn* moves. As defined by the author himself it is a 'song', the oldest English romantic story that remains to us. Behind it lies a historical world dominated by the Vikings, a world with precise political conceptions (kingdoms and marriages). But these are transported into a metahistorical universe, which is precisely that of romance. If the poem contains the mechanisms and the patina of chivalry, they exist within it at the level of the popular English romance.

In *Havelok the Dane*,[11] on the other hand, both the historical underpinning and the mimesis of the present are more substantial. In a clear and consistent way it recalls the period in which England and Denmark lived in close symbiosis, and there is an evident concern to describe the real life of the people – fishermen, cooks, servants – of the thirteenth century. Elements of the chivalric romance are reduced to the minimum: practically all that remains is the nocturnal vision, repeated three times, of the light and the cross – symbols of royalty – that shine on the sleeping Havelok. While the mechanism of the story is simpler than that of *Horn*, the romance is twice as long. This proves that the intention of the author and the attention of his audience are concentrated on details and not only on the plot. Three pairs of characters form the base of this mechanism: Havelok and Goldeboru, the son of the Danish King and the daughter of the English King; Godard and Godrich, the two usurpers, of the Danish and English thrones respectively; Grim the fisherman and Ubbe the baron, who save and help Havelok. When Godard hands Havelok over to Grim so that Grim can drown him, Grim has the first vision of the light and the cross and saves Havelok, carrying him with all his family to England – more precisely, to Grimsby in Lincolnshire. Here Havelok lives the humble life of a fisherman, and when there is a famine he exerts himself to contribute to his own and his family's survival by going to Lincoln, where he enters the service of the baron's cook Bertram. During the games that take place in connection with the Parliament, Godrich notices Havelok's physical vigour and decides to marry him to Goldeboru, in order to get rid of her. The girl complains of having married a man of such low social origin, but during the night the light shines on Havelok and the royal cross is clearly seen on his shoulder. An angel then appears to Goldeboru to inform her that Havelok will be king of England and Denmark. At the same time Havelok dreams of being in Denmark, on a hill, and of having arms long enough to embrace the whole kingdom. In another dream it is England that falls into his hands. The two dreams soon come true: accompanied by three of Grim's sons, the two go to Denmark; on landing they meet Ubbe, who at once decides to protect them. When they are attacked by robbers in the night, Havelok, Grim's sons, and Bernard, the protector assigned to them by Ubbe, manage to defeat them. Havelok, wounded, is carried to Ubbe's castle where, that night, the baron sees the light and the cross on his shoulder. Now convinced that Havelok is the king's son, Ubbe calls in the great men of the realm, invests Havelok as a knight and crowns him king. Then Godard is attacked, defeated and brought to justice. The Danes go to England, where they meet and fight the English forces of Godrich at Grimsby. The story ends with the usual marriages, the reward of those faithful to the conqueror, with the assignation of lands and titles, and the coronation of Havelok as king of England, while Denmark is entrusted to the governorship of Ubbe.

Havelok is, in short, a folk-tale thinly disguised as a romance. Havelok the hero, invested as a knight by Ubbe, is not a knight at all but, in the first part of the story, an upstart Dane who tries to get by in England by working at all trades. As he himself says to the cook Bertram:

> 'Goddot!' quoth he, 'leve sire,
> Bidde Ich you non other hire,
> But yeveth me inow to ete,
> Fir and water Y wile you fete,
> The fir blowe, and ful well maken;
> Stickes kan Ich breken and kraken,
> And kindlen ful wel a fir,
> And maken it to brennen shir;
> Ful wel kan Ich cleven shides,   *break boughs*
> Eles to-turven of here hides;   *skin eels*
> Ful wel kan Ich dishes swilen,
> And don al that the evere wilen.'
> (909–20)

However the Havelok who returns to England after having conquered

Denmark is reminiscent, and not only in name, of one of the Olafs
(Havelok←Abloc [Irish]←Olafr), perhaps Olaf Sictricson, called 'Cuaran',
a great Viking chief of the tenth century. It is he, the regal and warlike
Havelok, who 'shames' Godrich by cutting off his hand and has him
carried to Lincoln on an ass, facing the animal's tail, and finally burnt alive.
So *Havelok the Dane* is an adventure story with motifs typical of the genre
but at a level of mimesis and depth of characterisation that is more advanced
than that of *King Horn*.

Two romances that are chronologically quite far apart make up the next
pair: *Floris and Blancheflour*, which first appeared around 1250, and *Sir
Perceval of Galles*, which dates from the end of the fourteenth century.
These are here considered together, and at least implicitly compared,
because of the thoroughly romantic aura, impalpable and metahistorical, in
which they move.

Floris is a story that was quite widespread in the Middle Ages.[12] Possibly
of oriental origin, it concerns two youngsters, the son of a Saracen King
and the daughter of a Christian lady prisoner, who grow up together and
fall in love. To avoid a union between the two, the King sends Floris away
and sells Blancheflour to some oriental merchants, who deliver her to the
Amyral of Babylon. Floris returns and decides to recover his beloved at all
costs. He leaves for the East, enters Babylon and manages to get inside the
Tower of Maidens, where Blancheflour is being held. The two make love,
but they are discovered and condemned to death: one of them could be
saved by means of a miraculous ring given to Floris by his mother, but
each wants the other to use it. Touched by this supreme proof of love, the
Amyral frees the two condemned lovers, who get married and then return
to Spain, where Floris is crowned king on the death of his father. In other
words, this is a story of omnipotent love, which drives man to the most
arduous trials and even to the supreme sacrifice. In *Floris* exotic elements
are used to add more attraction to its theme. The Tower of Maidens, with
its guard of eunuchs, is the oriental harem; and still more fabulous is the
Amyral's garden, which contains a spring, the pure water of which turns to
blood whenever an impure girl washes her hands in it. In the garden there
is also a Tree of Love, whose flowers fall on the maiden who will be queen;
the Amyral uses this tree, with the aid of magic, to choose his favourite.
Even in its narrative devices *Floris* is full of charm and cogency: the only
way in which Floris (flower) can reach Blancheflour (white flower) at the
top of the Tower of Maidens is to have himself put into a basket of *flowers*
by the guardian of the Tower. Other devices and other scenes are typical
of the romance: for example, the miraculous ring that can save the life of
one of the lovers or the scene of Floris's return to his country after

Blancheflour has been sold to the merchants. In the latter case his father and mother make him think the girl is dead and take him to her supposed tomb; Floris faints three times and then takes out his sword to kill himself; then at last the truth is revealed to him. Another example is the brief *excursus* recounting the history of a goblet traded for Blancheflour: it is won by Aeneas at Troy, carried by him to Lombardy and given to his lady; then it is stolen from King Caesar by a thief and later exchanged for Blancheflour by that same thief.

Correspondences and repetitions govern the structure: in his search for the girl he loves, Floris three times receives information about her, and in very similar circumstances. The two crises of the romance – the return of Floris and the scene at the false tomb, and the scene where each of the lovers offers his life for the other – are dominated by the same theme, the wish to die for love.

A compact, coherent and charming work, *Floris* carries the romance into the realm of the exotic. *Sir Perceval of Galles* takes it into the world of Arthurian chivalry,[13] with its forests, duels and fairies. Lacking the coherent construction of Chrétien's *Conte du Graal* and the profundity of Wolfram's *Parzival*, *Sir Perceval* is a typical example of the English *roman d'aventure*, in which the salient features of the genre are given little prominence, or treated in a simple and ingenuous manner. The story is only a part of that commonly associated with the theme of Perceval: in effect it consists only of the training for knighthood of the naive and ignorant hero. But this is entirely pervaded by an extraordinary atmosphere of chivalry: knights and sorcerers, giants and sultans, the queen of the fairies, the ring, Arthur and his men. The whole romance is a series of adventures organised like a set of Chinese boxes, at times one within the other, at times simply set one after the other. The Red Knight kills Perceval's father; years later he is killed by Perceval. Perceval's mother gives him a ring, which he exchanges for that of the sleeping maiden; two years later he finds the girl, and the ring is the cause of a new adventure (the encounter with the giant), of his mother's madness and of his finding her again. In short, the story is guided by an extremely functional romantic *sen*: Perceval, wearing the armour of the Red Knight, is mistaken for him by the ten knights, who flee from him, but he catches up with one of them and reveals his true identity. This knight invites Perceval to his castle, where the messenger of Lufamour arrives on his way to Arthur. And this begins the adventure of Perceval in Maydenlande.

Certain lines are emblematic of the way this type of romance works. Here is Perceval leaving Maydenlande to look for his mother. One may well say, with Auerbach: 'The knight sets forth.'[14]

Now fro þam gun he ryde;
Þer wiste no man þat tyde
Whedirwarde he wolde ryde,
Ne whedir he wolde lende.
Forthe he rydes allone;
Fro þam he wolde euerichone:
Mighte no man with hym gone,
His sorowes to amende,
Bot forthe thus rydes he ay,
Þe certen sothe als i ȝow say,
Till he come at a way
By a wode-ende.
Then herde he faste hym by
Als it were a woman cry...
                    (1809–22)

This is in fact the image of the knight errant, who travels the world alone and arrives at the inevitable forest, where a new adventure suddenly opens to him. Encased in his armour, a stranger to all, he carries within himself a mysterious purpose, known to him alone, which he will in fact realise, but in a roundabout way – governed not by the logic of cause and effect but by a hidden *sen* – the logic of the *adventure*.[15]

If from the sphere of the exotic, and from the chivalry of *Floris* and *Perceval*, we move on to the Breton lay, we enter a still more rarified atmosphere – the extraordinary world of the *faerie*, of enchantment and magic. The romances of *Sir Orfeo*[16] and *Sir Launfal*[17] will serve as examples. Both these works (written around 1325 and 1350 respectively) have as their central theme the contact between human beings and the *faerie*. In both, the characters fall asleep in the shade of a tree and suddenly find themselves in an enchanted world. It is not a dream but another dimension of reality, with its kingdoms and its laws. Launfal, the knight of the Round Table, who has become poor through excessive liberality and has been tempted by Queen Guinevere, is overcome with love for the fairy Tryamour, and actively accepts the laws of her world. Heurodis, the wife of Orfeo, is kidnapped and carried off into the fairy world, and she accepts it passively, leaving to her husband the task of liberating her. In *Launfal*, the man enters the *faerie* and, although he has to leave it because he has failed to keep his pact with his beloved, he comes back as soon as he is allowed to, and there he remains. In *Orfeo* it is the fairies who abduct Heurodis, and the man, Orfeo, has to free her.

Thus the *faerie* has at least two values. In *Launfal* it is positive, and even counterposed to the Arthurian world. Launfal, the knight who is slandered, impoverished and menaced by Guinevere, is redeemed by the fairy with true love, riches and victory in battle. When he loses all this through publicly boasting of Tryamour's love, he risks death at Arthur's hands but is saved by the fairy, who thus offers him, unbidden, the supreme proof of her love. The figure of Guinevere, the Queen famous for her adulteries, who tries to ensnare Launfal, is contrasted with that of Tryamour, the kind, generous, faithful fairy who is more beautiful than Arthur's lady.

In *Orfeo*, on the other hand, the *faerie* has a negative value or at least a mysteriously equivocal one. In the garden of the king of the fairies Orfeo finds, together with Heurodis, people going about without heads, without arms, wounded, mad, on horseback, strangled, drowned, burnt; 'eche was þus in þis warld ynome, wiþ fairi þider ycome'. It is the irresistible power of enchantment, which conquers all without regard to the will of the subject, which spellbinds and freezes human beings in a state of passive suspension. This is the power conquered by Orfeo, the harpist King who has abandoned his Court in order to search for Heurodis or to wait for her to reveal herself to him in the wilderness, together with the *faerie*. When this enchanted world does appear to him he enters it as a minstrel, and thanks to the music of his harp he manages to rescue Heurodis from the enchanted garden. The harp that charmed the beasts of the forest conquers the *faerie*, and Orfeo and Heurodis return to their kingdom, where the faithful steward awaits his King. Love and music triumph. The Breton lays, says one of the manuscripts of *Sir Orfeo*, speak of the 'feyre', but above all, 'of alle þing þat men may se, most o love forsoþe þey be':

> When þey [the Bretons] myght owher heryn
> Of aventures þat þer weryn,
> Þey toke her harpys wiþ game,
> Maden layes and ȝaf it name.
>
> (17–20)

What we have in *Sir Orfeo*, is the genre celebrating itself: the harp of the Breton minstrel is the harp of Orpheus, a harp of 'feyre' and of 'loue', by means of which classical myth is transferred to the Celtic world.

These values, which are implicit in *Orfeo* and *Launfal*, would not emerge so clearly but for the fact that the major fascination and richness of meaning in these works centres on certain focal points: the representation of the two different *faeries*, which for the contemporary reader or listener must have been the main attraction. In *Orfeo*, for example, what strikes us is the violence with which the *faerie* first manifests itself: when Heurodis falls asleep under the fateful tree, she falls into a sort of catalepsy, which lasts all afternoon, from which she awakens in tears and 'reueysed out of hir witt'. It is she herself who later tells Orfeo how, as she slept, the king of the fairies, with a hundred knights and a hundred ladies, carried her against her will to his palace, and told her to present herself under the tree on the following day for the final journey. This scene, then, contains a dramatic element, which is intensified when, the next day, Heurodis is snatched away before the very eyes of Orfeo himself and a thousand armed knights who had come to protect her. Then comes Orfeo's decision – equally dramatic – to abandon his kingdom and live in the wilderness, alone, poor and bearded like a hermit. When the *faerie* reappears, this time to Orfeo, the transition to the enchanted world is slower and more gradual: first of all the king of the fairies appears, hunting, without any game, and then vanishes into nothing; then comes a troop of armed knights, who disappear mysteriously; then a group of dancing ladies and men; then sixty ladies with falcons on their wrists, hunting for water birds. Amid all this – and here the drama reappears – Heurodis arrives on the scene, weeping at the sight of Orfeo in such a forlorn state. But Orfeo follows the group and penetrates into the land beyond the mountain, where he discovers the *locus amoenus* of the *faerie*, a green valley, 'as briȝt so sonne on somers day'. In the middle of it stands a castle with a hundred towers, all of gold and precious stones, which Orfeo thinks is Paradise. He enters as a minstrel, and the reality is revealed to him: in the garden, in fact, is the whole crowd of people kidnapped by the *faerie*.

In *Launfal*, on the other hand, the appearance of the *faerie* is gradual, gentle and rhythmic: as the knight sleeps, two beautiful girls come towards him, and Launfal greets them courteously. They ask him, 'yif hit were thy wille', to call upon Tryamour, and Launfal, 'curteisliche', accepts. The *faerie* is presented, in short, as the world of 'courtesy', the splendid ideal world of beauty and love. Into this world Launfal enters by way of the Saracen pavilion, where he finds Tryamour, naked to the waist, on a purple bed. She offers herself to him, together with wealth and honours, if he will love her exclusively and without vainglory. Launfal agrees, and after a marvellous banquet he at once reaps the fruits of love. The atmosphere here is not at all dramatic but rather elegiac and conciliatory: the *faerie* does no violence to the knight but restores him to himself. This also happens later, when, with the usual cadenced rhythm, ten maidens of fairyland arrive at Arthur's Court to announce the imminent arrival of their mistress, Tryamour, who is coming to save Launfal. And the knight chooses the *faerie* once and for all, retiring with his beloved to the enchanted isle of Oliroun, where, once a year, he appears to human beings. Thomas Chestre, the mysterious author of *Sir Launfal*, thus circumscribes the *faerie* within the world of chivalry and courtesy, of love and gentility.

Around the end of the fourteenth century or the beginning of the fifteenth, we find two romances in which the pervading atmosphere is slightly different: *Sir Degrevant* and *The Squire of Low Degree*. Both of these are basically love stories, full of the usual elements and tricks of the genre. But the first is inserted into a story of territorial conflict between two noble neighbours, and the second is essentially the story of the social rise of a squire through the love of the King's daughter. In both there is a tendency to exaggerate those elements which are common in the medieval romance. In a sense both *Sir Degrevant* and *The Squire* are mannerist works.

The plot of *Sir Degrevant* is very simple:[18] the protagonist, Sir Degrevant falls in love with Melidor, the daughter of a neighbouring Duke who has trespassed and hunted on Degrevant's lands. The two meet secretly, but they are discovered and betrayed to the Duke. Melidor is courted by another Duke, whom Degrevant must defeat in a tournament. In the end Degrevant and Melidor's father make peace, and the two lovers are married. Actually, part of the author's attention is concentrated on the life of the time: for example, it is clear that although Degrevant has an income from his lands of a hundred pounds and many other sources of status, his social position is slightly lower than that of Melidor, whose father is an Earl; another Duke, in fact, is offered as her suitor instead of Degrevant. Then there is the feud between Degrevant and Melidor's father. This begins with the high-handedness of the latter, who goes hunting on Degrevant's property while he is away in the Holy Land. When Degrevant comes back he inspects the damage, reimburses his tenants and tries to do everything legally by sending a letter to his neighbour. The letter is refused and so he takes up arms. On the Duke's next incursion, Degrevant attacks him, wins the battle and then goes over to raise havoc in his enemy's lands. These were very much the habits of some of the landed aristocracy of the time. The author's other interest lies in the opportunities for describing details of décor that the story allows: Melidor's dresses, her room, the foods and wines of the lovers' *tête-à-tête* dinner, the apartment where Melidor lives and receives Degrevant. Each of these is described in precise detail, which suggests a special interest on the part of the public.

We find the same characteristic in *The Squire of Low Degree*,[19] which is full of lists of objects – from the trees and birds of the royal garden, to the foods served to the King by his squire, to the details of the picnic which the King arranges for his daughter (more than a hundred lines), down to the musical instruments that are played when the two lovers meet. Like *Sir Degrevant*, *The Squire* has a rather simple and commonplace plot: the squire in question loves the King of Hungary's daughter and his love is returned. But the girl asks him to prove himself by feats of arms and adventures and promises to wait for him seven years. Meanwhile, the steward is also in love with the princess; he betrays them to the King and prepares an ambush for the youth. When the latter goes to say farewell to his lady, on the night before leaving, he is attacked at the door of her room, but he kills the steward and manages to escape. The girl takes the disfigured body of the steward for that of her lover, has it embalmed and worships it as a relic. Meanwhile, with the King's support, the squire goes off on his travels and then returns; the two meet again and are married. With this romance, the macabre enters English narrative – a brief but significant appearance. To attract its audience, the verse romance must now use not only the usual devices of the genre and long elaborate lists of luxuries and delicacies, but also the morbid fascination of death.

The eight romances so far examined are among the best examples of a type that, as I have said, cannot be defined precisely without analysing the whole body of existing material. But on the basis of these eight examples, I can draw a few conclusions, however cautious and provisional, about the nature and importance of the romantic genre in England. In the first place, the appearance of these works considerably broadened the English literary horizon with respect to the more circumscribed limits defined by religious narrative: in this sense the romance is, from *King Horn* on, the 'secular scripture' of which Frye speaks.[20] This broadening occurs especially in the cultural field: the romances, or some of them, transpose the motifs of French courtesy into an English key, but at the same time they move away from the formalism of the French models and introduce elements of English 'realism'. And then they use 'folk' material, traditional stories, popular tales. In this way unofficial culture begins to move out of the purely comic or 'carnival' sphere and draws nearer to the secular stream of official culture – that is, to the theme of chivalry. So in a certain sense the romances form a bridge between the two cultures, and it is a bridge solid enough to bear the weight of Chaucer in the fourteenth century.

For all these reasons, the romances, like the religious narrative, comprise a 'mixed' body of material, and this is reflected in their style. Their modes of versification are rather limited, but they are elastic, and within them anything can happen. From the beginning – and we have seen this in *Havelok*, for example – the language takes on a decidedly colloquial flavour. This is particularly evident in the techniques of transition and compression. The anonymous narrators of the romances, who tell their tales in their own voice and stand 'outside' the story,[21] appear to be innocently and unconsciously omniscient, but they are able to link one scene with another with increasing ease and naturalness. 'Tags', parataxis and direct presentation dominate in the romances, even the later ones. One example should suffice, from *The Squire of Low Degree*:

> The squier kneled on his knee,
> And thanked that lady faire and free;

And thries he kissed that lady tho
And toke his leve and forth he gan go.

The Kinges steward stode full nye
In a chambre fast them bye
And hearde their wordes wonder wele
And all the woing every dele.
He made a vowe to Heaven-kinge
For to bewraye that swete thinge
And that squier taken shoulde be
And hanged hye on a tree;
And that false stewarde full of ire,
Them to betraye was his desire.

(279–92)

Here, in fact, the transition is effected without a hitch, and the narrative procedure is clearly direct and paratactic.

However, we have also seen how *Horn* and *Havelok*, to cite only two examples, manage to compress the narration into very short spaces, where everything is functional to the story. Again, the structures being created, midway between those of the popular tale and those of the *roman* are not entirely ingenuous. From the use of parallelism (*Horn* and *Havelok*), and correspondences and repetitions (*Floris*), to an attempt at 'interlace' (*Sir Perceval*), the device that dominates is that which Shklovsky calls 'stringing',[22] but this is less and less mechanical and in any case always works towards a symmetrical and harmonic construction. The *sen* of these stories is, of course, not very profound – it remains simply mysterious and evocative in *Sir Perceval*, as well as in *Orfeo* and *Launfal*. Aspects of irony and ambiguity are not developed at all. These romances are simple *fabulae*, without temporal distortions (except for *Sir Perceval*) or any interest in spatial depths or character development. The characters are still types, pure narrative functions. The imagination that governs the narrations and descriptions is devoid of metaphorical élan: it is ruled, above all, by metonymy – that is, by contiguity and association.[23] Once the essential frame of reference is found, the stories proceed within it: within the world of the *faerie*, for example, in *Orfeo*, or within the theme of the 'flower' in *Floris*.

The main contribution of these romances to Middle-English narrative lies, therefore, essentially in their construction and in their use of monologue and dialogue. And in the simplicity and naturalness of these last are the roots of the 'homeliness' of so much English literature, including, first and foremost, Chaucer and Shakespeare.[24]

So far I have examined, first, some of the poles between which the medieval

English romance moved and, secondly, some of the romances that seemed most useful for the purpose of characterising the genre. My concern has been with the 'average' and the 'type', both from the thematic point of view and from the point of view of aesthetic evaluation. However, Chaucer's romances have been mentioned as eccentric deviations from the norm. Another work, equally eccentric, though in a different way, is *Sir Gawain and the Green Knight*, the most interesting and beautiful romance produced on English soil and certainly one of the best to have come out of the whole European romantic tradition. *Sir Gawain* comes from north-west England, far from the cultural centres of the gallicising south; it has survived in only one manuscript, Cotton Nero A x in the British Library.[25] The specific sources of *Sir Gawain*, are not known, if indeed there were any, either in England or in France, although some of the events that occur in it have parallels in other romances.

The story consists of two central nuclei based on themes that are not rare in medieval legends and romances: the 'Beheading Game' and the 'Temptation'. These are closely linked by a third narrative artifice, that of the 'Exchange of Winnings'. The poem is divided into four 'fitts', and its central themes are distributed geometrically: in the first and fourth 'fitts' the 'Beheading Game'; in the second and third, the 'Temptation' and the 'Exchange of Winnings'.[26] Moreover, *Sir Gawain* begins and ends with a reference to Troy and Brutus, thus providing a mythological and fantastic frame within which the whole *fabula* is situated.[27] Finally, binary and ternary structures organise the romance: 'There are two New Year's Days, two "beheading" scenes, two courts, two confessions'; 'three temptations, three hunts, three kisses, three strokes of the axe';[28] the second, third and fourth 'fitts' are constructed with parallel elements (investiture of arms, journey, description of the castle and the Green Chapel, three temptations and three axe-blows, confession).[29]

The Green Knight's initial challenge to the whole Court of King Arthur is accepted by Gawain; in the end it is again Gawain who alone confronts the danger – but, as the Green Knight himself makes clear, he does so on behalf of the whole Round Table, which is thus put to the test by Morgan le Fay. Between these two episodes, Gawain faces other challenges: the journey, danger and winter, the temptations. But it is the outcome of the temptations that determines the outcome of the great final encounter at the Green Chapel. So it is a tightly-woven plot, which hindsight shows to be determined by the principle of causality. The drama of the first 'fitt' is followed by an apparent pause in the second and third, but this in fact lays the groundwork for the new drama of the fourth. Suspense, in short, ties everything together. *Coups de théâtre* are everywhere: the arrival of the Green Knight; the head that goes on talking after being cut off; the discovery of the castle; the first of the three appearances of the lady in Gawain's chamber; the second appearance of the Knight; the Chapel, which turns out to be different from what Gawain expected; the final revelation of the identity of the Green Knight and Bercilak, and of the old lady and Morgan le Fay.

However, these elements, which already show a degree of artistic elaboration that is quite out of the ordinary, are only the visible signs of a much deeper design. The poet of *Sir Gawain* – and in this he is unique among all the English romance writers and perhaps among all those of medieval Europe – creates space and time within his narrative and does so with a sense of perspective and of different dimensions.

There are at least three temporal dimensions in *Sir Gawain*. The first, which is mythological and fantastic for us but was historical for the readers of the time, is that of the Arthurian past, and this itself is a phase of the great mythological past to which belong Troy, Aeneas, Romulus, Brutus and the ancestral roots of England:

Siþen þe sege and þe assaut watz sesed at Troye,	*After; ceased*
Þe borȝ brittened and brent to brondez and askez,	
Þe tulk þat þe trammes of tresoun þer wroȝt	*man*
Watz tried for his tricherie, þe trewest on erthe:	
Hit watz Ennias þe athel, and his highe kynde,	
Þat siþen depreced prouinces, and patrounes bicome	
Welneȝe of al þe wele in þe west iles . . .	
Ande quen þis Bretayn watz bigged bi þis burn rych,*	
Bolde bredden þerinne, baret þat lofden,	*that loved fighting*
In mony turned tyme tene þat wroȝten.	*mischief*
Mo ferlyes on þis folde han fallen here oft	*marvels*
Þen in any oþer þat I wot, syn þat ilk tyme.	
Bot of alle þat here bult, of Bretaygne kynges,	*dwelt*
Ay watz Arthur þe hendest, as I haf herde telle.	*noblest*

(1–26)

* *founded by this noble warrior*

Initially this past is evoked by the poet; at the end it serves to frame the story:

Þus in Arthurus day þis aunter bitidde,	*adventure*
Þe Brutus bokez þerof beres wyttenesse;	
Syþen Brutus, þe bolde burne, boȝed hider fyrst,	*came*
After þe segge and þe asaute watz sesed at Troye,	
iwysse,	
Mony aunterez here-biforne	
Haf fallen suche er þis.	

(2522–8)

The second temporal dimension is cyclic, seasonal, ritual and religious.

It is the year that passes between one New Year and the next, in which the seasons follow one another from winter to winter, and the winters are marked by the ritual festivals of Christmas and the dates indicated by the Church calendar (Christmas, Lent, Michaelmas, All Saints, St John):

> A ȝere ȝernes ful ȝerne, and ȝeldez neuer lyke, *passes swiftly*
> Þe forme to þe fynisment foldez ful selden. *beginning; end; seldom*
> Forþi þis ȝol ouerȝede, and þe ȝere after
> And vche sesoun serlepes sued after oþer ... *followed*
> (498–501)

Thus begins the passage that is perhaps the most beautiful of the poem, and certainly the most famous. It takes us back to an age of pastoral simplicity within which moved even the aristocratic company of the Round Table, and behind this lies the irremediable sense of the 'tacito, infinito andar del tempo',[30] that time which inexorably carries man to the decisive event, the critical point of his life and his death.

The third temporal dimension of *Sir Gawain* is ordinary time, which reigns during the second Christmas festival of the poem, from Christmas Eve to the New Year: here the days are distinct one from the other, the day separate from the night, the hours marked by different activities. Bercilak rises with his men before dawn for the hunt; Gawain stays in bed until sunrise and encounters his lady; then he gets up, dresses, goes to Mass, dines and amuses himself until the moon rises. At dusk Bercilak stops hunting; when it is dark he returns. Then follows the evening meal, a chat by the fire, then bed. In other words, this is real time, precisely underlined by the author. This time is already 'deep', divided and punctuated by human events, which are in their turn framed and dictated by natural events. Because of this dual time-dimension the reader–listener has a double perspective, through crossed co-ordinates, as it were, of both Bercilak's day and Gawain's day – one out hunting and the other in the castle. Between these the poet moves back and forth three times,[31] thus emphasising their contemporaneity, and then brings the lines together at a single centre in the evening.

Space in *Sir Gawain* is also multi-dimensional. In the two long months that take Gawain from Arthur's Court to Bercilak's castle, the space he travels through is fantastic, indefinite, filled with the objects common to the medieval romance:

> Mony klyf he ouerclambe in contrayez straunge,
> Fer floten fro his frendez fremedly he rydez. *removed*
> At vche warþe oþer water þer þe wyȝe passed
> He fonde a foo hym byfore, bot ferly hit were,
> And þat so foule and so felle þat feȝt hym byhode. *he had to fight*

Se mony meruayl bi mount þer þe mon fyndez,   *among the hills*
Hit were to tere for to telle of þe tenþe dole.   *hard; part*
                               (713-19)

This is the space, in fact, inhabited by dragons, wolves, giants and 'wodwos', moving against the immobile background of the frozen land: in this space, Gawain, like Auerbach's Knight, passes into eternity, as if he were a painted knight, a Guidoriccio da Fogliano[32] motionless on horseback in a mysterious, ceaseless peregrination. It is the space that Gawain will traverse in order to return to Arthur, the 'wylde wyez in þe worlde', full of adventures. In *Sir Gawain*, unlike most medieval romances, these peripheral adventures are not narrated but left implicit, so that the story's thread runs straight and does not have to be unravelled.

Yet this romantic space, bordering on stereotype, comes close to the known, the geographical: Gawain's itinerary takes him towards North Wales, 'þurȝ þe ryalme of Logres'. Keeping Anglesey on his left, he passes Holy Head and enters the 'Wilderness' of Wirral. This route must have been recognisable for the poem's audience, though it is hard for us to reconstruct it precisely.

The landscape of *Gawain*, however, is described in a significantly more precise manner. At a certain point, Gawain's first journey takes him, no longer simply through 'strange countries', but 'by a mountain...into an old, deep forest, weird and wild, high hills on either hand, and below them a holt of huge and hoary oaks...; hazel and hawthorn were twisted there all into one, and rough, ragged moss grew rampant all about, and many small sorrowing birds upon bare twigs piteously piped there for pain of the cold'.[33] This landscape is individualised and sharply focussed, full of natural objects depicted with their specific features (the *hoary*, *twisted* trees, the birds on the *bare* twigs numb with the cold). And in this very definite space we suddenly see the sharp outlines of Bercilak's castle: 'above a lawn, on a mound, locked under boughs of many a boar-proud bole that grew by the ditches'.[34] This castle is described in minute detail, with its lawn, its surrounding wall, its drawbridge, gates, bastions, towers, pinnacles. It is a structure solidly planted on the ground; the footings of its rough-hewn stone walls are under water. At the same time it is a most vivid building, with painted pinnacles scattered about and clustered together, looking 'like decoration cut out of paper'. This is also the space that dominates in the description of the Green Chapel and the landscape around it:

And þenne he [Gawain] wayted hym aboute, and   *looked*
    wylde hit hym þoȝt,
And seȝe no syngne of resette bisydez nowhere,   *shelter*
Bot hyȝe bonkkez and brent vpon boþe halue,   *sides*

And ruȝe knokled knarrez with knorned stonez;   *rugged crags; gnarled*
Þe skwez of þe scowtes skayned hym þoȝt.   *skies; rocks; grazed*
Þenne he houed, and wythhylde his hors at þat tyde,
And ofte chaunged his cher þe chapel to seche:
He seȝ non suche in no syde, and selly hym þoȝt,
Saue, a lyttel on a launde, a lawe as hit were;   *mound*
A balȝ berȝ bi a bonke þe brymme bysyde,   *smooth barrow*
Bi a forȝ of a flode þat ferked þare;
Þe borne blubred þerinne as hit boyled hade.   *bubbled*
(2163–74)

A sharply visualised landscape, which is delineated little by little as it gradually comes into Gawain's view.

But the spatial sensitivity of the *Gawain*-poet is deeper still: as in the case of time, it is a contrast that sets the perspective. The exterior and interior scenes, in fact, dominate the three days of the hunt, with Bercilak and his men in the forest, and Gawain and the lady in the bedroom. Shifting rapidly from one to the other, the poet contrasts open and closed settings, natural space and artificial, human space. In this way he lays down the co-ordinates of a space that is real or at least perceptible as such by the reader.

This creation and articulation of time and space in several dimensions, one of which tends to reproduce the time and space of common experience, are the first tangible signs of an artistic and intellectual consciousness that is moving towards maturity. The deepening of perspective that occurs in *Sir Gawain*, from the point of view of Auerbach's outline of the development of mimesis in Western literature, finds its fourteenth-century equivalents only in Dante, in Boccaccio and, at least partly, in Chaucer. This is no small achievement, especially if we remember the poem's geographical-cultural eccentricity.

In this light, we can appreciate more fully the value of such features as the clear and precise divisions of the romance, the articulation of the plot, the parallelisms, the binary and ternary rhythms, the blending of ritual formality with particularised reality. The festivals, banquets, hunts, masses, investitures, journeys – in short, all the conventional devices of the medieval romance – are presented in *Sir Gawain* not only as obligatory rites of a social world that is sublimated in narrative fiction but also as individual events, detached from the featureless background of convention. Each of them is endowed with a particular function and a particular meaning: *that* hunt, *that* banquet, differing from each other in a thousand details that the poet dwells upon, bringing them into relief one by one against the common backcloth or picking them out with a single illuminating touch. A good example of this technique can be seen in the two armings of Gawain, one before his journey from Camelot to Bercilak's castle, the other before the meeting at the Green Chapel. One is narrated at length and in meticulous detail, the other is given a brief and summary treatment; the first is dominated by the shield and the 'pentangle' – the five-pointed star – emblazoned on it, the second by the green girdle given by the lady. These, as we shall see, are signs of two different moral situations.[35]

After this reconstruction, however summary, of the basic co-ordinates of the poem – those which in fact create the dimensions within which its universe moves – I must now consider what characteristics are implied by this universe. Our panorama of the poem's mimetic co-ordinates will then be complete. First of all, the poet of *Sir Gawain* creates a new psychological depth: his characters are not purely superficial figures, moving according to social and artistic conventions. Nor are they simple *exempla* of moral qualities or character types, such as one finds in all – even the best – medieval literature. The characters in *Sir Gawain* possess, even within the 'types' consecrated by tradition, individual characteristics; their actions are motivated by particular impulses and reactions. Except for Morgan le Fay, none of the characters is really 'flat'. Even Arthur, who in other romances is almost exclusively a royal figure without human depth, here is 'joly of his joyfnes, and sumquat childgered'; he does not like to sit or lie still for long, as he is spurred by 'his ȝonge blod' and his 'brayn wylde'. The Green Knight and Bercilak, who at the end are discovered to be the same person, are distinguished by their different characters: the first arrogant and provocative, the second friendly, courteous and pleasant. Here is the Green Knight making his challenge to the Round Table:

> 'What, is þis Arþures hous,' quoþ þe haþel þenne,   *knight*
> 'Þat al þe rous rennes of þurȝ ryalmes so mony?   *fame*
> Where is now your sourquydrye and your conquestes,   *pride*
> Your gryndellayk and your greme, and your grete wordes?   *fierceness*
> Now is þe reuel and þe renoun of þe Rounde Table
> Ouerwalt wyth a worde of on wyȝes speche,
> For al dares for drede withoute dynt schewed!'   *blow*
> Wyth þis he laȝes so loude þat þe lorde greued . . .
> (309–16)

And here is Bercilak returning from the first hunt:

> Thenne comaunded þe lorde in þat sale to samen
>   alle þe meny,
> Boþe þe ladyes on loghe to lyȝt with her burdes   *maidens*
> Bifore alle þe folk on þe flette, frekez he beddez   *men*
> Verayly his venysoun to fech hym byforne,
> And al godly in gomen Gawayn he called,   *in courtesy; gaily*
> Techez hym to þe tayles of ful tayt bestes,   *tally; nimble*
> Schewez hym þe schyree grece schorne vpon rybbes.   *fine flesh cut*

'How payez you þis play? Haf I prys wonnen?
Haue I þryuandely þonk þur3 my craft serued?'   *thoroughly*
                    (1372–80)

As we discover at the end, these are two parts acted to perfection and
with extreme naturalness. In the same way, Bercilak's wife plays her part
as temptress, with actions and words, with the consummate ability of one
who can dodge playfully between sexual attraction and social convention.
The lady enters Gawain's room for the first time, opens the bed-curtains,
slips in, 'and set hir ful softly on the bed-syde'. When Gawain decides to
open his eyes, he asks her to let him get up and dress. Here is her reply, a
little masterpiece of the art of seduction:

'Nay for soþe, beau sir,' sayd þat swete,
'3e schal not rise of your bedde, I rych yow better,
I schal happe yow here þat oþer half als,   *tuck*
And syþen karp wyth my kny3t þat I ka3t haue;   *talk*
For I wene wel, iwysse, Sir Wowen 3e are,
Þat alle þe worlde worchipez quere-so 3e ride;
Your honour, your hendelayk is hendely praysed   *courtesy*
With lordez, wyth ladyes, with alle þat lyf bere.
And now 3e ar here, iwysse, and we bot oure one;
My lorde and his ledez ar on lenþe faren,   *far away*
Oþer burnez in her bedde, and my burdez als,   *knights; ladies*
Þe dor drawen and dit with a derf haspe;   *fastened; strong*
And syþen I haue in þis hous hym þat al lykez,
I schal ware my whyle wel, quyl hit lastez,
          with tale.
      3e ar welcum to my cors,   *body*
      Yowre awen won to wale,   *pleasure; take*
      Me behouez of fyne force   *sheer necessity*
      Your seruaunt be, and schale.'
                    (1222–40)

But it is in the protagonist of the romance, Gawain, that we find the
poet's most refined psychological perspective. From the moment when, to
the sad farewells of his companions of the Round Table, he replies, with
'god chere', 'why should one fly from fortune dark and drear? What can
man do but try?'[36] up to the very end, Gawain's reactions are always
shown to us. 'Compast in his conscience', the poet says of him: Gawain is
the first self-conscious, thoughtful hero of English romance. A prime
example is the episode – a masterpiece of psychological finesse – in which
Gawain, who has just seen his host's wife creep into his room, first pretends
to be asleep, then opens his eyes, feigns surprise, crosses himself and waits
for the lady to speak and explain why she has come. This is one of the
points where mimesis in the romance is perfect (1178–1203).

This goes well beyond Auerbach's courtly knight and reaches, at a stroke, the mimetic sensibility of a Boccaccio: every move is indicated, every sensation and thought is mentioned and described; Gawain's embarrassment is emphasised, as is his timid–playful–prudent calculation. The space is filled with objects – curtains, canopy, door – and the poet uses each of these objects to obtain the desired effect. And the room is full of sounds, from the 'littel dyn at his dor, and dernly vpon', to the lady's closing of the door 'ful dernly and stylle', to her stepping up 'stilly' to the bed: all is muted, equivocal and ambiguous, until Gawain makes the sign of the cross 'as bi his saȝe þe sauer to worthe'.

Of all the characters in the romance, only Morgan le Fay lacks any psychological perspective. She is introduced, without our knowing who she is, as a wrinkled and dignified old lady; then she is revealed as the motivating force behind the whole action and, as such, she remains on a plane above the conflict. Perhaps rightly, she is left out of the play of psychological motivations in which all the other characters are involved. However, as Bercilak reveals at the Green Chapel, Morgan has her own motives for setting events in motion. While one of these is, so to speak, terroristic – to frighten Guinevere to death and deprive all the members of the Court of their 'wyttes', of their capacity to react like human beings – the other is to put the pride of the Round Table to the test and thus determine the justice or injustice of its renown. Hence the action is a test of the moral qualities of a whole society, a trial of that society's ability to put its professed ideals into practice. While the Green Knight's challenge is first accepted by Arthur, the supreme leader of the society, his place is taken by Gawain, the 'pearl' of the knights, the perfect representative of the virtues which that society has elevated to principles of life. *Sir Gawain* thus acquires an ethical dimension that carries it beyond the simple entertainment that was almost always the main aim of English medieval romance and endows it with a seriousness and austerity that colour the whole action. In the end, after the narrow escape from tragedy, the reader remains deeply disturbed – like Gawain – by the small flaw that he, the flawless knight, has demonstrated. That flaw, which the Arthurian society at once absorbs and transforms into a heraldic conceit, remains, on the individual plane, as the mark of the knight's humanity and his human fragility.

This moral dimension becomes the basis of a profound and subtle design. When Gawain departs in search of the Green Knight, he puts on his armour piece by piece and lastly takes up his shield, on which is painted the famous 'pentangle'. Here the poet stops to explain its meaning: the star is an emblem designed by Solomon 'in bytoknyng of trawþe'; it is a figure with five points, in which every line crosses and interweaves with the others, and it is composed of one endless line, so that the English call it 'þe endeles knot'. This is most appropriate to Gawain, who is always faithful in five ways and five times in each way, and, 'as golde pured', without flaw and adorned with virtues: he has proved himself stainless in his five senses, has never failed in his five fingers, has always had faith in the five wounds of Christ and has always derived his courage from the five joys that the Virgin had in her Son. Moreover, Gawain is endowed with five virtues: 'fraunchyse' (liberality), 'felaʒschyp' (love for one's neighbour), 'clannes' (purity), 'cortaysye', and 'pité' (piety). Beyond the play of symbolism, which the poet does dwell on, this passage opens an illuminating perspective on the action of the romance: because the first virtue that Gawain must prove in the course of his experience is precisely that 'trawþe' symbolised by the five-pointed star – which is not only faith, but also truth to one's word, honour, the cardinal virtue of the feudal knight. For the sake of this faith Gawain must respect his commitment to the Green Knight; for its sake he must refuse the advances made to him by his host's wife; for its sake he must carry out the exchange of winnings to the very end. And again, 'cortaysye', 'clannes' and 'trawþe' are challenged when Gawain is tempted by Bercilak's wife. In fact it is clear that the temptations are primarily of a sexual nature (and one could devote a whole chapter to the extraordinarily brilliant way in which the poet represents this attempt at seduction, perhaps the finest in medieval European literature) and that therefore it is Gawain's purity that is put to the test. But it is also clear that while Gawain has to refuse the lady's offer for the sake of his own purity and the 'trawþe' that binds him to his host, he cannot, in so doing, contravene the rules of 'cortaysye', which for example require him to accept the kiss and the gifts. In other words, private ethics and social ethics are inextricably mixed, to the point of provoking conflicts. To this relatively explicit dilemma is added another, subtler and more obscure one, which is ultimately decisive: Gawain, who has ably extricated himself from the tangle of the contrary demands of 'clannes', 'cortaysye' and 'trawþe', is surprised by an attack on another front, that of fear. Like every other knight, and more than any other, he must be completely fearless. So it is that Gawain, to protect his own life, which he knows to be in danger, accepts the green girdle from the lady and does not give it up in the exchange of winnings of the third day: 'but for ʒe lufed your lyf', as Bercilak tells him. For love of his own life Gawain has, in the end, failed in 'lewté' (loyalty) and in 'trawþe'. The girdle has become more important than the shield and the pentangle; Gawain curses his own cowardice. The ethical code of the society has been broken by the sin of one individual, who, for that matter, pays for this amply with deeds (the three axe-blows) and words (the confession to Bercilak). Gawain will wear the girdle forever as a symbol of his own failure. The Round Table will adopt it, transforming it into a chivalric decoration, like that Garter with the motto of whose Order the romance is concluded. The girdle, at first a typical token of an exchange of love, a chivalric object *par excellence*, is then laden with moral significance and finally returns to the courtly sphere. Gawain is absolved, first by the priest, then by Bercilak and finally by the society to which he belongs, which thereby absolves itself.

Up to now I have considered the spatial, temporal, psychological and moral profundity of *Sir Gawain*; we must not forget the social aspect, which constitutes such a large part of the fascination of the romance. In this sense *Sir Gawain* is, of course, one-dimensional. The society it depicts is almost exclusively aristocratic – 'the best', as all the poem's superlatives go to show: everything takes place in rich, refined and beautiful surroundings. But this uniformity is not flat, not an unchanging tableau. Each situation has its own characteristics and its own movement. The two Courts of *Sir Gawain* participate in the same world and have everything in common; yet it is clear that Bercilak's is a provincial Court, though a large one, which welcomes with open arms the knight from the famous Round Table, partly because he is one of Arthur's knights, a master of courtly manners. (Ironically, it is Bercilak's Court that must pronounce judgement on that of Arthur.) The most significant fact, however, is that the elements of this aristocratic and courtly world, which in other romances are taken for granted, in *Sir Gawain* are specified and described with scrupulous attention. Thus the rich and elaborate garments of the various characters are never the same, but each is suited to the occasion and the character – for example, the *décolletage*, front and back, that Bercilak's wife displays on her third visit to Gawain. The 'social' conversations too, always have a well-defined character – take for example those in Bercilak's castle. Even the verbal fencing between Gawain and the lady is never generic, never just vague 'love talk'; while remaining within the courtly framework, it always turns on a specific point – the kiss, or the gift – and the accompanying smiles, glances and embarrassments are constantly underlined. In short, the medieval courtly game of gallantry and chivalrous manners takes on a realistic depth that is very rarely found in the romances of the period. And this individuality, this specificity of the social dimension, is precisely what gives *Sir Gawain* the air of brilliant comic lightness that pervades it, contrasting deliberately with the seriousness and drama that lie beneath.

In fact *Sir Gawain* has one dimension that, for lack of a better word, can be called playful, which is at the same time both interior and exterior to the work. The whole action, not only the 'Beheading Game', is basically a *game* for the very people who live it: this is true at any rate of Arthur, who on New Year's Day refuses to sit down at the table until he is given some 'strange tale about some most mysterious thing, some monstrous marvel that merited belief, of the Old Ones, or of arms, or of other adventures, or until some stout lancer had sought of him some sure knight to join with him in the joust and in jeopardy lay mortal life against life'.[37] The arrival of the Green Knight offers just the adventure the King is waiting for, and thus the action of the romance is presented as an entertainment, a game of 'chance': this is what Arthur demands, and once it begins he can open the banquet. What we have, in fact, is an interlude recited for a year, which ends with Gawain's story and, still more significantly, with the whole Court laughing over the story of the girdle: a deliberate jest within the narrative fiction.

This 'double' aspect of the fantastic and the jocose, within the action itself, already shows an extraordinary artistic mastery. But, in addition, it is reflected at an external level in the 'frame' that the poet imposes on the romance from outside. He does this by placing the work in mythical-fantastic time, by calling it a 'laye', thus defining its action as one adventure among many others of the past. It is linked on the one hand with a long oral tradition ('I shal tell hit as-tit, as I in toun herde / with tonge / As hit is stad and stoken / in stori stif and stronge / With lel letteres loken / In londe so hatz ben longe') – and on the other hand with the world of books ('þe best boke of romaunce' and 'þe Brutus bokez'). The poet is in fact playing with his poem: and in this first shy glimmering of artistic self-consciousness we have the conclusive proof, if proof be needed, that with *Sir Gawain*, the isolated masterpiece of a provincial literature, the English medieval romance has reached maturity. It has taken firm possession of those mimetic co-ordinates that were evolving in Western culture, which in Italy found expression in the works of Dante and Boccaccio.

4

Dream and Vision

One literary genre, now extinct, was cultivated with particular interest in the Middle Ages. This was the genre in which a dream or vision constituted the framework, in form and substance, of the work of art. It was inherited from the classics and from Scripture: the *Somnium Scipionis* in Cicero's *De Re Publica* and the commentary on it by Macrobius, the visions of Ezekiel, Paul and John, and Alain de Lille's *De Planctu Naturae* are examples of a tradition that did not die out until the end of the Middle Ages. The vision and the dream are artifices whereby the artistic ego can speak to the reader through two voices that may be quite different – that of the poet and that of the dreamer. These modes generally indicate a penetration of the human spirit into a realm beyond the confines of ordinary experience, into a dimension where one discovers absolute truths and ontological realities, which appear only in veiled form in the sensible universe. In the dream there is always an underlying seriousness, which is not entirely cancelled even by a relatively light-weight subject. The vision always carries an important message from the author to his audience; nearly always there is a prophecy to be extracted and decoded. The genre is so elastic that, in the course of its development in the Middle Ages, it was not limited merely to themes of philosophical discussion, the experience of the other world and the mystic or apocalyptic vision. From the twelfth century on it was also adapted to the favourite theme of medieval poets – the theme of love, the religion of which was cultivated with such meticulous ritual. One need only think of the *Roman de la Rose*, which after the Bible was the work most widely read in all European countries in the Middle Ages.

The secular dream and the vision were passionately cultivated in France, and they also penetrated English culture, which was closely linked to that of the Continent. They had the honour of being introduced into the English language by Chaucer, who is generally believed to have translated the *Roman de la Rose* (or at least part of it) and the *Consolation* of Boethius and who set so much of his own narrative in dream form. However, this 'visionary' literature, which may be called secular and romantic, is not what I intend to deal with here. I should like rather to consider two works, both written in the last quarter of the fourteenth century, which in different ways

71

belong to the biblical–religious tradition of visions: *Piers Plowman* and *Pearl*. As we have seen in the first chapter, the dominant religious ideology of medieval Europe had already produced the traditions of hagiography, biblical paraphrase, and confession handbooks. *Piers Plowman* and *Pearl* are based on the same impulse: it is significant that *Pearl* was probably written by the same hand as *Patience, Purity*, and perhaps *Sir Gawain* and *St Erkenwald*, and that the tone of *Handlyng Synne* anticipates that of *Piers Plowman*. In any case, we are dealing with the same level of intellectual and artistic consciousness. Fourteenth-century English narrative faces the most difficult problems of its time in *Piers Plowman* and *Pearl*. This kind of narrative is no longer entertainment – like comic or romance narrative – nor is it written simply within an already-given code and genre (like the religious). It becomes problematic – the intention is to describe the pursuit of truth and justice or of man's ultimate aim, the supreme vision. In these poems, the narrative becomes philosophical. The organisation of the story thus follows very different lines from those we have come across so far. On the one hand, it is inspired by the logic of a dream or vision, which works through subterranean connections – labyrinthine, mysterious and yet meaningful – as, for example, the appearances and disappearances of Piers Plowman or the link between the Maiden and the jeweller. On the other hand, the whole story is orientated towards a fixed pole, which is never lost sight of. It thus becomes teleo-logical narrative and, more precisely, theo-logical (Truth in *Piers Plowman*, the Heavenly Jerusalem in *Pearl*). These are therefore difficult and complex works that require particular attention, with regard both to their themes and to the problems of narrative structure and style that they raise.

I

Piers Plowman is the poem that best represents one of the cultural trends with which a fourteenth-century Englishman might identify himself: the fact that about fifty manuscripts of it have survived is a sure testimony of this, and of the poem's popularity. *Piers Plowman* is also the most courageous intellectual undertaking in the whole history of medieval England. The fact that its author, William Langland, kept revising and rewriting it for nearly a quarter of a century – producing the three different versions known as A, B and C – is a sign of the poet's devotion to his task and of the difficulty involved in carrying it out.

The B text of *Piers Plowman* is perhaps the most complete and artistically coherent, and in accordance with the critical practice of the last thirty years, I shall focus on B.[1] In this version, the poem consists of a Prologue and twenty *passus* of irregular length, totalling around 7,200 lines. It is generally divided into two parts, of which the first, comprising the Prologue and seven *passus*, is known as the *Visio*, and the second, containing the other thirteen *passus*, is called *Vita de Dowel, Dobet and Dobest*.[2] It is a series of dreams, awakenings, and dreams-within-dreams, in the course of which the protagonist, the first-person narrator called Will, passes much of his life. In the *Visio* the dream points the way towards the building of a better society and the search for Truth. In the 'faire felde ful of folke' in which the dreamer finds himself at the outset, the King tries to establish the rule of Reason and Conscience, condemning Lady Mede. Meanwhile the Seven Deadly Sins confess, and Piers Plowman, before guiding the people towards Truth, asks that his half-acre should be ploughed, and tries to organise the work in a just and economical way. These efforts fail, and in the *Vita* Will devotes himself to the search for Dowel, Dobet and Dobest, through a series of fundamental encounters and conversations with various characters (such as Thought, Imagination, Dame Study, Scripture, Nature, Conscience etc.), each of whom has lessons to impart and definitions to offer. After being corrupted by Fortune and living a life of perdition for forty years, Will, still in dream, meets Faith, Hope and Charity, follows Piers Plowman to Jerusalem, and witnesses Christ's Passion, death and descent to Hell. Then he sees Pentecost, in which Jesus pours Grace on Piers and his people. The construction of Unitas, the Church, the Society of God, is attacked by the forces of evil, which cannot be defeated decisively. Conscience then decides to become a pilgrim and to set out in search of Piers, 'and siþþe he [Conscience] gradde after Grace til I gan awake'. The poem ends with the beginning of another quest.

This is a poem that encompasses the individual and society, Heaven and Earth, Good and Evil; even its allegorical personifications function as characters: it is the forces of Good and Evil, Old Age, the Plague and Death that give the finale its emotional tone and provide the narrative tension of the last two *passus*.

In fact this finale is a good point of departure from which to penetrate deeper into *Piers Plowman*. *Piers Plowman* ends a moment before the tragedy – the death of Will and the victory of the Antichrist – and two moments before the final jubilee – the resurrection of the dead, including Will, and the coming of Christ as judge. *Piers Plowman* ends in the historical present – Langland's time – and in the eternal present, in which everything is suspended as the search begins again, in the moment when Conscience cries out for Grace, and Will, old but now pure, awakens. In the world of dream, the search recommences; in the world of reality, life continues. A brilliant solution, this – matching the brilliance of Dante's beatific vision, of 'l'amor che move il sole e l'altre stelle,'[3] and that of the solitary way taken by Adam and Eve at the end of *Paradise Lost*. Only after reading to the end does one comprehend the enormous intellectual power of Langland as he feels his way along his path, with no *a priori* certainties and no predetermined goals, step by step, *passus* after *passus*, continually preaching, satirising, crying out his message of admonition and encouragement.

Let us begin, then, with the primary dimensions of a work of art, those of space and time. The space of *Piers Plowman* is the flat, unchanging space of dreams, devoid of any mimetic or imaginative depth. All that is defined, in a couple of brief strokes, is the beginning and end of the 'faire feld', the tower and the abyss, and the fortress-walls of Unitas. These are the only objects that occupy this space – it is really an immaterial space, without limits. On just four significant occasions it suddenly takes on a more definite form: in the 'faire felde ful of folke', in Piers Plowman's half-acre, in the Jerusalem of the Passion and in the citadel of Unitas. But these are merely wrinkles in the backcloth, which cannot give real depth to the one-dimensional scene. They are like islands marked on a map, enclosed spaces against a flat background.

Real time is marked by Will's falling asleep and waking up. Within this arc of time years pass – for example, the forty-five years in which Will follows Fortune – and the liturgical forty days from the beginning of Lent to Easter, the millennia that constitute sacred history and salvation, the thirty-three years of Christ's life, the three days of His Passion, death, descent into Hell and Resurrection, the days of the liturgy that follow, until Pentecost. Time is thus richly articulated in Langland's poem, yet it never has a mimetic function. It is used to indicate a profound, absolute significance: it is time in a symbolic and transnatural sense – in philosophical terms, the time of being, not of existence.

Again, *Piers Plowman* is a poem without any scenic background: in it there is no continuity of colours, lights, objects. Colours are indicated when they carry the message of the word, as in the case of Lady Mede's clothes. Light, a special light, appears only at the gateway of Hell just before the arrival of Jesus. Objects – the plough, the Cross, the Bill of Pardon – exist when they carry a burden of meaning; apart from that they are inert, non-existent. *Piers Plowman* is really a poem of voices – the voice of Langland, the voice of Will, the voices of all the allegorical personifications in eternal conversation, the voices of the cooks crying 'hote pies, hote'. *Piers Plowman* is the poem of the word; thus it reaches a tremendous climax when Christ, at the gates of Hell, pronounces his irresistible command:

> A vois loude in þat light to lucifer crieþ,
> 'Prynces of þis place, vnpynneþ and vnloukeþ,
> For here comeþ wiþ crowne þat kyng is of glorie.' (xviii, 263–5)

Eft þe light bad vnlouke and Lucifer answerde
'*Quis est iste?*   *Who is this?*
What lord artow?' quod Lucifer; þe light soone seide
'*Rex glorie,*   *The king of glory*
[The] lord of myght and of ma[y]n and alle manere vertues,
Dominus virtutum.   *The lord of virtues*
Dukes of þis dymme place, anoon vndo þise yates
That crist may come In, þe kynges sone of heuene!'
(xviii, 317–20)

Similarly consistent is the way the poem ends, with the great cry of Conscience calling for Grace.

It is in these very special primary dimensions, then, that the action of *Piers Plowman* takes place. Within this framework appear the allegorical personifications – projections of the individual, like Conscience and Reason, or projections of society, like Lady Mede and Holy Church, or distillations of human virtues and vices, like the Seven Deadly Sins. These figures are constantly arguing amongst themselves – a debate of essences in the world of being, of archetypes, without psychological depth. As we read we tend to get lost in this 'faire feld' of speaking statues, but Langland constantly brings us back to earth – the earth of workers, kings, knights, peasants, monks, rich and poor. There is a constant interplay between the world of being and the universe of existences, so that the personifications, or at least some of them, such as the Seven Sins, become individuals: for example Gluttony becomes a glutton who spends his time in the pub. It is in this movement back and forth from the abstract to the concrete that the quest – the poem's primary dimension – develops.[4]

The quest in *Piers Plowman* proceeds along two lines that constantly intersect – the social line and the individual line. The first starts from a point of fact – contemporary society in its corruption – and moves towards a perfect society on earth, the rule of the king aided by Conscience and Reason, and Piers's attempt at organising work in his half-acre. When this attempt fails, the search ends in the perfect society of the early Church and the corrupt society of the present Church – represented by Unitas, besieged by the Antichrist and about to collapse. That is to say, the social quest ends where it began, though on a different plane. The second quest is that of Will. It begins with his question to Holy Church, 'How I may saue my soule', and then moves towards Truth. Later it is transformed into the wider search for Dowel, Dobet and Dobest, and it ends when Will takes refuge in Unitas, only to witness its downfall. In reality, the two searches are closely interwoven one with the other. The protagonist of *Piers Plowman* is in fact Will, an individual who is also a representative of the whole human race, a social animal and an individual soul. Piers is the second main actor. With true genius he is characterised as a ploughman and thus represents the economic fulcrum of medieval society, but he is also a former servant of Truth, Christ, Peter and pontiff, and is therefore again a figure in which the social and the individual are inextricably interwoven. Precisely because the protagonist is Will, in whom the social and individual aspects of man come together, the quest in *Piers Plowman* is based on a fundamental impulse – the one that drives Will himself when he formulates his question, 'How I may saue my soule.' It is kept in motion through the whole course of the poem by a sort of central mechanism, which is expressed in the words pronounced by Scripture, 'multi multa sciunt, et seipsos nesciunt' (XI, 3) ('Many know many things, yet do not know themselves'). For what he – Will the dreamer – has to discover, he discovers bit by bit, taking a number of knocks in the process. He always fails to realise that the indirect answers, which he receives by the dozen during his dreams, are precise indications – that they are not just theoretical notions but are meant *for him* (for us), so that *he* (we) can act accordingly: and he must find them *within himself*. This unconsciousness of self is a basic element in the great machine of *Piers Plowman*; it is actually the fulcrum of what Lawlor has called the 'imaginative unity' of the poem.[5]

The double search in *Piers Plowman* can be followed on various different planes. The first, and most obvious, is the plane of the life of Will, who in the *Visio* appears substantially as an observer, while in the longer *Vita* he has a more active role to play. It is he who encounters Thought, Intelligence, Study and Learning, who is led astray by Fortune and its followers, who speaks with Nature and Imagination, who in some way witnesses the meeting between Patience and Haukyn, who listens to the speech of Anima, who contemplates the Tree of Charity, who meets Abraham, Moses and the Samaritan (Faith, Hope and Charity), who is present at the Passion and the Descent into Hell, the foundation of Unitas and the coming of the Antichrist. This is the plane encompassing the growth and education of a human being, who at first lacks self-awareness and who then discovers himself and who inexorably, and physically, grows old.

On another plane we can follow the quest of *Piers Plowman* through the mysterious, elusive figure of its second actor, Piers – his eternal pilgrimage, his sudden appearances and disappearances – flashes that give a glimpse of the world of the eternal. He is a *figura*[6] of the peasant Everyman, of Christ, of Peter, of the ideal pontiff and again of the pilgrim. We follow his efforts to organise the work on his half-acre; we see him making his will and tearing up the Bill of Pardon; we hear him mentioned by Anima, to Will's trepidation and joy; we see him enter Jerusalem. In fact we enter with him into a dimension that we do not fully understand but yet perceive as fundamental, because Piers, the faithful servant of Truth (that is to say, of God, as Langland explains), allows us to see into the plan of history conceived by God, and His intervention in it.

Yet again, we can reconstruct the poem's quest from the point of view of sacred history, which runs through it as a thread that is slender but never lost; and we find Adam and Eve, Cain, Noah, Abraham, Moses, Saul, David, Gabriel and the Virgin Mary, the disciples, Mary Magdalen, Peter, Christ and Lucifer – in short, all the fundamental episodes of a story which in the Middle Ages was absolute and certain and could be interpreted in four different ways: literal, allegorical, anagogical and moral.[7] It was the fount of truth and the guide to the redemption of all.

And sacred history carries us to the plane of the liturgical year: from Christmas (*Passus* xvi) to Epiphany, to Lent, the Passion, Easter, Pentecost (xix) and once again to Advent (xx). Thus we can follow 'the process of ritual being turned into drama',[8] in an operation typical of the Middle Ages – think of the Miracle Plays, for example. And, finally, we can reconstruct the moral journey of Will and of all humanity by tracing the line from the presence of the Seven Deadly Sins (*Passus* v) to the meeting with the three theological virtues, Faith, Hope and Charity (*Passus* xvi and xvii), and lastly to the gift made by Grace, after the foundation of the Holy Church, to Piers and to all men, of the four cardinal virtues of Prudence, Temperance, Fortitude and Justice (xix).

These, then, are the different levels on which we can follow the double quest of *Piers Plowman*. The poem thus reveals a multiplicity of dimensions, which enrich it and make it fascinating and at the same time form a design that is followed despite all the apparently confusing digressions, sermons and invectives. It is a plan that reveals itself little by little, becoming fully clear perhaps only at the end, when Will has had the *Visio*, passed through all the experiences of the *Vita*, and obtained all the answers he needed. To analyse this design, it will be convenient to divide *Piers Plowman* into two sections: because it is clear that while 'The *Visio* is concerned with the *animalis homo* and with the first stage in his regeneration, the *Vita de Dowel, Dobet et Dobest* is concerned with the spiritual life proper.'[9]

So I shall begin with the *Visio*:[10]

The first section (the *Visio de Petro Plowman*) is a study of human life in the active world as it existed before Langland's eyes; it concerns itself particularly with the following problems:

(1) What, in this business of honest and dishonest moneymaking that seems to keep the Field of Folk on the move, is to be rendered to Caesar, and what to God? (Prologue, i)
(2) How is a corrupt administration to be set to rights? (ii, iii, iv)
(3) How is society in general to purify itself? (v)

(4) The problem of labour versus famine and the twin problems of the shirkers and the impotent. (VI)

(5) Whether the solutions offered to these problems as they arise are pleasing to God, and, if so, what is the meaning of pardon, and what disciplines or virtues underlie these solutions? (VII) *This subsection may be regarded as the hinge upon which the poem turns toward an abstract consideration of Dowel, Dobet and Dobest.*

All these problems are considered *sub specie aeternitatis* and are riders to the principal problem – the grand subject of the poem – namely, how is man to work out his salvation? Thus far the first major section, which concerns the existing order of the active life in the world as lived by all men, but particularly as lived by the laity.

We can attempt to answer such questions schematically, with reference to the text of the poem itself: (1) Reason and common sense should regulate a man's conduct with regard to the question of what to render to Caesar and what to God (I, 54–7). One should also remember 'Give; and it shall be given to you' (I, 199). (2) Corrupt administration can be reformed by eliminating Mede and having the king rule with the aid of Conscience and Reason (III–IV). (3) Society can purify itself by confessing and repenting the seven deadly sins (V). (4) Labour should be divided among all people for the general good, and all should take part in it in order to avoid famines. Absenteeism should be punished, and those who are weak and incapable should be aided in a spirit of charity (IV). (5) The solutions given to these problems are pleasing to God (Truth), who grants the Bill of Pardon to Piers and to all those who have laboured with him. Yet the Pardon itself, 'And they that have done good shall go into life everlasting: and they that have done evil into everlasting fire', is a sentence from the Symbol or Creed of St Athanasius. It refers to the Universal Judgement, thus shifting the terms of the divine answer into an eschatological perspective, removing the Pardon from the *hic et nunc* of the society led by Piers. For this reason, Piers himself tears up the Bill and decides to devote himself to a life of prayer and penitence, while Will concludes that the Pardon is valid for a man's salvation, but not as efficacious as Dowel.[11]

This, then, is the structure of the *Visio*, and here, at the end of it, begins the *Vita*, with its triple quest for Dowel, Dobet and Dobest. The structure of the *Vita* has been clear to scholars since 1929, when Henry W. Wells, in his study of the construction of *Piers Plowman*, formulated the theory according to which Dowel corresponds to the active life, Dobet to the contemplative life, and Dobest to the mixed life. Since then, beginning with a further analysis by Wells himself,[12] the definitions of Dowel, Dobet and Dobest have multiplied. According to Coghill, the three lives are those of the layman, the cleric and the bishop; Meroney called them purgative, illuminative and unitive; Dunning and Donaldson, referring respectively to the A and C versions of the poem, maintain that the 'active–contemplative–mixed' and the 'purgative–illuminative–unitive' triad can both be applied together to Dowel, Dobet and Dobest; Roberston and Huppé bring in the three traditional modes of interpretation of biblical *sententia* – allegorical, tropological and analogical – thus producing a series of triads that apply not only to the *Vita* but to the poem as a whole;[13] finally, Hussey maintains – and I agree – that Dowel, Dobet and Dobest are not 'different "lives" or "states" but…degrees of the same thing'. Dowel, he says, is 'Langland's main concern throughout the poem'; Langland understands it as 'something like "living a good life in whatever state you are called" '.[14] Hussey does not deny that Langland wished to give us various definitions of Dowel, Dobet and Dobest, but he states that such definitions are not systematic, whereas the basic orientation of the poem is proved by the definition that Thought gives of them in the eighth *Passus*. This definition is the first of a whole series, and it remains substantially the same in all three versions of the work. It is worth remembering the salient points of the passage:

> Whoso is [meke of his mouþ, milde of his speche],
> Trewe of his tunge and of his two handes,
> And þoru3 his labour or his land his liflode wynneþ…
>   …dowel hym folweþ.
> Dobet [þus dooþ], ac he dooþ muche moore…
> Dobest is aboue boþe and bereþ a bisshopes crosse.
>
>   (VIII, 80–96)

In any case it is clear that the structure of the *Vita* consists, so to speak, of three great arches, devoted respectively to Dowel, Dobet and Dobest. However, these arches are not all of the same size. If we eliminate *Passus* VIII, which is really a prologue, Dowel extends from *Passus* IX to XIV, Dobet from XV to XVIII, and Dobest for the last two *Passus*, XIX and XX. This amounts to a sort of geometric 'regression', with six *passus* devoted to Dowel, four to Dobet, and two to Dobest. In the text, moreover, the definitions of these are all contained in the *Vita de Dowel*, except for one, which appears in the section devoted to Dobest. In fact, the definition provided by Thought, the first of the whole series, appears in *Passus* VIII, which is the prologue to all three of the 'lives' (perhaps that is why it is the most comprehensive, and, as Hussey says, the one that best reveals the nature of the three stages). In any case, we have fifteen definitions in all, of which two are offered by Will himself and rejected respectively by Scripture and Imagination. So it is clear that Langland gives greater weight to Dowel than to Dobet and Dobest: this is proved by the greater length of the section and the greater number of definitions (thirteen, apart from those in the prologue) given in that section. The reason for all this, I believe, lies in the fact that Dowel constitutes the foundation of the whole edifice – that is to say, Will's journey is much more difficult at the beginning, when he lets himself be led astray by Fortune and when he most needs the help of theoretical definitions to point out his goal. Once he has passed through this first, most delicate, phase, the way can become smoother and the traveller can do without theories: he can now *see* the Tree of Charity, *meet* Faith and Hope, *accompany* the Samaritan, *witness* the Passion and the Descent to Hell, *contemplate* the foundation of the Church and at last *enter* it. In other words, he can pass from listening to the word, to direct vision, and finally to participation. The last phase is again difficult for Will, and it contains the last act of a drama in which Langland was particularly interested – the drama of the Church established and immediately endangered, the fourteenth-century Church in which the poet already saw the arrival of the Antichrist. For this reason another definition of Dowel, Dobet and Dobest is offered to Will and to all mankind. In this section Dobest is, not without reason, precisely the foundation of the Church by Christ, His transmission of His own powers to Piers:

> And whan þis dede was doon do best he [þouȝte],
> And yaf Piers [pardon, and power] he grauntede hym,
> [Myght [men] to assoille of alle manere synne[s],
> To alle maner men mercy and forȝifnesse]
> In couenaunt þat þei come and knewelich[e] to paie
> To Piers pardon þe Plowman *redde quod debes*.
> (XIX, 182–7)

This is Conscience's last message to Will: 'redde quod debes' ('pay me that thou owest'), and, shortly afterwards, the words of the *Pater Noster*: 'dimitte nobis *debita* nostra, sicut et nos dimittimus *debitoribus* nostris' ('forgive us our trespasses as we forgive them that trespass against us'). This is an all-inclusive religion. Langland sees it as an absolute covenant, which is as valid on the spiritual as on the temporal plane, both for eternal salvation and for the good of society. 'Redde quod debes': Langland quite intentionally chooses the hard words of the servant whose master has forgiven him a debt of ten thousand talents, but who will not forgive his fellow servant the debt of a hundred pence, 'and he laid hands on him, and took him by the throat, saying, Pay me that thou owest' (Matthew xviii, 28). The master, hearing of this, is angry and has his servant thrown into prison 'till he should pay all that was due unto him. So likewise shall my heavenly Father do also unto you, if ye from your hearts forgive not every one his brother their trespasses' (verses 34–5). This is the law of the Kingdom of Heaven but also of earthly kingdoms, because 'haþ Piers power...To bynde and vnbynde...And assoille men of alle synnes *saue of dette one'* (xix, 188–90).

Langland's mental attitude in confronting the self-imposed problem of Dowel, Dobet and Dobest is inspired basically by two criteria – one practical and one, so to speak, philosophical. The first is exemplified by a phrase in which Dame Study reproves her husband, Intelligence:

And þo þat vseþ þise hauylons [for] to blende mennes wittes,	*tricks; blind*
What is dowel fro debet, [now] deef mote he worþe,	*become*
Siþþe he wilneþ to site whiche þei ben [alle].	
But he lyue in þe [leeste degre] þat longeþ to dowel	
I dar ben his bolde borgh þat dobet wole he neuere,	*surety*
Theiȝ dobest drawe on hym day after ooþer.	*Though*

(x, 134–9)

This is, in fact, the attitude dictated by common sense: it is pointless to pursue abstract definitions; one must *live* the life of Dowel. On the other hand, there is the position represented by Piers himself – and hence extremely authoritative – which reveals a deeper meditation:

And [demeþ] þat dowel and dobet arn two Infinites,
Whiche Infinites wiþ a feiþ fynden out dobest,
Which shal saue mannes soule; þus seiþ Piers þe Plowman.

(xiii, 128–30)

Thus Dowel, Dobet and Dobest are defined quantitatively (in fact Dobest is equal to two infinities plus faith):[15] therefore they are *a priori* unknowable, and to get an idea of them one can only approach them by *approximation*. And that is just what Will does, or is forced to do: each of the definitions he hears is an approximation, a part of the truth, each of them confronts the problem of Dowel, Dobet and Dobest from a different angle and each of them reveals a new answer. This philosophical attitude shows one of Langland's fundamental principles, one that goes beyond the structure identified up to this point: philosophically, *Piers Plowman* is a spiral that *tends* towards the knowledge of Dowel, Dobet and Dobest. Thematically, it traces yet another spiral, the axis of which is the Cross, the expression of Christ's *humanitas*. In its Christ-centred revolution, the Passion three times forms the fulcrum of the poem.[16]

While the three-part structure mentioned earlier may not be noticed at once by the reader, one is immediately aware of the way Will's experiences revolve around his problem – the unceasing centripetal tension that dominates both the *Visio* and the *Vita*. *Piers Plowman*, as critics have repeatedly stressed, is not a linear construction with clear, definite outlines but proceeds by way of a series of sermons, digressions, comments and asides. The method that governs the poem might be called Socratic or dialectical, but there is a model to which it corresponds much more precisely. This is the Gospels, in which the protagonist, Jesus, proceeds through questions and answers, actions and sermons, without a precise or clearly identifiable structural thread, and where His answers to the questions put to Him are often indirect (i.e. parables) or downright paradoxical. And this, on the whole, is the dimension in which *Piers Plowman* moves. Thoroughly permeated with the Gospels, the poem has the same radical intention, intolerant of compromises, and is wholly based on a divine, not human, logic. Of course this mode is also filtered through fourteen centuries of Christianity, so it is no surprise to find in the poem the typical features of the *questiones disputatae* of the medieval universities, with their special vocabulary of 'I pose', *'contra'*, and *'ergo'* – as, for example, when Will replies to the monks that Dowel certainly cannot live among them:

> 'Contra!' quod I as a clerc and comsed to disputen . . .
> (VIII, 20)

Nor is it strange to find Will and Thought, the tireless peripatetics, 'disputyng vppon Dowel day after other' for three days as they walk along in search of Intelligence. The 'scholastic' dimension is indeed present in the poem, providing a reflection of contemporary reality and the structural-stylistic framework of single episodes such as those cited above. Some of the themes that most preoccupy Langland – those of free will, the nature of merit, rewards on earth and in Heaven, and God's foreknowledge – are the central themes of the debate, inside and outside the Schools, that left its stamp on the logic of the *moderni* – that is, those philosophers who used the logic of language in the analysis of doctrinal and biblical problems, whose most famous exponent was William of Ockham. In this sense, *Piers Plowman* mirrors a reality that is no longer the exclusive patrimony of the 'clerkes' but has by now extended to the 'cultured' laymen, whose numbers had increased tremendously in fourteenth-century England. This can be seen in the following passage:

> I haue yherd hei3e men etynge at þe table   *noble*
> Carpen as þei clerkes were of crist and of hise my3tes,   *powers*
> And leyden fautes vpon þe fader þat formede vs alle,
> And carpen ayein cler[gie] crabbede wordes: *ill-tempered*
> 'Why wolde oure Saueour suffre swich a worm in his blisse   *serpent*
> That bi[w]iled þe womman and þe [wye] after,
> Thoru3 whic[h werk and wil] þei wente to helle,
> And al hir seed for hir synne þe same deeþ suffrede?
> Here lyeþ youre lore?' þise lordes gynneþ dispute,   *teaching*
> 'Of þat [ye] clerkes vs kenneþ of crist þe gospel:

82

*Filius non portabit iniquitatem patris &c.**
Why sholde we þat now ben for þe werkes of Adam
Roten and torende? Reson wolde it neuere!
*Vnusquisque portabit onus suum &c.'***

(x, 104–17)

* *The son shall not bear his father's sin.*
** *Every one shall bear his own burden.*

The problem of defining Dowel, Dobet and Dobest is also confronted by
the *moderni* – it is a central theme in their writings. They formulate it with
the question, 'quid sit facere quod in se est?' ('What is meant by doing
what is in you?'). And 'rendering what you owe by doing your best, doing
what is in you', is in fact the answer *Piers Plowman* provides for the meaning of the Dreamer's quest after Dowel, Dobet and Dobest. The logic of the
moderni no longer allows the construction of perfectly coherent and complete systems of thought – taking in everything from theology to physics –
and *Piers Plowman*, which is for the most part philosophically selective and
synthetic, cannot have the architectural coherence of a *Divine Comedy*.
Piers Plowman is, in form and substance, the expression of the crisis of
the fourteenth-century English and European intellectual, the tormented
search for rational systems that can no longer be constructed, the total
reliance on will, grace and love. There is a crucial and highly dramatic
moment in the poem: after Scripture has paraphrased the parable of the
Marriage Feast that ends when Christ says, 'Multi enim sunt vocati, pauci
vero electi' ('For many are called, but few are chosen'), Will, his heart
trembling and full of doubt, asks himself, 'whether I were chosen or nouȝt
chosen', and begins to argue this tremendous question in his own mind,
speaking to Scripture (xi, 103–35). Their conclusion is that every Christian
may ask to be admitted to the Kingdom of Heaven, by virtue of the blood
with which Christ redeemed us and by virtue of baptism. Scripture concludes that 'may no synne lette Mercy alle to amende and mekenesse hir
folwe'. But Trajan, the Roman Emperor who was thought in the Middle
Ages to have been saved, bursts in at this point and exclaims:

> ... clerkes wite þe soþe
> That al þe clergie vnder crist ne myȝte me cracche fro helle, *snatch*
> But oonliche loue and leautee and my laweful domes. *justice*
> (xi, 143–5)

Only love, good faith, and the exercise of lawful judgement: Trajan completes, and at the same time reverses, the conclusions of Will and Scripture.[17]
    This is why one of the central themes of *Piers Plowman* is divine love, on
which subject Langland's poetry sounds with greatest fullness and warmth:

[For þus witnesseþ his word; werche þow þerafter.]   *act; accordingly*
For truþe telleþ þat loue is triacle of heuene: *healing remedy*
May no synne be on hym seene þat vseþ þat spice,
And alle hise werkes he wrou3te with loue as hym liste;
And lered it Moyses for þe leueste þyng and moost lik to *dearest*
  heuene
And [ek] þe pl[ante] of pees, moost precious of vertues.
For heuene my3te nat holden it, [so heuy it semed],
Til it hadde of þe erþe [y]eten [hitselue].
And whan it hadde of þis fold flessh and blood taken   *earth*
Was neuere leef vpon lynde lighter þerafter,
And portatif and persaunt as þe point of a nedle   *portable; piercing*
That my3te noon Armure it lette ne none hei3e walles.   *armour*
Forþi is loue ledere of þe lordes folk of heuene
And a meene, as þe Mair is, bitwene þe [commune] &   *intermediary*
  þe[kyng];
Right so is loue a ledere and þe lawe shapeþ.

                (I, 147–61)

This is the love of the God who becomes man and sacrifices Himself for man. But love is also the foundation of the ideal society of which Conscience speaks.

Ac kynde loue shal come 3it and Conscience togideres
And make of lawe a laborer; swich loue shal arise
And swich pees among þe peple and a parfit truþe . . .

                (III, 299–301)

Such quotations could be multiplied, down to the famous words that Christ addresses to Lucifer, one of the high points of the poem:

For I þat am lord of lif, loue is my drynke,
And for þat drynke today I deide vpon erþe.

                (XVIII, 365–6)

Thus love, for Langland as for Dante, is a universal force, an objective principle of human life, which wants to 'trasumanar' – to pass beyond humanity.

The other great conception that fills *Piers Plowman*, the one most loved by its author, is Poverty – the poverty of the Gospels and of St Francis of Assisi, the poverty so much debated in the fourteenth century. Langland begins, of course, with the beatitudes: 'Beati pauperes, quoniam ipsorum est regnum celorum' (XIV, 214: 'Blessed are the poor: for theirs is the Kingdom of heaven'). But the discourse at once broadens out, echoing Vincent of Beauvais:

'*Paupertas,*'quod Pacience, '*est odibile bonum,*
Remocio curarum, possessio sine calumpnia, donum dei sanitatis mater;

                84

Absque solicitudine semita, sapiencie temperatrix, negocium sine dampno;
Incerta fortuna, absque sollicitudine felicitas.'

(XIV, 274)

('Poverty is a good – yet a hateful one: the removal of anxieties; possession without calumny; a gift of God; the mother of (good) health; a path free from worry; mistress of wisdom; business without losses; amidst fortune's uncertainty, happiness without worry' (trans. Schmidt).)

When Patience finishes explaining this passage to Haukyn in English, listing and discussing the nine 'points' of Poverty, *Activa Vita* weeps hot tears of repentance. The whole of *Passus* XIV is, in fact, devoted to the praise of Poverty, and with this Langland reaches moments of intense pathos. The poverty he contemplates is not just an abstraction, it is poor people in the flesh, and his poetry becomes decidedly evangelical:

> For muche murþe is amonges riche, as in mete and cloþyng,
> And muche murþe in May is amonges wilde beestes;
> And so forþ while somer lasteþ hir solace dureþ.
> Ac beggeris aboute Midsomer bredlees þei [soupe],
> And yet is wynter for hem worse, for weetshoed þei [gange],*
> Afurst soore and afyngred,** and foule yrebuked
> And arated of riche men þat ruþe is to here.   *scolded by*
> Now, lord, sende hem somer, and som maner ioye,
> Heuene after hir hennes goyng þat here han swich defaute.
>
> (XIV, 157–65)
>
> * *they go wet-shod*
> ** *sore thirsty and hungry*

This is what George Kane calls Langland's 'tenderness',[18] from which his best poetry springs. From the poor he passes to poverty, which is like a nut that has a bitter shell and a sweet kernel (XI, 251–4), then to God, who has often shown Himself in the garments of a poor man or a pilgrim (XI, 232–7), to the whole of humanity in its pilgrimage (XI, 234), to all men, poor and rich:

> For alle are we cristes creatures and of his cofres riche,   *coffers*
> And breþeren as of oo blood, as wel beggeres as Erles.
>
> (XI, 199–200)

And finally to the animals, to nature, to all creation, with an impulse that is once again evangelical and Franciscan – a view of the 'little threshing-floor that makes us so fierce':[19]

> And on a mountaigne þat myddelerþe hiȝte, as me [þo] þouȝte,
> I was fet forþ by [forbisenes] to knowe
> Thorugh ech a creature kynde my creatour to louye.
> I seiȝ þe sonne and þe see and þe sond after,
> And where þat briddes and beestes by hir mak [e þei] yeden,   *went*

85

Wilde wormes in wodes, and wonderful foweles
Wiþ fleckede feþeres and of fele colours.
Man and his make I myȝte [se] boþe.
Pouerte and plentee, boþe pees and werre,
Blisse and bale boþe I seiȝ at ones,
And how men token Mede and Mercy refused.

(xi, 324–34)

So that from love we pass to intellectual curiosity, 'probably the most important single factor in determining the plan of the poem', 'responsible for at least one of the finest passages of poetry in the Lucretian tradition that the Middle Ages produced':[20]

Briddes I biheld þat in buskes made nestes;
Hadde neuere wye wit to werche þe leeste.   *man*
I hadde wonder at whom and wher þe pye   *magpie*
Lerned to legge þe stikkes in whiche she leyeþ and bredeþ.
Ther nys wriȝte, as I wene, sholde werche hir nes[t] to paye;   *craftsman*
If any Mason made a molde þerto muche wonder it were.
Ac yet me merueilled moore how many oþere briddes
Hidden and hileden hir egges ful derne   *covered*
[For men sholde hem noȝt fynde whan þei þerfro wente;
In Mareys and moores [manye] hidden hir egges]
For fere of oþere foweles and for wilde beestes.
And some troden, [I took kepe], and on trees bredden,   *copulated*
And brouȝten forþ hir briddes al aboue þe grounde.
And some briddes at þe bile þoruȝ breþyng conceyued,   *bill*
And some caukede; I took kepe how pecokkes bredden.   *trod*
Muche merueilled me what maister [þei hadde],
And who tauȝte hem on trees to tymbre so heiȝe   *build*
Ther neiþer burn ne beest may hir briddes rechen.
And siþen I loked on þe see and so forþ on þe sterres;
Manye selkouþes I seiȝ ben noȝt to seye nouþe.   *wonders*
I seiȝ floures in þe fryth and hir faire colours
And how among þe grene gras growed so manye hewes,
And some soure and some swete; selkouþ me þouȝte.
Of hir kynde and hir colour to carpe it were to longe.
Ac þat moost meued me and my mood chaunged,
That Reson rewarded and ruled alle beestes
Saue man and his make . . .

(xi, 345–71)

Thus we come to the intellectual key of the poem, the almost Faustian spirit that pervades it through and through:

Alle þe sciences vnder sonne and alle þe sotile craftes
I wolde I knewe and kouþe kyndely in myn herte.

(xv, 48–9)

Kenelm Foster has defined Dante as 'the mind in love',[21] and so is Langland, in a way that is at once quite different and quite similar. Langland too has a boundless love for human beings, for the created world, for knowledge; like Dante, he takes enormous pleasure in disputing, reasoning, seeking, defining. But Langland does not manage to resolve the contradictions involved in being an intellectual, a poet and a consistent Christian – as Dante does when he elevates his poem to the level of a sacred prophecy and himself to an Aeneas and a St Paul. Dante too, of course, proclaims:

> State contenti, umana gente, al *quia*:
> ché se possuto aveste veder tutto,
> mestier non era parturir Maria . . .
> *(Purgatorio,* III, 37–9)

('Rest content, race of men, with the *quia*: for, if you had been able to see all, there was no need for Mary to give birth . . .')

But Dante never doubted his art, his right to work at it: indeed, he transformed this right into a moral duty, the duty to tell the truth.[22] Langland, on the other hand, doubts his very right to write:

> And þow medlest þee wiþ makynges and myȝtest go seye þi sauter,
> And bidde for hem þat ȝueþ þee breed, for þer are bokes y[n]owe
> To telle men what dowel is, dobet and dobest boþe,
> And prechours to preuen what it is of many a peire freres.
>
> (XII, 16–19)

Thus speaks Imagination, and the poet replies that if only someone would tell him what is the nature of Dowel, Dobet and Dobest, he would stop writing and give himself up entirely to the Church and to prayer (XII, 26–9). If there is a solution to Langland's aesthetic problem, it is severely limited:

> It is *licitum* for lewed men to [legge] þe soþe   *lawful; affirm*
> If hem likeþ and lest; ech a lawe it graunteþ,   *canon*
> Excepte persons and preestes and prelates of holy chirche.
> It falleþ noȝt for þat folk no tales to telle
> Thouȝ þe tale [were] trewe, and it touche[d] synne.
> Þyng þat al þe world woot, wherfore sholdestow spare
> To reden it in Retorik to arate dedly synne?   *reprove*
> (XI, 96–102)

Langland sets precise limits on human knowledge – much more severely than Dante and St Thomas Aquinas, with their faith in human reason (which after all was God's own creation). Langland places himself in a different, biblical and Augustinian tradition, and yet again he reflects the crisis of metaphysics that started in the fourteenth century. When Will proclaims his desire to know all the sciences, *Anima* replies: 'Thanne artow imparfit...and one of Prydes kny3tes. For such a luste and lykyng Lucifer fel from heuene' (xv, 50–1). And after Will has contemplated the wonders of nature, Imagination points out to him the precise limits of human reason:

> And so I seye by þee þat sekest after þe whyes
> And aresonedest Reson, a rebukynge as it were,   *argued with*
> [And willest of briddes & beestes and of hir bredyng knowe...]
> Clergie ne kynde wit ne knew neuere þe cause,
> Ac kynde knoweþ þe cause hymself, no creature ellis.   *Nature*
> (xii, 218–26)

Then, when his desire for knowledge is directed towards the ways of the Lord – that is to say, when he enters the sphere of metaphysics – Dame Study at once quotes Paul and Augustine, 'Not to be more wise than it behoveth to be wise', and censures the philosophers explicitly, without mincing words:

> For alle þat wilneþ to wite þe [whyes] of god almy3ty,
> I wolde his ei3e were in his ers and his [hele] after...
> (x, 127–8)

In his fervour, Langland approaches the position of St Augustine, whose words he repeats in the tenth *Passus*: 'Lo, the ignorant arise and take Heaven by force, while we, with all our wisdom, are plunged into Hell.' The Christian paradox,[23] of which this is an example, is followed through to the end, and Langland, who always loves the humble, completes the quotation with the justly famous lines:

> ...Than Plowmen and pastours and [pouere] commune laborers,
> Souteres and shepherdes; [swiche] lewed Iuttes   *ignorant people*
> Percen wiþ a Paternoster þe paleys of heuene
> And passen Purgatorie penauncelees at hir hennes partyng   *death*
> Into þe [parfit] blisse of Paradis for hir pure bileue,
> That inparfitly here knewe and ek lyuede.
> (x, 466–71)

The problem of knowledge and wisdom is, in short, presented entirely within the perspective of faith and ethics. As we have seen, it is only in this way that the self-consistent Langland was able to justify his art; now he justifies wisdom and intelligence. If, in fact,

> Clergie and kynde wit comeþ of si3te and techyng
> As þe book bereþ witnesse to burnes þat kan rede:
> *Quod scimus loquimur, quod vidimus testamur.**
> Of *quod scimus* comeþ Clergie, [a] konnynge of heuene,
> And of *quod vidimus* comeþ kynde wit, of si3te of diuerse peple
> (xii, 64–8)

> * *We speak what we know and we testify what we have seen.*

– if, in other words, wisdom and intelligence are *naturalia*, they are still 'to commende...And namely clergye, *for crystes loue þat of clergye is roote*' (XII, 72–3). So in the end knowledge is justified by means of a parable proposed by Imagination: let two men be taken and thrown in the Thames; one knows how to swim and the other does not. Will the one who knows how to swim not save himself?

> 'Right so', quod þe renk, 'Reson it sheweþ
> That he þat knoweþ clergie kan sonner arise
> Out of synne and be saaf, þou3 he synne ofte,
> If hym likeþ and lest, þan any lewed [sooþly].
> For if þe clerk be konnynge he knoweþ what is synne,
> And how contricion wiþoute confession conforteþ þe soule...'
>
> (XII, 170–5)

Knowledge, in short, is justified as a means of salvation, as a moral instrument. This is why Will's quest, which might at first sight seem to be a search for knowledge and truth, is really an essentially moral one: a search for the Truth, which is God, and for the active way (*D*owel, *D*obet, *D*obest) in which man can save himself and finally reach that Truth.

Following two of the themes that run through *Piers Plowman*, those of poverty and love, we have gradually arrived at the intellectual key of the poem and the contradictions that characterise Langland's attitude to the problems of art, knowledge and wisdom. As the work that best expressed the crisis of late fourteenth-century England, *Piers Plowman* was very popular in its time. Its audience has been identified as the clergy and the new bourgeoisie, rich and well educated, of the latter half of the fourteenth century and then the fifteenth century.[24] This is the class that Langland himself describes:

> Ac if þei carpen of crist, þise clerkes and þise lewed,
> At mete in hir murþe whan Mynstrals beþ stille,
> Than telleþ þei of þe Trinite [how two slowe þe þridde],
> And bryngen forþ a balled reson, taken Bernard to witnesse,   *crafty argument*
> And puten forþ presumpcion to preue þe soþe.
> Thus þei dryuele at hir deys þe deitee to knowe,
> And gnawen god [in] þe gorge whanne hir guttes fullen.
>
> (X, 52–8)

The popularity of *Piers Plowman* among its contemporaries means two things: that the problems discussed in the poem aroused the passionate interest of both 'clerkis' and 'lewed', and that the readers were attracted, even fascinated by the *way* in which these problems are discussed and the way in which the poem is built. In short, they must have found its form as aesthetically pleasing as they found its content compelling. Furthermore, if one accepts what has been said here about Langland's attitude to 'aesthetic' and 'epistemological' problems, the poem was intended by its author both as a work of art and as the vehicle of a moral and religious message. Critics must take account of this; *Piers Plowman* can no longer be considered at best as a satire and at worst as a boring allegorical–moralistic tract. Recent criticism has approached the problem with greater subtlety, beginning with Kane's theory of the four impulses, down to Bloomfield's identification of six formal traditions in which the poem participates.[25] Both these approaches are based on the same fundamental distinction, between art or literature on the one hand, and religion on the other. This distinction is very dangerous when carried to its logical conclusions – one cannot help being reminded of Croce's division between structure and poetry in Dante, with its disastrous consequences for Italian criticism.[26] In actual fact, notwithstanding the moral doubts of its author, *Piers Plowman* was intended and conceived as a work of art, of literature, of narrative. This is proved by its general design and structure, and by the centripetal tension that I have tried to bring out. It is not a tension involving abstract ideas alone: it affects a human being, Will Langland (who is a poetic *persona* – like Dante Alighieri) and a chameleon-like man–god *figura*, Piers the ploughman. These two characters are followed, on their troubled and mysterious journey, with an intent that is clearly dramatic and narrative, not simply didactic. The fact that the poem also expresses a moral and religious message (not to mention a social and political one) is quite natural at a time when the very dimensions of ideology were those of ethics and religion: again one thinks of the *Divine Comedy*.[27] And if the aesthetic value of a work is based on the multiplicity of meanings that may or may not be drawn from it, I think it is clear beyond any doubt that *Piers Plowman* is just as rich in this sense as the *Divine Comedy*, though, of course, in quite a different way. It is certainly true that the six formal traditions described by Bloomfield are present in the poem; in fact one could add others, such as that of the spiritual autobiography that began with Augustine's *Confessions*, or that of the Gospels, or that, suggested by Bloomfield himself, of the Apocalypse. And yet *Piers Plowman* is an original formation, more 'original', in the final analysis, than *Paradise Lost* or *Pilgrim's Progress* or even its contemporary, the *Canterbury Tales*.

Perhaps the 'aesthetic' problem of Langland's poem can be illuminated by referring to Dante, for example the *Epistle to Cangrande* in which he explains the principles on which the *Divine Comedy* is constructed. Dante maintains that the philosophical dimension of his poem is essentially an ethical one, that the work has a subject that can be considered from the literal and from the allegorical point of view, and finally that 'the form or method of treatment is poetic, fictive, descriptive, digressive, transumptive and likewise proceeding by definition, division, proof, refutation and setting forth of examples'. Taking these definitions purely as a model, let us try to see how they apply to *Piers Plowman*. The moral nature of the quest narrated in this work has already been demonstrated; a summary exposition of the literal subject of the poem would take a couple of dozen pages. The existence of an allegorical plane in *Piers Plowman* is self-evident: indeed, Robertson and Huppé find in it a consistent and continuous anagogical and tropological structure.[28] Less radically, Elizabeth Salter, after tracing some of the work's fluctuating and dramatically conceived allegorical themes, concludes that 'an over-all multiple meaning for the poem can still be defended' and goes on to give a summary indication of its various 'meanings'.[29] I agree with her argument and quote some of her more important observations:

As far as the second mode of significance, the allegorical, is concerned, the poem examines powerfully the special relationship of man and Christ: Christ the Redeemer, the way to God, the moat of Mercy, the pilgrim Piers, who is both human and divine [...] As far as the third level is concerned, the tropological, moral sense, the poem teaches on the Christian virtues around which a man's life should be set – selflessness, patience, charity. It shows how sin can be cleansed through prayer and repentance: so the Seven Deadly Sins repent, the cloak of the ordinary unreformed man, Hawkin, is scoured fresh, and he is set on the right path [...] When we turn to the fourth level, the anagogical, mystical significance, the poem 'shadows forth' how the mystic's life develops – from active good deeds, to dissatisfaction with this (as Piers turns from ploughing to prayer in Passus VII), on to harsher disciplines (the self-analysis, the difficult inquiries of Passus VIII–XV). Then comes the gradual revelation of God's love; the discovery, by means of love, of God or Truth within the soul.[30]

Elizabeth Salter has thus elucidated the multiple meaning of Langland's poem with precision and yet with the elasticity that is necessary in any interpretation.

It now remains to be seen whether, and in what measure, one can apply to this poem the model of the *modus tractandi* provided by Dante's *Epistle to Cangrande*. This in no way invalidates other 'models', such as, for example, the one codified in the *artes predicandi*, of the 'modern' or 'university' type of sermon referred to by Owst and Spearing.[31] The point is simply to use a model worked out specifically for a *poetic* work, in fact for a poem – the *Divine Comedy* – which has certain characteristics in common with *Piers Plowman*. In this sense, the first four *modus tractandi* of the *Comedy* can easily be applied to Langland's work. If *poesis* and *fictio*, which are practically synonymous, are taken to mean a composition (*fingere-facere-poiein*) that is 'poeticised' through rhetoric and music,[32] then *Piers Plowman*, which Langland himself alludes to (XII, 12) as a 'makynge' (akin to *facere-poiein*) and as a thing 'to reden in *retoryke*' (to be proclaimed openly in 'poetry': XI, 97-8), is certainly 'poetic' and 'fictive'. Nor can it be doubted that *descriptio* and, more abundantly, *digressio* function in it. The first, for example, appears in the description of the 'faire feld', of Lady Mede, the Seven Deadly Sins and Haukyn's 'coat'. Digression is prominent in *Passus* XV, which is centred on the theme of charity. Here Anima attacks proud clerics and corrupt priests, then the *passus* returns to the theme of charity, then it turns again to praise the Desert Fathers, to lament the decadence of wisdom and finally to point out the responsibilities of priests. It should also be noted that, unlike the *Divine Comedy*, *Piers Plowman* makes very limited use of the visual element, and that therefore *descriptio* is not a primary principle in the poetic imagination of this work. *Digressio*, on the other hand, is much more prominent than in Dante; it is almost a structural method, or at least a procedure functional to the overall plan of the poem.[33] It is not, as has been often said, a question of uncontrolled 'utterance'; digression is used deliberately as a means of opening up new spaces within the poem. These generally belong to the sphere of the historical present, especially in a moral–political direction. An example that can serve for all is the continuous invective against the rich and against the corruption of the Mendicant Orders, which, to cite just one case, actually sent their members to the University to learn logic 'and lawe and eke contemplacioun, / And preche men of Plato and preue it by Seneca, / That alle thinges vnder heuene ou3te to ben in comune' (XX, 271-4). Here Langland satirically hints at the appropriation of intellectual and political power by the Friars,[34] in the context of their degradation, as he sees it, with respect to the ideals propagated by Dominic and Francis (XV, 409-15) – and, still more broadly, of the decadence of the whole Church (XV, 409-600). This is a leitmotiv that runs throughout *Piers Plowman*, as it does, for that matter, in the *Divine Comedy*. Precisely through the digressions, the spiritual vision and the temporal one (kingdom, riches, commerce, manual labour) acquire a certain coherence in terms of a radical orthodoxy based on a return to their original meanings.

The fifth 'method of treatment' of the *Epistle* is *transumptio* (or *translatio* in the classics), which is defined as

metaphorical expression, primarily referring to the broader and more complex type of metaphor which goes beyond the semantic transposition of the single word.

In fact, *transumptio* is a fundamental element in the language of Dante's images ... understood as *transumptio* 'orationis', it is directly related to personification and prosopoeia; it is the rhetorical medium of allegory, which, when it does not originate as a *figura* in the Biblical sense, corresponds to a prolonged metaphor according to a definition already present in classical rhetoric.[35]

If Dante's journey and the dark wood are examples of *transumptio*, it is clear that some important moments of Langland's poem are also based on it – for instance the 'faire feld', the half-acre, Unitas and the structure of the quest itself. The allegorical personifications of *Piers Plowman* also belong to the sphere of *transumptio*. In other words, the mental process that governs the construction of Langland's poem is certainly metaphorical, and in this structural sense *transumptio* occupies an important place in the language of *Piers Plowman*, which, 'at its highest...explores the central problems of the universe through metaphor'.[36] But in fact, despite the presence and even prominence of metaphorical expressions, Langland's poem is largely based on words – discourse, dialogue, debate and sermon – and it is precisely for this reason that it tends towards the metonymic pole of language. That is to say, it is based more on contiguity than on similarity.[37] Hence we shall find in *Piers Plowman* four more of the 'methods of treatment' mentioned by Dante, that is, *definition*, *division*, *proof* and *refutation*, which are used in a specifically technical sense – totally functional, as in scholastic argumentation, to the demonstration of a particular case or a particular truth. These are the methods used in medieval disputations, and examples can be drawn from the poem. Dowel, Dobet and Dobest are defined many times, and these definitions often constitute the starting-point for a discussion between Will and the allegorical personifications he meets. For example, in *Passus* x (331ff) Will concludes from what Scripture is saying that Dowel and Dobet are lordship and knighthood (*definition*), but Scripture replies that she has nowhere read that 'kynghod ne kny3thod...helpeth...to heueneward one heres ende'. She then quotes Paul, Solomon, Cato and the Apostles to prove her point (*proof*) but, in so doing, opens up another debate, for she maintains that the poor have 'heritage in heuevene, and bi trewe ri3te' whereas the rich can claim no right but have to gain Paradise through mercy and grace. Will replies with a *refutation*:

> '*Contra!*' quod I, 'by crist! þat kan I [wiþseye],
> And preuen it by [þe pistel þat Peter is nempned]:
> That is bapti3ed beþ saaf, be he riche or pouere.'
>
> (x, 349–51)

Scripture answers distinguishing (*division*) between pagans who are baptised on the point of death and Christians: the former are saved for their true belief, but the latter must first have love and faith and fulfil the Law – baptism is not enough for them. At this Will launches into a long harangue against theologians and learned men (using many authorities to prove his argument) and concludes that learning is useless for salvation since both

93

the good and the wicked are in the hand of God. It is at this point (at the beginning of *Passus* XI) that Scripture replies with the quotation from the Pseudo-Bernard, 'multi multa sciunt et seipsos nesciunt'. This phrase, more than any strictly logical refutation or distinction, is alone sufficient to make Will weep 'for wo and wrathe' and to plunge him into the deeper dream where he will follow Fortune for forty-five years.

With the *example*, the last of the *modus tractandi*, we enter a sphere to which Langland gives a particular orientation. 'The *exemplum*, which belongs to the category of digression, can be a narration ("res gesta"), the simple mention of a well-known fact, "inductio" – that is, adducing a more or less substantial example of that which one intends to prove, in order to get the advantage of demonstration – a simile, or "auctoritas", when an authority is quoted.'[38] In *Piers Plowman* the most frequent form – to the point of becoming obsessive – is certainly *auctoritas*. It is intimately woven into Langland's mode of expression, an innate tendency cultivated and amplified by his thought. At a rough calculation it constitutes about 30% of the text of the poem (chiefly the Latin quotations). The *res gesta* naturally takes the form of the *parabola* modelled on the Gospels, from the story of the rats and mice in the Prologue to the three parables used by Imagination (XII, 160ff; 237ff; 262ff); Skeat calculates a total of twenty-seven parables for the three versions. Another form of the *res gesta* appears in the *ensample* taken from the *Legenda Sanctorum* (as in XV, 263ff). Thus we return, once again, to the language of the Bible and the Gospels, which Langland uses as naturally as Dante uses the language of philosophy and theology. In *Piers Plowman* this field of reference occupies all the space that in the *Divine Comedy* is divided among the religious, classical–mythological and philosophical worlds. In this sense, Langland's language is one-dimensional: on the stylistic level it recreates, in fourteenth-century English, the *sermo humilis* of the Scriptures[39] – a fusion of styles that had once shocked the classical *literati*.

In *Piers Plowman* we also find the 'humble' object signifying a 'high' truth, as in the famous passage in which the Samaritan explains the Trinity to Will:

> [For] to a torche or a tapur þe Trinite is likned,
> As wex and a weke were twyned togideres,   *wick*
> And þanne a fir flawmynge forþ out of boþe.
> And as wex and weke and [warm] fir togideres
> Fostren forþ a flawmbe and a fair leye
> [That serueþ þise swynkeres to se by aniȝtes],   *workmen*
> So dooþ þe Sire and þe sone and also *spiritus sanctus*
> [Fostren forþ amonges folk loue and bileue]
> That alle kynne cristene clenseþ of synnes.   (XVII, 206–14)

And as glowynge gledes gladeþ noȝt þise werkmen   *cheer*
That werchen and waken in wyntres nyȝtes
As dooþ a kex or a candle þat caught haþ fir and blaseþ,
Na moore dooþ sire ne sone ne seint spirit togidres
Graunte no grace ne for[g]ifnesse of synnes
Til þe holy goost gynne to glowe and to blase . . .

(xvii, 221–6)

Here the sublime is evoked through the humble. This occurs throughout the poem. Of course, Langland's tone is by turns satirical, eloquent, homiletic, dramatic, prophetic: examples of this range appear in almost every page of this chapter. And of course Langland uses rhetorical figures; he has a special fondness for word-play,[40] he loves to insert and repeat a key word for a whole series of lines, he quotes abundantly in Latin – in short, he has his personal idiosyncracies. But what remains constant through the whole poem is the way he never shrinks from the humble, the common, the proverbial – or even the ugly, the obscene and the grotesque – as long as it serves ultimately to enhance the sublimity of the poem. One constant characteristic of *Piers Plowman* is that which Elizabeth Salter has called the 'naturalness' of his language and which Lawlor describes as 'speech'.[41] The special alliterative technique used by Langland is quite different from the 'precious' one in *Sir Gawain*. The cadence of its lines is based on the natural flow of the spoken language; its 'prosaic' quality increases until it reaches the 'divine rhetoric' of sublime humility. All these elements make *Piers Plowman* one of the first poetic works in which an English writer expresses himself through the common language, the spoken word. With this language William Langland recreates the *sermo humilis* of the Scriptures: it is a 'translation' that will prove exemplary for English poetry. Of all his merits this is perhaps the greatest, the one that gives his poem the tone and authority of the 'classic'. One need only reread the beginning and the end of *Piers Plowman*:

In a somer seson whan softe was þe sonne
I shoop me into [a] shrou[d] as I a sheep weere;   *dressed*
In habite as an heremite, vnholy of werkes,
Wente wide in þis world wondres to here.

(*Prologue*, 1–4)

'By crist!' quod Conscience þo, 'I wole bicome a pilgrym,
And [wenden] as wide as þe world [renneþ]
To seken Piers þe Plowman, þat pryde [myȝte] destruye,
And þat freres hadde a fyndyng þat for nede flateren
And countrepledeþ me, Conscience; now kynde me avenge,   *oppose*
And sende me hap and heele til I haue Piers þe Plowman.'   *luck; health*
And siþþe he gradde after Grace til I gan awake.

(xx, 380–6)

This is the language with which Langland faces a subject to which, else-where, 'both heaven and earth have set their hand':[42] it is this that makes his poem one of the central reference points of fourteenth-century culture and one of the first 'classics' in English literature.

II

Turning now from the Vision of Piers the Ploughman to that of *Pearl*, we find ourselves in a world which, though it shares the dimension of dream and vision, is altogether different. The very language of *Pearl*, unlike that of *Piers Plowman*, is a jewel of precious refinement, carefully polished and balanced.[43] *Pearl* consists of twenty sections, each composed of five stanzas (except the fifteenth, which has six); each stanza contains twelve lines rhymed according to the scheme *ababababbcbc*; each line normally carries four stresses. Alliteration is added to the rhyme, though this is not constant. The stanzas of each section are linked by the repetition (sometimes with variation or punning) of a word from the last line of every stanza in the first line of the next. Finally, all the stanzas of each group end with the same line, or one nearly the same. An example will make the mechanism clear:

Perle, plesaunte to prynces paye	*delight*
To clanly clos in golde so clere,	*to set flawlessly*
Oute of oryent, I hardyly saye,	
Ne proued I neuer her precios pere.	*equal*
So rounde, so reken in vche araye,	*radiant in every setting*
So smal, so smoþe her sydeȝ were,	
Quere-so-euer I jugged gemmeȝ gaye,	
I sette hyr sengeley in synglere.	*apart as unique*
Allas! I leste hyr in on erbere;	*garden*
Þurȝ gresse to grounde hit fro me yot.	*grass*
I dewyne, fordolked of luf-daungere	
Of þat pryuy perle* wythouten spot.	

$$(1-12)$$

* I suffer, wounded by the power of my love for my own pearl

This is the first stanza of the poem. The first line of the next stanza is:

Syþen in þat *spote* hit fro me sprange

and the last repeats:

My priuy perle wythouten spotte.

Thus there is a double link among each of the five stanzas of a group. This is a highly artificial construction, which imposes a considerable effort on the poet. We are very far from *Piers Plowman*. *Pearl* contains 1,212 lines in all. A numerical structure has been found in it, based on 3, 4 and 12. This is probably modelled on the construction of the heavenly Jerusalem in the *Book of Revelation* by St John (21), which is so important in the poem. In this sense,

each stanza has twelve lines and three rhymes. Each line has four stresses and often three or four alliterating words. Of the hundred and one stanzas, ninety-nine are divided, like the *Divine Comedy*, into three groups of approximately equal length and two as an epilogue. The 101 is made up of 33 in part 1, + 32 in part 2, + 34 in part 3, = 99 + 2 = 101 (or perhaps, as P. M. Kean has suggested, 1212 lines).[44]

Dorothy Everett, on the other hand, divides the poem into three parts: the first four sections present the state of mind of the dreamer and then describe the dream country and Pearl herself; the twelve central sections are devoted to discussion and exposition; the last four sections again contain a description, this time of the New Jerusalem, ending with the poet's reflections. In any case, the structure of *Pearl* is a clear one, a *divisio* firmly planned and executed, with none of the 'openness' of *Piers Plowman*. We are dealing with an artist who imposes order on his creation and builds a 'difficult' poem.

The narrative content of *Pearl* may be briefly summarised. The poet, weeping for the loss of his pearl in an 'erbere', a garden, falls asleep, and while his body remains sleeping on the ground, his spirit 'springs in space':

My goste is gon in Godeӡ grace
In auenture þer meruayleӡ meuen.[45]   *exist*
(63–4)

He finds himself by the bank of a river, amid a marvellous and rich landscape. At the foot of a shining crystal rock sits a young girl whom he knows well. Amazed, the dreamer sees her rise and approach from the other side of the river. Her clothes are adorned with pearls; a magnificent pearl gleams on her bosom. The poet, who knows that she is 'more near akin than aunt or niece', at once speaks to her. He asks if she is really the pearl he has lost, for which he shed so many tears. Here begins a series of questions and answers, in which the Pearl constantly reproves and corrects the words of the dreamer. To his first question, she replies that it was a grave error to consider her lost:

For þat þou lesteӡ watӡ bot a rose   *lost*
Þat flowred and fayled as kynde hyt gef.   *nature; allowed*
Now þurӡ kynde of þe kyste þat hyt con cloѕe   *chest; encloses*
To a perle of prys hit is put in pref.   *it has proved to be*
(269–72)

The jeweller–dreamer apologises and declares that now he has found her he will never again let her go. But the Maiden reproaches him for speaking without thinking: before he can remain forever with her, he must die, and then, perhaps, he too will be allowed on the other side of the river. The poet, again apologising, asks the Maiden a series of questions about her present state. This introduces the central debate of the poem: the Maiden tells the dreamer–jeweller that he knows how 'ȝong and tender of age' she was at the moment of her death. The Lamb has taken her and made her queen. The poet asks in amazement if the Virgin Mary has been dethroned. The answer is that all those who enter the Kingdom of God are kings or queens: this is an answer given by Christ Himself in the parable of the Labourers (Matthew xx, 1–16), which the Maiden in fact repeats in full (495–576). The dreamer is not convinced, so she has to add that the innocents enter the Kingdom of God by right, because they are baptised but have not had time to sin. Christ himself has said: 'Suffer little children to come unto me', and has affirmed that no one shall enter his kingdom unless he has first become as a child. Finally, with a significant shift from innocence to spotlessness, the Maiden replies to the jeweller's question with another parable, in fact the one about the Jeweller and the Pearl.[46] It is worth quoting this passage, which is central for an interpretation of the poem. By reading it we can understand the way in which the poet thinks out his images and organises the symbolism of his poem:

'Iesus con calle to hym hys mylde,	*gentle (disciples)*
And sayde hys ryche no wyȝ myȝt wynne	*kingdom*
Bot he com þyder ryȝt as a chylde,	
Oþer elleȝ neuermore com þerinne.	
Harmleȝ, trwe, and vndefylde,	*innocent; faithful*
Wythouten mote oþer mascle of sulpande synne,	*polluting*
Quen such þer cnoken on þe bylde,	*knock; building*
Tyt schal hem men þe ȝate vnpynne.	*quietly; unfasten*
Þer is þe blys þat con not blynne	*chase*
Þat þe jueler soȝte þurȝ perré pres,	*with precious jewels*
And solde alle hys goud, boþe wolen and lynne,	
To bye hym a perle watȝ mascelleȝ.	
'This makelleȝ perle, þat boȝt is dere,	*matchless*
Þe joueler gef fore alle hys god,	
Is lyke þe reme of heuenesse clere:	*kingdom of heaven*
So sayde þe Fader of folde and flode;	*land; sea*
For hit is wemleȝ, clene, and clere,	*spotless*
And endeleȝ rounde, and blyþe of mode,	*serene*
And commune to alle þat ryȝtwys were.	
Lo, euen inmyddeȝ my breste hit stode.	
My Lorde þe Lombe, þat schede hys blode,	

He py3t hit þere in token of pes.   set; peace
I rede þe forsake þe worlde wode   advise; mad
And porchace þy perle maskelles.'

(721–44)

Thus, from the innocence of children to the absence of 'mote' or 'mascle'
to the 'mascelle3' pearl: from the parable of the children to that of the
jeweller, while the pearl, first an ornament and then a symbol of purity and
innocence, becomes a parable of the Kingdom of Heaven. The poet then
asks what the pearl's function is. The Maiden replies that it is the sign that
the Lamb has chosen His bride, that she is one of the 144,000 virgins seen
by John 'in gostly drem', which he described in the Apocalypse. And so a
new space opens up: the Maiden speaks at length about the New Jerusalem.
The jeweller-dreamer feels a very strong desire to see it and he implores the
Maiden to take him there. The poet is then led to a hilltop from which, like
John, he can contemplate the City of God, though he does not enter it.
He describes it to us in detail, showing how his delight increases until his
human mind is reduced to paroxysm and delirium. At this point, he decides
to cross the river and try to enter the City but, as soon as he begins running
towards the shore, his dream vanishes and he finds himself back in the
'erbere', where he laments his lost vision and submits himself to the
'Prince's' will. The poem concludes with a modified repetition of the first
line:

Ouer þis hyul þis lote I la3te,   fortune; had
For pyty of my perle enclyin,   lying
And syþen to God I hit byta3te   committed
In Kryste3 dere blessyng and myn,
Þat in þe forme of bred and wyn
Þe preste vus schewe3 vch a daye.
He gef vus to be his homly hyne   household servants
And precious perle3 vnto his pay.

(1205–12)

Thus the vision of *Pearl* is fundamentally different from that of *Piers
Plowman*: it proceeds linearly, as the poet–dreamer–jeweller gradually
progresses towards the vision of the Heavenly Jerusalem and the Lamb.
The action is marked by three salient moments: his falling asleep and the
beginning of the dream, the meeting with the Maiden and the dialogue-
debate that follows it, and the vision of the New Jerusalem. This action
unfolds in three main places: the 'erbere' in which the poet falls asleep; the
fabulous landscape on the river bank, where he meets the Maiden; and the
resplendent City of God of the Apocalypse. At the end of the poem, we find
ourselves again in the garden, on the 'mound', the grave of the little girl,
where everything began.[47] But a coherent interpretation of *Pearl* must

follow at least three interwoven lines of development: the first is the transformation undergone by the central symbol of the poem, the pearl; the second is the inner change of the protagonist; the third is the development that takes place in the nature of the vision itself. Let us try to reconstruct these lines.

At the start the pearl is the incomparable jewel that the protagonist has lost in the 'erbere', which has penetrated 'þurʒ gresse to grounde' ('through the grass into the earth). It is round, 'reken in vche araye', small and smooth (5–6). Here the language in which the symbol is described already suggests a person: 'smoþe' in fact refers not to a neutral surface, but to the 'sydeʒ', the sides, the limbs of the pearl–Maiden. Moreover, speaking of his grief over the loss of this immaculate jewel, the poet says he has been 'for-dolked of luf-daungere' ('wounded by the power of love') – an expression that belongs to the courtly love lyric. When the poet sees the girl in his dream, he knows that he knows her, he has seen her before (164), and the more he looks at her the more he recognises her (167–8): she appears 'so smoþe, so smal', that is, with the characteristics of the pearl lost in the garden, and 'a precios pyece in perleʒ pyʒt' ('a precious person adorned with pearls'). Pearls are everywhere on her clothes and on her crown; her face is the colour of pearl; a pearl of indescribable splendour shines on her breast. The poet reveals that his girl was 'more near akin than aunt or niece'. When he speaks he apostrophises her:

> 'O perle', quod I, 'in perleʒ pyʒt,
> Art þou my perle þat I haf playned,
> Regretted by myn one on nyʒte? . . .'
>
> (241–3)

The pearl, then, is a person: perhaps, as the language of this part of the poem seems to suggest, she is the lady, loved by the poet, who has died and now reappears in dream. But the girl's answer begins to suggest a deeper truth, another level of the symbol. The pearl is a person, but, as it were, in the earthly world – the universe of the jeweller, his garden. Here, 'in Paradys erde', she is something more:

> For þat þou lesteʒ watʒ bot a rose
> Þat flowred and fayled as kynde hyt gef.
> Now þurʒ kynde of þe kyste þat hyt con close
> To a perle of prys hit is put in pref.
>
> (269–72)

No longer a rose ('et, rose, elle a vécu ce que vivent les roses, l'espace d'un matin'),[48] but truly a Pearl by virtue of the jewel-box that holds her. On earth, this was the buried coffin, which forever enclosed the petals of the rose and which carried her through death to Paradise. Here, in the universe of the eternal and the incorruptible, it is the love of the Lamb who took her as His bride, giving her complete blessedness, and made her His queen. But in the world of the jeweller, that world from whose 'raysoun bref' he does not wish to depart, the pearl is still a person, and, indeed, the poet reveals to us one of her fundamental features: she is a little girl less than two years old (483). Suddenly the ambiguity of the courtly love language ceases to have any concrete reference: henceforth it remains only as a sign of the 'earthliness' of the protagonist. However, while the dreamer continues to think and speak as a being of this world, there, in the other world, the symbol takes on a further dimension. From the emblem of an individual soul who is saved by her own innocence and acquires the perfection and incorruptibility of a pearl, it is now transformed into a parable of the whole Kingdom of Heaven:

> 'This makelle3 perle, þat bo3t is dere,
> Þe joueler gef fore alle hys god,
> Is lyke þe reme of heuenesse clere . . .'
>
> (733–5)

This parable reveals the tropological, or moral, significance of the pearl: the Kingdom of Heaven, which one acquires by giving away all worldly goods, everything that belongs to the earth. It is only after the long dialogue with the girl – after all the lessons imparted to him – that the jeweller of the dream, the protagonist, is given visible proof of the moral truth that the jeweller of the parable has shown by his actions. He now contemplates the Heavenly Jerusalem, whose twelve gates are each made of a single pearl, 'a parfyt perle þat neuer fate3' (1037–8). Thus the entrance to the City of God is open to the jeweller who has abandoned the things of this world. The pearl is like the Kingdom of Heaven – not only metaphorically in terms of the parable but also visually. In the solemn and radiant procession of virgins that the dreamer sees passing through the streets of the City, every maiden is adorned with pearls. On every breast is fixed 'þe blysful perle wyth gret delyt', just as on the breast of the Pearl (1102–4), and finally even the garments of the Lamb look like precious pearls (1112). The pearl has become a symbol of beatitude, of the joy of the saints, of love, of gentleness, of the serenity of the Lamb. Now it is a mystic, anagogical sign of supreme joy. As Dante saw Beatrice in the crown of the blessed, the jeweller–dreamer can see his 'little queen' amid the crowd that follows the Lamb. And at the moment of the supreme vision, the language of the poet again becomes earthly, paternal, and full of love:

> Þen sa3 I þer my lyttel quene
> Þat I wende had standen by me in sclade.   *valley*

> Lorde, much of mirþe watȝ þat ho made
> Among her fereȝ þat watȝ so quyt!   *companions*
> Þat syȝt me gart to þenk to wade   *made me resolve*
> For luf-longyng in gret delyt.
>
> (1147–52)

It is only after returning to the garden, finding there true humility and total abandon to God's will, that the dreamer prays to his Lord to make all men 'precious perleȝ vnto his pay'. The pearl thus returns to earth as a sign of prayer, of humility, which has accepted the existence of a truth beyond its own world.

In tracing the line of development of the symbol of the pearl, I have often had to refer to the poem's protagonist, who is both narrator and actor of the whole episode. These references were deliberate since the poem develops on different planes, according to a scheme of intersecting, rather than parallel, lines. I have also noted that the central characteristic of this protagonist throughout the poem is his 'earthliness'. This quality appears above all in the sentiments of love and sorrow that pervade the whole first part of *Pearl*, which are announced at once in the first stanza:

> I dewyne, fordolked of luf-daungere
> Of þat pryuy perle wythouten spot.
>
> (11–12)

And they are amplified in the second, in an inconsolable lament:

> Syþen in þat spote hit fro me sprange,
> Ofte haf I wayted, wyschande þat wele,   *precious thing*
> Þat wont watȝ whyle deuoyde my wrange *drive away; sorrow*
> And heuen my happe and al my hele.   *heighten; happiness; well-being*
>
> (13–16)

These are the elegiac accents of a kind of poetry, the themes of which are not unlike those of Petrarch's sonnets and *canzoni* on the death of Laura. In fact, here the poet's attitude already reflects – as Petrarch's so often does – an inner conflict between human feeling and Christian faith:

> I playned my perle þat þer watȝ spenned *imprisoned*
> Wyth fyrce skylleȝ þat faste faȝt;   *arguments; fought hard*
> Þaȝ kynde of Kryst me comfort kenned, *taught*
> My wreched wylle in wo ay wraȝte.
>
> (53–6)

This conflict is evident in the dreamer's attitude towards the Maiden, when he finds her again in the dream, and it produces the second part of the poem, in which she teaches him the doctrine of salvation, while at the same time correcting his earthly impulses. But seeing his Pearl again gives the dreamer a very human shock, and he stands there silent and motionless, in awed astonishment (175–87). Only when she approaches him is he filled with boundless joy (231–2), but when he opens his mouth to speak to her he immediately underlines his grief: 'pensyf, payred, I am forpayned'. The Maiden's reproaches begin. It is at this time that the protagonist first refers to himself as a 'jeweller' (252 and 264): 'Fro we in twynne wern towen and twayned,/ I haf ben a joyle3 juelere.' In the girl's reply, the word 'jeweller' is accompanied by an adjective, first 'gentyl' (264) and then 'kynde': she is already thinking of the parable of the truly noble and courteous Jeweller, which she will later explain. The dreamer, however, is thinking of himself and he uses the adjectives 'joyle3' or 'joyful'. In other words, while for him the title of jeweller is entirely literal, or at most a metaphorical play on the part of the poet, for her it is already parabolic, exemplary, moral. These two dimensions, as I have said, remain constant in *Pearl*, where the protagonist is unable to go beyond the letter of the vision, while the tropological and anagogical aspects are shown to him. While his 'longing' and his grief continue to manifest themselves (325–6), he begins to apologise and even becomes humble (390), to the point where he recognises his 'earthliness' in a phrase that is both literal and metaphorical: 'I am bot mokke and mul among' (905). But what the Maiden tells him, before beginning her explanation about the innocents and the Kingdom of Heaven, remains substantially true almost to the end of the poem: 'I halde þat iueler lyttel to prayse / Þat leue3 wel þat he se3 with y3e' ('I have little praise for the jeweller *who believes what he sees with his eyes*'). Even after the apocalyptic vision, the protagonist is still in this state: after the Maiden's explanations he knows and understands more, but he needs to *see* the Heavenly Jerusalem before he can believe once and for all. Nor, in fact, do his human impulses cease during and after the vision: it is these that impel him to cross the river ('for luf-longyng': 1152) and thus to end his dream. With these impulses he awakens in the garden: 'a longeyng hevy me strok in swone' (1180). Only at this point does he finally realise that, if he had submitted to the will of the Prince, he would have been allowed to penetrate further the mysteries of God (1189–94). At the end of his experience he discerns the moral and mystical significance of his dream and his vision (that is, the meaning beyond pure earthly pleasure). He is able to find consolation even in the daily event, humble and yet sublime, of the consecration of the bread and wine. On earth, he humbly accepts that mystery which even in the vision had been shut off from him by his earthly will. The true jeweller thus prays that he may become, together with all men, a pearl for the pleasure of the Prince.

While the symbolism of the pearl changes and while, at the same time, the inner experience of the protagonist unfolds, the nature of his vision is also gradually changing. In the first section of the poem (1–60), the poet's eyes see a natural 'erbere' in the full bloom of summer: this, then, is a perfectly normal 'vision', physical and immediate. But the characteristics of this garden are quite special: to a considerable degree it represents the conventional *locus amoenus* of the courtly lyric, but into this

The poet introduces another note. The description of the garden is connected with the passage from John, 12, 24: 'Except a corn of wheat fall into the ground and die, it abideth alone; but if it die, it bringeth forth much fruit.' The pearl is equated both with a grain of wheat, the symbol of resurrection, and with the seed from which spring up the flowers and spices of the garden.[49]

The 'erbere' therefore functions at two levels, the courtly-secular and the religious. Now the protagonist's vision of it is, as it were, split in half: in his grief for the loss of the pearl, he fails to see the profound significance of the whole garden. He is fascinated only by the gorgeous flowers and exotic spices, so that when he falls among the flowers their perfume goes to his head, and he drops into a deep sleep (57–60). Although this is a 'bodily vision', the protagonist is partly insensitive to its meanings.

This 'natural' vision ends when the jeweller falls asleep. And at once we enter another dimension, which can be read in two different ways, according to the punctuation of the following passage:

> Fro spot my spyryt þer sprang in space;
> My body on balke þer bod [;] in sweuen [.]   *mound*
> My goste is gon in Godeȝ grace
> In auenture þer meruayleȝ meuen.   (61–4)

If one follows Gordon in reading the second line without a semicolon but with a full stop, the passage would mean: 'From that place my spirit leapt into space; my body remained there on the mound *in sleep*. By the grace of God, my spirit ventured forth to see marvels.' On the other hand, if we accept the reading of Kean and Spearing,[50] and retain the semicolon but not the full stop, the meaning becomes: 'From that place my spirit leapt into space; my body remained there on the mound; *in dream* my spirit ventured forth to see marvels.' 'Sweuen' may, in fact, be read either way. Whichever interpretation is chosen, clearly the poet wants to indicate first of all that his body remains behind, while the spirit enters another dimension. The question is whether this is an oneiric dimension or, more precisely, a visionary one. The issue is complicated by the fact that the passage is made to echo a central moment in Christian literature and visionary theology, the vision of which Paul speaks in the Second Epistle to the Corinthians (xii, 1–5):

It is not expedient for me doubtless to glory. I will come to visions and revelations of the Lord. I knew a man in Christ above fourteen years ago, (*whether in the body, I cannot tell; or whether out of the body, I cannot tell*: God knoweth;) such an one caught up to the third heaven. And I knew such a man, (whether in the body, or out of the body, I cannot tell: God knoweth;) how that he was caught up into paradise, and heard unspeakable words, which it is not lawful for a man to utter.

The *Pearl* poet wishes to emphasise that his vision is 'out of the body'. And up to this point all is well: the poet later tells us that he finds himself in Paradise (137 and 248) and that he cannot describe the glory of what he has seen, because the human tongue is not equal to the task (99–100). In fact, we have come very close to Dante:

> Nel ciel che più della sua luce prende
> fu' io, e vidi cose che ridire
> né sa né può chi di là su discende.
> (*Paradiso*, I, 4–6)

('I have been in the heaven that most receives His light and I have seen things which whoso descends from up there has neither knowledge nor power to re-tell.')

And indeed, throughout the *Paradiso* Dante suggests Paul's *raptus* until the beatific vision: he does so with scholastic coherence and with increasing poetic fervour, *without ever mentioning a dream*. For in biblical exegesis Paul's *raptus* (rapture) has never been considered a dream: Augustine speaks of it as 'ecstasy' and classifies his vision as 'intellectual'; Thomas Aquinas maintains that Paul's *raptus* was contemplation of divine truth 'in sua essentia'.[51] So if the author of *Pearl* meant to establish a parallel between his vision and that of Paul – and there is no doubt that he did mean to in verses 61–4 – then 'sweuen' was not the word he should have used. This poet is not ignorant of the rudiments of the theory of visions: when speaking of the vision of John in the Apocalypse, he calls it a 'gostly drem' (790), which corresponds perfectly to the 'visio spiritualis' of which Augustine speaks in connection with the Apocalypse.[52] Therefore, if he uses 'sweuen', either he means 'sleep' (as Gordon's punctuation would indicate), or he intentionally places the whole situation in an ambiguous light. For the moment let us skip forward to the jeweller–poet's vision of the New Jerusalem, according to the model of the Apocalypse. At the end of this, he refers to it as a 'drem' (1170) and shortly afterwards as a 'veray avysyoun' (1184). As this is a vision modelled on that of John, which has already been called a 'gostly drem', both these definitions are exact, though the adjective is missing. A little later he says that if he had submitted to the will of the Prince and had not desired more than what was given to him, he would have been 'drawen to Goddeȝ present' and would have penetrated further into 'his mysterys' (1189–94). The nature of this part of the vision as a 'visio spiritualis' is clarified beyond a shadow of a doubt by lines 1081–92, where the whole problem is taken up again and elucidated, as Spearing has noted,[53] with the aid of technical terms:

> An-vnder mone so great merwayle
> No fleschly hert ne myȝt endeure,
> As quen I blusched vpon þat bayle,   *gazed; walls*
> So ferly þerof watȝ þe fasure.   *marvellous; form*
> I stod as stylle as dased quayle
> For ferly of þat frelich fygure,   *frail; vision*
> Þat felde I nawþer reste ne trauayle,
> So watȝ I rauyste wyth glymme pure.
> For I dar say wyth conciens sure,
> Hade bodyly burne abiden þat bone,   *favour*
> Þaȝ alle clerkeȝ hym hade in cure,
> His lyf were loste an-vnder mone.
>   (1081–92)

Here, in fact, the word 'rauyste' deliberately echoes *raptus*, and 'glymme' can be set beside that *lumen gloriae* which is necessary in order that the creature may, in *raptus*, contemplate the divine essence.[54] So this is a 'visio spiritualis' in which, as for John (Apocalypse i, 10) the body is absent, remaining below in the 'erbere'. It resembles the final moments of Dante's beatific vision, which in other respects is so differently conceived. Delight pervades the eye and the ear, the human mind dissolves in a sort of madness:

> Delyt me drof in yȝe and ere,
> My maneȝ mynde to maddyng malte.
>   (1153–4)

Which brings to mind Dante:

> se non che la mia mente fu percossa
> da un fulgore in che sua voglia venne
>   (*Paradiso*, XXXIII, 140–1)

('had not my mind been smitten by a flash wherein came its wish')

With the difference that Dante's vision ends with a total surrender of his desire and will to the love that moves the sun and the other stars, whereas the jeweller's vision ends with a rude awakening in the 'erbere', before he bows to the pleasure of the Prince (1189). The jeweller's vision is not, in short, a beatific one; still less is it a vision of God 'in His essence'.

Let us now return to the second section of *Pearl*, in which the protagonist finds himself in a marvellous landscape, which he himself calls Paradise, where he then meets the girl. This fantastic landscape has many of the characteristic elements of medieval descriptions of the Earthly Paradise, but at the same time it contains, as Pamela Gradon has pointed out, elements common to the literature of romance and chivalry and to the exotic literature of travels. 'Such a world', says Gradon,

> could be a prelude to a love vision. And, as the vision proceeds, the poet subtly hints at all these, suggesting the uncertainty of the dreamer himself, as well as the dreamlike quality of blended fantasy and reality, characteristic of a dream.

So that

> in the earthly paradise and the debate, we have two levels of understanding, the earthly and the heavenly, the natural and the supernatural. Here the imagery is still ambiguous, pointing, on the one hand, to the world of romance which is the level of the dreamer's understanding and the divine, which is its true significance. In the debate section we have the dual interpretation of the preceding scene.[55]

The ambiguity disappears only in the final vision, which is modelled on the Apocalypse. Now we can understand the true meaning of 'sweuen' in line 62: it either means 'sleep', in which case it refers to the body that remains on earth, or it denotes a *somnium*, which Macrobius, one of the first classifiers of dreams, described as 'quod tegit figuris et velat ambagibus non nisi interpretatione intelligendam significationem rei quae demonstratur' ('something that conceals by means of images [or 'allegories'] and veils with ambiguity the true meaning of the thing revealed, which cannot be understood without interpretation').[56] This seems to be precisely the dimension of the 'sweuen' of the jeweller, especially in the light of Pamela Gradon's interpretation cited above. However, it seems rather doubtful that this *somnium* is a *somnium mentis*, as Spearing asserts, citing Richard of St Victor in support of his view.[57] The *somnium mentis* leads, through ecstasy, to the contemplation of divine things, which happens only in the last section of *Pearl*. The dreamer of the second part sends his spirit forth 'in auenture þer meruayleȝ meuen', like a knight in search of adventures and marvels; his 'sweuen' is, as Gradon has shown, fundamentally ambiguous – half romantic and half religious. So if we wish to synthesise into a formula the three successive moments of *seeing* in the poem, we might use the terms 'natural sight', *somnium*, and *visio spiritualis*. To these correspond the 'erbere', the Earthly Paradise and the Maiden, and the Heavenly Jerusalem. Ambiguity reigns in the first two, clarity in the third. In the first the image of the pearl is associated with the vegetable world and with death, and it is filtered through the language of courtly love; in the second it is immersed in a world of crystal, of precious stones, of life eternal and incorruptible, and its language takes on a chivalric dimension; in the third it finally enters fully into the sphere of the divine, which has already been suggested, subtly in the first part and strongly in the second. Thus *Pearl* moves from nature to God (in the consciousness of the jeweller and in the language that expresses it), and at the same time it is always, when interpreted with the linguistic keys provided by the poet, an epiphany of truth on the levels of reality, dream and vision.

I have already shown how the poet's mode of thought proceeds by associations: this was the case in lines 721–44, where the theme of the innocence of children led to the absence of 'mote' or 'mascle', and this in turn led to the 'mascelle3' pearl, bringing the poet from the parable of the children to that of the Jeweller. This procedure is typical of *Pearl*: for example, the theme of the jeweller is suggested in the first five stanzas, where the narrator repeatedly emphasises his possession of the pearl, whereas the word 'juelere' appears only later (252 and 264), with different connotations according to whether it is spoken by the protagonist or the Maiden, and it is in this second meaning that it leads to the parable of the Jeweller (730). And the theme of the Heavenly Jerusalem is also introduced before the narrator's vision of it: in fact it is the Maiden who, in sections xiv–xvi, illustrates the significance of the Apocalypse for the benefit of the jeweller; his own description of it follows immediately, in sections xvii–xix. The images themselves often echo one another, through similarity, contrast or variation, each time acquiring a wider significance. We may recall, for example, one of the most important and most beautiful responses made by the girl to the narrator:

> For þat þou leste3 wat3 bot a rose
> Þat flowred and fayled as kynde hyt gef.
> Now þur3 kynde of þe kyste þat hyt con close
> To a perle of prys hit is put in pref.
>
> (269–72)

The Maiden's explanations evidently change the protagonist's attitude, for he becomes very humble. He takes up the image of the rose again in order to contrast his own 'earthliness', made as he is of filth and mud, with the beauty of the girl. He uses an image that might come from a love lyric, as if the Maiden had not pointed out, some 600 lines earlier, the mortal and earthly nature of the rose:

> I am bot mokke and mul among
> And þou so ryche a reken rose.
>
> (905–6)

So the two crucial moments of the dream and the vision, the moment of the appearance of the girl and that of the *raptus*, are marked by the same silent, awed immobility on the part of the protagonist. They are described in two similes constructed in the same way and with the same kind of images:

I stod as hende as hawk in halle   *still*
(184)

and

I stod as stylle as dased quayle
(1085)

In fact, even the central image of the poem, the pearl, seems to have been formed in the poet's mind through a process of association between two passages of the New Testament, the parable of Matthew and the description of the gates of the New Jerusalem in the Apocalypse. To these must have been spontaneously added the exotic element that the pearl inevitably brought with it in the Middle Ages and the association with the themes of love: beautiful women adorn themselves with pearls, and the queen of love in Chaucer's *Legend of Good Women* has a crown 'of a perle fyn, oriental' (F 221). Then, too, the external form of *Pearl*, in which several words or a whole line of one stanza are repeated in others within the same section, or across sections, means that associations are manifested rhetorically through *repetitio* and *variatio*. This permits a chain-like progression of images, which sometimes culminates in points of baroque intricacy but which nevertheless retains all the meanings of a particular image:

'O maskeleȝ perle in perleȝ pure,
Þat bereȝ', quod I, 'þe perle of prys . . .'
(745–6)

This way of setting forth the semantic and imaginative structures of the poem is far removed from the metonymic use of language, which as we have seen is the tendency in *Piers Plowman*. *Pearl* is decidedly metaphorical. The poem's imagery is, as Johnson maintains,[58] basically divisible into two groups, one of the earthly and vegetable world and the other of light and gems: the metaphorical inventiveness is highly developed. Consider the description of the 'erbere':

Þat spot of spyseȝ mot nedeȝ sprede,
Þer such rycheȝ to rot is runne;
Blomeȝ blayke and blwe and rede
þer schyneȝ ful schyr agayn þe sunne.   *brightly*
Flor and fryte may not be fede
þer hit doun drof in moldeȝ dunne;   *dark brown earth*
For vch gresse mot grow of grayneȝ dede;
No whete were elleȝ to woneȝ wonne . . .   *barn; brought*

To þat spot þat I in speche expoun
I entred in þat erber grene,
In Auguste in a hyȝ seysoun,
Quen corne is coruen wyth crokeȝ kene . . .   *cut*
(25–40)

These are extremely dense images, in which the full life of summer is immediately transformed into death. Conversely, as the Gospel allusion indicates, it is death, the physical decay of the pearl in the dark-brown earth, which allows life to propagate and flower: in this there is an almost baroque sense of contrast, and the same colours that should belong to life are, in part, those of death. Notice the black flowers, for example, and also the way the image ends, with the ripe grain cut by the scythe, again suggesting death.

In contrast, let us look at the description of the Earthly Paradise:

> Towarde a foreste I bere þe face,
> Where rych rokkeȝ wer to dyscreuen.
> Þe lyȝt of hem myȝt no mon leuen,
> Þe glemande glory þat of hem glent;

Dubbed wern alle þo downeȝ sydeȝ	*adorned; hill*
Wyth crystal klyffeȝ so cler of kynde.	*by nature*
Holtewodeȝ bryȝt aboute hem bydeȝ	*woods; are set*
Of bolleȝ as blwe as ble of Ynde;	*trunks*
As bornyst syluer þe lef on slydeȝ,	*slid open*
Þat þike con trylle on vch a tynde.	*quivered; branch*
Quen glem of glodeȝ agaynȝ hem glydeȝ,	*clear patches of sky*
Wyth schymeryng schene ful schrylle þay schynde.	*dazzlingly; shone*
Þe grauayl þat on grounde con grynde	
Wern precious perleȝ of oryente:	
Þe sunnebemeȝ bot blo and blynde	*dark; dim*
In respecte of þat adubbement.	

Þe fyrre in þe fryth, þe feier con ryse	*further; wood; fairer*
Þe playn, þe plontteȝ, þe spyse, þe pereȝ;	
And raweȝ and randeȝ and rych reuereȝ,	
As fyldor fyn her bonkes brent.	*gold thread*

> (67–106)

All this is based on the play of light in its various gradations and reflections: it is truly, as Spearing has said,[59] 'a science-fiction landscape', 'planetary or lunar', full of similes of metals and precious stones (109–16). Thus the other world is realised in terms of metaphorical *audacia*; the effect is attained through the use of earthly images, but these are precious and remote, like the gems 'as glente þurȝ glas þat glowed and glyȝt', or 'as stremande sterneȝ ... staren in welkyn in wynter nyȝt'. This is a very high level of visual imagination, a play of light worthy of Dante's *Paradiso*. It is continually reworked by the *Pearl*-poet, as when the girl appears:

> Suche gladande glory con to me glace ...
> (171)

The imagery is changeable, however, according to the situation: though the background remains the same, the girl's approach becomes a gesture of courtly grace:

> He profered me speche, þat special spece,   *precious; person*
> Enclynande lowe in wommon lore,   *bowing*
> Caȝte of her coroun of gret tresore   *took off*
> And haylsed me wyth a lote lyȝte.   *greeted; joyful cry*
> (235–8)

And once again the play of light begins, accompanying the gesture: a light that 'glows', 'glints', 'glitters', 'gleams', 'shimmers', and so forth. But the imagination is not concentrated only on light: the jeweller's conversation with the Maiden is dominated by rhetorical contrasts and extraordinary verbal syntheses:

> Pensyf, payred, I am forpayned,   *sorrowful*
> And þou in a lyf of lykyng lyȝte,   *settled*
> In Paradys erde, of stryf vnstrayned.
> (246–8)

When the man expresses his wish to remain there forever, the girl replies with a chilling image: first, she says,

> Þy corse in clot mot calder keue.
> (320)

The conversation itself, with the pearl-Maiden's long sermon, is more discursive, dominated by the language of the wine-growers of the parable and by the girl's serene and contained argumentation. But even here there are some images of melancholy beauty and others that evoke a typically religious sort of contrast. When the Maiden speaks of the innocents, for example, she says that as soon as they are born, they are baptised: then, suddenly, death comes. These are two perfect lines, which could have been written by Milton:

> Anon þe day, wyth derk endente,   *inlaid*
> Þe niyȝt of deth dotȝ to enclyne.   *sinks*
> (629–30)

Salvation, too, is summarised in two lines, in which blood and water are counterposed: the blood of Christ on the Cross, and the water of baptism – the one necessary for the other:

> Ryche blod ran on rode so roghe,   *cross; cruel*
> And wynne water þen at þat plyt.
> (646–7)

Finally, we enter the sphere of the vision of the Heavenly Jerusalem: here the poet has precise self-imposed limits, based on John's description. *Pearl* follows the apostle as faithfully as possible, omitting a few details. But the most interesting aspect is the *amplificatio*, at times quite baroque, of John's text. Take, for example, a very concise simile from the Apocalypse (xxi, 18): 'and the city was pure gold, like unto clear glass'. In the poem this succinct phrase, with its touch of mystery, becomes:

> Þe borȝ watȝ al of brende golde bryȝt
> As glemande glas burnist broun ...
> (989–90)

in which the simple 'aurum' of the Vulgate expands into 'brende golde bryȝt', and the glass becomes 'glemande glas burnist broun'. Again, John says (xxi, 23): 'And the city had no need of the sun, neither of the moon, to shine in it; for the glory of God did lighten it, and the Lamb is the light thereof.' The metrical scheme forces the poet to repeat, but he does it with obvious pleasure:

> Such lyȝt þer lemed in alle þe strateȝ
> Hem nedde nawþer sunne ne mone.
>
> Of sunne ne mone had þay no nede;
> Þurȝ hym blysned þe borȝ al bryȝt.   *lamplight*
> Þe Lombe her lantyrne, wythouten drede;
> Þe self God watȝ her lombe-lyȝt,   *shone*
> (1043–8)

Two stanzas later, *Pearl* returns to this image, with no justification in the text of the Apocalypse, for pure poetic enjoyment:

> The mone may þerof acroche no myȝte;   *steal no light*
> To spotty ho is, of body to grym,
> And also þer ne is neuer nyȝt.
> What schulde þe mone þer compas clym   *Why; circuit; make*
> And to euen wyth þat worþly lyȝt   *vie*
> Þat schyneȝ vpon þe brokeȝ brym?
> Þe planeteȝ arn in to pouer a plyȝt,
> And þe self sunne ful fer to dym.
> (1069–76)

With respect to the Apocalypse, the first expression of this concept in *Pearl* involves only 'technical' repetition; here, however, it is magnified in a rhetorical crescendo (moon–planets–sun), and the moon is particularised in a completely artificial way. The author of *Pearl*, of course, had no telescope or spaceship that could enable him to see the 'grimness' of the moon: for him it was always a brilliant light, or else total night.

The technique, style and images of *Pearl* reveal for the first time an English poet who faces – in the 'erbere', in the Earthly Paradise, and in the New Jerusalem – the main problems that might present themselves to a medieval poet: the description of *loci amoeni*, which also carried other meanings, and the use of light to describe divinity. This was one of the methods codified by Dionysius the Aeropagite, 'per sensibiles similitudines' ('physical likenesses') (which may, in fact, be 'igne' ('fiery') or 'electrine' ('amber')), as happens 'in imaginativis visionibus'.[60] The problematic scheme is that of Dante's *Paradiso*. *Pearl* introduces *courtoisie* into the religious dream and vision. It is an elegy for the death of a baby daughter, a romantic search for the lost Eden, a parable of salvation, a *consolatio*,[61] a theological debate, a spiritual vision. With this poem, English literature acquires a 'classic' altogether different from *Piers Plowman*, one of which the language is not that of humble, ordinary speech but finely wrought and mounted in a setting of rigorous construction. *Pearl* tends, in miniature, towards the kind of poetry Dante created in the *Divine Comedy*. Together with the other works of the *Gawain*-poet – *Patience*, *Purity* and perhaps *St Erkenwald* – it constitutes one of the highest points reached by fourteenth-century English poetry. But this unknown poet, who brought new light to the romance, the homily, the biblical narrative, the elegy and the vision, was to remain the isolated fruit of a dying tradition: the pearl, to use his own metaphor, did not become the grain that dies and germinates. Without fruits and without followers, it came to light, archaeologically intact, five centuries after its first flowering, and, instead of becoming an inspiration for poetry, it has remained the object of historical and critical study.

5

The Narrative Collections
and Gower

Along with the narrative elements so far examined – the *exemplum*, biblical paraphrase, hagiography, romances and visions – the fourteenth century saw the beginning of a completely new phase in the development of English narrative. This was the collection of stories set in a narrative frame. As we have already seen, the century opened, in 1303, with Robert Mannyng's composition of *Handlyng Synne*. But this work, adapted from the French, represents an intermediate stage, in which the organising principle is still purely abstract and doctrinal. *Handlyng Synne* is a collection of *exempla* meant to illustrate sins, sacraments and the advantages and the grace of confession; as its title indicates, it is a *manual*, the ultimate aim of which is the conversion of the sinner, his repentance and confession. I have also noted that Mannyng's work had a precise 'political' purpose: to provide a collection of stories that could successfully compete with the popularity of those entertainments that were judged 'illicit' by the Church authorities. Therefore *Handlyng Synne* contains a mixture of minutely realistic scenes of daily life and *exempla* designed to arouse the reader's curiosity and at the same time persuade him to reform his own life without further delay.

What changes in the course of the fourteenth century, and not only in England, is the character of the frame within which the stories are assembled: the frame itself becomes a narrative device, and at the same time an embryonic dramatic element. The characteristics of the first phase of this development have been outlined by Viktor Shklovsky:

There are several types of frame-tales, or, more precisely, several methods of inserting one story inside another. The most common procedure consists of telling stories or tales in order to delay the accomplishment of some action ... In the *Thousand and One Nights* Sheherezade tells stories to put off her own execution ... In the *Thousand and One Nights* the story cycles are constructed according to a system: that of *delay* ... Another system for setting one story inside another is the dispute, in which both sides tell stories to prove or to refute an idea. This procedure is interesting because it can be extended to include other material, such as verses or aphorisms. These are devices which can only be used in written literature ... Fairly early in European literature there appeared collections of stories joined into an organic whole by one story that served as a *frame*. The oriental collections, imported from the East by the Arabs and the

Jews, introduced many exotic tales into Europe, where they undoubtedly encountered many similar ones of native origin. During the same period a *European type* of frame-tale arose, in which storytelling is *an end in itself*. I am referring to the *Decameron*.[1]

Shklovsky thus indicates two fundamental types of story collections, which were once both current in Europe. One is based on a narrative device with some motivation, for example that of delay or dispute, which has a definite purpose and tends to be dramatic. In the other type the narrative device (the frame) is occasional or based on pure entertainment. Alongside these we may set the old type of collection of *exempla*, such as *Handlyng Synne*, the organising principle of which is clear but abstract and doctrinally inspired. This type was in fact very widely circulated, normally at first in a Latin or French version and later in an English translation. The fifteenth century saw, for example, the English versions of the *Gesta Romanorum*, *Jacob's Well*, the *Alphabet of Tales* and the *Book of the Knight of La Tour Landry* – all inexhaustible sources of stories, pious or otherwise, for the preacher and the reader. They are all in prose, all without any design beyond the mechanical succession of stories (*Gesta Romanorum*), or the structure imposed by the alphabetical list of themes (Abstinentia, Accidia etc.: *Alphabet of Tales*), or the knight's instruction of his daughters (*Book of the Knight of La Tour Landry*). It would be a mistake, however, to dismiss these works because of their rudimentary structures. 'Their frequency, their structural shape, their stylistic modes, the character of their content, the intentions determining their form – all these elements come together to establish a very precise literary tradition, and a firm testimony of the medieval mentality.'[2] It is within this sphere – already explored by G. R. Owst[3] – that a taste for narrative as such, no longer dominated by religion and morality, developed in England as in other European countries. 'The roots of narration', as S. Battaglia has said, 'lie precisely in this incessant curiosity about reality – as action, character, feeling – that is, in the perpetual re-evocation of vitality.'[4]

On this common foundation the English narrative collections of the fourteenth century not only grew but took on forms of their own. Let us return for a moment to Shklovsky's classification. In England we find notable examples of both types of collections, those with motivated frame-devices and those with occasional ones. To the first group belong the anonymous *Seven Sages of Rome*, Gower's *Confessio Amantis*, and Chaucer's *Legend of Good Women*; to the second, the *Canterbury Tales*. I shall set Chaucer aside for the moment, as his narrative works go far beyond these types: they will be discussed in the next chapter. Meanwhile, one fact seems rather significant: both Gower and Chaucer conform – the former consistently, the latter only momentarily – to the first of these narrative models, one which, on the European cultural scene, is by now being left behind. For example the *Decameron* (*c.* 1350) has a frame-tale in which, as Shklovsky says, 'storytelling is an end in itself'.

The case of the *Seven Sages of Rome* is different. This work, of oriental origin, was classified as a 'metrical romance'. It was re-elaborated in English, by way of Latin and French, during the course of the fourteenth century.[5] The plot of the frame-tale is simple: the Emperor Diocletian sends his son away from the Court to be educated by seven sages. When the boy returns, he is accused by his stepmother of trying to seduce her. Her magic arts render him mute for seven days, and he is condemned to death. On each of the seven nights that pass before the execution, the stepmother tries to convince the Emperor that his son is threatening to depose him: to support her argument she tells seven appropriate stories. But on each of the seven mornings, the seven sages in turn tell stories showing how dangerous it is to trust a woman. Diocletian does not know what to do and repeatedly changes his mind. Meanwhile his son regains his power of speech and exposes the queen's plot, whereupon she is condemned and burned alive. The frame that provides the occasion for the stories makes use, in Shklovskian terms, of both the *delay* and the *dispute*. One of the reasons why the seven sages narrate their *exempla* is to gain time and delay the boy's execution after the sentence is passed; in addition, the lady and the learned masters have two opposite theses to prove. The frame-tale receives a double dramatic impulse, which is manifested in the narration: 'The anxiety of the sages, sharpened by the woman's hatred, communicates itself to the reader.'[6] Thus begins the embryonic drama mentioned at the beginning of this chapter, which is to be a prominent feature of the frame-tales in Gower's and Chaucer's narrative collections. More important than the frame, however, are the stories of the *Seven Sages*. From the point of view of cultural history, the most important feature of these stories is the fact that while they are certainly *exempla*, the morality that they represent is entirely secular. It is not based on the rigid doctrinal categories elaborated over the centuries, but on the principle – still within the fundamental distinction of good and evil – that George Kane has called 'hard shrewdness': a mixture of ability, astuteness and human intelligence. The target, which has remained the same from the original oriental collection through all the various versions, is, again in Kane's words, 'not so much vice as stupidity'. In this sense the *Seven Sages of Rome*, which in its time was classified as a 'romance', is in fact closer to the comic mode, where (as I have shown in chapter 2) the primary value is what Detienne and Vernant, speaking of the Greek *metis*, call 'les ruses de l'intelligence'.[7] This represents an event of great significance for English cultural history. It becomes even more significant when we consider that the *Seven Sages of Rome* is one of the romances contained in the Auchinleck manuscript, compiled between 1330 and 1340, which is thought by some to be the product of a 'bookshop', perhaps intended to satisfy the tastes of the mercantile class. This was a public that accepted both *Handlyng Synne* and the amoral *exemplum*.

To pass from the *Seven Sages* to John Gower may seem contradictory, if not actually irreverent. Because whereas the *Seven Sages* presents a view of humanity that goes beyond conventional morality, Gower was the 'moral' poet *par excellence* of the English fourteenth century.[8] He wrote not only a collection of stories but also two other weighty and important works. He was, in fact, one of the greatest intellectuals and artists, as well as one of the chief critical minds, of his time. I should make it clear that Gower is introduced at this point simply because the narrative device that frames his great collection of stories, the *Confessio Amantis*, is of the same type as that used in the *Seven Sages*. We have a character, the lover, who prays to Venus to relieve him of the pain caused by Cupid's darts; Venus, before satisfying him, demands that he should make a full confession to her priest, Genius, in order to prove his value as a lover. In hearing his confession, Genius uses the conventional method of examining the seven deadly sins one by one, dividing each one into its five aspects, and meanwhile tells exemplary stories *ad hoc*. When the confession is finished, the lover receives full absolution and liberation from the pains of love. Here, then, the frame has a motivation corresponding to Shklovsky's first type – fictitious, of course, as is the frame of the *Seven Sages*. The device used is essentially that of delay, with Venus as its motive force. In this sense, the *Confessio Amantis* belongs to the stage of narrative development in which I have placed the *Seven Sages*. Here the likeness between the two ends and the differences begin.

The first difference is that this particular frame is obviously influenced by the tradition of the manual of confession. I began this chapter by referring back to *Handlyng Synne*, the most systematic product of that tradition in its original abstract and religious form, and it is irresistibly tempting to place all three works in a single narrative triangle, which moves diachronically through the century and synchronically shows a very fascinating play of affinities and divergences. But the game does not end there, because, while Genius is as 'thorough' a priest as the Fourth Lateran Council or Robert Mannyng could have wished, he is also a character derived from the *Roman de la Rose*. So this confession cuts both ways: it is, as it were, sacramental but, as the title indicates, it is also a confession of love. These two terms are not as contradictory as they seem: from the twelfth century on it was fashionable to speak of love as a religion. The important thing is that the *Confessio Amantis* partly belongs to the tradition of *courtoisie*, which permeated the language and cultural life of medieval Europe. Furthermore, the first-person narrator, the lover of the poem – the fictitious John Gower – becomes a true *dramatis persona*. Through the dialogue with his confessor and Genius's priestly interferences, the protagonist undergoes a noticeable change. The phases of this development are dictated essentially by irony – self-irony, as we shall see. Here one cannot but see a shadow of Chaucer, the great inventor of Geoffrey the dim-witted, Geoffrey the lover who knows nothing of love. The first version of the *Confessio Amantis* was sent to Chaucer, as Chaucer had sent Gower his *Troilus*:

> 'And gret wel Chaucer whan ye mete,
> As mi disciple and mi poete:
> For in the floures of his youthe
> In sondri wise, as he wel couthe,
> Of Ditees and of songes glade,
> The whiche he for mi sake made,
> The lond fulfild is overal:
> Whereof to him in special
> Above alle othre I am most holde.'[9]   *grateful*

Here, through John Gower, Venus speaks to Geoffrey Chaucer and advises him to forget about love in his old age, to make his 'testament of love'. This sharing of a feeling, a convention, a fiction – this association, which as far as we know is the first such friendship between two great English poets – was in itself the sign of a new consciousness. The two writers themselves, like Petrarch and Boccaccio, were aware of its significance to the extent of writing about it. And here one begins to see the whole range of complexities that Gower represents.

Gower, as I have mentioned, was the author of other weighty and important works apart from the *Confessio Amantis*: the *Mirour de l'Omme* (or *Speculum Meditantis*) and the *Vox Clamantis*, written in French and Latin respectively. He is a writer who first expressed himself in the two 'noble' languages of England and medieval Europe; only later did he come to the English vernacular. He has often been reproached for this fact, which has been taken to indicate a certain cultural backwardness and lack of sensitivity. But these accusations do not stand up: the *Confessio* is not a clumsy effort, groping for a tongue and an idiom, but the full expression of a writer who has complete command of his vernacular. The use of Latin and French in his earlier works reflects a certain cultural commitment, as in the case of Brunetto Latini's *Tresor*, or Dante's Latin writings: it expresses the integrated mentality of a European intellectual, who consciously chooses the languages of international culture and handles them with perfect ease. These are the languages of the encyclopedists and the philosophers, and it is with such ideals in mind that the 'moral' Gower uses them. At the same time, the use of French, and the quality of Gower's Latin, clearly delimit the cultural range within which he moved: we are far from Petrarch or even Boccaccio – far, in other words, from the proto-humanism that was taking shape at that very time in Italy. In this sense Gower was not an advanced intellectual; he was closer to the outlook of the late thirteenth century than to the new experiments of the fourteenth.

These, in any case, are the aspects of Gower that emerge from even a summary examination of the *Mirour de l'Omme* and the *Vox Clamantis*.[10] It may have been the poet himself who, in a marginal note that appears in Latin at the end of several manuscripts of the *Confessio*, briefly describes the content and intentions of his earlier books:

The first book, written in French, is divided into ten parts. It treats of the vices and virtues and of the various states of this world. It seeks to show the true way by which the sinner who has strayed must return to the knowledge of his Creator. The title of this little book is *Speculum Meditantis*.

The second book, composed in Latin verse, treats of the various misfortunes that occurred in England during the reign of Richard II, when not only did the nobles and the people suffer, but the cruel king was ruined through his own fault, falling into the trap he himself had made. The title of this second book is *Vox Clamantis*.[11]

These are the works, respectively, of a teacher and of a prophet – 'vox clamantis in deserto' – purely intellectual arrangements of material that is 'the same raw material as Chaucer's and Langland's'.[12] The *Mirour* is concerned, first of all, with the seven capital sins and the seven virtues (theological and cardinal), each in its five aspects: but these are treated in a narrative manner, through a plot that is naturally based on the device of personification. It is the Devil, for example, who sends Sin and his seven daughters (the capital sins) into the world to fight against the divine plan and to corrupt humanity. Various scenes describe the diabolical council, to which Man is invited, and where he is tempted by the Devil, by Sin and by the World; the struggle between Flesh and Spirit; the marriage of the seven daughters of Sin with the World; the marriage of the Seven Virtues with Reason; the battle between the children of the one union and the other. At this point Gower goes into a description of the corruption of the world: he examines all the states of society and condemns them all, and the author confesses that he is himself a sinner. Finally, the way of salvation is pointed out; it can be attained only through the intercession of Mary. The work ends with a prayer-hymn to the Virgin, like the *Divine Comedy* and Petrarch's *Canzoniere*:

> O mere et vierge sanz lesure,
> O la treshumble creature,
> Joye des angles gloriouse,
> O merciable par droiture.
> Restor de nostre forsfaiture,
> Fontaine en grace plentevouse,
> O belle Olive fructuouse,
> Palme et Cipresse preciouse,
> O de la mer estoille pure,
> O cliere lune esluminouse,
> O amiable, o amourouse
> Du bon amour qui toutdis dure...
> (29917–28)

So the *Mirour de l'Omme* has a solid structure, derived in part from manuals of confession such as *Handlyng Synne*, and a basically didactic orientation, tending on the one hand towards the *Summa* and on the other towards allegorical narration. The intellectual and emotional centre of this narration which in fact stands at the very heart of the work, in the second of the three parts – is concerned with the traditional motif of *contemptus mundi*, in an ethical-political dimension: king, clergy, merchants and workers are all corrupt. These are the great themes of *Piers Plowman*, but here they are explored without Langland's fervour and dramatic language. And the spark of allegorical narrative soon dies out, as can be seen in the following short passage from the wedding procession of the daughters of Sin – which may be compared with the appearance on the scene of the same character, Gluttony, in *Piers Plowman*:

> Bien tost apres il me sovient
> Que dame Gloutonie vient,
> Que sur le lou s'est chivalché,
> Et sur son poign un coufle tient,
> Q'a sa nature bien avient;
> Si fist porter pres sa costée
> Beau cop de vin envessellé...
> (913–19)

In the *Vox Clamantis* Gower again takes up, in part, the themes of the *Mirour*, giving them a decidedly prophetic-political force; between the two works the Peasants' Revolt of 1381 had broken out, and *contemptus mundi* was transformed into terror, anger and satiric ferocity. Not Fortune but Man is responsible for his ills: and Man, in all his social states, is corrupt. The young King Richard II is exhorted to rule with justice: but years later, in revising the text, Gower saw 'ipse crudelissimus rex suis ex demeritis ab alto corruens' ('through his own fault the cruellest of kings rushing from the heights towards his downfall') and he replaced the exhortations with reproaches and threats. Nebuchadnezzar's dream is the central prophetic metaphor of an apocalyptic vision of human history: the golden head, silver chest, bronze belly and feet of iron and clay are the ages of the world. Richard II's England, his splendid festive Court with its art and literature,[13] stands at the centre of a world in crisis, of iron and clay. Man, created by God but unconscious of himself, only moved his limbs, turning his gaze upon 'the face of the earth and its various aspects'. He was a nominalist Adam: 'quia non nouit nomina, nescit eas' ('not knowing their names, he did not know them'). Now he lifts his eyes to the sky, wonders at the stars and their motions, and suddenly asks himself what all this means. Nature gives him the answers, telling him what is a human being, his ends, his place in the universe. And Man finally burns with love for the Creator and *understands* what it is to love God.

> Erexit vultus, os sublimauit in altum,
> Se rapit ad superos, spiritus vnde fuit:
> Miratur celi speciem formamque rotundam,
> Sidereos motus stelliferasque domos:
> Stat nouus attonitus hospes secumque reuoluit,
> Quid sibi que cernit corpora tanta velint.
> Noticiamque tamen illi natura ministrat;
> Quod sit homo, quod sunt ista creata videt:
> Quod sit ad humanos vsus hic conditus orbis,
> Quod sit ei proprius mundus, et ipse dei.
> Ardet in auctoris illius sensus amorem,
> Iamque recognouit quid sit amare deum.
>
> (vii, 555–66)

This being (here described with sure strokes, evoking a sense of the primordial discovery of his spirit, in eloquent, 'philosophical' Latin),[14] this human microscosm, yet suffers corruption after death, and the world is as corrupt as his corpse. The *Vox Clamantis* cannot but end with a vision of death and Hell. The animal-like peasants of the Revolt, with whom Book 1 opens, at the end of the work find a universal correlative:

> Quidam sternutant asinorum more ferino,
> Mugitus quidam personuere boum;
> Quidam porcorum grunnitus horridiores
> Emittunt...
>
> (i, 799–802)

(Some sneeze in the bestial manner of the ass, others bellow like oxen, others emit the horrid grunts of pigs...)

The vision of the *Vox Clamantis* is in part magnified by the commonplaces of medieval tradition, and its horror is amplified – swollen, as it were, by Latin rhetoric. Nevertheless, it testifies not only to the objective state of crisis and decadence that acutely affected the reign of Richard II but also to the instinctive reaction of one of its greatest intellectuals. The poet, who in his youth had fabricated 'les fols ditz d'amours...dont en chantant je carolloie', was forced to turn his attention to graver matters. But it was time to find a middle way.

The *Confessio Amantis* is, in fact, this middle way, as the author himself was aware:

> I wolde go the middel weie
> And wryte a bok betwen the tweie,
> Somwhat of lust, somwhat of lore,   *pleasure*; *learning*
> That of the lasse or of the more
> Som man mai lyke of that I wryte:
> And for that fewe men endite
> In oure englissh, I thenke make
> A bok for Engelondes sake.
> (Prologue, 17–24)[15]

The thematic compromise, then, is between love and knowledge, wisdom and erudition: significantly, it is expressed in English. We have already seen how the narrative construction of the *Confessio* functions, how it is based on the device of confession and motivated by an eminently moral impulse. Ethical, scientific and narrative motives are explicitly mixed in the work, which begins, like its predecessors, by describing the state of crisis in the present world, a world 'reversed' – the world of the past turned upside-down:

> Men se the world on every syde
> In sondry wyse so diversed,
> That it welnyh stant al reversed,
> As forto speke of tyme ago.
> (Prologue, 28–31)

Gower introduces himself with the usual formula of humility as a 'burel clerk' ('a mediocre intellectual') and announces his intention to write a book 'after the world that whilom tok long tyme in olde daies passed', which will also touch on 'the world which neweth every dai' – in other words, a work dealing with past and present. He certainly does not mean to say that the *Confessio* will find an equilibrium between these two dimensions. In fact all but one of the stories narrated in the book are set in the mythological, biblical, historic–legendary past. The scientific excursuses are either atemporal or historical. What Gower means is, in the first place, that he will not avoid references to the present and, above all, that the whole narrative and scholarly apparatus will constantly aim to throw light on the present. In short, the past is the measure of the present. Thus the Prologue of the *Confessio*, which is over a thousand lines long, after indicating the intentions and aims of the poem, opens with a broad political–moral discussion of the state in which the country's spiritual and temporal governments and the 'commons' find themselves now, in the reign of Richard II. It is here, for example, that we find the first reference to the Lollards, later defined as 'Antichristes'. But the Prologue itself goes on to narrate the dream of Nebuchadnezzar and to give it the interpretation we have already seen, in terms of the progressively worsening ages of the world. Finally it returns to the present and to the principal cause of the crisis, which is the division among men.

This process is evident throughout the *Confessio* and of course it corresponds to the moral purposes of the work. The structure of the poem, as we have noted, produces a coherent ethical construction. But Gower's aim is more ambitious: the work is organised around various different 'systems', though only one of these, apart from the moral one, attains a particular compactness of exposition. First of all, in the *Confessio* there is the effort to construct a historical view: already in the Prologue, as noted above, we are presented with a 'prophetic' vision of the history of the world, the central image of which is represented by the statue in Nebuchadnezzar's dream and by the ages of the world that it symbolises. But in Book v, for a good 1200 lines, Genius expounds a vision of his own. This might be called a vision of religious history, which goes from the Chaldees, through the Egyptians and the Greeks, with a parenthesis on idolatry, and on to the Jews and the Christians. It represents a notable attempt at synthesis (for example, the catalogue of Greek gods); but the result is often confused, because of the lack of precise information or the superficial interpretation of sources. In Book IV, on the other hand, Gower moves towards the construction of a history of culture, giving different lists of 'inventors' or founders of the various arts: 'Cham', who first 'found the letters' (the alphabet), who wrote in Hebrew and founded natural philosophy, 'Heredot', who discovered metre, rhyme and cadences, 'Zenzis' the painter, Prometheus the 'sculptor' and so on – a mixture of names, of which some are invented, others misunderstood, corrupt, pseudo-historical, mythological or biblical. In the same passage the author attempts a description of alchemy and the three philosophical stones, and ends with a short exposition of the story of letters and languages, from Aristarchus, Donatus and Dydimus to 'Tullius with Cithero' and Ovid, prince of love poets.

Gower's second attempt at systematising occurs in Book VII, where, referring to the education of Alexander, and taking his construction and material from Brunetto Latini, he divides philosophy into its three 'Aristotelian' parts – theory, rhetoric and practice. Here we find a sort of miniature encyclopedia of medieval knowledge, popularised for a moderately cultivated audience: the creation of the four elements, the composition of the human body, the soul, geography, astronomy and astrology (planets, signs and stars), rhetoric (divided into grammar and logic), and finally practical philosophy, sub-divided into ethics, domestic economy and politics. With respect to this last, five 'points' are indicated: truth, liberality, justice, piety and chastity – all qualities of the ideal king. The exposition is interlarded with *exempla* and explanatory stories: in the first version of the poem, for example, lines 2329–37 refer to the rebuff given by Dante to a flatterer (and this is the only reference to the 'grete poete of Ytaille', as Chaucer calls him, in the entire *Confessio*). Here in Book VII the exposition, briefly outlined above, assumes the organic character of a real compendium: it is here that the 'lore' promised by Gower in the Prologue finds its rational arrangement. It is here too that the language becomes scientific – without the rigour, of course, of professional philosophy but in simplified terminology and syntax, with a clearly instructional aim. Here is a revealing passage, the diluted and simple language of which may be compared with the dense and rigorous language of the 'scientific' Dante; in this discourse the only technical term is 'Ylem', the Aristotelian *ule*, 'matter':

> Tofore the creacion
> Of eny worldes stacion,
> Of hevene, of erthe, or eke of helle,
> So as these olde bokes telle,
> As soun tofore the song is set   *sound*
> And yit thei ben togedre knet,
> Riht so the hihe pourveance   *Providence*
> Tho hadde under his ordinance
> A gret substance, a gret matiere,
> Of which he wolde in his manere
> These othre thinges make and forme.
> For yit withouten eny forme
> Was that matiere universal,
> Which hihte Ylem in special.
> Of Ylem, as I am enformed,
> These elementz ben mad and formed,
> Of Ylem elementz they hote
> After the Scole of Aristote.
>
> (VII, 203–20)

The theme is slightly different, but this exposition of Gower's may be compared with the beginning of Dante's version of Thomas Aquinas's discourse on creation:

> Ciò che non more e ciò che può morire
> non è se non splendor di quella idea
> che partorisce, amando, il nostro sire.
>
> (*Paradiso*, XIII, 52–4)

('That which dies not and that which can die are naught but the splendour of that Idea which in His love our Sire begets.')

The difference between the discursive and the 'high' style could not be more obvious.

Gower's third attempt at synthesis is mythological: in Book v, as we have seen, in the course of his 'history of the religions', the poet devotes about 600 lines to an annotated catalogue of the Greek divinities, according to a classical model transmitted and transformed in the Middle Ages by Isidore, Fulgentius, the Vatican Mythographer and finally Boccaccio. Gower's work in disseminating the classics was of considerable cultural importance, especially in fourteenth-century England. J. A. W. Bennett has brought this out very well:

Gower's fondness for classical myth and story is a further reason for revising the general view of him as essentially mediaeval. It is not only that he is the first English transmitter of so many of the classical themes which Renaissance poets and painters were to embroider – giving us as he does not merely the common references to Helen and Dido, Phaethon and Pygmalion, Actaeon and Achilles, but the ampler tales of Ulysses, Penelope and Telegonus, Demetrius and Persius, Orestes and Diogenes; it is also that in his modest way he provided in the fifth book of his *Confessio* an English equivalent to Boccaccio's more elaborate *Genealogia Deorum* – a work likewise professedly undertaken by royal request. In that very book Boccaccio had remarked that in mythological learning the English were as yet *studiis tardi*; and Thomas Walsingham's *De generatione et natura deorum ... cum interpretatione Ovidii* (post 1386) ... is still apologetic in tone. But the Gower who presents Ovid without undue regard to the moralizing interpretations that festooned the medieval *Metamorphoses*, stands at no great distance in spirit from later humanists and translators. It is not surprising that Ben Jonson read widely in the *Confessio*, and – perhaps because he remembered Gower's own evocation of Ovid's *aurea prima aetas* – introduced the poet into the masque *The Golden Age Restored*.[16]

Gower's catalogue does not have the encyclopedically systematic quality or the breadth of erudition of Boccaccio's *Genealogy*, nor do we find in it the mythographic novelty of the short passage in Petrarch's *Africa* where the poet depicts some of the classical gods.[17] It does, however, correspond to the internal requirements of the *Confessio*: it provides a sort of concise analytical index that once and for all characterises the poem's intricate mythological world, and once again it fits into a scheme of cultural exposition that is one of the main aims of this work, and one of the reasons why it stands among the most notable documents of fourteenth-century English history. It is a vernacular poem with a solid moral framework and a broad, if unsystematic, spectrum of historical, scientific, philosophical and mythological references. The 'middel weie' refers not only to the compromise between 'lust' and 'lore' in the *Confessio*, but also to the educative function of 'lore'. And here we see the substantial difference between Gower's work and Boccaccio's *Genealogia*, which is a treatise in Latin, with two books devoted to the defence of poetry and poets – a work written for intellectuals. The difference, indeed, goes well beyond Gower and Boccaccio: it might be seen as emblematic of the difference between two cultures that took two different directions at the end of the fourteenth century. This had important consequences for the future history of the two literatures: the English never went beyond the 'middel weie', while the Italian inclined for a long time to humanism, erudition, Latin – a literature that was no longer national and popular.[18] The Boccaccio of the *Decameron* went on to write the *Genealogia*; the Gower of the *Mirour* and the *Vox* went on to write the *Confessio*: two opposite paths.

Apart from his importance as an intellectual, as an organiser and dis-seminator of culture, and as a moralist–prophet, Gower must be assessed as a narrative poet. In the fourteenth century literature was affected by numerous developments in the art of narrative, and there is no doubt that if it were not for Chaucer and the *Gawain*-poet, Gower would stand out as the best narrative poet of his time. His stories are always straightforward and well-constructed, without complications, digressions or superfluous embroidering: one might almost say that the English poet had gained an instinctive feeling for classical principles through his assiduous reading of Ovid. The story of Canace (III, 143–356), for example, is taken from Ovid's *Heroides*. It proceeds directly from beginning to end: Canace and Macareus, children of Aeolus, grow up together and fall in love with each other; the girl becomes pregnant and her brother flees. When the child is born, Aeolus is furious and has Canace killed by one of his hirelings. Then he enters the room, finds the baby crying amid all the blood and has him abandoned in the forest, a prey to the wild beasts. A tragedy, in other words, entirely based on the fury of Aeolus, which is in fact the 'malencolie' that Genius wants to censure. But in this tale we can begin to see some of the constant features that characterise Gower as narrator: far from concentrating on the horror of incest, for example, the poet gives all his human sympathy towards the two young people, who have always lived together and cannot escape the law of nature. Their situation is described in a series of images of

extreme delicacy: one is left with an impression of that 'enchantment' which
is the wizardry of nature:

> Nature, tok hem into lore
> And tawht hem so, that overmore
> Sche hath hem in such wise daunted,
> That thei were, as who seith, enchaunted.
> And as the blinde an other ledeth   *blind man*
> And til thei falle nothing dredeth,
> Riht so thei hadde non insihte;
> Bot as the bridd which wole alihte
> And seth the mete and noght the net,   *food*
> Which in deceipte of him is set,
> This yonge folk no peril sihe.
> (III, 175–85)

The structural lines are clear and straight, and the mode of narration is
correspondingly even, smooth and artfully simple; C. S. Lewis has noted
this in a comment that has become classical:

He [Gower] is our first considerable master of the plain style in poetry, and he
has the qualities and defects that go with such a style. He can be dull: he can
never be strident, affected, or ridiculous. He stands almost alone in the centuries
before our Augustans in being a poet perfectly well bred.[19]

Gower's sentences are almost always constructed smoothly, without syntactic
twists and turns; characterising elements follow one another in good order,
polished and levelled, to form the discourse of the 'polite and easy society',
as Lewis calls it, of the fourteenth-century upper class. Here is a typical
example, taken from the story of Jason and Medea in Book v. Jason has
conquered the Golden Fleece, and the Greeks await his return:

> The dai was clier, the Sonne hot,
> The Gregeis weren in gret doute,
> The whyle that here lord was oute:
> Thei wisten noght what scholde tyde,   *happen*
> Bot waiten evere upon the tyde,
> To se what ende scholde falle.
> Ther stoden ek the nobles alle
> Forth with the comun of the toun;   *commons*
> And as thei loken up and doun,
> Thei weren war withinne a throwe,
> Wher cam the bot, which thei wel knowe,
> And sihe hou Jason broghte his preie.
> (v, 3752–63)

A period like this essentially meets the narrative requirement of functional-
ity, and in this sense it corresponds perfectly with the structural organisation that Gower gives his stories: Derek Pearsall has observed that one of
the characteristics of Gower's narrative is precisely that of 'cutting the

antique moorings and isolating the tellable tale, akin to Malory's technique in handling the polyphonic or interwoven Arthurian narratives'.[20] This is no small merit considering the development of the romances in England and the dominant influence that French literature exercised on Gower. It is a step forward towards the type of narrative that will prevail in the modern age, a narrative based on logic and consequentiality, far from the rule of chance and hidden *sen* in the medieval romance; a function, one might say, akin to that which Ockham's razor performed in philosophy during the same period. This procedure, moreover, is not confined exclusively to the mythological stories of the *Confessio*: we also find it in tales with a completely different setting, such as that of Pope Boniface (II, 2803–3037) and that of Constantine and Sylvester (II, 3187–496). The former, for example, has, to use Dorfman's terminology,[21] a sub-structure clearly divided into two parts, each containing three successive *narremes*, linked together by cause and effect: (1) on the death of Nicholas, when Celestine is elected, Boniface begins to think of 'supplantacioun'; (2) the trick to force Celestine to abdicate is set in motion; (3) Celestine makes what Dante calls 'the great refusal', and Boniface becomes Pope. In the second part: (1) Boniface has a 'querelle' with King Louis of France; (2) there follows a French expedition against him; (3) Boniface is imprisoned and dies. The three-part movement is repeated at the end of the story in the (by then almost proverbial) comment on the Pope's career:

> Thin entre lich the fox was slyh,   *beginning*
> Thi regne also with pride on hih
> Was lich the Leon in his rage;
> Bot ate laste of thi passage
> Thi deth was to the houndes like.
> (II, 3033–7)

Gower's choice of structure and his stylistic approach may have made it impossible for him to develop further the mimetic aspect of the *Confessio*. The work lacks spatial and temporal depth, and it lacks the graphic quality that could have been provided by the more-or-less prominent presence of objects, sounds and colours. While there is some attempt at psychological profundity, as in Florent's uncertainty whether or not to accept the old woman's proposal (I, 1568–80) and Constantine's monologue-prayer (II, 3243–300), this dimension had existed in European literature since the twelfth century – for example, in the interior monologues of the *Roman d'Eneas*. Gower's approach was actually different from that of mimesis in the true sense of the word: Lewis rightly maintains that the poet of the *Confessio* 'sees...movement, not groups and scenes, but actions and events'.[22] For example, here is the moment when Tereus, after eating his son's flesh, throws himself upon Procne and Philomela; everything is realised in terms of movement and action:

> With that he sterte up fro the mete,
> And schof the bord unto the flor,
> And cauhte a swerd anon and suor
> That thei sholde of his handes dye.
> And thei unto the goddes crie
> Begunne with so loude a stevene,
> That thei were herd unto the hevene;
> And in a twinclinge of an yhe
> The goddes, that the meschief syhe,
> Here formes changen alle thre.
>
> (v, 5928–37)

Another of Gower's narrative skills in the *Confessio*, complementary to the first, lies in creating an atmosphere at the beginning of a story, within which the whole narrative unfolds. In the story of Rosiphelee, for example, everything is enveloped in a rarefied air of enchantment and pensive melancholy. The maiden comes out of the house before dawn, and all is silence:

> Whan come was the Monthe of Maii,
> Sche wolde walke upon a dai,
> And that was er the Sonne Ariste;
> Of wommen bot a fewe it wiste,
> And forth sche wente prively
> Unto the Park was faste by,
> Al softe walkende on the gras,
> Til sche cam ther the Launde was,
> Thurgh which ther ran a gret rivere.
>
> (iv, 1283–91)

Now the scene is set for the advent of the faerie: Rosiphelee looks around her and sees a procession of ladies, mounted on white horses. Gower's touch becomes most delicate, and the atmosphere condenses in one of the most famous verses of the poem:

> Here bodies weren long and smal,
> The beaute faye upon her face
> Non erthly thing it may desface . . .
>
> (iv, 1320–22)

In the same way, in the story of Jason and Medea, the conquest of the Golden Fleece is marked by four lines that suggest a mood of exultation:

> The Flees he tok and goth to Bote,
> The Sonne schyneth brythe and hote,
> The Flees of gold schon forth withal,
> The water glistreth overal.
>
> (v, 3731–4)

In the same story, Medea, the sorceress, goes out at night to gather the herbs that will rejuvenate Jason's aged father; here, the poetry of movement blends with poetry designed to create a particular mood:

> Thus it befell upon a nyht,
> Whan ther was noght bot sterreliht, *starlight*
> Sche was vanyssht riht as hir liste,
> That no wyht bot hirself it wiste,
> And that was ate mydnyht tyde.
> The world was stille on every side;
> With open hed and fot al bare,
> Hir her tosprad sche gan to fare,
> Upon hir clothes gert sche was,
> Al specheles and on the gras
> Sche glod forth as an Addre doth. *snake*
> (v, 3957–67)

Finally, in the *Confessio* there is the poetry of the Lover, who confesses and discourses with Genius: this is the thread that links all the stories, but it is not only a functional element. It provides a delicately-drawn portrait of a 'gentil herte' at the mercy of love, a courtly but very human love: when the poet–lover, in the evening, has to take leave of his lady, after dancing and playing and reading about Troilus, he does so reluctantly, turning back to snatch a second kiss; then he curses the night and lies wide awake in bed, thinking of the nightingale that by nature does not sleep, because of love; and finally

> Into hire bedd myn herte goth,
> And softly takth hire in his arm
> And fieleth hou that sche is warm, *feels*
> And wissheth that his body were
> To fiele that he fieleth there.
> (iv, 2884–8)

A good dose of self-irony adds vivacity to this portrait of the lover: when Genius preaches against 'lachesse' (glossed in the marginal notes as 'tardacio': 'procrastination') and recommends to the penitent that he should take care to avoid this if he wants to win the love of a lady, the poor poet replies that he has never had a chance to commit this sin because his lady has never allowed a tryst:

> Mi fader, that I mai wel lieve.
> Bot me was nevere assigned place,
> Wher yit to geten eny grace,
> Ne me was non such time apointed.
> (iv, 270–3)

Again, Genius condemns the cowardice of those lovers who are afraid to ask anything of their ladies: here, the poet frankly admits his guilt (IV, 355–63). But when Genius speaks of laziness, of failure to take the initiative, of idleness, the lover replies that he has exerted himself greatly, but with no result:

> For everemore I finde it so,
> The more besinesse I leie,
> The more that I knele and preie
> With goode wordes and with softe,
> The more I am refused ofte.
>
> (IV, 1746–50)

This character (for such he becomes in the course of the *Confessio*) is timid, unlucky in love, a little comic, at times deliberately ridiculous; but as the poem proceeds he gradually matures, until at the end he realises that he is now an old man and must abandon love. It is in the final part of the *Confessio* that we see the greatest quality of Gower as man and poet: his humanity becomes self-comprehension, as he renounces illusions and quietly resigns himself to the reality of old age. When Venus reappears at his prayer, she says to him:

> Er thou make eny suche assaies
> To love, and faile upon the fet,
> Betre is to make a beau retret...
>
> The thing is torned into 'was';
> That which was whilom grene gras,
> Is welked hey at time now.
> Forthi mi conseil is that thou
> Remembre wel hou thou art old.
>
> (VIII, 2414–39)

The poet feels a sudden chill, swoons and dreams. He dreams of the lovers of the past, of whom he has sung in his poem – the young lovers of mythology and then the old, ridiculous in their love. Cupid arrives and extracts his arrow from the lover's heart, and Venus makes him contemplate himself in a mirror. The old man recalls the seasons of his life as if they were seasons of the year and he knows that winter is upon him. When he awakens, Venus asks him, smiling, what is love. He does not know how to answer: thus, at last, he understands:

> 'Ma dame,' I seide, 'be your leve,
> Ye witen wel, and so wot I,
> That I am unbehovely
> Your Court fro this day forth to serve...'
>
> (VIII, 2882–5)

He asks Genius for absolution; when he obtains it, he kneels before the goddess and wants to take his leave:

> Bot sche, that wolde make an ende,
> As therto which I was most able,
> A Peire of Bedes blak as Sable
> Sche tok and heng my necke aboute;
> Upon the gaudes al withoute
> Was write of gold, *Por reposer.*
>
> (VIII, 2902–7)

'Enclosed in a sterred sky', Venus rises to heaven, and the poet, rosary in hand, returns home 'a softe pas', and concludes his work with a prayer for his land, taking leave of his poem and of earthly love, to rise, finally, to celestial love:

> Such love is goodly forto have,
> Such love mai the bodi save,
> Such love mai the soule amende,
> The hyhe god such love ous sende
> Forthwith the remenant of grace;
> So that above in thilke place
> Wher resteth love and alle pes,
> Oure joie mai ben endeles.
>
> (VIII, 3165–72)

Science, ethics, mythology, narrative and the whole story of the poet, are stilled in the prayer and in the vision of infinite joy: this is the path travelled by John Gower, the 'moral Gower'. With him travels his friend, Chaucer.

6

Chaucer

With Chaucer English medieval narrative reaches full maturity; in Chaucer English literature finds the author who, despite all the fluctuations of critical opinion, will always be considered its 'father', its Homer. The cultural and poetic atmosphere of the latter half of the fourteenth century favoured the formation of a 'classic' paradigm, for the first time, in the English vernacular. Even apart from the blind alley represented by the *Gawain*-poet, we have seen this process beginning with Langland and Gower. But Chaucer, in his own lifetime (about 1340–1400) and in the generations following, acquired a special importance: a host of poets, in England and Scotland, explicitly imitated him and celebrated him as their master. Part of the reason for this success was undoubtedly the fact that Chaucer wrote in a dialect, that of London, which was about to become the national literary language: certainly his success at Court and among the gentry also worked in his favour. Of course the themes of his works had a general interest, and the elegance and refinement of his poetry evoked a ready response in society. All this, however, is not sufficient to make a classic, still less to assure that it remains one when the vernacular in which it is written becomes archaic and hard to understand, when the society that formed its audience has disappeared, when some of its themes have lost their importance and its forms have been superseded by others. Chaucer has not held the position enjoyed in later generations by Dante, Boccaccio and especially Petrarch: for the great fourteenth-century Italian writers had the advantage of a linguistic continuity that was perhaps unique in Europe. Nor has it been possible to construct an image of Chaucer based on an autobiography or collection of letters; there is nothing like the myth of Beatrice or Laura or Fiammetta, no characteristic events and acts comparable with Dante's exile and political struggles, or Petrarch's laurel wreath and his passionate search for the buried texts of ancient masters. All that remains of Chaucer is his tomb in Westminster Abbey, where, as a clear sign of official favour and consecration, he was received after his death – in an age when Poets' Corner did not exist and the place was reserved for royal sepulchres. There remains the *persona* that he created for himself in his narrative works: the polite and timid dreamer; the voracious reader of all sorts of books, lacking experience of the world and of real love but faithfully serving a conventional and literary love; the pilgrim who keeps his eyes on the ground, who cannot put together a decent rhyme; the poet clinging to his sources, his 'auctoritees'. This is a comic character, humbler than that required by the formulae of humility used in his time, modest and wise in his *aurea mediocritas*; a competent, rather pedantic intellectual, a Christian to the point of repudiating, as did Boccaccio, his 'enditynges of worldly vanitees'.

And, as postwar criticism has recognised, it is precisely here, in this *persona* that is not the real Chaucer, that the first sign of the real Chaucer's originality and importance can be seen. Here is a poet who hides behind a mask, who constructs his own character with perfect and coherent narrative irony. It is a narrative device that reveals, in the ambiguity between what he says, what he says he does not say, and what he accidentally lets drop, the first extraordinary self-consciousness in English literature. Chaucer constructs this image of himself, the image to be delivered to his readers, without solemnity or apparent inner torments, without extravagances of a heroic, political, mystical or poetic kind. He invokes the Muses for the first time in the literature of his country but he does not aspire to a laurel crown; he invents new metres and stanzas but claims that he cannot make a rhyme; he has experience of several environments and trades but pretends to have lived 'as an heremyte'. And in this humour, in this 'playing it down', he makes the first assertion of a distinctive English cultural identity.

Indeed, before beginning to analyse his narrative writings, we must take note of the fact that Chaucer had a very wide range of experience. The son of a wine merchant, he was familiar with commerce and mercantile life on an international scale; he lived in the royal Court and was on intimate terms with one of the great figures of the realm, John of Gaunt; he fought in the war against the French and was taken prisoner; he went to school and perhaps to a university; he travelled all over Europe on political and commercial missions; he was in contact with English, French and probably Italian intellectuals; he was employed in the Customs and in the king's constructions and forests, and even took part in making arrangements for a tournament; he was a member of Parliament; he knew the Church and its sermons, the public square and the 'pleyes of myracles'; he retired to the country; he had a wife and children; he was even accused of a lady's *raptus*: altogether, he had a full life – of which, in fact, we only know the general outlines. Chaucer was one of the most widely cultured people of his century, at least in England: he was competent in medicine, alchemy, astrology and astronomy; he knew something of ancient and 'modern' philosophy, dialectics and *disputatio*, and kept up with the debates of the time; he especially liked Boethius and Alain de Lille. Of course he had read the Scriptures and patristic literature, and he had assiduously studied the texts of Macrobius, Martianus Capella, the grammarians and the authors of the *artes poeticae*, especially Geoffrey of Vinsauf. He knew the encyclopedias and mythographical works; he loved the Latin classics, especially Ovid, Virgil and Statius; he had gone deeply into the legend of Troy, reading the most important authors on the subject, from Dares to Guido delle Colonne to Geoffrey of Monmouth. He was familiar with the romance tradition, Arthurian and otherwise, French and English; he himself probably translated part of the *Roman de la Rose*, and he loved and imitated French poets including Machaut, Deschamps, Grandson, Froissart and Deguileville. He was the first Englishman to take an interest in the Italian *avant-garde*, studying Dante, Petrarch and Boccaccio. The list of authors and works cited by him exceeds the sixty or so which he claimed to possess, though some of these are works he had only heard of. The authors and works that he did not mention, but obviously knew, are far more numerous.[1]

Chaucer knew four languages; English, French, Latin and Italian. He used the first with consummate experience and naturalness, as if it were a fully-developed vernacular; what he actually did was to absorb it and re-invent it at the same time, enriching it with words, expressions, turns of phrase and *modes of thought* garnered from the other three languages.[2] Chaucer mastered the various traditions of French literature, the courtly and the bourgeois, the love tradition and that of the *fabliau*;[3] he used the classics, especially Ovid, as an inexhaustible mine of stories, myths and images; from the Italians he learnt style, new perspective on the real and the imaginary, the importance of poets and poetry: a lesson that was truly to change the course of English literature. Finally, Chaucer knew the tradition of his own country; he appreciated the heritage of the metrical romances, he read Gower, alluded to alliterative poetry and may have seen *Piers Plowman*.[4] What is most important, Chaucer thoroughly assimilated all this into his own personal itinerary and into his own image of poetry and the poet: starting from the conventions of courtly love, he moved away from them, contaminated them, completed them, mocked them and exposed their tragic contradictions;[5] starting from the concept of 'remembrance,' he defined the activity of the poet within the tradition, between nature and artifice, between form and substance, between poetry and morality and science. He was a craftsman of rhetoric and the ironic interlocutor of his own readers.

Chaucer was, finally, the first English writer to experiment with almost all the literary genres at his disposal, trying his mettle with verse and prose, adapting or inventing metres, rhythms and stanzas, creating different structures in the heart of his narrative. Chaucer translated Boethius's *De Consolatione Philosophiae*, Innocent III's *De Contemptu Mundi*, part of the *Roman de la Rose*, and the homily *De Maria Magdalena* attributed to Origen, not to mention an unknown number of French poems, so many that Deschamps called him a 'grant translateur'. Chaucer wrote visionary poems – elegies and poems of philosophy and love – (*Book of the Duchess, House of Fame, Parliament of Fowls*, the Prologue to the *Legend of Good Women*); he wrote every kind of romance, from the lay to the tragic to the burlesque (*Knight's Tale, Man of Law's Tale, Wife of Bath's Tale, Clerk's Tale, Squire's Tale, Franklin's Tale, Sir Thopas, Troilus and Criseyde*); he wrote *fabliaux* (*Miller's Tale, Reeve's Tale, Cook's Tale, Shipman's Tale*), stories based on traditional, popular and contemporary elements (*Friar's Tale, Summoner's Tale, Merchant's Tale, Canon's Yeoman's Tale*), stories based on mythology and classical history (*Physician's Tale, Manciple's Tale, Legend of Good Women*); he wrote a series of 'tragedies' (*Monk's Tale*), an *exemplum* (*Pardoner's Tale*), a sacred legend (*Prioress's Tale*), the life of a saint (*Second Nun's Tale*), an animal fable (*Nun's Priest's Tale*), a sermon on penitence with an appended treatise on the capital sins (*Parson's Tale*), a prose translation of the *Livre de Melibée et Dame Prudence* (*Tale of Melibee*), and one or two scientific treatises (*Treatise on the Astrolabe* and perhaps *Equatorie of the Planetis*). In the General Prologue to the *Canterbury Tales*, Chaucer took advantage of the tradition of the estates satire;[6] he composed, as he himself said, 'many a song and many a lecherous lay', which have not survived; and he wrote *planctus*, love ballads and 'moral' poems, metrical epistles and an epigram to his scribe, Adam, which have come down to us. Chaucer inherited the first of his metrical schemes from the English and French tradition – that is, the four-accented octosyllabic distich (two iambic tetrameters), but he literally invented the five-accented decasyllable (iambic pentameter), bearing in mind the French and Italian schemes as well as the natural rhythm of the English language. Within this metre he combined two basic units, the heroic couplet (*aabbcc* etc.) and the seven-line stanza or rhyme royal (*ababbcc*), but he also experimented with stanzas of five, six, eight, nine and ten lines, adding for good measure the *terza rima* imitated from Dante, the 'rym dogerel' of *Sir Thopas* and the metrical romances that it parodied, and the roundel; and, lastly, he used cadenced prose.[7]

Chaucer, in other words, stands at the centre of the Middle English tradition; in himself he summed up the cultural, linguistic and stylistic tendencies of England at the end of the fourteenth century. He developed these and enriched them with elements drawn from continental traditions, carrying them to new achievements. He evolved a decidedly personal poetic model of such strength that it established him as the first English classic.

Chaucer's narrative and its structures, which are the object of the present study, contributed preponderantly to the formation of this paradigm. His narrative works may be initially divided into three categories: the dream poem, the collection of stories and the romance. These three forms fall entirely within the medieval English narrative tradition, as outlined in the preceding chapters. But Chaucer, apart from Boccaccio in the *Amorosa Visione*, the *Decameron* and the *Filostrato*, was the only European fourteenth-century artist to use all three of these in his narrative works. Still more significantly, Chaucer internationalised all three of these traditional forms: he was the first in England to use the French courtly conventions in a dream poem; his romance was articulated on the broader European scale (*Troilus* has the breadth of the romances of Chrétien, Gottfried von Strassburg and Boccaccio); with the *Canterbury Tales* he introduced the framed composition as an end in itself. As he carried out this work of bringing English literature up to the level of the great European tradition, Chaucer at the same time overthrew the international models on which his work was based, creating a set of structural stereotypes and a narrative problematic that were all his own. These I shall now examine in detail.

1 The Dream Poem

The dream is one of the 'type-cadres' of medieval literature,[1] whose fundamental line of development I have mentioned in chapter 4, distinguishing schematically the religious and the secular traditions. The latter, that of the love dream, found its first full formulation in the *Roman de la Rose*, especially in the first part of that work, written by Guillaume de Lorris. In an allegorical frame, this section of the *Roman* traduces and perverts the religious vision in narrative and in debate about love: the poet becomes a dreamer, he contemplates the rose (his lady) in a garden that is erotic and at the same time mirrors the Garden of Eden. He is struck by the darts of the God of Love and becomes a lover. Throughout the work, the story tells of the attempts made by this poetic *persona* to win the rose. The story takes shape through the actions and words of the first-person narrator, together with various allegorical personifications representing qualities of the human soul, such as, for example, Delight, Reason, Fear and Fair Welcome, or mythological characters like Venus, or 'philosophical' deities like Nature. In the second part, written by Jean de Meun, the scheme expands in digressions that touch a wide variety of broadly moral and philosophical problems, thus constructing an all-comprehending vision. The *Roman* consecrates once and for all, in the vernacular, certain key *topoi* of the European tradition, such as that of May and that of the Garden.[2] Fusing the classical heritage with medieval Christian patterns of thought and the conventions of courtly love, it creates a model that held a central place in the imagination of the Middle Ages.

Variations on these themes are developed by the fourteenth-century French poets, Machaut and Froissart, in their dream poems and *dits amoureux*.[3] In Machaut's *Dit dou Vergier*, for example, the poet's *persona* enters a garden. Here he has a vision in which the God of Love explains his attributes to him and introduces him to his followers, and then narrates a wholly allegorical love story. The poetic mechanisms are thus essentially unchanged and the theme of love remains at the poem's centre, while the *persona* of the narrator–lover, the 'I', gradually takes on more importance. In Froissart's *Paradys d'Amour* this *persona* is presented as a poet: thus the love dream turns back on itself and becomes an increasingly self-conscious meditation on poetry.

Within the type of the dream we can identify two other thematic traditions, separate from that of love. The first is the more generally philosophical one, the most significant examples of which are the *Somnium Scipionis* and the *De Planctu Naturae*. The *Somnium Scipionis* makes up the last sixteen chapters of Cicero's *De Re Publica*, in which Scipio dreams of his grandfather Africanus after a conversation with Masinissa: in the dream, Africanus prophesies to his grandson the latter's military and political rise, urges him to strive for the good of the 'res publica', shows him the heavens and gives him a physical and spiritual view of the universe. The central point of the *Somnium*, crowning a philosophical–political treatise, are precisely these: the need to work for the good of the state, the winning of beatitude and the 'aevum sempiternum' in Heaven after death, the vision of the 'definitum locum' in which this is to happen, and the physical laws that govern it. In other words, the *Somnium* is a philosophical vision of the natural order, aiming to harmonise political, moral, scientific and metaphysical interests into a coherent whole. In Alain de Lille's *De Planctu Naturae* a personified Nature stands at the centre of the vision; she laments the corruption and perversion of men, who no longer belong to her order. Nominated by God as his vicar, she has made Venus her minister, flanked by Hymenaeus and Cupid. But Venus, intended for love and procreation, has degenerated into pure sex and sexual perversion. Briefly, the work is centred, as Spearing has said,[4] on 'sexual love considered in the context of general philosophy'; it provides a bridge between the themes of love and the natural order, which was later used by Jean de Meun in his part of the *Roman de la Rose*.

Lastly, within the tradition of dreams and visions, one particular tendency emerged in the fourteenth century as a typically Italian phenomenon. This was the 'triumph', invented by Boccaccio in the *Amorosa Visione* and taken up by Petrarch in the *Trionfi*. Boccaccio was by no means unaware of the visionary genre as it came down to him, but

he profoundly renewed it; he did not cast it in the form of pageants in the other world, or of prophetic visions, but expounded his intention and his moral-allegorical credo in a new way. The *Amorosa Visione* contemplates the greatness, the splendour and the vanity of earthly goods in grandiose scenes, in which figures symbolising Wisdom, Fame, Wealth, Love and Fortune are surrounded by some of the great personages who enjoyed them or suffered from them, often represented in their most famous actions.[5]

Going even further than the analogous tendency that was manifest in the Italian painting of the time, Boccaccio meditated on the forces and passions that dominate man, in a fresco that blends medieval allegorism with the classicising images of a culture moving towards the Renaissance. Petrarch adopted his friend's design, varying its central subjects and their succession so as to make them correspond to an organic conception that reflected his personal experience and his philosophy: Cupid, Pudicitia, Mors, Fama, Tempus and Aeternitas celebrate their triumphs (surrounded by the biblical, classical and medieval heroes of the poet's erudite world). Within these triumphal visions both Boccaccio and Petrarch reserved a special place for poets and writers in general – a touch reflecting their mentality and the cultural climate they created.[6] So here, too, in a world already far from the dream of love, the vision touches on the theme of poetry: this time not in terms of the narrator's *persona* but as the triumph of the cultural tradition on which the poet is nourished, and which through him is often 'reborn' as a central human activity.

These, then, are the traditions of dream and vision, mutually interconnected in their inspiration, sources and common motifs, within which Chaucer worked. Even if he had not read or even seen the *Amorosa Visione* and the *Trionfi*,[7] it is significant for the story of fourteenth-century European culture that some of the themes of his dream poems coincide with those that interested Boccaccio and Petrarch. In his works, however, Chaucer fused the traditions and themes that I have schematically indicated, and his dreams are concerned with love, nature, philosophy, fame and poetry. The first, the most frequent and perhaps the most original of the narrative stereotypes used by Chaucer, is the one Robert Payne has codified with the formula 'book–experience–dream',[8] occurring in the *Book of the Duchess*, the *House of Fame*, the *Parliament of Fowls* and the Prologue to the *Legend of Good Women*. All four of these works have some common characteristics, which Payne has brought out clearly: first, they 'are ironic in a special sense which is a direct consequence of their structural peculiarities'; secondly, the problems examined in them are 'as much aesthetic as ...moral or philosophical'; and finally, 'none of these four is strictly speaking a narrative poem in the sense that *Troilus and Criseyde* is, or *Anelida and Arcite* sets out to be. In none of the four is there any "plot" as we ordinarily understand that term in connection with fiction.'[9] The Prologue to the *Legend*, however, constitutes the frame for a collection of stories, and hence it belongs, structurally, to another narrative stereotype: it will be examined later, in the appropriate context, with the particular attention due to a work that combines two narrative models.

The *Book of the Duchess* stands apart – despite the similarities – from the other two poems included in the dream stereotype, the *House of Fame* and the *Parliament of Fowls*. This is not only because it is certainly the earliest work, and because, according to the old division of Chaucer's works into three periods, it does not seem to reflect any Italian influence, but above all because it is almost certainly linked to a specific occasion and deals with a well-defined central theme. It is almost certain, in fact, that Chaucer composed it in memory of Blanche, the Duchess of Lancaster and the wife of John of Gaunt. The 'Deth of Blaunche the Duchesse', as Alceste calls it in the Prologue to the *Legend*, could have been presented in traditional terms as a *planctus* or a *consolatio* or an elegy: in effect it does include elements characteristic of these forms. But Chaucer approaches them in a very oblique way: whereas originally they were lyric forms, he makes them emerge from a narrative. If it is true that Chaucer wrote many lyrics – including love lyrics – that have not survived, and if it is true that the *Book of the Duchess* is the earliest of his surviving narrative works, then we can see in it a transposition of lyric into narrative. The transformation takes place before our eyes, and yet it emerges as a finished, organic product, as if it had reached perfection through long practice.

The plot of the *Book of the Duchess* is linear – a series of scenes unified by the presence of the same protagonist – but complicated by the insertion of two narrative episodes within the narration. It unfolds according to a logic that seems to correspond to that of dreams. The 'I' of the poem is a writer who has suffered from insomnia for eight long years, presumably because of love. One night he begins reading what he calls a 'romance', which is actually Ovid's *Metamorphoses*. He concentrates on one of the stories, which he immediately relates to us: it is the story of Ceyx and Alcione. Ceyx loses his life at sea, and his wife, Alcione, asks Juno to put her to sleep and to show her husband to her in a dream. Juno sends a messenger to Morpheus to ask him to take the mortal form of Ceyx and appear to Alcione; the latter, after seeing her husband again, dies within three days. The sleepless reader, amazed and rather sceptical, decides to offer a featherbed to Morpheus and Juno if they will put him to sleep. Hardly has he formulated his vow when he falls asleep over his book and begins to dream: it is a morning in May and he is lying in bed quite naked, with birds singing all around him, in a room whose walls are covered with frescoes depicting scenes 'of al the Romaunce of the Rose', 'bothe text and glose', and whose windows are storiated with scenes from Trojan history and its heroes, and Jason and Medea. The sun is shining and the air is 'blew, bryght, clere'. Suddenly he hears a horn, shouts, dogs and horses: sounds of the hunt. The protagonist mounts a horse, rushes out and finds that the Emperor Octavian is going on the hunt; he follows the company. Then he finds himself standing near a tree in the middle of the forest, with a small dog; trying to catch the dog, he arrives in a 'floury grene', a grassy clearing in the full bloom of spring – the classical *locus amoenus*. Here, leaning against a great oak, stands a man dressed in black, a knight, reciting a 'compleynte' for his dead lady. The Knight at first does not notice the presence of the man; when he does, he begs his pardon. Apologising in his turn, the protagonist tries to start a conversation about the hunt, but the Knight replies that his thoughts are far from such things. The protagonist delicately and courteously remarks that he has noticed this, offers his assistance and asks the Knight to speak of his grief and so relieve his own heart. But the Knight declines with thanks and abandons himself to another lament, this time directed mainly against Fortune, who has beaten him at chess by taking his 'fers' (queen?).[10] The other man tries to comfort him, reminding him of how Socrates despised Fortune and mentioning a series of famous lovers who committed suicide for love: no man would make such a complaint for a 'fers'! And the black-clad Knight replies:

> 'Why so?' quod he, 'hyt ys nat soo.
> Thou wost ful lytel what thou menest;   *know*
> I have lost more than thow wenest.'
> (742–4)

The protagonist then asks him to tell the whole story in detail. The Knight makes him swear to listen attentively and proceeds. A faithful servant of love, he had fallen in love with a lady, a 'chef patron' of beauty and a model of 'courtoisie', whose name was White. He speaks of her in a passionate eulogy completely in line with the canons of the time. Interrupted and prodded by the protagonist, the Knight then describes his first meeting with the lady, his courtship, his declaration and her refusal. For a year he continued to serve her in sorrow, until she gave him 'the noble gifte of his mercy': in marriage the two had lived for years in perfect felicity. And then the protagonist asks where she is now:

> 'Sir,' quod I, 'where is she now?'
> 'Now?' quod he, and stynte anoon.   *stopped*
> Therwith he wax as ded as stoon,
> And seyde, 'Allas, that I was bore!   *born*
> That was the los that here-before   *loss*
> I tolde the that I hadde lorn.
> Bethenke how I seyde here-beforn,
> "Thow wost ful lytel what thow menest;
> I have lost more than thow wenest" –
> God wot, allas! ryght that was she!'
> 'Allas, sir, how? what may that be?'
> 'She ys ded!' 'Nay!' 'Yis, be my trouthe!'
> 'Is that youre los? Be God, hyt ys routhe!'
> (1298–310)

At this point the protagonist hears that the hunt is ended. The Knight goes off to his castle, where the bell strikes twelve. The dreamer awakens to find himself in bed with the book of Alcione and Ceyx beside him, and decides to put his dream into rhyme.

Thus the dream turns back on itself: the sensation one has after reading the *Book of the Duchess* is, typically, a dual one. On the one hand, it is clear that the dream was the predetermined object of Chaucer's poetic intention: we know this from the moment we take in hand a volume entitled *The Works of Geoffrey Chaucer*. But one has an equally strong impression that in some way this dream has caused the poet to mature within the protagonist – it seems in fact to create its own author. At the outset, the 'I' of the poem is an insomniac who at once proves to be an assiduous reader of romances. In other words he is a person who likes to be entertained, who enjoys art and 'thinges smale', as he himself says, stories of kings and queens. But reading on we discover, from what this 'I' tells us, that he is actually quite an intellectual: he knows Macrobius (though not very well, for Scipio was never 'kyng'), he knows the Bible, Ovid, the history of Troy, the *Roman de la Rose*, Socrates, mythology; in short, for his time he is a fairly cultivated man. At the end of the poem he decides to put his dream into rhyme, and it is precisely the 'quaynt...sweven' that stimulates him to do so. The dream awakens within him the creative potential latent in his passion for reading and in his culture; the dream, with its revelation of human experience, makes him a poet. And at the end of the book we find ourselves back at the beginning: the protagonist has become the author, again in his bed with the book of Alcione and Ceyx in his hands.

This perfect circularity is only the first, all-encompassing, dimension of the poem, in which the Chaucerian formula of the 'old books–experience–dream' is realised for the first time, with the first version of the ambiguous *persona* in which the author and his protagonist are combined. The originality of this approach already goes well beyond the underlying French and Ovidian cultural and poetic influence that permeates the *Book of the Duchess*.[11] But it must be added at once that the poem is ruled by two forms of logic, probably interrelated but different in purpose, each of which is expressed in a stylistic method. The combination of these, in the work as a whole, produces a fabric that is quite unique. The first is a logic typical of dreams: not only do the single scenes correspond to the courtly models of the dream as a literary genre, but the passages that link them seem to reproduce the apparently chaotic and disconnected quality that characterises the dream as a human psychic activity. This occurs, for example, in the way the protagonist, hearing sounds typical of the hunt, jumps out of bed, presumably naked, and mounts a horse that is presumably in his bedroom; or in the allusion to the Emperor Octavian, which is then completely abandoned; or the way the protagonist suddenly finds himself on foot, the sudden disappearance of the dog, the shift of scene from bedroom to garden to wood to meadow to castle. To some extent this representation is based on the conventional technique of the genre, derived essentially from Machaut. Within this there is a slight mimetic-impressionistic impulse, whereby the poet passes with rapid strokes over the hunt, the dog, the *locus amoenus*, the detail of the great oak by which the Knight is sitting, with his back to it, the approach, as if emerging from the depths of the forest, of the 'long castel with walles white' (first indicated only as a 'place'), with its bells that strike twelve times. In this way Chaucer endows an otherwise derivative mode with the freshness that so many readers have found in the poem. Modern criticism, however, has noted a much more significant characteristic of the dream logic, in what is revealed as the central mechanism of the poem: the sleepless reader, as soon as he is transformed into a dreamer, forgets the 'oppressive sorrow' that burdened him before he fell asleep and 'transfers' it to the Knight in black. In the words of Bertrand Bronson, who first developed this view,

> By a wonderful leap of psychological insight, and in strict accord with truths rediscovered in our own century, his private grief has been renounced by the Dreamer, to reappear externalised and projected upon the figure of the grieving knight. The modern analyst, indeed, would instantly recognise the therapeutic function of this dream as an effort of the psyche to resolve an intolerable emotional situation by repudiating it through this disguise. The knight is the Dreamer's surrogate.[12]

This, in effect, is the keystone of the whole *Book of the Duchess*: since the one character is nothing but the projection of the other, the two are presented in a series of descriptive parallelisms with regard to their emotional situation. But in reality, as Bronson himself and others have seen, this key motivates the very construction of the poem. The reading of Ovid's story of Ceyx and Alcione, which involves the *death* of the husband and the *dream* of the wife, forms a bridge between the reader's *dream* and the story of the Knight and his Blanche, which ends with her *death*. At the same time, the story of the ducal couple is the projection of that of Ceyx and Alcione. There is an equally profound connection between the theme of sleep, the central problem of the protagonist, and the theme of death, which is the Knight's torment. And finally, as John Lawlor has observed, there is a fundamental contrast between the Dreamer, a 'doctrinaire servant of love', and the Knight, an 'experienced servant of love';[13] this is in fact a version of the Chaucerian 'old books–experience–dream' formula of which Payne speaks. Only by listening in his dream to the Knight's story, the true story of a perfect love, can the sleepless reader learn the true nature of love-service and happiness in love, which he, by his own admission, has not experienced in life. This contrast, in turn, reveals the consolatory design of the poem: the consolation offered to the Knight, and through him to John of Gaunt, is that of the 'happiness of requited love', which compensates for the cruel joke of Fortune and the final blow of death. The mechanism of the *poem*'s construction may thus be synthesised in a series of parallels:

protagonist	knight
Ceyx and Alcione	knight and Blanche
sleep	death
doctrine of love	experience of love
book	dream

This deep logic, which I shall call 'binomial', governs not only the whole complex scheme of the *Book of the Duchess* but even its details. The dream, which is the fundamental scenic nucleus of the poem, is completely permeated with it: in it the bedroom and the garden are followed by the wood and the meadow; the horse precedes the dog; the hunt takes place before the meeting and conversation with the Knight. The Knight's story itself unravels by means of a dialogue in which the dreamer, who from the start knows the outcome of the story (the death of the beloved lady), has the function of continually prodding the Knight to go on and reveal more and more. In fact it is the dreamer's insistent questioning that structures the narration in its fundamental moments: his offer to help is followed by the description of the Knight's grief and his chess game with Fortune; his invitation to tell all ('telle me al hooly / In what wyse, how, why, and wherefore / That ye have thus youre blysse lore'), produces the story of love-service; in reply to the crucial question ('What los ys that? / Nyl she not love yow? ys hyt soo? / Or have ye oght doon amys / That she hath left yow?') the Knight recounts his courtship and its success, and the final question ('Sir...where is she now?') produces his trembling answer: 'She ys ded!' Dialogue thus becomes a narrative principle. It becomes particularly dense in certain exchanges that form the dramatic focal points of the work (for example the one cited above, at the end of the summary of the poem – but there are two others, lines 714–58 and 1112–43).

Within this dia-logic (binomial and dialogue logic) the depths of the dream reveal still more significant contrasts: the grief of the present is set against the happiness of the past, and, within the same temporal dimension, the present springtime of life – in the *locus amoenus* – is contrasted with the present reality of death – the Knight's solitary lament by the great oak. And again, broadening the 'pattern of consolation' of which Lawlor speaks, love comes into relief, in memory, against a background of death. Against Fortune is set not wisdom –- as recommended by the dreamer who mentions Socrates – but Love with a capital *L*, the perfect experience and the perfect happiness of the passion lived in full adherence to courtly canons – *courtoisie* par excellence. And here we can see two further dimensions of the poem, closely linked to each other: one specifically human, the other more particularly cultural. The dia-logic of the *Book of the Duchess* functions because, despite the social difference between the two characters (the poetic *persona* of Geoffrey Chaucer and that of John of Gaunt, the most powerful duke of the realm), their profound humanity brings them together in sorrow and love. The dreamer offers understanding and attention: the Knight accepts these and, in exchange, gives him the true story of a perfect love. But this dia-logic is realised only through a poetic–social attitude that Patricia Kean has rightly seen in the 'urbane manner', of which the *Book of the Duchess* is perhaps the best example in medieval English literature,[14] and through an equally significant community of culture. What takes place between the dreamer and the Knight is in fact a true meeting – not only human, courtly and urbane, but also cultural: when one of them cites an author or a character, the other responds in the same key, on the same wavelength; when one speaks of Ovid, Orpheus or Daedalus, the other replies with Socrates, and then with Jason and Medea, Dido and Aeneas, Samson and Delilah; if one thinks that reading romances is better than playing chess, the other builds his story of Fortune's intervention in his life on the extended metaphor of a chess game. This is the first appearance of a dimension that is to be typical of Chaucer's works, the presence of a cultural fabric that seems lightly woven, as it were *en passant*, by means of allusions, asides and ironic remarks. The method can be illustrated with a single example: the Knight is telling how, during his courtship, he has composed many songs for his lady; he drops a cultured reference, which he at once complicates with a parenthesis, then concludes with: 'But it does not matter':

> Althogh I koude not make so wel
> Songes, ne knewe the art al,
> As koude Lamekes sone Tubal,
> That found out first the art of songe;
> For as hys brothers hamers ronge
> Upon hys anvelt up and doun,   *anvil*
> Thereof he took the firste soun, –
> But Grekes seyn Pictagoras,
> That he the firste fynder was

Of the art, Aurora telleth so, –
But thereof no fors, of hem two.   *matter*
                    (1160–70)[15]

From this dimension arises the last of the basic contrasts that govern the *Book of the Duchess*, that between literature and reality – and, more specifically, between romance and reality. The protagonist of the poem tells us, at the outset, that to while away the hours of his insomnia he has asked someone to give him a book:

> And bad oon reche me a book,
> *A romaunce*, and he it me tok
> To rede, and drive the night away;
> For me thoughte it beter play
> Then play either at ches or tables.   *backgammon*
> And in this bok were writen *fables*
> That clerkes had *in olde tyme*,
> And other poets, put in rime
> To rede, and for to be in minde,
> *While men loved the lawe of kinde.*   *natural law*
> This bok ne spak but of such thinges,
> Of quenes lives, and of kinges,
> And many other *thinges smale.*
>   (47–59)

We are, then, in the world of literature, a literature that is romantic, fabulous, entertaining – above all, an ancient literature that was created when men loved and followed natural law. Here, in a nutshell, we find two of the directions in which the poem will move: the book, the 'romaunce', the *Metamorphoses*, sets the reader on the path of natural law, that sleep which has been denied him by illness and the pain of love (lines 16–21); in the same way this very book, with the dream of Alcione that it contains, also provides the Knight indirectly with his example of how to recover that harmony with nature which he has lost through his lady's death (lines 466–9 and 511–13): because death is, precisely, the 'lawe of kinde', as the story of Ceyx and Alcione demonstrates.[16] Two other oppositions thus govern the poem: that between insomnia and nature and that between sorrow and nature. Both are resolved in death, a natural law in the book and in the dream. And, on the other hand, the romance is the dimension within which, by preference, the protagonist moves: even in dream he lives in this literary world, amid stained-glass windows illustrating the story of Troy and other myths, and walls painted with the *Roman de la Rose*. When the Knight appears to him and tells his story, in the marvellous meadow where behind literary conventions reigns the full-blown spring of nature, literature and romance take on new dimensions. For the Knight, even as he describes a love story in perfect harmony with poetic and social models, hastens to make it clear that Blanche was never the type of lady who sent her faithful cavaliers off to the ends of the earth, as happens in the romances:

> Ne, be thou siker, she wolde not fonde
> To holde no wyght in balaunce   *suspense*
> By half word ne by contenaunce,
> But if men wolde upon hir lye;
> Ne sende men into Walakye,
> To Pruyse, and into Tartarye,
> To Alysaundre, ne into Turkye,
> And byd hym faste anoon that he
> Goo hoodles to the Drye Se
> And come hom by the Carrenar,
> And seye 'Sir, be now ryght war
> That I may of you here seyn
> Worshyp, or that ye come ageyn!'
> She ne used no suche knakkes smale.   *tricks*
> (1020–33)

Here is an irony that also dominates other parts of the poem, at times becoming a real *vis comica*.[17] Through it romance is counterposed, in dream, to reality, and literature is sensibly put in its place. The dream, far from being an illusion, proves to be a sort of litmus paper that measures the deepest reality. The following diagram completes the binomial logic that dominates the dream itself – the nucleus of the *Book of the Duchess* – and extends outwards to the whole poem and beyond, *trans textum*, to the meta-literary plane:

The Dream

descriptive structure

bedroom and garden	wood and meadow
horse	dog
hunt	meeting

narrative (dialogical) structure

I offer of help	chess game with Fortune
II invitation to tell all	love service
III didn't she want to love?	courtship and success
has she left you?	
IV where is she now?	she is dead

deep structure

present – sorrow	past – happiness
present – sorrow	present – spring
death	love
Fortune	courtesy

The Poem

thematic structure

insomnia ━━━━━━━━━━━━━━━━━━━━━━━━━━━━━━━ nature
                              │ death │
sorrow ━━━━━━━━━━━━━━━━━━━━━━━━━━━━━━━━ nature

deep structure

reality   literature (romance)

dream   book

And with this last binomial we have returned to the final terms of our first scheme. But the final step remains to be carried out: the protagonist who, departing from the book, has learned through his dream the reality of the complete experience of love and death, decides to transform his dream into a poem. The reader becomes, as I said at the beginning, a dreamer and a poet. Or, in conclusion: the book is transformed, through the dream-reality, into the Book: the *Book of the Duchess*.

The *House of Fame*, the second of Chaucer's dream poems, is an extremely complex creation, and not only because it is formally incomplete. Its construction has often given the impression of total disorder. At first sight it is impossible to understand; after reading it the least one can say is that it is puzzling. We cannot rule out the possibility that this was precisely one of the effects that Chaucer had in mind in presenting it to the public. He sets up a series of problems that are not treated organically but rather announced, hinted at, withdrawn and now and then plucked up again from forgotten depths, to emerge finally in one grand question-mark that makes us ponder and re-read. Nor can we exclude the possibility that the formal incompleteness of the poem is the sign, more or less conscious, of a work that is 'open' in intent and effect. Whereas the *Book of the Duchess* uses the methods of allusion, implicit statement and ambiguity, and is ruled by the logic of dreams, in the *House of Fame* all these are extended and refined. As in the earlier poem, irony is not only a device for producing humour but also the principle inspiring Chaucer's thought and the measure of his wisdom. In the *House of Fame*, however, the cultural background that nourishes the work has been renewed and has acquired greater density. Alongside the continuing French influence appears that of Dante and perhaps a first acquaintance with Petrarch and Boccaccio. This contact with the Italian writers did not produce a radical alteration or dramatic change of direction in Chaucer's poetry, but it broadened the poet's horizons and provided a stimulus within his own cultural sphere. It not only suggested the figure of the guiding eagle but urged a deeper consideration of the activity and the dignity of poetry. For example, the authority and success of Dante confirmed that poetry could be used to discuss even physics; it stimulated a more profound study of the medieval thought with which Chaucer was already familiar (Boethius, Alain de Lille). It contributed to a greater knowledge of the classics, especially of Virgil's works, with which the whole of Book I is imbued and from which a good part of the *ecphrasis* of Fame is derived.[18] Indeed, the central nucleus of Book III is born in the shadow of Virgil and Ovid, with the division of Fame into 'Fame' and 'Rumour', whose house is constructed according to the description in the *Metamorphoses*.[19]

The central design of the *House of Fame* is clear: it is a dream that the protagonist has on the night of 10 December, in the course of which he, here 'Geffrey' Chaucer in person, visits certain places in an imaginary world. Modelled perhaps on Dante, the poem is divided into three books, each of which opens with an Invocation (the first to the god of sleep and a prayer to God, the second to Venus, the Muses and Thought, the third to Apollo, god of science and light). Book I begins with a Proem in which the nature and cause of dreams is discussed and then passes from the Invocation to the description of the Temple of Venus. There, beside the portrait of the goddess and many 'curious portreytures, and queynte maner of figures', the poet can read the opening lines of the *Aeneid*, on a bronze tablet, and then admire the whole story of Virgil's poem, especially the episode of Dido, which is painted on the walls. When he comes out of the temple the protagonist finds himself in a sandy desert, and sees a golden Eagle preparing to descend towards him. In Book II, the Eagle grasps the poet 'in his fet', and transports him, stunned and frightened, higher and higher into the sky. The Eagle has been sent expressly by Jove to carry Geoffrey to the House of Fame, so that he can have 'som disport and game' in return for his 'labour and devocion' towards Cupid. The Eagle explains that the House of Fame is suspended between heaven, earth and sea, and that in it the poet will find 'mo wonder thynges' and 'of Loves folk moo tydynges' than he can imagine. The poet does not believe this, and so to prove it the Eagle embarks on a logical–scientific exposition of the theory of sounds, constructed with perfect coherence of argument: in the natural order everything has its own 'kyndely stede' (its own port, Dante would say)[20] towards which it moves by natural inclination. Now, the word is a sound, and sound is nothing but 'eyr ybroken'. Like water into which a stone is thrown, it ripples, forming a circle, which then produces others, wider and wider. So every word moves the air, which in turn disturbs other air, carrying each sound towards its 'port', suspended between heaven, earth and sea – in other words, to the House of Fame. When this demonstration is finished, the Eagle points out to Geoffrey the distant earth, by now no more than a 'prikke', and the galaxy above with the 'ayerissh bestes'. Finally they come into view of the house and hear the 'grete swogh' coming from it. The Eagle sets the poet down near the palace and says goodbye, promising to wait for him. Book III is devoted to the two houses, that of Fame and that of Rumour: the first is a castle of fantastic Gothic architecture, surrounded by musicians and magicians; the interior, all of gold, is filled with coats of arms. In the 'halle' is Fame in person, surrounded by the Muses, with the escutcheons and the names of Alexander and Hercules on her back. On both sides arise metal pillars, on each of which a famous author holds on his shoulders the 'fame' of some subject or 'matere': Josephus Flavius and seven others, then Statius, Homer, Dares, Dictys, Guido delle Colonne, Geoffrey of Monmouth, the mysterious Lollius, Virgil, Ovid, Lucan and Claudian. As he contemplates this scene, Geoffrey witnesses the arrival of nine groups of men, who, kneeling before Fame, ask her in turn to grant them glory, or to cancel their names from the memory of men, or to give them fame contrary to their merit. The goddess, attended by Aeolus (who blows one of his two trumpets, 'Clere Laude' and 'Sklaundre', to broadcast good and bad names respectively), replies to these requests in an extremely voluble manner. The last to arrive is the man who burned the temple of Isis in Athens.[21] A stranger turns to the protagonist, asking who he is and if he has come to acquire fame. Geoffrey says no, he has come

> Somme newe tydynges for to lere,
> Somme newe thinges, y not what,
> Tydynges, other this or that,
> Of love, or suche thynges glade. *joyful*
> (1886–9)

Following the man, the poet finds himself below the castle, in a valley, before an extraordinary house made of twigs, 60 miles long and continually revolving. It is full of murmurs, voices and sounds. At this point the Eagle reappears and lifts the poet through a window into the house. There a large crowd is gathered, in which each person is telling his neighbour 'a new tydynge'; news and stories spread rapidly in a continual crescendo and then fly out through a window and a crevice to arrive at the castle, where Fame gives them a name and a duration 'after hir disposicioun'. This House of Rumour is full of sailors, pilgrims, pardoners and messengers, with packs full of stories. As he moves about and listens to some of these stories, the poet hears a great noise in one corner of the room, 'ther men of love-tydynges tolde'. He approaches, while all the others rush over, crowding and trampling one another, and he finally sees a man whom he does not know, but who seems to be 'of grete auctoritee'. And here, at line 2158, the poem ends, incomplete.

One way of making a first approach to the *House of Fame* is to enjoy its rich surface and movement, the visual element and the sounds that define its atmosphere. This should not be an impressionistic reading but a necessary exploration of the imaginative and linguistic co-ordinates that govern the poem. As the Proem reminds us with its easy, yet learned, Macrobian discussion, we must never forget that we are in a dream and that the author's hand is guided by the same superficial dream logic that we have seen at work in the *Book of the Duchess*. The first scene offered to us is that of the Temple of Venus: here silence reigns. Amid the fantastic architecture of the 'chirche', with its extravagant decoration, the frescoed wall painting stands still and mute – Venus naked in the great sea, garlanded with roses, with a comb in her hand, accompanied by Cupid and Vulcan; the bronze tablet with the solemn opening lines of the *Aeneid*; the painted story of Virgil's poem displayed on the walls and relived by the poet in his memory. Thus Dido's words and the laments resound, not in space, but in the mind, in an absolute physical silence. They echo in thought, which can then digress and extend to famous cases of betrayed heroines: Chaucer drops the formula 'saugh I grave' precisely at the beginning of the Dido episode, picking it up again as soon as the latter is finished. In silence the *Aeneid* is recreated and lives on the walls, enriched by the poet's pity, external and intimate at the same time. Not even Geoffrey dares to break this silence and, when he marvels at the nobility and the richness of the images, he does so in thought, just as in thought he turns to Christ for salvation 'fro fantome and illusion' when he finds himself in the sandy desert that surrounds the temple. There the complete silence and solitude signify aridity, sterility, the absence of life:

> Then sawgh I but a large feld,
> As fer as that I myghte see,
> Withouten toun, or hous, or tree,
> Or bush, or grass, or eryd lond;
> For al the feld nas but of sond
> As smal as man may se yet lye
> In the desert of Lybye;
> Ne no maner creature
> That ys yformed be Nature
> Ne sawgh I, me to rede or wisse.
> (482–91)

On the threshold of a *phantasma*, a dream dictated by evil spirits, the poet prays to Christ, raising his eyes, and suddenly the heavens appear 'd'un

altro sole adorno' ('adorned with another sun'): Dante's Eagle has arrived.[22]
At the appearance of Jove's messenger, the still and silent scene of the now-
ended book bursts into life again; the Eagle descends like a lightning bolt
without thunder, silent and intent, and seizes the poet; images abound
(534–44). Then begins the dialogue, or rather the Eagle's monologue,
broken now and then by the replies of an air-sick Geoffrey. It is a discourse full of humour and verve; life opens out again in the familiarity
and the humanity of the communion between the two. As they fly
through space the Eagle's words ring out – pure voice – speaking of sound
and air, of water and natural laws, while below the earth is seen, diminish-
ing to a point as they move farther and farther away. There is an underlying correspondence between the images of the Eagle's speech, the
shattered air, the stone dropping into the water and rippling, and the earth
fading away in the distance: little by little the words become detached
from immediate reality and are rarefied, transported to the plane of pure
thought. At first earthly images are still in focus; thus, if the word is
reduced to the thin substance of air, if

> Soun ys nought but eyr ybroken,
> And every speche that ys spoken,
> Lowd or pryvee, foul or fair,
> In his substaunce ys but air;
>
> (765–8)

the comparison is still based on flame and smoke, and the proof by association makes use of musical instruments (774–80). The image of water-
ripples is a silent one (788–803). The monologue is interrupted by a lively
exchange, and when it begins again, the view broadens out; on one side,
the distant world:

> And y adoun gan loken thoo,
> And beheld feldes and playnes,
> And now hilles, and now mountaynes,
> Now valeyes, now forestes,
> And now unnethes grete bestes;
> Now ryveres, now citees,
> Now tounes, and now grete trees,
> Now shippes seyllynge in the see . . .
>
> (896–903)

On the other, the galaxy and the creatures of the air:

> Tho gan y loken under me
> And beheld the ayerissh bestes,   *aerial*
> Cloudes, mystes, and tempestes,

153

Snowes, hayles, reynes, wyndes,
And th'engendrynge in hir kyndes...
(964–8)

Thought seems to have transcended the elements, as the poet himself, recalling Boethius, seems to imagine. This could be the threshold of a higher vision, as the quotation from Saint Paul would appear to indicate,[23] and as in effect happened to Dante. But Geoffrey is thinking of his beloved books, of Martianus Capella, of the *Anticlaudianus*. And the Eagle interrupts him with 'Lat be...thy fantasye!' The spell is broken, and the dialogue is beginning again with renewed spirit, when the noise of the House of Fame is heard. The silence, echoing with the two solitary voices, is broken; the Eagle describes the new sound, and Geoffrey, finally perceiving it, indulges in two similes:

'Herestow not the grete swogh?'
'Yis, parde!' quod y, 'wel ynogh.'
'And what soun is it lyk?' quod hee.
'Peter! lyk betynge of the see,'
Quod y, 'ayen the roches holowe,
Whan tempest doth the shippes swalowe;
And lat a man stonde, out of doute,
A myle thens, and here hyt route;
Or elles lyk the last humblynge   *humming*
After the clappe of a thundringe,
Whan Joves hath the air ybete...'
(1031–41)

Thus closes Book II, announcing the tremendous noise that will pervade the following book. But the first thing to strike the reader in Book III is once again the visual spectacle: the rock on which the castle stands is made of ice, like bright crystallised alum; a cold shadow preserves the names written on the mountain, while the other side melts in the heat, and finally there is the castle itself, a fantastic structure that recalls and surpasses the Temple of Venus:

Temple	*Castle*
But as I slepte, me mette I was	Al was of ston of beryle,
Withyn a temple ymad of glas;	Bothe the castel and the tour,
In which there were moo ymages	And eke the halle and every bour,
Of gold, stondynge in sondry stages,	Wythouten peces or joynynges.
And moo ryche tabernacles,	But many subtil compassinges,
And with perre moo pynacles,	Babewynnes and pynacles,
And moo curiouse portreytures,	Ymageries and tabernacles,
And queynte maner of figures	I say; and ful eke of wyndowes,
Of olde werk, then I saugh ever.	As flakes falle in grete snowes.
(119–27)	(1184–92)

Both edifices are products of the same architectural imagination, but the second is perhaps even richer, more extraordinary, than the first, and the final simile of thickly-falling snowflakes is like a last burst of fireworks, preparing us for the visual feast that follows.

Noises begin at once: minstrels telling 'tales both of wepinge and of game'; harps, bag-pipes and trumpets; then the songs of the Muses, the cries of those who praise Fame, the arrival of the postulants buzzing like bees, their prayers, the trumpets of Aeolus, the words of Fame (some of them actually vulgar), Geoffrey's exchange with the stranger. These are all human sounds, in some way ordered, sounds that still have meaning – music, words, conversation. The postulants are arranged in groups, as if for an audience; they kneel in courtly ceremony. There are coats of arms of the 'chevalrie' of the whole world and of all times: in short, the place is ordered like a catalogue. And, against a background of walls, floor and ceiling covered with gold 6 inches thick and studded with all the gems of the lapidary, sits Fame herself on her imperial ruby throne. She is the 'monstrum horrendum ingens' of Virgil: a female creature less than a cubit in height, who grows longer and wider until she touches the floor with her feet and the sky with her head. She has as many eyes as a bird has feathers, or as the beasts of the Apocalypse; her hair is golden and curly; she has innumerable ears and tongues; her feet are winged. She is a capricious woman, the sister of Fortune, quite different from Boccaccio's 'Gloria' and Petrarch's 'bella donna' – an iconographic nightmare, an apocalyptic beast that Chaucer is the first English writer to recreate.

With the *ecphrasis* of Fame, the world of the vision seems to go mad, to explode according to a clearly premeditated plan. This is what happens in the House of Rumour, where the visual fantasy and the 'sound-track' are magnified, where all order is shattered, the space is filled with swarms of people and the air is full of voices in continual crescendo, an almost Rossinian effect.[24] It continues almost to bursting-point, until the 'tydynges' rush out through the window and the cracks in the wall, until the whole building is revealed as a sort of 'faire felde ful of folke' like Langland's, dominated not by activity but by the word. The last thing we see is the running crowd, which ends up in a heap of figures trampling each other; their cries are the last thing we hear. Then, mysteriously, appears the man of authority, who remains suspended in our imagination. The Ovidian impulse that lies behind the description now breaks free. The house, Domus Dedaly, is labyrinthine, marvellous and strange. It is made of multi-coloured twigs, with entrances as numerous as the leaves of trees in summer and a thousand holes in its roof. Open night and day, 60 miles long, it is built to last as long as may please Chance:

> ... ever mo, as swyft as thought,
> This queynte hous aboute wente,
> That never mo hyt stille stente.
> ...
> And the noyse which that I herde,
> For al the world, ryght so hyt ferde,
> As dooth the rowtynge of the ston
> That from th'engyn ys leten gon.
>
> (1924–34)

Like a cage, then, turning round and round, full of murmurs, stories, whispers and babblings and chatterings; from within, in a curious relativistic effect, it proves to be immobile. There sound is associated with individual human beings:

> And every wight that I saugh there
> Rouned everych in others ere
> A newe tydynge prively,
> Or elles tolde al openly
> Ryght thus, and seyde: 'Nost not thou
> That ys betyd, lo, late or now?'
> 'No,' quod he, 'telle me what.'
> And than he tolde hym this and that,
> And swor therto that hit was soth –
> 'Thus hath he sayd,' and 'Thus he doth,'
> 'Thus shal hit be,' 'Thus herde y seye,'
> 'That shal be founde,' 'That dar I leye' ...
>
> (2043–54)

This bit of bravura is not an end in itself; it lays the foundation for the description of the 'tydynges' that spread from one person to another and yet another, constantly increasing like the ripples described by the Eagle, until

> ... Thus north and south
> Wente every tydyng fro mouth to mouth,
> And that encresing ever moo,
> *As fyr is wont to quyke and goo*
> *From a sparke spronge amys,*
> *Til al a citee brent up ys.*
>
> (2075–80)

The *House of Fame* is, then, an extraordinary *tour de force* of language and creativity, in which selected authors set the theme and serve to spark off an imagination that is always ready to burst into flame: the simile that ends the above quotation is, as it were, its emblem. This reading of the poem clarifies at least two things: first, the *House of Fame* has a precise plan (what else could explain such a careful arrangement of visual and aural effects and images?); secondly, this plan does not correspond to a fixed and rigid unity of theme and mode. Both these aspects make the *House of Fame* a many-sided work – ambiguous and, perhaps deliberately, in-finite. What is the connection between Venus and the *Aeneid*, between these and Fame and Rumour, and between all of these and the Eagle's flight and his science? What are the 'tydynges' that Jove has promised to Geoffrey? What is the relevance of the Proem? Is there an overall meaning in the *House of Fame*? These are some of the questions that, with the help of scholars, I must try to answer.

First of all, it is clear that within the French and Macrobian dream type, the poem is an exploration of two central themes, Love and Fame. In Middle English the meanings of the word 'fame' include 'renown', 'rumour', and 'ill-repute'. Its dual nature is expressed by the figures of Fame and Rumour, whose two houses occupy Book III. With the maximum simplification, we can hazard a definition of the work in terms of cultural references: at first sight, the *House of Fame* is a Dantean journey (Book II) from the *Aeneid* (Book I) to Virgilian Fame and Ovidian Rumour (Book III). The Proem contains a discussion of the nature of dreams; in this context the poem is also an exploration of various types of dream. If the general impression is, as Spearing says,[25] that the type is that of the *somnium coeleste*, of a *visio*, it is equally evident that while Book I resembles the *love dream*, the second, with its reminiscences of Dante and St Paul,[26] seems to come close to a *beatific vision*, and the third partakes of the *apocalyptic vision* as well as the dream typical of the *Roman de la Rose* and other French poems,[27] ending with what may be seen as the overture to a Macrobian *oraculum*. But of course these are only approximate lines, indications of tendency: the dream of love is disturbed by features outside the tradition, and it is also quite clearly a literary dream; the courtly dream is complicated by an inclination towards the triumphal vision; and the *oraculum* does not have time to get started. The *House of Fame* is therefore a composite dream; this is indicated clearly in the Proem, which merely mentions various types without taking any position. Chaucer's typical method is to use allusion and implicit statement: proclamation and explicitness are as far from him as from T. S. Eliot.

The structural pattern that works in the *Book of the Duchess* and the *Parliament of Fowls* is recognisable in the *House of Fame*, with certain modifications: Chaucer inserts the *book* (the *Aeneid*) *within* the dream and widens the erotic and literary sphere of *experience* to include the world of natural science (the Eagle's demonstration 'be experience', and the 'preve by experience' that Geoffrey has during the journey and then in the world of the two houses), as well as the real and verbal world (2121–30). By this means, he suggests for his poem a more specific, and at the same time

vaster, dimension which goes beyond the dream, beyond love and fame.
Venus and Fame are the first areas explored by Chaucer. Venus and Dido:
the connection between the two is longstanding, both because in mythology
Virgil's Aeneas is the son of the goddess and the queen's lover, and
because the *Aeneid* was, for the Middle Ages, essentially the story of Dido's
tragedy. The naked Venus of the *House of Fame* is, therefore, love: an
iconography that has nothing to do with the Renaissance[28] places her in a
scene resembling that of Botticelli's painting, within a Gothic architectural
setting. Venus is rich, naked and mute: the sphinx of love. She is not
presented as the personification of one particular type of love – sensual,
Platonic or courtly – but as an ambiguous deity, beyond morality. In and
of herself, she does not suggest negative connotations – indeed, she is an
attractive figure, but she is accompanied by a 'blind' Cupid and a 'brown'
Vulcan who slightly disturb the atmosphere of perfect beauty that reigns
in the temple, and she is surrounded by walls decorated with the story
of Dido – a story of betrayal, of 'untrouthe' in love; of death for love.
Finally, her 'chirche' stands, not in the middle of a *locus amoenus*, but at
the centre of a sterile and uninhabited waste land, which almost transforms
the poet's dream into a *phantasma*, a nightmare of evil spirits. The love of
the *House of Fame* – that of Aeneas and Dido, of Demophon and Phyllis,
of Achilles and Briseis, of Jason and Medea, of Theseus and Ariadne – is
not the love of the knight and his Blanche. This love is beautiful, yet
presages tragedy: it is a glass temple in an arid desert, a two-faced Venus.
And this Venus is not, as some have said, rejected *tout court* by Chaucer –
for he invokes her, calling her 'faire blisfull', in the Proem to Book II.
Lastly, Venus is linked with Fame by similarity and at the same time by
difference. On the one hand, as we have seen, the temple of the goddess
and the Palace of Fame are similar in their architecture and decoration; on
the other hand, fame destroys love between two human beings through
their desire for 'synguler profit', fame seals the tragedy of love with the
shame of a lost reputation. Chaucer's Dido proclaims this aloud in her
planctus, slightly but significantly modifying the sense given the phrases
by her Virgilian ancestor. Every man, she says, is unfaithful: he would
like to have a new lover every year, or even three:

> As thus: of oon he wolde have fame
> In magnyfyinge of hys name;
> Another for frendshippe, seyth he;
> And yet ther shal the thridde be
> That shal be take for delyt,
> Loo, or for synguler profit. *private (individual)*
> (305–10)

Dido's name will be slandered, while the story of her abandonment will be read and sung 'over al thys lond, on every tonge'.

> O wikke Fame! for ther nys
> Nothing so swift, lo, as she is!
> O, soth ys, every thing ys wyst,
> Though hit be kevered with the myst.
> (349–52)

In reading Virgil to himself, the poet has evoked the horrible and infamous monster, Fame: he is destined to admire her at close range and to exorcise her, when he reaches her palace. Meanwhile, Dido and her 'faire toun' fade into the distance, and the queen is reduced to one of the many Shades that Aeneas will meet in the 'inferno' of Dante, Claudian and Virgil (439–50). Her tragedy becomes but one of the many adventures in the *Aeneid*, of minor importance in the general context of the poem (427–65); after all, it had not even been mentioned in the solemn opening lines on the bronze tablet. Meanwhile Aeneas, who betrayed her and caused her suicide, successfully completes his 'aventure', with the help of Jove, called up with consummate irony by the timely prayers of Venus (461–5). This goddess of love is a real sphinx, and before her Geoffrey can do nothing but pray her to 'alwey save us, and us ay of our sorwes lyghte!'

Chaucer's Fame is equally ambiguous: in the first place, she is divided between the two dwellings, of which the second, the House of Rumour, is but the House of Fame raised to the nth power; in the second place, we are shown two aspects of Fame herself, one passive and one active. The minstrels and the 'gestiours' who swarm round the castle

> ... tellen tales
> Both of wepinge and of game,   *joy*
> Of al that longeth unto Fame.
> (1198–200)

Wizards, witches and enchanters 'by such art don men hen fame'. Above all, poets bear on their shoulders the fame of the various subjects treated in their works. This is how fame is created. C. S. Lewis has compared the attitude of the medieval public with that of the humanists; the latter, exemplified by Pope, shows the 'literariness' of its whole cultural outlook. In the context of his own time, Chaucer's attitude can more significantly be compared with the 'triumphs' of Petrarch and Boccaccio, which began the tradition to which Pope belonged. The difference emerges clearly, says Lewis, if one compares Chaucer's *House of Fame* with Pope's *Temple of Fame*:

In Pope the great poets have the place we should expect: they are present because they are famous. But in Chaucer it is not the poets but their subjects that have the fame. Statius is present to bear up the fame of Thebes, Homer to bear up the fame of Troy, and so forth. Poets are, for Chaucer, not people who receive fame but people who give it. To read Virgil sets you thinking not about Virgil but about Aeneas, Dido, and Mezentius.[29]

Fame becomes, for Boccaccio, 'la *Gloria* del popol mondano' ('the glory of worldly folk'). But although Chaucer's attitude is basically the one identified by Lewis, there is something in the House of Fame that slightly modifies it in the new direction: the coats of arms displayed on the armour in the palace are those

> *Of famous folk* that han ybeen
> In Auffrike, Europe, and Asye,
> Syth first began the chevalrie.
> (1338–40)

Fame herself bears on her shoulders

> Bothe th'armes and the name
> Of thoo that hadde large fame:
> Alexander and Hercules . . .
> (1411–13)

Finally, it is Calliope and the other eight Muses who sing the praises of the 'goddesse of *Renoun* or of *Fame*', while their very presence seals the close connection between poetry and fame. The Muses, here depicted in the attitude of the angelic choirs of the *Praefatio* and the *Sanctus*, are, precisely, the *angeloi*, the angels, harbingers of fame.

On the other hand, there is no clear disjunction between the creation of Fame and her creative and destructive activity. The effects of Fame's activity are already seen on the slopes of the rock on which the castle stands, in the half-cancelled names ('so unfamous was woxe hir fame') and in those that are preserved, 'as fresh as men had writen hem here / The selve day ryght'; and again, in the beryl of the palace walls, which magnifies everything:

> . . . walles of berile,
> That shoone ful lyghter than a glas
> And made wel more than hit was
> To semen every thing, ywis,   *look*
> *As kynde thyng of Fames is.*   *natural*
> (1288–92)

And finally on the portal, decorated with unprecedented richness, which reveals the two laws of fame, because

> ... it was be *aventure*   *chance*
> Iwrought as often as be *cure.*   *care*
>   (1297–8)

The potential power of Fame is revealed, however, in her figure – and it is shown in action in the audience she grants to the postulants: a small and enormous monster, animal–woman–bird, who sees all, hears all and repeats all. She is contradictory and voluble, her motives are inscrutable (1541–2), she knows no justice (1820) and administers her favours with no regard for good and evil. Fame gives or refuses herself impartially to the first group of postulants, who have all done 'good workes', to the indolent of the sixth and seventh groups and to those in the eighth and ninth groups who, together with the violator of the temple, have sinned, as Dante would say, through 'malizia' and 'matta bestialitade'. She cancels a name forever, or spreads it far and wide, truly or falsely:

> Non è *il mondan romore* altro ch'un fiato
> di vento, ch'or vien quinci e or vien quindi,
> e muta nome perché muta lato.
>   (*Purgatorio*, XI, 100–2)

('*Earthly fame* is naught but a breath of wind, which now comes hence and now comes thence, changing its name because it changes quarter.')

This, then, is Fame – like Venus, beyond morality. She is Fortune's true sister (1547), omnipresent and fragile, the magnifying beryl and the nullifying silence, a trumpet of gold and black, won by chance and by effort, the creation of poets and the glory radiated by the Muses. She sows and she reaps: the 'grete swogh', the murmur, the sigh, the moan, the grumble, the great 'breath of wind'; 'fame', precisely, 'renown', 'ill-repute'. And now *Rumour*: this is a composite, atomised Fame, reduced to its essential particles, centrifuged in that sort of gigantic cyclotron which is the revolving house in the valley, totally dominated by chance, the 'moder of tydynges'. *Rumour* is the world in which stories are gathered, hearsay, news, words, true and false, pronounced by human beings, by common mortals – pilgrims, sailors, pardoners. These, now, are the *angeloi*, the 'messengers', who in the palace were impersonated by the Muses and the poets. It is a world of swarming crowds, broken up into separate voices, reflected in exaggerated stories: not the world of reality but a mirror of it, a 'boyste crammed ful of lyes' like those carried by couriers, a pack of words, to which Fame will give 'duracioun, somme to wexe and wane sone, / As doth the faire white mone'.

In fact this is, basically, the theme that Chaucer explores in the *House of Fame*: the disorder of the human universe in contrast with the order of the natural cosmos, the theme of reality and illusion. The books of Fame, Love and Rumour are set against the book of nature, Book II. Here, in contrast to the sterility that surrounds the Temple of Venus, is the realm of life, the 'engendrynge' of the 'ayerissh bestes', God's creation, recalled by the making of Adam (970). While the world of Fame and Rumour is governed by Fortune, here, as Dante says, reigns the order in which 'all natures have their bent', each with 'an instinct given it to bear it on' towards its 'stede', its port in the 'great sea of being':

> 'Geffrey, thou wost ryght wel this,
> That every kyndely thyng that is   *natural*
> Hath a kyndely stede ther he   *place*
> May best in hyt conserved be;
> Unto which place every thyng,
> Thorgh his kyndely enclynyng,   *inclination*
> Moveth for to come to . . .'
>
> (729–35)

This is the order of light and heavy objects, of hands and stones, of fire and smoke, of rivers, fishes, trees, air and sound, of the whole earth, of the galaxy: it is an order that can be disturbed only by a human being, Phaethon, the 'fool'. It is the world of Aristotle, Plato, Boethius, Martianus Capella, Alain de Lille – the world of philosophy and science, of thought that soars to heights beyond all the elements, of demonstration by experience, of truth. Chaucer was a realist in the medieval sense of the word, not in the modern sense, and he refused to go beyond reason and abandon himself to mysticism. At the same time, he clearly saw all the ambiguity of reality and illusion in the human universe, magnified in the dream of Venus, Fame and Rumour. The temple is made of glass: the story of Dido and Aeneas is a matter of 'apparence. . . fals in existence', of 'trouthe' and 'untrouthe', of 'trouthe' and 'godlyhede in speche'; the desert that surrounds the 'chirche' arouses the fear that this world of love is 'fantome and illusion'. And, again in the Palace of Fame, illusion dominates without opposition: when Geoffrey asks if the noise he hears there is produced by people, the Eagle replies with a speech that should condition our whole reading of Book III:

> Loo, to the Hous of Fame yonder,
> Thou wost now how, cometh every speche;
> Hit nedeth noght eft the to teche.
> But understond now ryght wel this,
> Whan any speche ycomen ys
> Up to the paleys, anon-ryght
> Hyt wexeth lyk the same wight
> Which that the word in erthe spak,

Be hyt clothed red or blak;
And hath so verray hys lyknesse
That spak the word, that thou wilt gesse
That it the same body be,
Man or woman, he or she.

(1070–82)

Here there are three phases: we pass from the human being to the word
to the 'lyknesse' of the human being. The flesh is made word, and the
word resembles the flesh but is not body. And then, of course, the beryl
magnifies: names vanish or remain, being is distorted, everything *seems*
'more than it *was*'. Finally, in the world of Rumour, the word reigns
supreme, and the contrast between illusion and reality is carried onto its
plane – the plane where truth and falsehood are inextricably 'compouned'
in rumours (2702, 2108–9), where the verbal system is multiplied and
inflated, raised to the nth power, beyond its original essence ('more than
hit ever *was*'; 2067). Thus the word contains the same ambiguity as
reality. And the world of the *House of Fame* is revealed as if in a gigantic
anamorphosis, as the distorted world, far from nature, of the Macrobian
phantasma:

The 'phantasma', or 'visum', comes upon one in the moment between wakeful-
ness and slumber, in the so-called 'first cloud of sleep'. In this drowsy condition
a person thinks he is still awake, and imagines he sees *forms* rushing at him or
wandering vaguely about, *differing from natural creatures in size and shape, and
hosts of diverse things, either delightful or disturbing* (trans. W. H. Stahl (New
York, 1952), p. 89, slightly modified).[30]

The conflict between reality and illusion, however, assumes another aspect
in the personal dimension of the poet–protagonist, the poetic *persona* that
Chaucer creates for himself. Geoffrey, says the Eagle, has served Love and
Venus 'ententyfly' and has used all his wit ('although that in thy hed ful
lyte is') to compose 'bookys, songes, dytees, / In ryme. or elles in cadence'
in homage to Love, although he has very little experience in the art of
love (615–28). In fact his passion for books has led him to neglect even
that reality which is nearest him (644–60). Here the contrast is between
the poetry of love and the experience of love, between books and experience
of reality: a poet of small wit, a bookworm, who goes from business
('labour' and 'rekenynges') to the four walls of his home and does
nothing but read. The *persona* of the *Book of the Duchess* is here further
enriched.

Through this personal dimension we can discern the last of the fields
explored by the *House of Fame*, that of poetry. The *House of Fame* begins
with a finished work of art, an earlier poem, Virgil's *Aeneid*, expounds a
theory of sounds and words, exhibits the famous poets with their subjects

and finally illustrates the formation and growth of 'tydynges'. The work of art is dissolved and fragmented into its constituent elements, and then an attempt is made to put the pieces together in a new unity. This is the process that goes on in the poem, and within it the nature, principles and mechanisms of poetic creation are discussed. It is not a system but a series of allusions and hints that define a complex of problems.

After a discussion 'on the degree of truth and falsehood in dreams, traditionally associated with poetic creation',[31] Chaucer invokes Morpheus, the father of dreams, and God, who, as becomes clear in Book II, is the father of Man and of the whole universe (970–1). Book I is the book of the *Aeneid*, the most important subject of which is love (Dido's story), but which also deals with 'armes' (151–73 and 451–65) and with Hell (439–50). The Proem to Book II invokes Venus and (with precise references to Dante) the Muses and Thought. In the course of the book the eagle speaks of sound and of words, and Geoffrey contemplates the natural world and its laws. In Book III the invocation is to Apollo, 'god of science and of lyght', and the protagonist observes musicians, minstrels, 'gestiours', the Muses, and the poets: these are the poets of the Hebrew tradition, of arms (Statius), of Troy, of Aeneas, of love, of Rome and of Hell. The field of poetry has been diversified and extended, but it is still organised into 'matters'. Finally, in the House of Rumour, the range of the work of art is broadened to include all of reality:

> And over alle the houses angles
> Ys ful of rounynges and of jangles   *whispering; chatter*
> Of werres, of pes, of mariages,
> Of reste, of labour, of viages,
> Of abood, of deeth, of lyf,
> Of love, of hate, acord, of stryf,
> Of loos, of lore, and of wynnynges,
> Of hele, of seknesse, of bildynges,
> Of faire wyndes, and of tempestes,
> Of qwalm of folk, and eke of bestes;   *plague*
> Of dyvers transmutacions
> Of estats, and eke of regions;
> Of trust, of drede, of jelousye,
> Of wit, of wynnynge, of folye;
> Of plente, and of gret famyne,
> Of chepe, of derthe, and of ruyne;   *ample supply; dearth*
> Of good or mys governement,
> Of fyr, and of dyvers accident.
>   (1959–76)

These are the 'half-baked stories, the rumours and travellers' tales', the 'raw material' on which poets must work. We have arrived at the beginning of poetry, and in particular of narrative poetry, at the multiplicity and confusion of the real, to which the ordo of the *Aeneid* and the 'matters' is counterposed. Has the 'man of grete auctoritee', who appears at the end, come to restore some sort of order? The *House of Fame* does not answer this question: it will be answered, in two completely different ways, by *Troilus* and the *Canterbury Tales*. In the *House of Fame* Chaucer is interested rather in *exploring* the world of art, without constructing systems. He is making a journey, a 'quest', not a 'Grecian Urn'. We sense, for example, that his search – and the poetry adumbrated in it – has a cultural–scientific dimension and a moral dimension: the Eagle tells him that what is happening to him is 'for thy *lore* and for thy *prow*', and later he invokes the grace of God that it may do him 'some *good* to lernen in this place'. And in fact the flight offers the poet a scientific theory, and his visit to the Temple of Venus and the Palace of Fame sharpens his moral conscience.[32] We understand too that, although he assigns to poetry and poets a prominent place in the human order, he rejects, with witty modesty, the prophetic and supernatural dimension that Dante had made his own. When Dante demurs from the unearthly journey by saying he is neither Aeneas nor St Paul, Virgil replies by recounting Beatrice's mission of mercy; Dante, who repeatedly declares the impossibility of telling what he has seen, proceeds to describe the beatific vision; to Dante, who, if he speaks truly, fears 'di perder viver tra coloro che questo tempo chiameranno antico' ('to lose [my] life among those who will call these times ancient'), Cacciaguida replies that his 'grido farà come vento, che le più alte cime più percuote' ('cry...shall do as the wind, which strikes most on the highest summits'), and that his life shall far outlast the punishment of his enemies. When Geoffrey feels afraid, remembering that he is neither Elijah nor Romulus nor Ganymede, the Eagle calms him with the reply:

> 'Thow demest of thyself amys;
> For Joves ys not theraboute –
> I dar wel putte the out of doute –
> To make of the as yet a sterre...'
> (596–9)

When Geoffrey, echoing St Paul, says that there beyond the planets he knows not whether he is flesh or spirit, the Eagle cries, 'Lat be...thy fantasye!' To the stranger who asks him if he has come in search of fame, Geoffrey, as if answering Cacciaguida, declares:

> 'Nay, for sothe, frend,' quod y;
> 'I cam noght hyder, graunt mercy,
> For no such cause, by my hed!
> Sufficeth me, as I were ded,

That no wight have my name in honde.   *accuse*
I wot myself best how y stonde;
For what I drye, or what I thynke,   *suffer*
I wil myselven al hyt drynke,
Certeyn, for the more part,
As fer forth as I kan myn art.'
(1873–82)

This is not simply a formula of humility, but the noble expression of a full and totally human self-awareness and responsibility. Not a 'sacred poem to which both heaven and earth have set their hand', but a discourse that unfolds 'lewedly to a lewed man': this is the Eagle's orientation and Chaucer's. The most important thing is not the 'art poetical', not the 'craft', but the 'sentence', the profound meaning. As long as the rhyme is 'lyght and lewed', and, in short, 'agreeable', there is no need for

... any subtilite
Of speche, or gret prolixite
Of termes of philosophie,
Of figures of poetrie,
Or colours of rethorike...
(855–9)

Of course, as Dorothy Everett has demonstrated,[33] this is deliberate self-irony on Chaucer's part, as well as a mild jest at the reader's expense; but it is not simply a case of what Alice Miskimin calls 'allegorical irony'.[34] The key is in the two words, 'gret prolixite'. The *ars poetica*, which Chaucer knows very well and which, as the *House of Fame* itself shows, he can use to perfection, should not be overdone:

For hard langage and hard matere
Ys encombrous for to here
Attones...
(861–3)

What matters is the effect of the poetry, to which a 'craft', well-measured and concealed, contributes. Poetry should be 'palpable':

'A ha!' quod he, 'lo, so I can
Lewedly to a lewed man
Speke, and shewe hym swyche skiles   *arguments*
That he may shake hem be the biles,
So palpable they shulden be...'
(865–9)

This is what the Eagle has just demonstrated in his speech, making poetry of a logical–scientific proposition: his arguments ('skiles') have in effect become palpable.

166

Yet Chaucer knows quite well that the 'palpability' of art is, above all, a problem. It is this problem that he sets himself in the second part of the *House of Fame*, when the finished work of art, the *Aeneid*, is broken down into its primary elements, words. The Modistae maintain, to summarise in a formula, that 'dictio includit in se vocem tamquam sibi materiam et rationem significandi tamquam sibi formam' ('a word includes in itself its sound as it were its matter and its meaning as its form').[35] The Eagle's speech describes with precision the mechanisms of the verbal *materia*, that is, the *vox*, the nature and propagation of sound. But a moment before leaving Geoffrey on the threshold of the Palace of Fame, the Eagle, in reply to one of his pupil's questions, also mentions the *forma*, proposing a theory of *significatio* and, more particularly, of *suppositio*, i.e. of the relationship between a sign and that which it signifies: a word (in the *suppositio*, a noun) substitutes for a thing, a person, an event. This is the passage, already cited, in which Chaucer, or at any rate the Eagle, maintains that when a 'speche' reaches the palace, it becomes *like* the person who has pronounced it (1073–82). The imagination working here seems to resemble that of Swift, who invented the Academy of Lagado, where professors go about carrying things instead of speaking words. But Chaucer is more ambiguous than Swift, and his ambiguity is summed up in the term he uses to define the relationship between a sign and its meaning, the word '*lyknesse*':

> And hath so *verray* hys lyknesse
> *That spak the word*, that thou wilt *gesse*
> That it the same *body* be . . .
>
> (1079–81)

In this image all the ambiguity of the language is enigmatically crystallised: the hearer ('thou') thinks he recognises ('gesse') a relationship of identity between 'body' and 'word', because the 'speche' manifests an extraordinary resemblance ('verray lyknesse') to the thing: it is in fact a *guess*, not *knowledge*.

This ambiguity dominates the world of art: if the walls of beryl magnify everything, if they make all things *seem more* than they are, then signs are also subject to that effect. So everything that fills the hall of the palace, all the different forms of art, appear as though seen through a magnifying-glass – another anticipation of Swift. Everything that belongs to art is gathered around or within the palace: musicians, minstrels, magicians, Muses and poets, the creators of art and their products, the 'tales', funny and sad, of the minstrels, the musicians' sounds, the magicians' images, the poets' 'matters' and, again, the written 'gestes' (1515). It is a composite world: alongside the classics 'of digne reverence', the great, mythical inventors of music, we find the famous pipers of Holland; together with the trumpeters of the Bible and of Virgil are those, equally famous, of Catalonia and Aragon; and finally magicians and witches. It is all 'art', a human, not a natural thing – an *arti*fact: it has various aspects, different degrees of organisation, order and dignity; it has functions of celebration, entertainment, accompaniment, manipulation; but there is a common ground. It is the art of Homer (whose sincerity and objectivity are here, as elsewhere in the Middle Ages, doubted), of Orpheus, Circe – all art that, more or less markedly, counterfeits nature: 'craft countrefeteth kynde' (1213).

On reaching the House of Rumour, we find ourselves in a world where reality is transformed into verbal and narrative units: all reality, war, peace, journeys, winds, animals, hatred, love, cleverness and madness, and a thousand other aspects; all the phenomena of the natural and human world, feelings, relationships, events, have become 'tydynges', news, rumours, stories. Here there is no art, no 'craft' to organise the verbal material: the 'tydynges' are children of Chance, of 'Aventure' (1982–3); they increase and multiply as they spread. Their birth is arbitrary, their growth, through human beings, is a geometric progression: their nature is ambiguous. The 'tydynges' are composed of both truth and falsehood (2108–9). When they are brought inside the house by those sailors, pilgrims and pardoners who will tell the *Canterbury Tales*, the 'tydynges', in the form of winged monsters (2118) fly to the Palace of Fame, to be set in order by her – that is, to be given form and meaning by the poets. The crowd rushes up to see and listen to the man who appears, a stranger to Geoffrey: is it by chance that even for him the word *seem* is used ('But he *semed* for to be / A man of great auctorite')? Venus is ambiguous, so is Fame, so is the *significatio* of the word, so is art, so is the fabric of stories, and the man of authority remains unidentified. The only certainties in the *House of Fame* are Nature and her laws, the creative power of God and the substance of the word. Is it legitimate for a twentieth-century reader, educated in Prospero's school of 'thin air', to interpret the following lines, beyond the literal meaning, as Chaucer's ironic comment on the ambiguity of reality, of dream, of poetry?

> Soun ys noght but eyr ybroken,
> And every speche that ys spoken,
> Lowd or pryvee, foul or fair,
> In his substaunce ys but air.

Reading the *Parliament of Fowls* after the *House of Fame*, one gets an impression of extraordinary completeness of both form and content, a completeness of craft and of *sentence*. The poem is not incomplete, it is short (699 lines), it is compact; the octosyllabic distichs of the *Book of the Duchess* and the *House of Fame* give place to stanzas of seven decasyllables – the expansive, majestic, flexible 'rhyme royal', in which the English voice is heard for the first time in its fullness, natural and elastic like the Italian of the *terza rima* or the Petrarchan sonnet. The opening of the *Parliament* is broadly conceived and beautifully worked out, with an air of 'classical' perfection. This, one feels, is poetry that has reached maturity, equal to any in the great European tradition:

> The lyf so short, the craft so long to lerne,
> Th'assay so hard, so sharp the conquerynge,   *attempt*
> The dredful joye, alwey that slit so yerne: *slides away*
> Al this mene I by Love, that my felynge
> Astonyeth with his wonderful werkynge
> So sore, iwis, that whan I on hym thynke,
> Nat wot I wel wher that I flete or synke.   *float*
>   (1–7)[36]

The close of the work is equally formal, with the roundel sung by the chorus of birds before they disperse, whose 'note', as the poet explicitly declares, 'imaked was in Fraunce':

> 'Now welcome, somer, with thy sonne softe,
> That hast this wintres wedres overshake,
> And driven away the longe nyghtes blake!
>
> 'Saynt Valentyn, that art ful hy on-lofte,   *above*
> Thus syngen smale foules for thy sake:
> Now welcome, somer, with thy sonne softe,
> That hast this wintres wedres overshake.
>
> 'Wel han they cause for to gladen ofte,
> Sith ech of hem recovered hath hys make,
> Ful blissful mowe they synge when they wake:
> Now welcome, somer, with thy sonne softe,
> That hast this wintres wedres overshake,
> And driven away the longe nyghtes blake!'
>   (680–92)

The poem's structural scheme is simpler than that of the *Book of the Duchess* and the *House of Fame*: after the *ouverture* on the theme of love, the narrator introduces himself (as usual) as an assiduous reader, and he briefly describes the plot and themes of the book he has been reading all day, the *Somnium Scipionis*. When night comes he falls asleep and begins to dream: Scipio Africanus appears to him and leads him to a marvellous park, dominated by the Temple of Venus. The poet describes the temple with a wealth of detail, then leaves it and continues alone on his way (Scipio has inexplicably disappeared after their entry into the park). He finds himself on a flowery hillside, where the goddess Nature presides over the parliament of fowls, convoked on St Valentine's day so that each may choose his mate. The fowls are arranged according to their 'degree', with the birds of prey at the top and the worm-eaters, seed-eaters and water fowl arranged in ranks below them. When three 'tercel' eagles of different grades choose the same noble 'formel', a debate begins – at first disorderly, then directed by Nature according to parliamentary rules: each class of birds chooses a representative, who states his opinion on the problem of the three suitors. When they fail to reach a conclusion as to which one best loves the beautiful 'formel', Nature interrupts the discussion and leaves the choice to the female, advising her to choose the 'royal tercel'. The formel asks for a year's time in which to decide, and this is granted. The other birds are assigned their companions by Nature; then they sing their roundel celebrating the arrival of summer and the mating season and fly away, awakening the poet with their cries:

> And with the shoutyng, whan the song was do
> That foules maden at here flyght awey,
> I wok, and othere bokes tok me to,
> To reede upon, and yit I rede alwey.
> I hope, ywis, to rede so som day
> That I shal mete som thyng for to fare
> The bet, and thus to rede I nyl nat spare.
>
> (693–9)

Thus we return to the original structural stereotype of Chaucer's dream poems: the book is outside the dream – indeed it is instrumental in producing the dream. The poet, who is in real life inexperienced in love, but an attentive observer of its literary manifestations (8–12), reads in order to learn (20), and the dream helps him, as Scipio says, if not to 'do', at least to 'se'. It also provides him, if he has any ability, with 'mater of to wryte' (167–8). As in the *Book of the Duchess*, the book becomes the Book, and the dream becomes a poem.

This is a poem that conforms more closely than its two predecessors to a specific tradition, that of the love vision. We find in it the *locus amoenus* and the Temple of Venus of the courtly convention, and, inscribed in the frame of the celebratory poem for St Valentine's day, a *demande d'amour*. At the same time, in the second part of the poem there is a metaphorical device whereby the birds stand for human beings ordered in a hierarchical, feudal and chivalric society and the *demande* is debated in a parliamentary context similar to that of the real English Parliament.[37] Of course, in using these traditions Chaucer subtly modifies them so as to suggest a different and broader meaning, as can be seen from the cultural and iconographic references: here, alongside the *Roman de la Rose* and the courtly tradition in general, the Ciceronian and Macrobian *Somnium Scipionis* serves to widen the field of inquiry through its preoccupation with the cosmic, the ultramondane, the political in the broadest sense of the word (the 'commune profit', the 'bonum commune', the 'res publica' of which Africanus speaks). Boethius and Alain de Lille's *De Planctu Naturae* are brought in with their emphasis on the great chain of being and the 'principle of plenitude'; Dante not only suggests the form of the two inscriptions on the garden's portal but transforms the park into an earthly Paradise, and Boccaccio's *Teseida* is used, probably for the first time, both as a formal, linguistic and metrical point of reference and as the source of the iconography of Venus and her temple.[38] This, then, is the broader tradition within which Chaucer, as if following Eliot's theories in 'Tradition and Individual Talent', avowedly operates:

> For out of olde feldes, as men seyth,
> Cometh al this newe corn from yer to yere,
> And out of olde bokes, in good feyth,
> Cometh al this newe science that men lere.
> (22–5)[39]

And just as every year new corn grows out of old fields, Chaucer's *Parliament* is new with respect to the tradition: above all, because its different and sometimes intrinsically conflicting aspects are played off against one another, or superimposed, so as to create a whole that is again fundamentally problematical, open and ambiguous – this time doubly so. For whereas the problematic aspect of the *House of Fame* found its counterpart in the formal openness of the poem, the *Parliament* is both closed and open: the 'inferior' kinds find their mates and celebrate the principle of plenitude in their splendid French roundel, but the *demande d'amour* is unresolved, the eagle's choice postponed, and, above all, the narrator's search remains unsatisfied. Having begun with the reading of the 'olde book totorn', 'a certeyn thing to lerne', the narrator finds himself in a dream situation that mirrors that of the protagonist of the book he has in his hands. One expects, perhaps, an answer to the problem of love as clear as that offered by Scipio on the problem of the universe and the other world. But Africanus, in this *somnium*, promises only to let the dreamer 'se', not to explain, and he very soon disappears. What the narrator sees does not entirely clarify the problem: after reading the *Somnium* he had prepared for bed 'fulfyld of thought and busy hevynesse', whereas now, when the dream is ended, he takes up other books in the hope of finding in them 'som thyng for to fare / The bet'. The search, in short, is by no means ended:

the narrator has returned to the beginning of the circle ready to set off again, like Conscience at the end of *Piers Plowman*.

By comparison with the *House of Fame*, therefore, the *Parliament* presents its audience with two further tricks. While, in the former, the insertion of the story into the traditional model was disregarded from the start and then continually postponed until it remained suspended forever, in the latter the game is more subtle. The first two stanzas, in fact, create the expectation of a poetic dream of love, which is at once frustrated by the summary of the book, the *Somnium Scipionis*; the park and the Temple of Venus seem to return us to the traditional path, but Nature and her parliament of fowls immediately carry us away, only to bring us near to it again with the *demande d'amour*, then cut us off from it with the conclusion. As Gerard Manley Hopkins in his poems uses counterpoint in leading the reader to expect a rhythm and then withholding it, Chaucer uses counterpoint on a semantic level. The continual counterpoint culminates in the last section of the poem, which as I have said is both open and closed. The reader is satisfied, but he is also frustrated: he is dissatisfied with his satisfaction, which is more than what happened in the *House of Fame*. He finds himself, like the narrator after reading the *Somnium*,

> Fulfyld of thought and busy hevynesse;
> For bothe I hadde thyng which that I nolde,
> And ek I nadde that thyng that I wolde.
>
> (89–91)

Thanks to these two features, the overall effect of the *Parliament* is more 'perverse': while the disquiet that the reader feels at the end of the *House of Fame* prompts him to reread it in order to grasp its structural and thematic secrets, the lack of complete satisfaction in the *Parliament* does not only provoke 'thought and busy hevynesse'. It also directs us to the world outside the poem, to the 'othere bokes' to which the poet himself finally turns: the books that stand immediately behind the work and those to which they in turn refer.[40] In short the *Parliament* stimulates a sort of reverie and inspires a research project in the field of the history of ideas.

This research has been carried out by others at various levels and on the different strata of the poem, so there is no need to go into it here in depth. It is indispensable however, to identify the principal object of that search within the poem and the various forms in which it appears during the course of the work. It is clear from the first stanza of the *Parliament* that this object is love, and from the very first lines it is clear that this love is polyvalent and at the same time comprehensive ('*Al* this mene I by Love'). Love is 'dredful joye, alwey that slit so yerne', 'assay...hard' and

'sharp...conquerynge'; its 'werkynge' is 'wonderful'; its phenomena
are 'myracles' and 'crewel yre'. It is an ambiguous world, in which one
lives in perpetual uncertainty and in absolute impotence:

> ... that whan I on hym thynke,
> Nat wot I wel wher that I flete or synke.
>
> (6–7)

> I dar nat seyn, his strokes been so sore,
> But 'God save swich a lord!' – *I can na moore.*
>
> (13–14)

But Love is also a power that dominates everything: even one who, like
the narrator, does not know love 'in dede', can get from books an idea of
how 'he wol be lord and syre'. Love is really human life – all of it, albeit
short; it is an art – the *ars amandi* – that is long and difficult to learn.
And finally, as is implied by the reference to *ars longa, vita brevis*, love is
the art of poetry itself, and often the object of literature:

> Yit happeth me ful ofte *in bokes* reede
> Of his myracles and his crewel yre.
>
> (10–11)

In other words, love is not only a feeling, even the dominant one in man's
short life, but also a real culture, with its conventions and its laws: this
is the ultimate horizon of the difficult craft, of the *ars longa*. The *Parliament* is an exploration of these themes and in particular the theme of
happiness and unhappiness in connection with love.

In this process, Chaucer's first move is to shift the whole problem onto
another level: if love is 'short life' and 'dreadful joy that soon passes',
there is a blissful place, after *this* life, where love finds 'joye...that last
withouten ende'. The picture is reversed: if life is short in the first line of
the poem, now Africanus, in the *Somnium*, declares that 'oure present
worldes lyves space / Nis but a maner deth', and to this he counterposes
the eternal joy of the blissful place, Heaven, immortality. The love that is
here rewarded – and this is the key to the passage – is love for the 'commune profyt':

> ... what man, lered other lewed
> That lovede commune profyt, wel ithewed,   *of good habits and virtues*
> He shulde into a blysful place wende,
> There as joye is that last withouten ende.
>
> (46–9)

> ...'Know thyself first immortal,
> And loke ay besyly thow werche and wysse
> To commune profit, and thow shalt not mysse

> To comen swiftly to that place deere
> That ful of blysse is and of soules cleere.'
>
> (73–7)

This, then, is a love that must be exercised on Earth but must be explicitly detached from worldly pleasure (64–6), though it is linked with morality and law.[41] Clearly it is not sensual love, because the initial condition of the 'likerous folk' after death is different from that of the 'rightful folk'. It is, rather, love directed towards the *bonum commune*, love that goes beyond the individual, whose object is society and the state. The latter should be understood in the Roman sense, to which the Ciceronian *Somnium* obviously refers, and which was partly incorporated into the language of the English Parliament.[42] Love is the salvation and aggrandisement of the *res publica* – or, in a wider sense, of the whole of mankind. As far as the 'commune profit' is concerned, the narrator's account of the *Somnium* reveals nothing more specific than that, and in this context the position of sensual love is left unresolved: in fact, after an initial 'purgatory' of sorrowful rotation around the Earth, the 'likerous folk' will be 'foryeven al hir wikked dede' and will reach the place of eternal happiness. On this point, Chaucer limits himself to repeating Cicero's view, without in any way clarifying the exact meaning of 'likerous' ('lustful') and without entering into distinctions of the Dantean type, although his reminiscences of the *Divine Comedy* in the *Parliament* show that he knew them quite well.[43] So Chaucer's reticence is deliberate, an intentional suspension of the problem.

If the narrator's first operation is to shift the question of love onto the plane of the *bonum commune*, of the immortal and eternal, the second, simultaneous operation is to give it a cosmic background and perspective. This is the sense of Scipio's dream experience when, like Geoffrey in the *House of Fame*, he contemplates the galaxy and the 'lytel erthe' and the nine celestial spheres, and listens to their music: love is a universal force; its point of reference is the whole universe. This is the context in which the various aspects of love are to be explored.

Against this broad background, after the invocation to Cytherea (Venus: 113–19), the dream opens with the first of the two scenes in which love reveals its various natures. The two inscriptions, one gold and one black, over the portal leading into the park 'walled with grene stone', echo the movement of Dante's inscription 'Per me si va...', but their meaning is completely different:

> 'Thorgh me men gon into that blysfyl place
> Of hertes hele and dedly woundes cure;
> Thorgh me men gon unto the welle of grace,

There grene and lusty May shal evere endure.
This is the wey to al good aventure.
Be glad, thow redere, and thy sorwe of-caste;
Al open am I – passe in, and sped thee faste!'

'Thorgh me men gon,' than spak that other side,
'Unto the mortal strokes of the spere
Of which Disdayn and Daunger is the gyde,   *Scorn; Disdain (Reserve)*
Ther nevere tre shal fruyt ne leves bere.
This strem yow ledeth to the sorweful were   *weir*
There as the fish in prysoun is al drye;
Th'eschewing is only the remedye!'   *avoidance*

(127–40)

Chaucer plays on the expectations of his readers and listeners, who have heard of a park and look for the *locus amoenus*, which they know re-presents the conventional scenario of love. Without ever mentioning love itself, he thus reintroduces its ambivalence, which he had suggested in the first two stanzas. The park is at once a happy and a mortal place, which heals the heart's wounds but also inflicts them – an Eden of eternal, flourishing life and a world of total sterility, a source of grace, the way to a happy end, and a 'sorweful were' in which the fish dies in the prison of aridity. The 'blysful place' of the *Somnium* (48–9) is shown here to be quite near (127–8), but there is also a presentiment of its negative nature. Beginning with the inscriptions, the park takes on a complexity of allusion, which is soon translated into precise images: the sphere of love that it represents is linked to other spheres. It is clear, for example, that the 'grene and lusty May' goes beyond the simple topical connotation of Eros. It is enriched with a vaster aura: the season of love and life, of lush greenery, of joy, the place of eternity, that 'shal evere endure'. Ultimately, it is the source of grace. The sphere of love is widened through a series of allusions, until it takes in the whole of natural life and its sublimation in the terrestrial Paradise. In the second inscription, the link between love and nature is again introduced, though in negative form: here the trees never bear leaves or fruit, and the fish suffocates in a weir. In other words, we are already informed by these 'vers of gold and blak' that love will be identified and defined according to its positive or negative relationship with the world of nature. At the same time, the second inscrip-tion establishes a contact between love and a particular cultural world, the world of courtesy. This is here represented by the two personifications, derived from the *Roman de la Rose*, of Disdayn and Daunger.

Moving with the narrator into the interior of the park itself, we find that here the atmosphere changes as one or another of these elements is more or less emphasised with respect to the others. As we gradually penetrate deeper into the park, and then into the temple, the scene changes: at first the traditional features of the garden of love remain in intimate contact with the natural world, also seen in sublimated form as a garden of Eden. In the second phase these features are detached from nature and identified in a more artificial world, the essential sphere of human beings, the universe of myth and courtesy – civilisation as distinct from nature. Chaucer bases the whole passage (172–294) on the lines – and perhaps also on the glosses – of Book VII of the *Teseida*, in which Boccaccio describes the Temple of Venus, the seat of the 'concupiscible appetite' and in particular of lasciviousness, that is to say of desire that is not 'honest and lawful', as is that of 'having a wife in order to have children'.[44] The elements that Chaucer uses in his description have a precedent or source in the *Teseida* – a fact of extraordinary cultural and stylistic importance – but Chaucer greatly widens the sphere of natural references in the first part of the passage and in the same section recalls Dante's earthly Paradise.[45] The object, we must remember, is always love but not only lasciviousness: it is the whole of Eros, as a fundamental element of the natural order (in this sense it is seen also in its original and eternal essence, as embodied in the earthly Paradise) and of a particular human civilisation.

In a structural sense, too, Chaucer's *descriptio* is a re-ordered version of Boccaccio's. It begins with a catalogue of trees in full bloom, the leaves of which 'ay shal laste' and the attributes of which are linked with human activities: thus the rhetorical figure (as, for example, in 'the byldere ok') is used to indicate a fundamental harmony between the world of nature and that of Man, which is completely covered, in a summary way, by the wide scope of the list and the attributes themselves.[46] The vegetable world is further represented by the green meadow full of flowers of every colour and again projected into eternity ('there as swetnesse *evermore* inow is'). It finds a response in the animal world: a world of life ('nothyng dede'),[47] variety of species, play and 'gentillesse', a world of procreation,[48] and angelic harmony:

> A gardyn saw I ful of blosmy bowes
> Upon a ryver, in a grene mede,
> There as swetnesse everemore inow is,
> With floures white, blewe, yelwe, and rede,
> And colde welle-stremes, nothyng dede,
> That swymmen ful of smale fishes lighte,
> With fynnes rede and skales sylver bryghte.
>
> On every bow the bryddes herde I synge,
> With voys of aungel in here armonye;
> Some besyede hem here bryddes forth to brynge;

The litel conyes to here pley gonne hye;   *rabbits*
And ferther al aboute I gan aspye
The dredful ro, the buk, the hert and hynde,
Squyrels, and bestes smale of gentil kynde.

(183–96)

Here Chaucer's imagination and ability to represent the natural world in all its colours, which were already evident in the *Book of the Duchess*, are further refined through the poet's experience of Boccaccio and Dante, to produce a vision of extraordinary pictorial density.

The repeated hints of Paradise are now made explicit (197–210): the garden is filled with the music of stringed instruments 'in acord', a soft breeze murmurs in the leaves in harmony with the song of the birds, the air is mild, spices and herbs grow everywhere. Joy reigns supreme, there is no illness or old age, night never falls. This is truly the 'blysful place' promised in the *Somnium*: we are brought there by stages, from the galaxy and the music of the spheres to the garden of singing birds, to the eternal Eden with its string music and its 'sweet air'.

As we approach the temple, however, the scene changes: the only animals that remain are pairs of white doves, sitting on top of the great jasper pillars that support the structure of copper (Venus's metal). Ladies in flowing garments dance all around as the personifications and mythological incarnations of Eros gather; fiery sighs, generated by desire, run through the whole building, producing a 'swogh' like the one heard in the House of Fame and igniting fires on the altars. Cupid enters, followed by Voluptuousness, Lasciviousness, Flattery, Bribery and Foolhardiness, on the one side, and Courtesy, Beauty and Youth, on the other. Priapus stands 'in sovereyn place', naked as on that Ovidian night when the ass's bray surprised him beside Vesta, 'and with hys sceptre in honde'. The phallic image provides a prelude to the inner recesses of the temple, where the darkness thickens. There Venus, wrapped in a golden aura, with her hair unbound, her body half-covered by a film of transparent lace, reclines on her couch until sunset. She embodies all the various aspects of Venus: courtly, planetary, sensual. And tragic too: Bacchus and Ceres stand beside her, two youths kneel before her in supplication and all around lie the broken bows of the virgins of Diana who have sacrificed their chastity in her service; the walls are frescoed with stories of love and death. Semiramis, Dido, Cleopatra, Helen, Paris, Achilles, Troilus, Tristan and Isolde, 'And al here love, and in what plyt they dyde'. The lines written in black on the park's portal have now revealed their full meaning: the weir where the fish lie suffocated is the violent death of lovers. Love can also be the negation of life, the reversal of nature. The fiery heat of the sighs of desire is the opposite of the cool brooks in which rainbow-coloured fishes swim and of the mild air that reigns in the garden; their indistinct noise ('swogh') is contrasted with the angelic voices of the birds, the harmonies of the strings and the sweet murmur of the breeze; the gold that surrounds Venus is far from the flowers of white, blue, yellow and red, far from the red fins and silvery scales of the fish.

All this, then, is love – complex and ambiguous but always represented outside human action, projected in images of nature, personifications, mythology – in iconographic form, in fact. The second part of the *Parliament*, on the other hand, approaches the problem of love through the debate, dealing with a specific case – that of the eagle loved by three birds at once: a courtly context *par excellence* but broadened by means of two devices – the introduction of Nature and the extension of the discussion to all the birds, including the less noble ones. The occasion, the annual mating of the birds on St Valentine's day, already places the *demande d'amour* within the universal natural order and places love itself in a perspective that is more properly philosophical: the eagles' courtly love is only one aspect of the general economy of nature, mating, procreation and the perpetuation of the species. By taking in the lower classes together with the nobility, the poet brings the problem into the sphere of the social order, giving it an ideological dimension: the birds of inferior rank freely express their views on the solution of the problem in hand, suggesting hypotheses that may or may not fit into the courtly code. Above all, they indicate – first by their impatience and then by flying away satisfied – the basic irrelevance for them of the problem itself and the socio-cultural convention it represents:

> The noyse of foules for to ben delyvered
> So loude rong, 'Have don, and lat us wende!'   *go*
> That wel wende I the wode hadde toshyvered.
> 'Com of!' they criede, 'allas, ye wol us shende!   *ruin*
> Whan shal youre cursede pletynge have an ende?   *argument*
> How sholde a juge eyther parti leve
> For ye or nay, withouten any preve?'
>
> (491–7)

Nature, however, is more patient; she evidently sees the courtly code as an instrument for achieving those ends which, by divine deputation, she has assigned to living beings. Thus, in suggesting to the eagle that she should choose the 'royal' male, she takes up the logic of 'gentilesse':

> 'But as for conseyl for to chese a make,
> If I were Resoun, certes, thanne wolde I
> Conseyle yow the royal tercel take,

> As seyde the tercelet ful skylfully,
> As for the gentilleste and most worthi,
> Which I have wrought so wel to my plesaunce,
> That to yow hit oughte to been a suffisaunce.'
>
> (631–7)

This logic is in perfect accord with 'Resoun' and with the inner order of creation, in which the royal eagle has been fashioned to the full satisfaction of Nature and hence of that God whose 'vicaire' she is. The social order is in substance nothing but an aspect of the natural order; its hierarchical scale is a reflection and a part of the *scala Naturae* of which Thomas Aquinas speaks:[49]

A thing approaches the more perfectly to God's likeness, according as it is like Him in more things. Now in God is goodness, and the outpouring of that goodness into other things. Therefore the creature approaches more perfectly to God's likeness if it is not only good, but can also act for the goodness of other things, than if it were merely good in itself: even as that which both shines and enlightens is more like the sun than that which only shines. Now a creature would be unable to act for the goodness of another creature, unless in creatures there were plurality and inequality: because the agent is distinct from and more noble than the patient. Therefore it was necessary that there be also different species of things, and consequently different degrees in things.[50]

This is the idea of the *catena aurea*, the great chain of being, which Chaucer could not but absorb from much of the philosophical tradition that was accessible to him,[51] and which in any case he would have found in the Macrobian comment on the *Somnium Scipionis*.[52] Later, in the *Knight's Tale*, the poet was to call this 'the faire cheyne of love', and it stands at the centre of the world of the *Parliament*. There, as if by chance, the narrator indicates the basic function of Nature:

> Nature, the vicaire of the almyghty Lord,
> That hot, cold, hevy, lyght, moyst, and dreye
> Hath knyt by evene noumbres of acord,
> In esy voys began to speke and seye,
> 'Foules, tak hed of my sentence, I preye,
> And for your ese, in fortheryng of youre nede,
> As faste as I may speke, I wol me speede.
>
> 'Ye knowe wel how, seynt Valentynes day,
> By my statut and thorgh my governaunce,
> Ye come for to chese – and fle youre wey –
> Youre makes, as I prike yow with plesaunce . . .'
>
> (379–89)

As God's vicar, Nature knits all the elements together in harmony and presides at the mating of living beings, instilling in them the desire, the 'pleasaunce', which is therefore part of her order. For love and sex, if not distorted, are good things that serve to further the perfection of the universe. This perfection, as in the divine precept of Genesis, is identified with the increase and multiplication of living beings, which are to fill the earth, with that plenitude which Lovejoy sees as one of the principles of universal law that Plato had already identified. Plenitude and the gradation of beings, both necessary for universal perfection, are thus strictly joined in the natural order: 'Therefore it concerns the perfection of the universe, that there be not only many individuals, but that there be also different species of things, and consequently different degrees in things.'[53] It is clear, then, why the garden of love is also Eden and why Venus and Nature figure in the same poem. We can also understand the narrator's dissatisfaction after reading the *Somnium*, permeated as it is with *contemptus mundi*, in which everything is put off to the eternal world of the after-life. The presence of the *scala Naturae* reconciles the sense of the 'contemptible worthlessness of the world' with that of its 'love-guided perfection', according to the direction indicated by Macrobius in his *Commentary* on Cicero.[54]

And finally, we can see why Chaucer replaces the Roman terms of *res publica* and *patria* with the more general and philosophical notion of 'commune profyt', which retains a legal and political tone, though he applies it to a different field. Thomas Aquinas, here interpreting a very widespread view, clarifies the connection that the reader of the *Parliament* must work out by deduction on the basis of simple allusions:

It must also be observed that among natural acts generation alone is directed to the common good: since eating, and the discharge of superfluities, regard the individual: whereas procreation regards the preservation of the species. Hence, as the law is made for the common good, whatever regards procreation should be regulated before other things, by laws both divine and human.[55]

The 'commune profyt', then, is the well-being of the community, in the context of the wider order of natural economy, including the aspects of mating and procreation. In the socio-natural order it corresponds, in the last analysis, to the laws that regulate *generation* – in other words those of marriage, which was Chaucer's constant preoccupation and which, as we have seen in the *Book of the Duchess*, he considered in no way extraneous to the courtly convention.

The third phase of the *Parliament*, the broadest implications of which I have been examining, focusses in particular on one aspect of the second. In the first part of the park we saw the principle of plenitude in action, transported onto the meta-temporal plane: the trees, flowers, fish and animals all lived in harmony, populating the garden of Eden; some of the birds, in particular, put into practice the precept of 'generatio':

> Some besyede hem here bryddes forth to brynge.
>
> (192)

On the barren land at the top of the flowery hill where the 'noble goddess' sits – the 'empress' Nature, with features like those described by Alain – the birds gather and 'fill' the place: on this St Valentine's day, as every year, every bird 'that cometh of engendrure' has come to choose its mate. In other words, here the poet concentrates on the moment immediately preceding the generation that takes place in the park, on the *pluralitas*, the *plenitudo* and the *inaequalitas* that will be fully realised after the mating:

> For this was on seynt Valentynes day,
> Whan every foul cometh there to chese his make,
> *Of every kynde that men thynke may,*   [*pluralitas*]
> And that so huge a noyse gan they make
> That erthe, and eyr, and tre, and every lake
> *So ful was*, that unethe was there space
> For me to stonde, *so ful was al the place*.   [*plenitudo*]
> . . .
> That is to seyn, the foules of ravyne   [*inaequalitas*]
> Weere hyest set, and thanne the foules smale . . .
>
> (309–24)

Time, which had stopped in the park, is both the present (St Valentine's day) and a cyclical dimension (every year). Thus in the third phase of the *Parliament* we witness the process whereby natural impulses are realised in that 'engendrynge of...kyndes' that Geoffrey, in his flight towards the House of Fame, had contemplated in the 'ayerissh bestes'.

The courtly conflict of the three suitors, which it seemed would have to be resolved in a duel (538–40),[56] is instead to find its solution in purely natural terms. The problem is that Nature, in her own words, 'prike(s) with pleasaunce' all three of the lovers, so none of them can claim a greater natural right than the others. The solution is not difficult – indeed in a certain sense it can be taken for granted. It is proposed by the 'tercelet of the faucoun' (547–53) and seconded by Nature herself (631–7). Of the three, the eagle's mate should, provided she is satisfied, be

> . . . the worthieste
> Of knyghthood, and lengest had used it,
> Most of estat, of blod the gentilleste,
>
> (548–50)

which actually means the royal eagle, in accord with Nature's direction and the falcon's own allusion. As I have pointed out, the *scala Naturae* incorporates the feudal–chivalric order, so the problem should no longer exist. It arises precisely because Nature democratically opens the debate to the representatives of the lower classes, who have not absorbed the courtly code. The goose says the rejected suitor should choose another mate; the turtle-dove says he should remain forever faithful; the cuckoo recommends that all three should remain celibate. The only one who enters into the logic of the courtly code is the turtle-dove, by nature an amorous and gentle bird.[57] The duck, in reply to the turtle-dove, scornfully casts doubt on the whole code:

> 'Wel bourded,' quod the doke, 'by myn hat!   *jested*
> That men shulde loven alwey causeles,
> Who can a resoun fynde or wit in that?
> Daunseth he murye that is myrtheles?   *merrily; sad*
> Who shulde recche of that is recheles?   *reckless*
> Ye quek!' yit seyde the doke, ful wel and fayre,
> 'There been mo sterres, God wot, than a payre!'
> (589–95)

And the falcon justly answers, from within the convention:

> '. . . Thy kynde is of so low a wrechednesse
> That what love is, thow canst nat seen ne gesse.'
> (601–2)

Nature, though she recommends the royal eagle, leaves the choice to the female, which demonstrates not only her open-mindedness, but also her sensible realism: in the end, as the Wife of Bath will prove *ad abundantiam*, it is always the woman who chooses her partner. And the eagle is conscious of this, as can be seen from her tone, which is humble when she speaks to Nature but becomes almost arrogant towards the three suitors:

> '. . . This al and som that I wol speke and seye.
> Ye gete no more, although ye do me deye!'
> (650–1)

The conclusion of the *demande d'amour* rests on the *non possumus* of the lady, who, like Emily in the *Knight's Tale*, is unprepared for love:

> . . . I wol nat serve Venus ne Cupide,
> Forsothe as yit, by no manere weye.'
> (652–3)

But while in the *Knight's Tale* the philosophical and political considerations expounded by Theseus will prevail, in the *Parliament* the final answer is determined by the personal condition, the state of mind and the will of the female eagle. All that can be done is to postpone everything for a year, during which the three suitors will continue to 'serve' (659–65) – as happened to the Knight in the *Book of the Duchess* (1258), and as happens to many other knights in medieval romances and many lovers in every time. And the *Parliament* can only have a dual ending.

The type of narrative exemplified by Chaucer's dream poems is, perhaps, unique in fourteenth-century Europe. If, as Scholes and Kellogg maintain, all that is needed for a narrative work is a story and a narrator,[58] then the poems examined up to here are definitely narrative. But for a twentieth-century reader familiar with medieval narrative – and, I suspect, for a reader of Chaucer's own time – it would be difficult to place these works with scientific precision in any of the traditional genres. This problem is clearly set out by Derek Brewer:

> In *The Book of the Duchess, The House of Fame, The Parliament of Fowls,* which are modelled on French love-visions of the thirteenth and fourteenth centuries, he [Chaucer] shows himself in line with a general development of French poetry from lyric to narrative. Yet they are not purely narrative; nor are they full stories, for these love-visions may well be regarded as narratively expanded first-person lyrics, with the special expressivity that lyrics imply. The forms of Dream and Meeting were especially important in the thirteenth and fourteenth centuries. Chaucer approached even these narrative love-visions from the point of view of provincial English romances which, though he later mocked them, seem to have provided his earliest literary pleasure and to have conditioned his poetic diction.[59]

In the first place, then, Chaucer's dream poems are transitional forms, which originate in the lyric and move in a narrative framework: this development has been noted especially in the *Book of the Duchess*, where the elegiac element produces a consolatory narration. The *House of Fame* and the *Parliament*, mainly through a process of abstraction, take a sharper turn in this direction: love, which in the *Book of the Duchess* is considered in the human figures of the Knight and his Blanche, in the *House of Fame* and the *Parliament* is examined in the forms of personification, iconography and literature: Venus, the temple and Dido in the former; the park and the temple in the latter.

Works conforming to the love vision type were expected to follow a certain pattern. With respect to this, the *Book of the Duchess*, and still more the *House of Fame* and the *Parliament of Fowls*, produce a remarkable sense of 'strangeness'[60] on all levels – the thematic, the structural and the linguistic; at times, as in the *House of Fame*, this reaches explosive proportions. It is on this threefold 'strangeness' that the following observations are based.

The French dream poem is essentially concerned with love, and in it the poetic 'I' represents the fulcrum of an experience, real and fictional, of love. Chaucer reverses the convention, when in the *Book of the Duchess*, and still more clearly in the *House of Fame* and the *Parliament*, he declares himself inexperienced in love, both in the real world and in the fiction of dreams. The oneiric–poetic adventure thus takes shape in Chaucer not as the story of a love experience, or a *planctus* on an unhappy love, but as a discovery of love, either through others (*Book of the Duchess*) or in the abstract and in general through iconography, literature, animals. The lyric-narrative 'I' of the love visions is thus neutralised, but remains present with eyes and ears, seeking to know love through other things.

However, the 'strangeness' is more profound: whereas in the *Book of the Duchess* the love experience between the Knight and Blanche is still the centre of attention, in the *House of Fame* and the *Parliament* the erotic theme is shifted and becomes one element in a complicated set of thematic relationships. The presence of the problem of nature can already be felt, as we have seen, in the *Book of the Duchess*, where the *Natureingang* ('starting with a nature-setting') at the beginning of the dream is not only a traditional *topos* but has an underlying relationship with the 'lawe of kinde', exemplified by the ancient books, and with death. In the *House of Fame* nature acquires a central place of its own, in Book II, which is set against love in Book I and against the world of Fame and Rumour in Book III. In the *Parliament* the *Natureingang* of the park becomes the sign of a real enjoyment of Nature, and Nature, this time personified, is the pivot of the poem's system of thought and imagination. The *Parliament* tries in every way to find the *Stimmung* of harmony–grace–love–nature of which Spitzer speaks, and which for a moment can be glimpsed, in iconographic form, in the park sublimated into an earthly Paradise.[61] In other words, the central theme of Chaucer's dream poems is not only the discovery of love, but also – and more importantly – a quest for Nature. The thought and the sensibility through which this theme is expressed conform to the general tendencies of the art of the period.[62]

The 'tydynges' of love that are promised and sought in Books II and III of the *House of Fame* are extended, at the end of the poem, to cover everything that is susceptible of poetic resonance and attention, including poetry itself. Illusion and reality, order and disorder, poetry and nature, all form part of the fabric of the *House of Fame*, which produces an extreme sense of 'strangeness' by comparison with the conventional dream poem. The 'synguler profit' of which Dido accuses Aeneas in the *House of Fame* is counterposed to the 'commune profyt' of which Africanus speaks, and with which all of the Parliament is permeated. In the *Parliament*, too, we see in action that 'lawe of kinde' which in the *Book of the Duchess* had to be identified through literature and the past, and through death. In the dream poems, Chaucer takes two directions: he upholds the comprehensiveness of poetry against the exclusiveness of the theme of courtly love, as witness the passage in the *House of Fame* in which the 'tydynges' include feelings, natural and human phenomena, history and politics (1959–76), and, on the other hand, he takes up a series of philosophical problems circulating in the schools and translates them, in a totally unsystematic way, into poetic narratives. In him, the Court poet, courtly–chivalrous culture and scientific culture meet – an encounter which, as Duby says,[63] was typical of the Courts of the fourteenth century. In Chaucer, as in Gower, there is an instinctive impulse towards explanation and popularisation. Chaucer has all the earmarks of the new intellectual, as seen by Duby: he reads 'what for lust and what for lore' and writes 'tales of best sentence and moost solas', while at the same time bringing mythology, Boethius, Alain, Macrobius, Boccaccio, Dante and the classics within the reach of all.

In the form, the *type* of the dream, Chaucer crystallises – at least at first – his own narrative and philosophical interest. The Chaucerian dream, as we have seen, goes far beyond the conventional love dream; in its allusions it covers all, or nearly all, the types indicated by Macrobius, plus the type invented by Boccaccio and continued by Petrarch. It is not a question of homage to tradition but an enormous extension of the convention, producing an indeterminate and mutable form such as we find most markedly, for example, in the *House of Fame*. The dream is, clearly, both a mode of apprehension of reality and a type of discourse. In the dream Chaucer moves away from the everyday world, just as he does by submerging himself in his beloved books, and this is another aspect of the close link between these two experiences. This detachment allows him to confront reality in a certain sense *sub specie aeternitatis*: the dream is the path to a viewpoint beyond this world. But it is a path that always begins on Earth: the very situation in which the dream is produced, that of reading, is an 'authenticating device'.[64] Indeed, as we pass from the first to the last of these works, the artifice becomes more and more refined. While in the *Book of the Duchess* the passage from reading to dream is motivated by the vow to Morpheus and Juno, in the *Parliament* it is much more natural (85–91ff). It is, I believe, the first time in European literature that at nightfall, when all the animals go to their rest – a classical *topos* that Chaucer here takes from Dante – the reader is transported into the real situation of his predecessor in the pre-electric age. Night prevents him from reading. And for the first time in a work of art we see a man, indeed the narrator–protagonist, preparing to get undressed for bed.

In connection with the figurative art of France in the fourteenth century, Duby speaks of 'courtly dreams' in a paragraph that is worth quoting: 'But for these dreams to have some connection with the reality which they transposed into poetic fiction, it was necessary that amid the leaps and discontinuities of the line, just as amid the leaps and discontinuities of the *ars nova*, a few scrupulously observed fragments of reality should be easily recognisable.'[65] This refers to other authenticating devices, which Chaucer, even as he abandons himself in his dream poems to the most bizarre fantasies, uses with great astuteness: for example the dog and the detail of the man with his back to the oak tree in the *Book of the Duchess*, the Eagle's claws in the *House of Fame*, the colours of the fish scales and the 'Kek kek! kokkow! quek quek!' of the birds in the *Parliament* — authenticating fragments within a wholly invented universe.

The dream framework permits a double vision of reality, sublimated and distorted. It is sublimated in the *Book of the Duchess* where the *locus amoenus* is the perfect theatre for the narration of a perfect love story; it is again sublimated in the *Parliament*, where the park is the perfect and eternal seat of the laws of nature and love. It is distorted in the *House of Fame*, in the surroundings of Venus's temple and in the two houses, and again in the *Parliament* in the Temple of Venus. Distortion and sublimation are both, however processes of exaggeration, the arbitrary *reductio* of reality. Thus Chaucerian dreams implicitly refer to the world outside themselves, to the otherness of reality, while at the same time mirroring the truth. A good example is the revolving House of Rumour: a fantastic conglomeration of men and voices, an absurd cyclotron governed by chance, it is revealed as the mirror of a 'faire feld' denoting the true dimension of Man and his word, even though it is not in the least realistic.[66]

The structural technique corresponds perfectly to the dream framework. The narration, as we have seen, is articulated according to a logic that is precisely that of the dream: in the *Book of the Duchess*, through the device of surrogation; in the *House of Fame* and the *Parliament*, behind the sense of mystery and total uncertainty, lie three principles that may be called 'echo', 'contradiction' and 'transformation'. Thus, in the *House of Fame*, Dido's references to fame are magnified in the House (echo); the world ordered by Nature is contrasted to the chaotic world of Rumour (contradiction); and in the *Parliament*, Scipio's stoic, other-worldly, political concept of 'commune profyt' is transformed into the *bonum commune* of generation, and the dualism between *contemptus mundi* and the Godlike perfection of the universe is resolved in the chain of being.

The dream is, finally, a parable of poetry: through it, in the *Book of the*

Duchess, the book becomes a work of art; through it, in the *House of Fame,* the narrative is broken up and recomposed; through it, in the *Parliament,* the difficult *ars longa* is learnt, with uncertain result. Chaucer's dreams are not only instrumental to the creation of the works that they enclose and determine. They also enter into a purely literary dimension, the world of books and of tradition quite apart from their specific subject; in other words they constitute a meta-language. For Chaucer, the book (literature) both causes the dream and exists within it. And Chaucer was in fact the first European writer to use this formula, which was to become a distinctive feature, if not a *topos,* of Western culture.[67] At the beginning of the fourteenth century Dante, in the episode of Paolo and Francesca, had consecrated the book as an occasion for love, sin, murder and eternal damnation; now, in the second half of the century, Chaucer consecrates it as the key and integrating element of the dream experience – one of the fundamental activities of the human psyche – and on the basis of this the book becomes the occasion for the quest for love, nature and poetry. Thus, before Petrarch's humanism, or at least independently of it, literature became one of the driving forces of European civilisation.

On the structural level, the sense of strangeness is produced first of all by a technique linked on the one hand with dream logic, and on the other with thematic expansion. This technique is, in substance, that of the surprise effect. Chaucer generally presents a three-part structure: in the *Book of the Duchess* there is the episode of Ceyx and Alcione, then the first part of the dream, then the encounter with the Knight and his story (each preceded and followed by a 'personal' moment); in the *House of Fame,* we have the Temple of Venus, the flight with the Eagle and the Houses of Fame and Rumour (each preceded by an invocation, and the first by a Proem); in the *Parliament,* Scipio's dream, the park and the temple, and the parliament of birds. As I have observed in connection with the *Parliament,* Chaucer plays continually on the expectations of his readers, by using a contrapuntal technique. This method, based precisely on surprise, also functions in the *Book of the Duchess* and the *House of Fame.* In the former, the *Natureingang* at the beginning of the dream leads one to expect a love adventure; instead, the knight in black appears and recites his *planctus*; the love story comes only later and then does not entirely conform to past models. In the *House of Fame,* the desert around the Temple of Venus is a surprise in itself; then, when the talking Eagle glides over it, the surprise is total, and one begins to wonder where the story is going to end up.

Chaucer's dream poems are based on his own experience, real or imaginary. Narrated in the first person, they describe the dream experience of the narrator by counterposing it, among other things, to his experience in real life. He is the inexperienced lover who discovers love, the administrator and accountant who reads avidly and whom only Jove, through his Eagle, manages to remove from his room. Thus there are two levels of experience, of which the second, the dream level, is paradoxically and significantly nearer than the first to the truth of things. Chaucer introduces himself into his poems, creating the narrative *persona* we know so well, on which Brewer has made some revealing observations:

> in *The Book of the Duchess*, *The House of Fame*, *The Parliament of Fowls*, [Chaucer] follows Machaut and others and specifically includes himself within the action, thus establishing a real, though equivocal, relationship with the world outside the poem, which thus, through the poet, exerts a pull of validating originality. He slightly characterises himself as a dull man within the poem, which is obviously absurd. He thus both does and does not extend the autobiographical and expressive interest that was developing among his immediate French predecessors.[68]

In the dream poems, Chaucer is, as Genette says, a homodiegetic and intradiegetic narrator – that is to say, he is the 'I' who narrates and also the protagonist within the story.[69] But these functions change slightly as we pass from the *Book of the Duchess* to the *House of Fame* and still more when we come to the *Parliament*. In the first two poems, especially in the *Book*, the *persona* of the narrator is active, at least verbally: he converses with the Knight and the Eagle. Indeed, in the *Book* he keeps questioning the Knight to make him continue his story, so that the narrative structure of the dream is, as we have seen, dialogical. In the *House of Fame* the interlocutor is replaced by the guide, the Eagle; the dialogue between protagonist and deuteragonist remains but it is dominated by the latter, precisely because he is acting as a guide. At the beginning of the *Parliament* the guide is present but he has become much more enigmatic and much less talkative, and then Africanus disappears altogether. The narrative *persona* does not ask his guide any explicit questions, and there is no dialogue between the two. Although the 'I' is both narrator and protagonist, he limits himself to reporting what he has seen and heard and he never opens his mouth either in the park or in the debate. The questions he asked in the *Book of the Duchess*, and again, though to a lesser extent, in the *House of Fame*, are now externalised, projected into the description and the debate between other characters. They are, so to speak, implicit in the mode of presentation of the poetic object and in the situation of observer in which the *persona* finds himself. In this sense, Chaucer is moving from a basically dialogical form of narrative towards a monological form, which gives rise to polyphony.[70] The parliament is emblematic of this polyphony (the birds represent many points of view), which takes shape within a monologic narration – that is to say, one in which everything is seen through the eyes of the narrative *persona*, here reduced to the role of an observer.

In the *Book of the Duchess*, the dialogic form of the narration in the second part of the poem is the sign that within it a 'questioning quest' is going on[71] – one might call it a Socratic inquiry. The quest remains, as in *Piers Plowman*, the central form of the other dream poems, but the explicit questioning continually diminishes, until in the *Parliament* it completely disappears. Chaucer does not learn from the Eagle and Africanus in the way that Dante learned from Virgil, Statius, Beatrice and in fact all the characters in the other world. Dante falls silent only when he reaches the beatific vision; Chaucer does so much sooner, though he embarks on at least two journeys similar to that of Dante. Chaucer really behaves, in the narrative fiction, like the knights of courtly romance, like Perceval who does not ask the Fisher King the question that could save him. Instead, Chaucer searches into the things he sees and the books he reads: in a certain sense he verifies what he reads through what he sees in the world of dreams (the *Somnium* through the universe of the park and the debate) and at the same time confirms what he sees in dream by reference to what he has read (Nature appears just as she does in Alain's *De Planctu*). Thus his dream narrative is essentially problematic. Chaucer incarnates or pictorialises a problem and then, in his uncertainty, seeks a solution – which, if he then finds it, proves to have one or more different alternatives. In the *Book of the Duchess*, the problem is love, from which the narrative *persona* declares himself to be suffering and in which he is revealed to be inexperienced: the solution is offered by the story of the Knight and Blanche, but this ends with the death of the lady. In the *House of Fame*, the problem is again love, but Venus here proves to be such a sphinx that Jove has to send his messenger to carry Geoffrey into the world of the 'ayerissh bestes' and then into the universes of Fame and Rumour. Here, in other words, there is no solution, but there are different alternatives. In the *Parliament*, love is the problem yet again, but the *Somnium* gives it a meta-terrestrial perspective, the park places it in the sublimated universe of the earthly Paradise, the temple frames it in a strictly sensual dimension and the debate leaves the *demande d'amour* unresolved, while otherwise the natural function of the parliament is carried out. The quest, in short, never ends, except in the *Book*: in the *House of Fame* it breaks off at the end of a line, leaving everything to the imagination; in the *Parliament* it is referred to 'other books', that is, to a new search, like the end of *Piers Plowman*. In this, Chaucer again reveals himself as a man of his time: indefiniteness and incompleteness are characteristics typical of the Gothic mode.[72]

All this produces an extreme sense of 'strangeness' by comparison with traditional genres: the French narrative lyric has become a narrative quest (first by means of the dialogue, then by means of the guided journey, then by means of debate); the dream has gained a field of action – that of the *Bewegungsdrama*, the 'drama of movement,'[73] which it exploits by setting different scenes and visions side by side. The narrative poem has been reconstructed in a problematic framework; that 'I' of the narrator is gradually moving towards the novella and the novel.

In the stylistic sphere, the drama of movement produced by the dream logic of Chaucer's early poems is based on a series of *aposiopeses* or *reticentiae* – that is to say, interruptions of a train of thoughts and images, followed by something altogether different.[74] As I have shown, such changes of scene and mode, at times abrupt and enigmatic, are frequent in these narratives: for example, the transition from the *Somnium* to the park or from the awakening to the hunt. Key moments are marked by *percursio*, the enumerative accumulation of objects, each of which would merit a detailed treatment: the catalogue of trees, personifications, birds and lovers in the *Parliament*, the lists of artists and then of 'tydynges' in the *House of Fame*, the series of stories from romances on the walls of the bedroom in the *Book of the Duchess*. Another common figure is the *praeteritio*, the announcement that the author is going to omit part of the discourse. This is seen, for example, in the *Parliament*, when Chaucer tells us that there are many stories painted on the walls, but he will mention only a few of them (285–6),[75] or in the *House of Fame*, when he says he is not going to tell 'how they [Dido and Aeneas] aqueynteden in fere'.[76] Another technique common in these dream poems is that of 'emphasis', in which more is implied than is said. The most interesting case is that in which the 'allusion', the humorous intent, emerges within the emphasis: for example, when Priapus is described 'with hys sceptre in honde'. For that matter, as we have repeatedly seen in Chaucer's dream poems emphasis is really a way of structuring speech: this is the technique of implicit statement that I have often noted in the foregoing pages. In other words, in the dream poems Chaucer seems to invent a narrative method that we might call 'detractive', where *detractio* refers to 'the omission of thoughts fundamentally necessary to the purpose of communication'; *percursio*, *praeteritio*, *reticentia* and allusive emphasis are, precisely, the expressive means of *detractio*. It is no accident that the *House of Fame* and the *Parliament* tend to be obscure, and we need to break down and rebuild the texts in order to clarify their implicit and Pindaric passages, whereas in the *Book of the Duchess*, his first narrative work, this method is still being worked out.

The detractive method and its expressive means correspond to the construction of the meaning itself: the continual play of affirmation and negation, of reticence and allusion, creates ambiguity and multiple meanings. For example, the piling-up of possible interpretations produced by reticence creates a stratification of meanings with regard to the object itself: this is the case in the *Parliament*, where the *Somnium*, the park, the temple and the parliament each contribute to the definition of one of the values of love. In the *House of Fame*, on the other hand, the ambiguity rests on allusive emphasis and implicit statements: the result, as we have seen, is that Venus, Fame and art – all ambiguous – are all built on the basis of a series, which may begin with an *ecphrasis* but then uses hints, foreshortenings, apparently-chance phrases, echoes. In this sense, the stylistic method of the dream poems is detractive, and that which governs the construction of meaning may properly be called 'circumlocutory'.

Circumlocution can also be seen in the quotations, in the references to authorities and in the borrowings, imitations, translations and adaptations that are used so pointedly in Chaucer's dream narratives. Quotation has an internal purpose but at the same time it opens up an external space, establishing relationships with other texts and codes. The evocation of the *De Planctu Naturae* in the *Parliament* serves to complete, within the circumlocutory system, the identification of Nature that is at the centre of the poem, but, at the same time, it refers back to the philosophic individuality of Alain and places the *Parliament* itself in a cultural stream, a tradition. For that matter the *Parliament* is, as we have seen, an enormous 'quotation', in the sense that it continually calls for comparison with other texts. In the *Book of the Duchess*, however, the quotation from Ovid's story has an almost exclusively internal function, anticipatory and dialogical. In the *House of Fame*, the 'quotation' from Dante of the Eagle and his flight are an example of transcodification: Chaucer exploits the model but rejects its original significance. His is hardly a flight towards the beatific vision. This, in other words, is irony in the broadest sense of the word. Irony provides not only a breath of wit that makes the work more enjoyable, serving as a sort of extended *captatio benevolentiae*, but it permits Chaucer to point out the gap that separates the possible from the actual. Geoffrey's journey might result in a beatific or apocalyptic vision, in a *Paradiso* or a *Pearl*, but it never does; it remains the *House of Fame*, 'in myddes of the weye / Betwixen hevene, erthe, and see'. Irony, a function of Chaucer's consciousness, is the 'mesure' of his wisdom and common sense, and an indication of his inability to overcome the dichotomy between the ideal and the real. What was possible for Dante is no longer possible for Chaucer.

Irony thus figures as an authenticating device. In the *Book of the Duchess*, the Knight declares that Blanche never behaved like the heroines of romances, who send their knights off on crazy adventures to the four corners of the earth, and this lends credibility to the perfection of the lady and the love experience. In the *House of Fame*, the Eagle's mockery of professorial pedantry and language contributes to the plausibility of his presence and his discourse. In the *Parliament*, the statue of Priapus and the ironical remarks of the inferior birds balance the ideal world of the park and the *demande d'amour* of the aristocratic fowls.

The stylistic register of the dream poems cannot, therefore, be other than multiple.[77] The expression has to be high and low at the same time. The great overture of the *Parliament* must end with the colloquial 'God save swich a lord!' The Eagle, who speaks like an Oxford Master, uses expressions like 'Seynte Marye', 'Seynt Julyan', 'Seynte Clare', 'heven kyng' and 'Petre!' Even the highly educated Knight in the *Book* exclaims: 'A Goddes half!' These examples could be multiplied; they occur in every part of these poems. The truth is that Chaucer speaks 'lewedly to a lewed man', like the anonymous writers of the English romances for whom, as Brewer maintains,[78] he learned to manipulate the vernacular. In this sense even Dante's multiplicity of styles only confirmed the rightness of the path Chaucer had taken. The style is 'comic' precisely in the Dantean sense of the term; it is *spoudogelaion*, 'serio-comic' – 'Menippean satire', in short, according to Bakhtin's enlarged definition.[79] However, while in Dante multiplicity is the sign of a conciliation between the real and the ideal, which comes about because the poet, with a superhuman effort, sees the historical world *en bloc* from the plane of eternity, in Chaucer's dream poems it remains the sign of a dichotomy that is not overcome. That is why Dante can say that art is the grandchild of God, while Chaucer affirms that it counterfeits nature.

2 The romance

It is possible that Chaucer's *Anelida and Arcite* represents his first attempt at romance: at various points it is reminiscent of Boccaccio's *Teseida*, and it breaks off just as the author is preparing to describe the Temple of Mars, presumably also on the model of the *Teseida*. Chaucer, however, transforms the *Anelida* into a complaint, thus making it a substantially lyrical work, formally very elaborate. Chaucer must have realised that the story was getting out of hand and decided to abandon it. He may also have taken up the theme of the *Teseida* in a composition on Palamon and Arcite that he himself mentions in the Prologue to the *Legend of Good Women*, which later became the first of the *Canterbury Tales*, the *Knight's Tale*. None of this can be established with absolute certainty – Chaucerian chronology is an endless labyrinth – but that does not matter in the present context. It is reasonable to assume that Chaucer had experimented with romance before composing *Troilus*. Certainly *Troilus*, as we know it, shows that Chaucer had a good knowledge of the *Filostrato* and the *Teseida*. In any case – and this is the main point – *Troilus and Criseyde* is the only full-scale romance that Chaucer has left us, and as such, for the modern reader, it is perhaps his most important work. If it in fact dates from around 1385, *Troilus*, together with *Sir Gawain* (also composed in the last decades of the century), is the first great romance written in Europe after Boccaccio's *Filostrato* (1335?), *Filocolo* (1336?) and *Teseida* (1340–1). In fact *Troilus*, to a much greater extent and in a more obvious way than *Sir Gawain*, participates fully in the great European narrative current of the Middle Ages, as mediated by the work of Boccaccio.

It is quite well known that Chaucer based his *Troilus* on the story of the *Filostrato*, one of Boccaccio's early works. A great deal has been written on the relationship between the two works, and nothing – it would seem – needs to be added on the subject. However, a study of Chaucer's narrative fiction in the *Troilus* cannot proceed without some attention to its relationship with the work on which it is known to be modelled – especially as up to now criticism has insisted on certain aspects, of undoubted importance, while neglecting others that are equally significant.

Chaucer used the *Filostrato* without ever mentioning it; he attributed his source to a certain 'Lollius'. However, it is clear that he knew the title of Boccaccio's work, because he used it as a name – 'Philostrate' – in the *Knight's Tale*. In the *Filostrato*, Chaucer found not only a good story but a new way of telling it, and he used it to best advantage. It has often been said that Chaucer eliminates the autobiographical elements contained in the *Filostrato*, especially in the *Proemio* and in Part IX. If we accept the premise that these are not autobiographical elements but, as Branca has demonstrated,[1] a *senhal*, an artificial idealised story of love, which when repeated in other early works creates a real myth of the beloved lady (here Filomena, elsewhere Fiammetta), then this is true: Chaucer eliminates *that* convention. But Chaucer really uses Boccaccio's convention as a point of departure for his own. He defines himself as the 'servant of the servants of Love', whereas Boccaccio declares that he has been 'almost from childhood...in the service of Love'.[2] Chaucer apostrophises lovers and begs for their understanding, compassion and prayers (I, 22–56): the idea comes from Boccaccio (I, 6), who begs lovers to pray for him. One might even think Chaucer was playing with Boccaccio's convention when he declares that he wants to pray for the servants of love (I, 48) and to be considered their 'brother' (I, 51) – that is, the brother of that fictitious Boccaccio who proclaims himself the servant of love. In the light of the subtle relationship that the Narrator of *Troilus* establishes with his 'auctour', commenting upon him and using him as a foil, this hypothesis is not so very strange.

It has often been said that this Narrator is Chaucer's invention; and it is true that his complexity, as I shall demonstrate, is entirely new. But in itself the device of the narrator who remains outside the story, and yet manifests himself within it through comments and exclamations, is a device that comes from Boccaccio: no other medieval romance before the *Filostrato* gave such autonomy and solidity to the narrator, the 'I', as such. From the *Proemio* on, Boccaccio is present in his story, as he was later to be in the *Teseida*.[3] Chaucer developed and complicated this device with extraordinary skill, but the device itself can already be found in the *Filostrato*. In the same way, the Narrator's attitude towards his sources, his 'authorities', is developed and underlined by Chaucer, but its origin lies in that of Boccaccio, and also in the widespread practice of medieval authors. Boccaccio also speaks of the 'ancient tales' (*Proemio*, 27) and maintains that, apart from the (fictitious) identification of himself with Troilo and his beloved lady with Criseida, 'of the many other things beyond these, none...pertains to [him], nor is put there for [his] sake, but because the story of the noble and enamoured youth requires it'

(*Proemio*, 35). For that matter Chaucer's development of this theme is quite comprehensible. Boccaccio literally invented the love story of Troilo and Criseida, inspired by a marginal episode in Benoît; that is why he uses the expression 'the story requires it': not what the 'authority has written' but what is required by the narrative logic developed from the 'ancient tale'. Chaucer, however, had before him a fully elaborated story, that of the *Filostrato*, and he could not but feel, in the medieval way, the limits imposed by this pre-existing text. Chaucer greatly developed this element, which was already present in the *Filostrato*, making it an integral part of his form and creating a new world from it.

What Chaucer did with the *Filostrato* was what most modern cinema directors do when converting a book into a film, except that the director never talks about what he is doing during the course of the film. For example, the structural elements on which the story hinges are the same: Troilus falls in love with Criseyde after seeing her in the temple, and Pandarus serves as a go-between, arranging their meeting. Criseyde's father Calchas, a soothsayer who has fled to the Greeks, asks for Criseyde in exchange for Antenor, and against Hector's opposition the Trojan parliament accepts. Diomedes realises that Criseyde is in love with Troilus and courts her. Troilus dreams that Criseyde betrays him; then, when he sees the brooch he had given her on the arms that Deiphobus has captured in battle from Diomedes, he knows it is true. Troilus is killed by Achilles (this takes up only one line in both poems). The basic mechanism of the plot is the same. What Chaucer does, again, is to complicate it. For example, whereas the meeting between the two lovers is effected by Boccaccio's Pandaro through the conversation, the two letters and the direct encounter in Criseida's house, Chaucer's Pandarus uses not only the conversation and the letters but also Troilus's walk in front of Criseyde's window (in Boccaccio a chance event), the dinner in Deiphobus's house and the enmity of Poliphete, the supper at his (Pandarus's) house and Troilus's feigned jealousy. In other words, through the whole first part of *Troilus*, Chaucer amplifies and reinvents the narrative devices as if he were writing a play, with Pandarus as stage manager. Then in the second part he eliminates the episode in which Deiphobus, his brothers, Cassandra, and all the women of Troy become aware of Troilus's love and discuss it with him (vii, 77–103) – and he shifts the interpretation of Troilus's dream from Troilus himself to Cassandra.[4] In other words, Chaucer eliminates those elements that are not strictly functional to the plot.

Critics have often spoken, with good reason, of the lyrical element that Chaucer brought to *Troilus*: the two 'Cantici Troili', the *aubades*, Troilus's song (III, 1744–71). As Robert Payne has observed,[5] in Chaucer this lyricism forms a coherent design, and as such I shall have to deal with it later. But here, again, the idea comes from Boccaccio: if Chaucer uses one of Petrarch's sonnets for the first 'Canticus Troili', Boccaccio uses a canzone by Cino da Pistoia for one of Troilo's songs (v, 62–6). And, in general, it is Boccaccio's Troilo who abandons himself to songs and lyrical *planctus*, as does his Arcita later on. 'The exercise of the lyric keeps pace with the construction of Boccaccio's most complex edifices.' 'Again and again in Boccaccio, epitomising the unity of experience between the writer's lyrical *carnet* and his realisation of more extensive structures, we find lyrics used as a sort of embroidery over the whole fabric of each work.'[6] So Chaucer is simply retracing the path already marked out by Boccaccio, following it all the way back through Boethius, Machaut and the tradition of the *aubades*, but he gives a special coherence to this procedure. We may also note in passing that the melodramatic quality of Boccaccio's text by no means disappears in Chaucer's *Troilus*. Not only do the lyrical effusions, arias and duets remain and increase – so do the faintings, the lamentations and episodes like Criseyde's presumed death and Troilus's intended suicide. All those elements which Chaucer eliminated from the *Teseida* when writing the *Knight's Tale*, he used in the *Troilus*.

Even the character of Troilus seems to be partly remodelled in the style of Arcita: he is a more lyrical, more passionate, more profound Troilus than his model in the *Filostrato*, more like the gentle, suffering, pensive Arcita of the *Teseida* – who, like him, ascends to the eighth heaven and to a destiny dictated by Mercury. The fundamental traits of the four characters of *Troilus* are those already outlined in the *Filostrato*: Troilus enamoured, valorous, faithful and courteous; Criseyde beautiful and self-confident; Pandarus the unsuccessful lover, witty and clever; Diomedes bold and perspicacious. Here Chaucer has developed to the highest degree the potential inherent in Boccaccio's characterisation, especially when he changes Pandarus from Criseyde's cousin into her uncle and puts the soliloquy on predestination into Troilus's mouth.

The 'medievalisation' of which C. S. Lewis speaks[7] is, in this context, an ambiguous term. Chaucer in no way medievalises the social setting of the *Filostrato*: Troilo and Troilus are courteous knights, and both of them have 'kinsmen' and 'knyghtes'. The courtly convention followed, according to Lewis, by Chaucer's Troilus is by no means absent in Boccaccio's Troilo, and if the former is partly an incarnation of the allegorical process seen in the *Roman de la Rose*, the latter is modelled on the canons of the *dolce stil novo*[8] and has nothing to do with the Renaissance. Courtly love is at the centre of both poems.

There is no doubt that Chaucer embellished his text according to the rhetorical canons of the thirteenth-century *artes poeticae*. In particular, critics have noted that with respect to the *Filostrato*, Chaucer's text is richer in poetic invocations, similes and the use of mythology. This is undoubtedly true. However, once again it was Boccaccio who pointed the way. For example, the simile 'right as floures, thorugh the cold of nyght' (II, 966–70) can be traced to the *Filostrato* (II, 80)[9] and through it to Dante (*Inferno*, II, 137–9). Later Chaucer goes back to Dante, ignoring Boccaccio, just as in Book II he goes back to Boethius, who is not recalled in Boccaccio.[10] In short, the *Filostrato* served to stimulate Chaucer's adaptive imagination, through a process similar to the one he applied to the *Teseida* in writing the *Knight's Tale*.[11]

With regard to the use of mythology, Daniel Boughner has already shown how this was understood by Chaucer according to the practice of Dante and Boccaccio.[12] In fact one may easily suspect that Chaucer's way of using mythological references is due to his knowledge of the *Divine Comedy* and above all to the *Teseida* – two fourteenth-century models that might well have directed him back to classical canons. A typical and well-known case is that of *Troilus*, V, 8–13, which is derived from the *Teseida*, II, 1. But *Troilus*, V, 1016–20 also has something in common with the *Teseida* (III, 5), and many of the mythological allusions in *Troilus*, even when not directly derived from the *Teseida*, find their counterpart in Boccaccio's poem, which is a major source of mythological information, both in the text and in the commentary.[13]

Moreover, it seems that as he approaches the end of *Troilus*, Chaucer comes close to the *Teseida*: not only is the first line of Book V taken from Boccaccio's poem (IX, 1, 1), but this is followed at once by the mythological image already mentioned,[14] and later another; the process ends in the famous conclusion whereby Troilus ascends to the eighth sphere (V, 1807–27), which is taken entirely from the *Teseida* (XI, 1–3). Even in the poetic invocations the model of the *Teseida* and the *Filostrato* are present in *Troilus*, supplemented by the *Divine Comedy* and the *Thebaid*, which Boccaccio himself, especially in the *Teseida*, continually echoed.[15]

Finally, we should not overlook the importance for *Troilus* of the part played in the *Teseida* by Fortune and the 'Fates',[16] which Chaucer found confirmed in the *Filostrato* itself. Philosophical depth is certainly fundamental in *Troilus*, but even this could well have been stimulated by the *Filostrato*, and especially by the *Teseida*, and through it by Dante and Boethius, as happens in the *Knight's Tale*. Again, if the final perspective of *Troilus* is very broad and other-worldly, it is thanks to the *Teseida*, from which it derives Troilus's ascent and the *contemptus mundi* ultimately inspired by the *Somnium Scipionis*. The eighth sphere, denied to Arcite in the *Tale*, is granted to Troilus, whose Narrator, unlike the Knight, is not afraid to appear as a 'divinistre' with his own 'registre' of souls (*Knight's Tale*, 2809-14). Thus, for the Chaucer of *Troilus*, the *Filostrato* and the *Teseida* constitute a sort of combustion chamber, within which is generated a veritable chain reaction to drive the Chaucerian 'engyn'.

The episode in Chaucer's poem where he evokes the story of Thebes[17] represents a singular aspect of the presence of the *Teseida* in *Troilus*. When Pandarus finds Criseyde and her women listening intently to what Criseyde herself calls 'this romaunce...of Thebes', he refers to 'bookes twelve': these could be either Statius's *Thebaid* (which is in fact in twelve books), or the *Roman de Thèbes* ('romaunce'). It is even possible that while Pandarus refers to the former, Criseyde, with more verisimilitude in the fourteenth-century feminine context, speaks of the other. When in interpreting Troilus's dream Cassandra quite unnecessarily tells the story of Thebes,[18] omitted in the *Filostrato* (VII, 27), are we sure that the excursus is due to the *Thebaid* (as would seem to be indicated by a few manuscripts that, at this point, give a summary of Statius's poem in Latin verses) or should we not rather think of the *Teseida*, which is more and more prominent in Book V of *Troilus*, and which is constantly retelling the story of Thebes? Lewis maintained that in writing the *Troilus* Chaucer saw himself as a 'historical poet', contributing to the history of Troy and reconstructing, for his backward English audience, 'a new bit of the matter of Rome', whereas the Boccaccio of the *Filostrato* could get by with a passing mention of the story of Troy and other episodes, because his audience was 'fully conscious that all this is mere necessary "setting" or "hypothesis"'.[19] However, if that is the case, why the story of Thebes, which has nothing to do with Troy and Rome except the connection between Tydeus and Diomedes – a small matter that could be dealt with in three lines? There is, of course, the medieval narrator's fascination with digression and 'interlacing'. But that does not suffice to explain why the same Boccaccio who wrote the *Filostrato*, when writing the *Teseida* later, presumably for the same 'conscious' audience, chose to cram his narration full of mythological references, creating a 'historical' space for his poem among the classical 'matters'. Chaucer deliberately omits this mythologising in the *Knight's Tale*, while filling *Troilus* with it. Of course the two poems have different requirements of presentation and approach, but the fact remains that, where Chaucer has the necessary space at his disposal (i.e. in *Troilus*, where he amplifies – in the *Knight's Tale* he has to reduce), he is far from disdaining those mythological or 'historical' procedures which Boccaccio in the *Teseida*, by conscious choice, first included in vernacular romance. The narrator of the *Knight's Tale* repeatedly oscillates between two contrasting attitudes towards the past, one of which recognises its substantial difference from the present, while the other puts past and present on the same plane.[20] The Narrator of *Troilus*, on the other hand, shows that he is fully aware not only that customs change but also that language changes (II, 22–8), and from the height of his Christian faith he condemns the 'corsed olde rites' of the pagans.

To sum up, there is no more 'medievalisation' in *Troilus* than there is in the *Filostrato* and the *Teseida* (though there is more in the *Knight's Tale*). Nor, of course, is there a 'Renaissance' tendency, but there is the conscious effort by Chaucer to draw material from the areas of poetry, scholarship, and the whole range of medieval and contemporary problems (Boethius, Machaut, the *aubades*, Bradwardine's ideas on predestination), making full use of all the new tools that the Italian *avant-garde* could suggest to a late-fourteenth-century poet. Together with the canvas of the *Filostrato*, already full of ideas and atmosphere, in *Troilus* we find – albeit transformed – a Petrarchan sonnet (the first in English literature), the framework, method and language of the *Teseida*, and the echo of Dante, whose lines begin and end the last stanza of the poem. Dante, Boccaccio and Petrarch together in a single work: a unique event in early European literature.

Having said all this, it should at once be added, even at the risk of being obvious, that *Troilus* is not the simple arithmetical sum of its sources, nor a mosaic of literary references, but a new poetic and narrative system and, in the European context, a completely original one; in its unique success it could even be said to be isolated and abnormal. For three centuries afterwards the English literary tradition – from Caxton to Henryson to Shakespeare to Dryden – had good reason to return with perennial fascination, and at the same time with disquiet, to the story sung by Chaucer. This does not contradict what I have said about its literary sources: the characteristics of *Troilus* that have been mentioned up to now must be considered as integral parts of the whole universe of the work, which is *in toto* unique and unrepeatable. Since it is impossible to analyse the poem very closely here,[21] in the following pages I shall attempt to give a general view of the whole by examining certain key points, in order to establish the poem's place in the context of English and European medieval narrative.

At the centre of *Troilus* undoubtedly stands the Narrator, either Geoffrey Chaucer in person or a projection modelled more or less in his image. He is a narrator whose presence and whose importance are partly due to the material circumstances of the work's 'publication' – it was read aloud by the poet himself to a courtly audience and at the same time circulated in manuscript. The role of the Narrator is also partly inspired by the Boccaccian model and partly due to Chaucer's own genius and his plan of construction. In our day the question is further complicated. *Troilus* is now available in thousands of printed copies (even in English 'translation' – one wonders whether the author would have considered this a case of 'miswriting' or one of change 'in forme of speche... / Withinne a thousand yeer'). Since the book is always accessible on our own shelves, we react to the poem's Narrator in a way he could never have foreseen; we have been transformed into the type of reading public envisaged – and indeed created – by more recent narrators, such as Fielding and Sterne.[22] Thus the Narrator of *Troilus* becomes for us a sort of Tristram Shandy *ante litteram*, and his voice cannot but strike our ear with a slight Shandean resonance. Whereas in Chaucer's dream poems the narrator was homodiegetic and intradiegetic, here in *Troilus* he is extradiegetic and heterodiegetic[23] – but in a particular way. We might call him, with a rather unorthodox term that would undoubtedly please him (or at least Pandarus), a 'meene'.[24] He is a Narrator anxious to establish relationships with everyone and at the same time dominated by certain laws. In his own mind the Narrator makes the choice – presumably based on free will – of a given story, the story of the 'double sorrow' of Troilus. But this story has a preordained form and development, imposed by 'Lollius', who in this case stands for Boccaccio (and Petrarch), Benoît and Guido delle Colonne – but especially Boccaccio. This story is situated in a 'historial' cycle, that of Troy, which is also well defined by certain authorities: Homer (in fact unknown to the author), Dares and Dictys, as well as, again, Benoît and Guido. From the moment that he selects, from among many possibilities, the story of Troilus as told by Lollius, the Narrator is, in the medieval context, dominated largely by necessity; that is to say, he is no longer free to alter the *fabula* of the poem in any substantial way but must follow his authority's model. That is why, in speaking to his audience, the Narrator keeps referring to his author, almost to the point of declining any responsibility for his story:[25]

> Forwhi to every lovere I me excuse,
> That of no sentement I this endite,
> But out of Latyn in my tonge it write.

> Wherefore I nyl have neither thank ne blame
> Of al this werk, but prey yow mekely,
> Disblameth me, if any word be lame,
> For as myn auctour seyde, so sey I.   (ɪɪ, 12–18)

Since he is writing especially for ladies, he is particularly reluctant to follow his sources on the question of Criseyde's betrayal, although this is an integral part of the story (v, 1050–94). While he does not reprove Criseyde 'forther, than the storye wol devyse' (as Shakespeare was to do), and indeed tries to find excuses for her, the Narrator cannot escape this sort of literary predestination, according to which the lady's betrayal must be consummated. The most he can do is to say that if he could he would excuse her 'for routhe' – 'for she so sory was for hire untrouthe' (v, 1095–9) – and that he would much rather write of 'Penelopeës trouthe and good Alceste' (v, 1777–8). In other words, at the end of his work the Narrator seems to be on the point of repudiating it, of going back on the choice he made at the beginning, almost promising a completely different book about the fidelity of women. In fact Alceste later appears in the Prologue to the *Legend of Good Women*, where she herself apologises for the author to the god of Love, who has reproved him for writing *Troilus*. Thus we realise that the relationship of the Narrator with his story is, in part, a fiction and a game, even though constraint and necessity remain. In fact, the Narrator of *Troilus* frees himself from this necessity not only within the limits normally conceded and even suggested to medieval writers by the *artes poeticae* – that is, by amplification, displacement, removal and substitution – but also by giving the *fabula* itself a new twist, a sudden leap that is basically heterodox in the context of conventional literary canons. Troilus, who in the *Filostrato* dies and 'ends' with death, ascends to the eighth heaven, and is then taken by Mercury to a place that is not revealed to us. Chaucer's Troilus is a firm believer in predestination but as a creature of the Narrator, he frees himself from the literary *anankē* ('necessity') and leaps right out of the realm of tragedy.

Behind this Narrator, then, stands the story, before him lies his book, to which he says farewell at the end:

> Go, litel bok, go, litel myn tragedye...
> (v, 1786)

First comes the choice of the story; then constraint imposed on the story; and, lastly, free will. In reality even the original choice is more complex than it looks at first sight, for it is a choice of the 'matter', and hence of the framework and intonation of the work. The Narrator makes this point at the beginning and at the end of *Troilus* (I, 141–7 and v, 1765–71): perhaps thinking of Boccaccio and the *Teseida*, he explicitly rejects the epic, the 'geste'. His is a story of love, and the reader who wants a more precisely 'historial' dimension is referred at the outset to Homer, Dares and Dictys. The narrative system of *Troilus*, though it contains historical references and even follows the historical course of events, is in actual fact open to different points of view from the very beginning. The Narrator sets the reader, as it were, before a window: 'inside' is the story of Troilus, 'outside' is the whole history of Troy: the glass allows him to see both ways, provided he chooses his vantage point. The reader of *Troilus* is offered a comfortable seat 'inside', from which he can even see a bit of the landscape 'outside'; in any case he is given the key that enables him to go out on the terrace and take in the whole panorama.

Behind the Narrator stands the story, before him the book. Detached from both, yet enabled by the Narrator to reach both, are the listeners, the original audience of the poem. From the start the Narrator establishes an intimate relationship with this audience – 'al this compaignye', as he calls it at a certain point (I, 450). It is an audience he can count on, of connoisseurs, experts, for whom there is no need to spell everything out:

> Whan al was hust, than lay she [Criseyde] stille and thoughte
> Of al this thing; the manere and the wise
> Reherce it nedeth nought, for ye ben wise.
>
> (II, 915–17)

It is in fact, an ideal audience of servants of love, with whom the Narrator carries on a continual dialogue. He is only the servant of the servants of love (and hence, in the irony of the humility formula, also their Pope) and he dedicates his work to them, while at the same time inviting them to enter into the story, by relating the narrated events to their own experience. He, the Narrator, does not speak 'of sentement', but he begs his listeners to provide it themselves through their memory and add it to the story. He asks them to remember their 'pyte', their 'good entencioun' (I, 15–38). In other words, from the outset the Narrator not only involves his listeners in his poem but makes them to some extent co-authors. He continually calls upon them by asking them direct questions; he guides them through the scenes, indicating directions and changes,[26] he leaves the narration itself open to their 'discrecioun':

> But soth is, though I kan nat tellen al,
> As kan myn auctour, of his excellence,
> Yet have I seyd, and God toforn, and shal
> In every thyng, al holy his sentence;
> And if that ich, at Loves reverence,
> Have any word in eched for the beste,
> Doth therwithal right as youreselven leste.
>
> For myne wordes, heere and every part,
> I speke hem alle under correccioun
> Of yow that felyng han in loves art,

And putte it al in youre discrecioun
To encresse or maken dymynucioun
Of my langage, and that I yow biseche.
But now to purpos of my rather speche.
(III, 1324–37)

As we have seen, the narration, dominated by 'authorial' necessity, is already open to possibility, to 'historial' choice. Now it is opened at the receiver's end, on the side of the audience. The passage above, in which the Narrator stresses his intention to follow his author's whole 'sentence' and at the same time gives his audience of lovers the option of manipulating and recreating his language, perfectly illustrates the literary play of freedom and necessity that goes on in *Troilus.* This Narrator presents himself almost as a Pandarus of literature: a 'meene', a middle-man between the story and its audience. Above all he is a middle-man between the experience of Criseyde and his audience of women; he is forced – or pretends that he wishes – to reverse Boccaccio's moral in the *Filostrato* ('Giovane donna è mobile': 'Young women are fickle').

Bysechyng every lady bright of hewe,
And every gentil womman, what she be,
That al be that Criseyde was untrewe,
That for that gilt she be nat wroth with me.
Ye may hire giltes in other bokes se;
And gladlier I wol write, yif yow leste,
Penelopeës trouthe and good Alceste.

N'y sey nat this al oonly for thise men,
But moost for wommen that bitraised be
Thorugh false folk; God yeve hem sorwe, amen!
That with hire grete wit and subtilte
Bytraise yow! And this commeveth me
To speke, and in effect yow alle I preye,
Beth war of men, and herkneth what I seye!
(V, 1772–85)

Sterne would say: 'That's another story.' And so does the Narrator of *Troilus,* when he refers us to 'other bokes' and moreover declares his readiness to write about Penelope and Alceste.

The Narrator's relationship with this public gives *Troilus,* even for the modern reader, the quality of a story in the making, rather than an already bound and finished book. The audience, past and present, is continually apostrophised; it witnesses the making of the narration, the poet's work and that of his characters, the choices made by the Narrator as he goes along. From the beginning, for example, the audience knows what is in store for it:

> The double sorwe of Troilus to tellen,
> That was the kyng Priamus sone of Troye,
> In lovynge, how his aventures fellen
> Fro wo to wele, and after out of joie,
> My purpos is, er that I parte fro ye.
>
> (I, 1–5)

There is a constant reference to the 'matere' as the Narrator digresses to indulge in commentary and then finds the thread again (I, 260–6). In reality he plays deliberately and consciously with his 'matere' and the public's reaction to it. Though at times he claims to be uncertain or unable to say something (I, 492–3 and III, 1310–13), he is actually ruled by a teleology that dominates everything:

> But al passe I, lest ye to longe dwelle;
> *For for o fyn is al that evere I telle.*
>
> (II, 1595–6)

There is a reason even for the omissions (IV, 199–805), as is confirmed by a passage where the Narrator reveals all his literary self-consciousness:

> But now, paraunter, som man wayten wolde
> That every word, or soonde, or look, or cheere
> Of Troilus that I rehercen sholde,
> In al this while unto his lady deere.
> I trowe it were a long thyng for to here;
> Or of what wight that stant in swich disjoynte, *difficult position*
> His wordes alle, or every look, to poynte.
>
> For sothe, I have naught herd it don er this
> In story non, ne no man here, I wene;
> And though I wolde, I koude nought, ywys;
> For ther was som epistel hem bitwene,
> That wolde, as seyth myn autour, wel contene
> Neigh half this book, of which hym liste nought write.
> How sholde I thanne a lyne of it endite?
>
> (III, 491–504)

Here the whole problem of literary freedom, tradition and necessity takes on a fascinating formal complexity.[27] For the problem is, substantially, one of form as conceived by the literary tradition ('I have naught herd it don er this / In story non'). The 'sentence' of the 'auctour' will be fully conveyed, as we have seen, but its form is a particular problem, which is resolved by means of predetermination and teleology. Significantly the Narrator, without mentioning it, and indeed involving both himself and Pandarus, paraphrases an idea from Geoffrey of Vinsauf, 'maister soverayn' of the formal *ars poetica*:

For everi wight that hath an hous to founde
Ne renneth naught the work for to bygynne
With rakel hond, but he wol bide a stounde,   *rash*
And sende his hertes line out fro withinne
Aldirfirst his purpos for to wynne.
Al this Pandare in his herte thoughte,
And caste his werk ful wisely or he wroughte.
(I, 1065–71)[28]

The 'hertes line' governs the construction with a precise 'purpos', and the artist is an architect or, more modestly, a draughtsman, just as Dante, when he wants to measure the circle of the Incarnation, is the draughtsman of the beatific vision.

The self-consciousness of this Narrator is even expressed metalinguistically. He pays particular attention to language; when he wants to indicate that Criseyde stands out among all the beauties of Troy, he uses a linguistic simile: 'Right as oure firste lettre is now an A'. Nor can a Narrator who manipulates 'authorial' texts in three different languages – Italian, Latin and French – be unaware of the problem of translation. When he transcribes Petrarch's sonnet (attributing it to Lollius), he takes pains to point out that his version conveys not only the 'sentence', but 'plainly...every word', 'save oure tonges difference'. Later, when he declares that he will not write 'of sentement', he adds that he is translating 'out of Latyn in my tonge' (II, 14). And finally his linguistic consciousness is transformed into historical consciousness: language is the measure of time and difference:

Ye knowe ek that in forme of speche is chaunge
Withinne a thousand yeer, and wordes tho
That hadden pris, now wonder nyce and straunge
Us thinketh hem, and yet thei spake hem so,
And spedde as wel in love as men now do;
Ek for to wynnen love in sondry ages,
In sondry londes, sondry ben usages.
(II, 22–8)

This is not only a fictitious excuse: however contradictory it may seem, the Narrator and his characters are in fact speaking of love in the manner of noble fourteenth-century lovers (and, after all, the language of the poem is the English of that century!). But behind this contemporary or 'medievalised' language, as Lewis would call it, there is a great cultural stratification. Troilus, for instance, before his crucial meeting with Criseyde, fearfully invokes the aid of almost all the gods of Olympus, with a wealth of mythological references. And the Narrator does almost the same thing in his proems. In other words, this consciousness of language is not evident only *a posteriori*, six centuries after the book was finished. It is also there, *in fieri*, in the poem. Consider the episode when Pandarus encourages his friend and promises to do all he can to help him win Criseyde, and Troilus takes heart once more. Boccaccio writes:

> Udiva Troiol Pandaro contento
> sì nella mente, ch'esser gli parea
> *quasi già fuor di tutto il suo tormento,*
> e più nel suo amor si raccendea . . .
> (*Filostrato*, II, 29, 1–4)

Chaucer, obviously with an eye on his author, puts it this way:

> Whan Troilus hadde herd Pandare assented
> To ben his help in lovyng of Crysedye,
> Weex of his wo, *as who seith, untormented,*
> But hotter weex his love . . .
> (I, 1009–12)

According to the *Oxford English Dictionary*, this was the first appearance in English of the word 'untormented': this, and the presence of the so similar and yet so different Boccaccian model, are already significant facts. But the most important element of the expression is 'as who seith', which serves here not only to fill out the line and to underline the oral nature of the *Troilus* but also, and especially, to reveal Chaucer's whole linguistic operation, his reflection on the 'forme of speche', the way he translates and reinvents – 'save oure tonges difference' – his author's poetic language. We can imagine the effect 'untormented' must have had on his contemporary readers and listeners; the word 'torment' was of course not new to them (especially in the sense of 'physical torture'), but they had probably never heard the negative participle (nor, if they had, would Chaucer have prefixed 'as who seith').

Behind him the story, before him the book. All that lies in between, everything I have spoken about so far (including the audience) is the Narrator's 'matere'. Later, the sphere of the book will include him too, as we shall see. But meanwhile, the matter that takes shape before our eyes is extremely wide. It includes, for example, the relationship that the Narrator, modelling himself on Boccaccio, Dante and the classics, establishes with the forces that inspire the poem and dominate the proems of the first four books: Tisiphone, the 'cruwel Furie', the 'goddesse of torment', of whom the Narrator, in announcing the tragic theme ('the double sorwe') of the work, proclaims himself the 'sorwful instrument' (I, 7–11); Clio, the Muse of History, whom he invokes at the beginning of Book II; Venus and Calliope, to whom he turns in the Proem to Book III;

Venus, Cupid and all the Muses, whom he thanks at the end of the same book; the Erinyes, 'Nyghtes doughtren'; Mars, from whom he takes his inspiration in Book IV; and lastly the Parcae, who, though they are not invoked, are mentioned as 'executrices', at Jove's 'disposicioun' of the 'fatal destyne' of Troilus in Book v (1–7). These serve as indications of the specific narrative, poetic and emotional register that will govern a particular section of the work; at the same time they are parts of the complex system of forces that dominate the action; finally, they are instruments by which the poet tries to weave Heaven and Earth into his poem – aiming at the sublime style. The presence of Tisiphone, for example, is felt throughout the romance, which the poet himself will call a 'tragedy'; Clio, Muse of historical narration, corresponds to the 'neutral' progress of Book II; the Erinyes appropriately open Book IV, where the parabola begins its descending curve. But the most famous case, and the one that is best realised poetically, is that of Venus, who presides over Book III, and whose praises the Narrator sings with a magnificence only partly derived from Boccaccio:[29]

> O blisful light, of which the bemes clere
> Adorneth al the thridde heven faire!
> O sonnes lief, O Joves doughter deere, *beloved*
> Plesance of love, O goodly debonaire,
> In gentil hertes ay redy to repaire! *find a home*
> O veray cause of heele and of gladnesse,
> Iheryed be thy myght and thi goodnesse!
> (III, 1–7)

And so on for five more stanzas, in which Venus is hailed as the fount of peace, principle of virtue, unifying force and lawmaker of the universe. In this book is the culmination of Troilus's earthly story, and later he himself echoes his author's voice in his song, reminiscent of Boethius:

> 'Love, that of erthe and se hath governaunce,
> Love, that his hestes hath in hevenes hye,
> Love, that with an holsom alliaunce
> Halt peples joyned . . .'
> (III, 1744ff)

Moreover, the Narrator speaks directly of the forces that dominate the story of Troilus – first of all, that of love:

> For evere it was, and evere it shal byfalle,
> That Love is he that alle thing may bynde,
> For may no man fordon the lawe of kynde.
> (I, 236–8)

Here we see again the idea Chaucer brought out in the *Parliament of Fowls*. But a little earlier, also in Book I, a long proverbial exclamation by the Narrator, about Troilus's blindness in laughing at lovers, anticipates the parabola of the hero, who is now 'clomben on the staire' but soon will have to descend (I, 211–17). While Troilus's career is still in its ascending phase, and he passes, a knight in shining armour, before Criseyde's window, the Narrator casually introduces the theme of necessity that will dominate in the last two books:

> With that com he and al his folk anoon
> An esy pas rydyng, in routes tweyne,
> Ryght as his happy day was, sooth to seyne,
> For which, men seyn, may nought destourbed be *hindered*
> That shal bityden of necessitee.
>
> (II, 619–23)

And even in Book III, which magnificently celebrates the triumph of love, the Narrator clearly indicates, with an author's foresight, the forces that are now, and have always been, at work in the affair:

> But O Fortune, executrice of wyrdes,
> O influences of thise hevenes hye!
> Soth is, that under God ye ben oure hierdes, *shepherds*
> Though to us bestes ben the causes wrie. *concealed*
>
> (III, 617–20)

When these forces emerge clearly in the course of events, the Narrator can refrain from mentioning them himself – for example in the last two books, where he shifts his point of view from the 'distance' of which Bloomfield has spoken[30] to a greater 'impersonality'.

In this light, from the height of his omniscience, the Narrator can also address his characters directly, or speak of them in a tone of both detachment and empathy. Troilus, struck by the arrow of Love, is 'reduced' to a rebellious horse that has been tamed (I, 218–25). The Narrator wishes Troilus good luck, invoking the protection of Janus on him (II, 77). After Troilus has seen Criseyde leave Troy, the Narrator speaks to him directly (V, 27–8). And again, later:

> But Troilus, thow maist now, est or west,
> Pipe in an ivy lef, if that the lest!
>
> (V, 1432–3)

Thus Troilus is always accompanied by the sympathetic and ironically reductive comments of the Narrator. The latter's approach to Criseyde is different: she is the crucial personage in the whole system of characterisation in the work, the one who must necessarily play the part of the villain, but whom the Narrator, as we have seen, always tries to excuse. 'The most obvious and all-important fact about the narrator is that he loves Criseide; not as a lover, though he shares Troilus's boyish idolatry of her, but rather he loves her with something of the avuncular sentimentality that Dickens lavishes on several of his more intolerable heroines.'[31] Donaldson, with precision and brilliant intuition, has described the two types of logic, the logic 'of fact' and that of love, that govern the characterisation of Criseyde: at the end of *Troilus*, he says, Pandarus declares that he hates Criseyde (v, 1732–3), and Troilus that he loves her in spite of everything (v, 1695–9):

These are the two simple attitudes to Criseide that Chaucer has carefully nurtured – simple, but in combination infinitely complex. One of the principal ways he has nurtured them is through his narrator, making him so wholly loving of Criseide that he will do anything to excuse her, and then seeing to it that in the very process of excusing her he will suggest – sometimes most unfairly – reasons for us to distrust and to hate her.[32]

If Criseyde is such a complex character, whom 'every sensitive reader will feel...he really knows' and 'no sensible reader will ever claim...he understands', Troilus proves to be more complex than he appears at first sight. There is no doubt that he is the ideal lover spoken of by critics from C. S. Lewis on; he fully conforms to the courtly ideal, and not with puppet-like rigidity but with deep humanity. Totally overcome by love (truly *filo-strato*), Troilus trembles, blushes, weeps and sings; he becomes the incarnation of every virtue, rejoices, nearly goes mad with grief, despairs. When he finally realises he has lost Criseyde forever, he also understands the truth about his own love for her, that he *cannot* 'unloven' her in spite of all the pain she has made him suffer (v, 1696–701). Yet Troilus lives this love of his, and then Criseyde's departure and her betrayal, in a particular dimension – sentimental, lyrical, even philosophical, but not very active and, if the truth be told, not very 'real'. The Knight of *The Book of the Duchess*, a noble and ideal lover, is nevertheless real: he courts his lady, declares himself to her; even if it is she and only she who grants him her love, he takes the initiative. Troilus, on the other hand, puts all his trust in Pandarus, who literally chases him into Criseyde's bed and undresses him. Later, when he learns that Criseyde is to leave for the Greek camp, Troilus is persuaded by Pandarus to kidnap her and so prevent her from leaving, but only 'if hireself it wolde', and Criseyde persuades him not to do it. It is again Pandarus who persuades him to go and stay for a week with Sarpedon and who urges him to write to Criseyde. When Pandarus no longer knows what to do, Troilus seeks, and finds, death in battle. Charles Muscatine had already noted that no

French romance hero is so 'prostrated by love'; Donaldson, still more justly, calls Troilus the hero of paralysis and inaction.[33] Whether or not Chaucer revised the *Troilus*, and in whatever way,[34] the main additions regarding the character of Troilus, if there were any, are consistent with the character's original outline. The Troilus who, thanks to Pandarus, has finally reached the full happiness of love, sings philosophically, after Boethius, of the universal power of love, which binds all (III, 1744–71); the Troilus who remains after Criseyde's departure meditates, again according to Boethius, on predestination and free will (IV, 958–1078). In both these passages the character's personal, emotional situation is relived by him in terms of his own preoccupations and carried onto a general, philosophical plane. (All this is not really very different from the soliloquies of Elizabethan drama. For example, Hamlet's paralysis, though its motives are different, seems to have a certain affinity with that of Troilus.) Before the monologue on predestination, Chaucer makes his Narrator say that on that day Troilus was so deeply plunged in despair that he intended to die (IV, 954–5); then he has Troilus begin his monologue thus:

> 'For al that comth, comth by necessitee:
> Thus to ben lorn, it is my destinee...'
>
> (IV, 958–9)

The general meditation (958) is always linked with the personal situation (959) and the emotional state (954–5) of the character. Of course this does not mean that the problem of determinism[35] in *Troilus* is resolved simply by transferring it to the context of the character's inner life. It is undoubtedly reflected in the poem's whole action, as a projection partly of the author's own view and more generally of fourteenth-century philosophical polemics.[36] Like Boethius, Chaucer deals with the problem by raising it, in the end, to the plane of eternity. Troilus approaches this at the end, when, although he is 'lost' in terms of what he considers to be his destiny, he rises to the eighth sphere. Although Troilus's final ascent is conceived in terms of Christianity, it is in fact a pagan Troilus who rises to the eighth sphere and is finally sent by Mercury to an unrevealed destination. If Robertson were completely correct,[37] if the tragedy of Troilus were consistently that 'of every mortal sinner', then Minos, recalled by the Narrator (IV, 1188) to his Dantean role, would condemn him to the second circle of Hell, together with many other pagans.[38] Troilus, however, is destined by Mercury for something mysterious, which Chaucer does not wish to specify, but which is certainly not the Christian Hell. It is Chaucer who then rises to the Christian Heaven, to the 'uncircumscript' God. We are left with a fundamental uncertainty, regarding both the pagan Troilus and the Christian Narrator.

And the problem of love, so much discussed by the critics of *Troilus* also needs to be looked at afresh. It is true that both the Narrator (III, 1–42) and Troilus (III, 1744–71) 'celebrate human love as an aspect of the divine love that governs the universe',[39] while at the end of the work Troilus 'dampned al oure werk that foloweth so / The *blynde lust*' (V, 1823–4), and the Narrator, inviting the 'yonge, fresshe folkes' to love God, wonders:

> What nedeth *feynede loves* for to seke?
> (V, 1848)

In his Boethian song to Love, Troilus had said, among other things:

> And if that Love aught lete his bridel go,
> Al that now loveth asondre sholde lepe,
> And lost were al that Love halt now to-hepe.
> (III, 1762–4)

That is exactly what happens in Books IV and V of *Troilus*: love disappears and the whole world is identified by the Narrator with the image of 'brotelnesse' (V, 1832), of fragility; unity is shattered because there is no more love; the universe is in pieces. At the beginning of the same book, the Narrator had said:

> God loveth, and to love wol nought werne.
> (III, 12)

In his song, Troilus echoes and deepens this concept:

> So wolde God, that auctour is of kynde,
> That with his bond Love of his vertu liste
> To cerclen hertes alle, and faste bynde,
> That from his bond no wight the wey out wiste.
> (III, 1765–8)

Earthly love, the love between Troilus and Criseyde, is felt by Troilus and by the Narrator as a part and a reflection of the love that governs the universe. Both are binding forces, forces that create unity. God, who loves, has 'circled' every heart with his bond of love. It is a natural law, and God is the 'auctour . . . of kynde'. But this love is not the love for God and of God that Chaucer defends and celebrates at the end of *Troilus* as the only truth. That love lies beyond, it is more pure and exclusive than the love that governs nature and the human heart: it is love for God in Himself and for the love He has shown towards mankind. Between the two there is a huge qualitative leap, so that whoever manages to comprehend the second may ignore or despise the first. In the scale of perfection, the dichotomy again lies within Christianity.

As a couple, Troilus and Criseyde are affected by all the forces that dominate the action: love, the planets, Fortune. If love is what sets the story in motion, the planets are its aids, and Fortune determines the direction and the end of the whole movement. When Criseyde falls in love with Troilus, on seeing him return from the wars resplendent with the glory of battle, and exclaims, 'Who yaf me drynke?', the Narrator anticipates a possible objection by the audience, who may think:

> 'This was a sodeyn love; how myght it be
> That she so lightly loved Troilus,
> Right for the firste syghte, ye, parde?'
> (II, 667–9)

He replies that Criseyde has not given her love to Troilus, 'but that she gan enclyne / To lyke hym first' (674–9), and finally:

> And also blisful Venus, wel arrayed,
> Sat in hire seventhe hous of hevene tho,
> Disposed wel, and with aspectes payed,   *favourable*
> To helpe sely Troilus of his woo.
> (II, 680–3)

Later, for example, it will be a conjunction of the moon, Saturn and Jove in Cancer that cause the torrential rain that forces Criseyde to spend the night in Pandarus's house and thus favours the consummation of love between her and Troilus. But it is certainly Fortune that governs the love affair. The Narrator reminds us of this even when the two are happy (III, 1714-15). It is the wheel of Fortune, 'executrice of wyrdes', who overwhelms Troilus:

> From Troilus she [Fortune] gan hire brighte face
> Awey to writhe, and tok of hym non heede,
> But caste hym clene out of his lady grace,
> And on hire whiel she sette up Diomede.
> (IV, 8–11)

Together with him, together with Hector who dies, Fortune, the 'ministre general' of God, involves all of Troy in the *Dämmerung*:

> Fortune, which that permutacioun
> Of thynges hath, as it is hire comitted
> Thorugh purveyaunce and disposicioun   *providence*
> Of heighe Jove, as regnes shal be flitted
> Fro folk in folk, or when they shal be smytted,
> Gan pulle awey the fetheres brighte of Troie
> Fro day to day, til they ben bare of joie.
> (V, 1541–7)

Troilus's parabola belongs finally to the great parabola of 'history'. And the parabolic course of the action determined by Fortune explains why Chaucer calls *Troilus* a 'tragedy' (v, 1786). It is a tragedy in the terms indicated by the Monk in the *Canterbury Tales*, and by Boethius:[40]

> Tragedies noon oother maner thyng
> Ne kan in syngyng crie ne biwaille
> But that Fortune alwey wole assaille
> With unwar strook the regnes that been proude.
> (*Monk's Tale*, 2761–4)

What other thyng bywaylen the cryinges of tragedyes but oonly the dedes of Fortune, that with unwar strook overturneth the realmes of greet nobleye? (Glose. Tragedye is to seyn a dite of a prosperite for a tyme, that endeth in wrecchidnesse.)

> (*Boece*, ii, pr. 2, 60–70)

If these are the superior forces that govern the tragedy, there are other forces in the story itself, in the world in which it is set, that assist its development. I mean not only the 'authorial' and 'historical' necessity of which I have already spoken but the system of values incarnated in the society in which Troilus and Criseyde are placed by Chaucer. This is the feudal–courtly system, to whose rules the two lovers must conform. Once Troilus has fallen in love with Criseyde, and Pandarus has set in motion the mechanism of courtship, the first part of the action is more or less decided. Criseyde, left a widow while still young, cannot help feeling the urges of 'love of kynde', as Pandarus well knows. Nor can she help feeling the 'pite' for the suffering Troilus, which, combined with his valour, makes her 'incline' towards Priam's son. In short, 'l'amor, ch'a nullo amato amar perdona' ('love, which absolves no loved one from loving')[41] conditions Criseyde's behaviour. Troilus serves in love, always respectful of his lady's 'name', her honour. He becomes a model of all the knightly virtues, first and foremost of that 'trouthe' which he will never abandon. Just before leaving Troy for the Greek camp, Criseyde reveals to him, in their last conversation, the reasons that made her fall in love with him:

> 'For trusteth wel, that youre estat roial,
> Ne veyn delit, nor only worthinesse
> Of you in werre or torney marcial,
> Ne pompe, array, nobleye, or ek richesse
> Ne made me to rewe on youre destresse;
> But moral vertu, grounded upon trouthe,
> That was the cause I first hadde on yow routhe!
>
> 'Eke gentil herte and manhod that ye hadde,
> And that ye hadde, as me thoughte, in despit

Every thyng that souned into badde,
As rudenesse and poeplissh appetit,
And that youre resoun bridlede youre delit;
This made, aboven every creature,
That I was youre, *and shal while I may dure . . .*'
(IV, 1667–80)

The bond of 'trouthe' is just the point at which, 'slydynge of corage', Criseyde fails, succumbing to Diomedes's courteous and resolute 'avances' and his subtle persuasion. The result leads to the classic triangle of what will in later centuries be the novel of adultery: Criseyde loses her honour forever, Troilus and Diomedes try to kill each other in battle but are prevented by Fortune. Instead, Troilus is killed by Achilles. At the same time Troy is in decline. Antenor, exchanged for Criseyde, betrays the city, as it had initially been betrayed by the foresighted Calchas. The story of Troilus and Criseyde becomes a tragedy of betrayal.

Two characters in *Troilus* act as determining forces in the action, Pandarus in the first part and Diomedes in the second. Troilus and Criseyde are fundamentally victims of love, of the planets, of Fortune and of themselves. On the other hand, Pandarus and Diomedes, while they are also subject to these forces, are active characters. They use the forces for their own ends, though within the ambit of their society's conventions. When Diomedes, as he accompanies Criseyde to the Greek camp, realises from the looks exchanged by her and Troilus that the two are in love, he at once prepares for action, meditating to himself:

'Al my labour shal nat ben on ydel,
If that I may, for somwhat shal I seye.
For at the werste it may yet shorte oure weye.
I have herd seyd ek tymes twyes twelve,
"He is a fool that wole foryete hymselve." '
(V, 94–8)

'There's no harm in trying': Diomedes never forgets this. Unlike Troilus, he at once takes the initiative, exploiting Criseyde's solitude, her state of psychological prostration. Using a series of ably constructed and well-reasoned arguments (V, 106–75 and 855–945), he conquers Criseyde with words: not for nothing is he 'of tonge large'.

The great master of the word, however, is Pandarus, the most securely successful character in the whole work. It is impossible here to describe the wealth of ideas that Chaucer has lavished on this many-faceted character – the unsuccessful lover who laughs at himself, the merry, ironic, wise and comic gentleman, with an endless fund of epigrams and proverbs, master of the language of love, the language of the Court, the language of consolation and of pleasantry. Pandarus reigns supreme in the first three books of *Troilus*, taking inspiration from his own active philosophy of Fortune:

> Quod Pandarus, 'Than blamestow Fortune
> For thow art wroth; ye, now at erst I see.
> Woost thow nat wel that Fortune is comune
> To everi manere wight in som degree?
> And yet thow hast this comfort, lo, parde,
> That, as hire joies moten overgon,
> So mote hire sorwes passen everechon.
>
> 'For if hire whiel stynte any thyng to torne,
> Than cessed she Fortune anon to be.
> Now, sith hire whiel by no way may sojourne,
> What woostow if hire mutabilite
> Right as thyselven list, wol don by the,
> Or that she be naught fer fro thyn helpynge?
> Paraunter thow hast cause for to synge . . .'
>
> (I, 841–54)

Troilus had just said: 'Fortune is my fo'; and Pandarus replies using the mechanism of Fortune itself as a source of hope. Later, when he decides to reveal Troilus's love to Criseyde, Pandarus begins indirectly, telling her that she has had a bit of good fortune:

> 'For to every wight som goodly aventure   *chance*
> Som tyme is shape, if he it kan receyven;
> But if that he wol take of it no cure,
> Whan that it commeth, but wilfully it weyven,
> Lo, neyther cas ne fortune hym deceyven,
> But ryght his verray slouthe and wrecchednesse;
> And swich a wight is for to blame, I gesse . . .'
>
> (II, 281–7)

Afterwards, when Fortune's wheel has twice turned, first giving happiness to Troilus and then taking it away, Pandarus, even while contradicting himself by exclaiming that no one could have imagined such a quick reversal of Fortune (IV, 384–92), continues to exhort Troilus:

> 'Thenk ek Fortune, as wel thiselven woost,
> Helpeth hardy man to his enprise,
> And weyveth wrecches for hire cowardise . . .'
>
> (IV, 600–2)

Of course Pandarus cannot defeat Fortune, whose 'guidicio' ('sentence') is 'occulto come in erba l'angue' ('hidden like a snake in the grass').[42] But he can, so to speak, exploit Fortune's ups and downs, the favourable curve of the wheel. And this is precisely what he does in the first part of the poem: Pandarus is not only a go-between in the literal sense of the word, he is a 'middle-man' between Fortune and man; Pandarus is the architect of Troilus's success, the engineer of the innumerable tricks of the love comedy; above all, he is an engineer of words: in one of the most appropriate phrases used of him by the Narrator, 'This Pandarus gan newe his tonge *affile*'. Criseyde calls him a 'fox'. Pandarus is a Ulysses, almost the Ulysses of Shakespeare's *Troilus*. But there is more to this character: Pandarus acts as a sort of stage manager for the Narrator. He himself declares that through his efforts Troilus will be able to speak directly to Criseyde within two days; the expression he uses in this case is 'yet shall I *shape* it so' (II, 1363). Later the Narrator himself recognises the demiurgic function of his character; Troilus must pretend to be ill in Deiphobus's house, and despite the attentions and remedies offered to him he continues to behave according to Pandarus's directions: 'he held forth ay the wyse / That ye han herd Pandare er this *devyse*' (1547). In the end Pandarus is, if only in jest, as all-seeing as the Narrator and God Himself:

> But God and Pandare wist al what this mente.
>
> (II, 1561)

Pandarus is, implicitly, a Narrator–poet. When, at the end of Book I, he begins to think about how to help Troilus, the Narrator uses for him the simile I have already quoted, where he is compared to the 'wight that hath an hous to founde' – a simile taken from Geoffrey of Vinsauf's *Poetria Nova* and originally applied to the poet who has to organise his material before taking up his pen. Moreover, this simile is indirect. What Chaucer says is that Pandarus 'al this...in his herte thoughte' – that is, he was thinking about what we know, and Chaucer knew, are Geoffrey of Vinsauf's directions to poets. Are Books II and III of *Troilus* Pandarus's poem? Certainly both he and the Narrator often seem to think of his business as a 'tale' (II, 255–73, 305, 1193; III, 769), and certainly Pandarus is a 'maker' who uses words like a poet, to shape, devise and plan. It is significant that in Book IV, and still more in Book V, there is a gradual withdrawal of Pandarus – not so much from the scene, where he is always present, as from the function of shaping, from active and successful devising. Pandarus suggests to Troilus that he should kidnap Criseyde, but when Troilus replies, 'but if hirself it woulde', Pandarus consents. His words, from this point on, are no longer creative, but simply palliative. At the end Pandarus, in contrast to Troilus, can see reality: when Troilus, from the city walls, thinks he sees Criseyde returning, Pandarus points out that what he sees is only a cart. He even goes so far as to advise a *Realpolitik*: Criseyde has gone, so love another woman. But, as the sparrowhawk replies to the goose in the *Parliament*, Troilus responds with the logic of love: 'It lyth nat in his wit, ne in his wille.' Pandarus himself is caught in the toils of this logic, as Troilus points out to him; he can offer no further opposition. And when the factual confirmation arrives that Criseyde has betrayed Troilus for Diomedes, it is one of the saddest moments of the book, because Pandarus, for the first time, does not know what to say to Troilus (v, 1723-5). When he opens his mouth, it is only to condemn his niece; then, 'I kan namoore seye' (v, 1743). And with Pandarus's silence the comedy is really finished: from the end of the story, which, as he himself says, is 'every tales strengthe', Pandarus is absent.

The narrative structure of *Troilus* is profoundly different from that of the dream poems. First of all, the narration, no longer obliged to incarnate abstract problems, extends and broadens out in fullness and variety. The Narrator's voice, with its continual interventions, constitutes a constant point of reference to which the reader feels inexplicably attached. But there are many moments when the Narrator in person is absent, leaving space for his characters, their conversations, their monologues, their songs. Thus a narrative is created that is both bivocal (the Narrator versus all the other characters), and polyphonic. In any single moment of *Troilus*, messages reach the reader from every side. It is not necessary for all the speakers to be on the scene at that particular moment. The reader's memory is continually jogged by the Narrator with references and allusions, both conceptual and verbal. When Pandarus brings Criseyde to visit Troilus, as he feigns illness in Deiphobus's house, he reminds her to behave in a suitable manner:

> ... And inward thus, 'Ful softely bygynne,
> Nece, I conjure and heighly yow defende,
> On his half which that soule us alle sende,
> And in the vertu of corones tweyne,
> Sle naught this man, that hath for yow this peyne!
>
> 'Fy on the devel! thynk which oon he is,
> And in what plit he lith; com of anon!
> Thynk al swich taried tyde, but lost it nys.
> That wol ye bothe seyn, whan ye ben oon.
> Secoundely, ther yet devyneth noon
> Upon yow two; come of now, if ye konne!
> While folk is blent, lo, al the tyme is wonne...'
>   (II, 1732-43)

This hastily murmured little speech is full of references to Pandarus's earlier speeches. 'Sle naught this man', Pandarus had already told his niece (II, 322–5), and indeed the whole first line of attack on Criseyde's reticence was based on just this argument. The first two lines of the second stanza echo the thought of Criseyde herself, as expressed in the famous monologue:

'Ek wel woot I my kynges sone is he;
And sith he hath to se me swich delit,
If I wolde outreliche his sighte flee,
Peraunter he myghte have me in dispit,
Thorugh whicch I myghte stonde in worse plit.
Now were I wis, me hate to purchace,
Withouten nede, ther I may stonde in grace?'
(II, 708–14)

'I thenke ek how he able is for to have
Of al this noble town the thriftieste,
To ben his love, so she hire honour save.
For out and out he is the worthieste,
Save only Ector, which that is the beste;
And yet his lif al lith now in my cure.
But swich is love, and ek myn aventure.'
(II, 736–42)

The third line of the second stanza (II, 1739) refers back to another, more broadly philosophical, speech of Pandarus to Criseyde:

'Thenk ek how elde wasteth every houre
In ech of yow a partie of beautee;
And therfore, er that age the devoure,
Go love; for old, ther wol no wight of the.
Lat this proverbe a loore unto yow be:
"To late ywar, quod beaute, whan it paste";
And elde daunteth daunger at the laste.'
(II, 393–9)

In her monologue, Criseyde had expressed her fears about the dishonour that would result from a publicly acknowledged affair with Troilus (II, 799–805); here (II, 1741–2) Pandarus implicitly replies: no one knows anything yet. Finally, Pandarus's words, 'Sle naught this man, that hath for yow this peyne', recall the earlier laments of Troilus himself (I, 519–39), and the thought that rises spontaneously in Criseyde's mind when Troilus passes, all splendid, on his horse:

For of hire owen thought she wex al reed,
Remembryng hire right thus, 'Lo, this is he
Which that myn uncle swerith he moot be deed,
But I on hym have mercy and pitee.'
(II, 652–5)

And this, in turn, is the 'whi' that the Narrator himself, a few lines later, will offer to the audience as explanation of the first 'inclination' of Criseyde towards Troilus (II, 673–9). This, in fact, is just one example of a narrative technique used constantly throughout the poem, which dominates all the others and weaves a polyphonic web that enmeshes the reader.

The other instrument that Chaucer uses with obvious pleasure is that of conversation – brilliant examples of which can also be found, of course, in the *Book of the Duchess* and the *House of Fame*. In *Troilus*, however, it is not merely instrumental to the narration or the advancement of the action. I shall give just one example, but there are several moments in which conversation is introduced just for the sake of providing a social or convivial interlude, as occurs now and then in *Sir Gawain*. Normally, Pandarus is at the centre of the scene, as here, where he has just tucked Troilus's letter into Criseyde's bosom:

> ... And seyde hire, 'Now cast it awey anon,
> That folk may seen and gauren on us tweye.'
> Quod she, 'I kan abyde til they be gon';
> And gan to smyle, and seyde hym, 'Em, I preye,
> Swich answere as yow list youreself purveye,
> For trewely I nyl no lettre write.'
> 'No? than wol I,' quod he, 'so ye endite.'
>
> Therwith she lough, and seyde, 'Go we dyne.'
> And he gan at hymself to jape faste,
> And seyde, 'Nece, I have so gret a pyne
> For love, that everich other day I faste –'
> And gan his beste japes forth to caste,
> And made hire so to laughe at his folye,
> That she for laughter wende for to dye.
>
> (II, 1156–69)

Just as in this conversation we find humour and play, in others there is melodrama, weeping and despair. The mimetic intention may be more or less consciously present in the writer's mind, but for the reader accustomed to other English medieval romances the effect is undoubtedly one of mimetic liberation, effected without effort, without straining, without deliberately aiming at realism. Lightly, with a few strokes, Chaucer sketches a perspective that it is left to us to fill out and complete.

The same technique inspires the psychological construction of the characters. None of them is purely and simply a narrative agent, as are nearly all the characters of earlier romances. Each of them is sketched with a 'roundedness' of character and psychology: Troilus, Criseyde, Pandarus and Diomedes are human beings who, within the conventions that govern them, think and feel; indeed they were so conceived by Boccaccio. Their

asides, their interior monologues, their external attitudes, both generate
and reflect their motivations, and from the outside the Narrator, with his
continuous interventions, helps to define and deepen this perspective. But
there are limits to this realism, which led Schlauch to identify in *Troilus* a
sort of forerunner of the novel,[43] and these limits are mainly due to the
necessity imposed by the story. Until the author is completely free of
'authorial' ties, his characters cannot be fully rounded, because they must
carry out the narrative functions assigned to them by the source. Not only
that, but psychological realism as we understand it today was far from
the medieval mentality – even from that of Dante and Boccaccio – and it
was particularly alien to the Chaucer of *Troilus*, as it was to the author of
Sir Gawain. These writers were primarily concerned – as, in quite another
field, were Giotto and the Lorenzetti – to fill in the background and sketch
the perspective. Chaucer explicitly leaves it open to the reader to 'encresse'
or 'maken dymynucioun', even to 'correcte' his poem. The centre of
interest for Chaucer and the *Gawain*-poet was not yet the individual in
himself, to whom Ockham reduced all reality, nor was it Petrarch's tormented self-centredness.[44] The character is part of a complex and very
rich tableau, a system of forces as real as they are invisible, a total universe.
Troilus is not, like Piers Plowman, an 'Everyman'; he is Troilus, as
Gawain is Gawain; but primarily both of these are incarnations of ideal
models. And secondarily, especially in the case of Troilus, they are functions
of a much broader emotional and philosophical design – individualised, but
still instrumental.

   If this were not so, there would be no explanation for the lyrical pattern,
which Chaucer expands and makes more consistent in *Troilus* than was
the case in Boccaccio. There are ten lyrical sections in this romance: the
first *Canticus Troili* (I, 400–34), the song of Antigone (II, 827–75),
Criseyde's *aubade* (III, 1422–42), Troilus's *aubade* in reply (III, 1450–70),
Troilus's second *aubade* (III, 1702–8), Troilus's song to Love (III, 1744–71),
Troilus's monologue on predestination (IV, 958–1078), Troilus's *planctus*
(V, 218–45), Troilus's *planctus* on Criseyde's empty palace (V, 540–53), and
the second *Canticus Troili* (V, 638–58). These passages might seem to be
lyrical digressions, but Robert Payne gives a true picture of their nature
and structural aims when he observes that 'Taken as a group, apart from
their individual contexts, these ten lyrics constitute a kind of distillation
of the emotional progress of the poem, held together by a thread of thematic
imagery in much the manner of a very condensed sonnet sequence...
They interrupt the action at each major turn of events.'[45] Hence, given
the division, the structural *dispositio* in five books, and the parabolic curve
of the action with its peak in Book III – a curve that follows the turning of

Fortune's wheel – these lyrics serve as devices to reinforce the poem's organisation. The poetic invocations of the proems, of which I have already spoken, function in the same way. So do the dreams and the prophecies, always placed at strategic points, from the 'calkulynge' of Calchas at the beginning of Book I, through the continual admonitory references of the Narrator, to his direct prophetic intervention on Antenor's betrayal (iv, 201-10), to Calchas's prophecies recalled by Diomedes to Criseyde (v, 883-924); from Criseyde's dream after Antigone's song (ii, 925-31), to the dream of Troilus that prefigures the lady's betrayal (v, 1233-41), shortly after Pandarus's speech on dreams ('A straw for alle swevenes signifiaunce!'), followed by another reply from Pandarus himself regarding dreams and their senselessness (v, 358-85 and 1275-88). Thus the poem's framework is continually broadened beyond the limits of the narrative: the *romance* tends towards the *novel* by way of Boethian tragedy, Pandaresque comedy, sparkling social conversation, songs, lyrics, melodrama, philosophical monologue and the poetic invocation of the 'sublime' style and of the classics. It is undoubtedly unique in European narrative.

Let us consider, for example, the temporal and spatial dimensions of *Troilus*, as we have done in chapter 3 for *Sir Gawain*. Over thirty years ago Henry Sams pointed out that *Troilus* has a double time scheme.[46] There are two complete and concentric circles: one 'factual' and 'basic', of three years; the other, 'artistic', of one year, 'or the coming and departure of one summer'. The second is marked by a series of images and similes, beginning with winter:

> But also cold in love towardes the
> Thi lady is, as frost in wynter moone,
> And thow fordon, as snow in fire is soone.
>
> (I, 523-5)

These are followed by images of spring (ii, 764-8 and 967-82), and the series culminates with summer (iii, 351-7), to fall afterwards with Dante's autumn simile, which Chaucer, significantly, changes to winter:

> And as in wynter leves ben biraft,
> Ech after other, til the tree be bare,
> So that ther nys but bark and braunche ilaft,
> Lith Troilus, byraft of ech welfare,
> Ibounden in the blake bark of care.
>
> (iv, 225-9)

This temporal circle, like the lyrical one, 'plots out the curve of emotional tension through the poem' – that is, it serves to reinforce the organisation. But actually there are many strata of time in *Troilus*. There is mythological time, in which Troy exists and falls, and within which, projected forward, is Antenor's future betrayal; again within this time is a past that is both literary (the 'romaunce...of Thebes' read by Criseyde and her women)[47] and 'historial' (the story of Thebes evoked by Cassandra). Innumerable mythical and temporal parentheses open up every time a god or hero of classical mythology is evoked. From the narrative point of view, the mythological time of Troy is a 'historial' time, within which is situated the fictional time in which the story of Troilus and Criseyde takes place – that is, the first of the two circles described by Sams. Then, at the centre, there is the time of the author and his original audience, the 'here and now' of the performance, the present in which the Narrator addresses his listeners. And finally, there is the time of the book's language: first, the past, the thousand years that have changed the 'forme of speche' since Troilus's age (II, 22–49); secondly – a bridge between past and present – the story that becomes a book, *this* 'litel bok', which will take its place in the poetic tradition of the classics (v, 1786–92); and thirdly the link between present and future, when the author shows himself worried about his poem's 'miswriting' and 'mismetring' by future scribes (v, 1793–9), in other words about its publication in manuscript (and its future fame). As Chaucer wrote in his lines to Adam, his scribe:

> ... if ever it thee bifalle
> Boece or *Troylus* for to wryten newe ...
> But after my makyng thou wryte more trewe ...

At the end of the work, the various levels of time are united: Troy falls (v, 1541–8), *exeunt* Criseyde, Diomedes, Pandarus (v, 1085–1743). Troilus stands alone before Achilles and death. Without a narrative pause (but after a parenthesis of the Narrator), Troilus, still within fictional time ('and whan': v, 1807), is removed beyond time (v, 1807–27), to a meta-time towards which the Narrator directs his listeners, inviting them to turn towards God, who 'first starf, and roos, and sit in hevene above', introducing them to the 'archaeological' time-gap of civilisation, religion and literature ('Lo here, of payens corsed olde rites...': v, 1849–55) – in other words, he detaches them from earthly time, to make them leap to the 'oon, and two, and thre, eterne on lyve': from time to eternity, like Dante.

The treatment of the spatial dimension is slightly different. We have the 'here' of the recitation and the audience, defined by the Narrator with his continual interventions. This space is visualised by the modern reader as a sort of circle – in fact it was seen that way by the anonymous miniaturist of the manuscript of *Troilus* at Corpus Christi College in Cambridge.[48]

Here space, too, is functional to the narrative: Criseyde's window before which Troilus passes, the room in Deiphobus's house where the lovers meet, the 'stewe' in which Troilus hides in Pandarus's house, where their love is consummated – the classical *locus* of comedy. There is also an emotionally charged space: the garden where Antigone sings her song; Criseyde's empty palace, over which Troilus weeps; the walls of Troy, from which he sees the plain and the cart that passes through it instead of Criseyde. There is a dramatic space: Troy, on the one hand, the Greek camp on the other, 'upon that other syde', as the Narrator, like a playwright, says: the Greek camp prevails towards the end of the story; Troy dominates the whole poem emotionally, until Troilus and Diomedes meet in battle on the open field. There is a social space: the temple where the Trojans worship the Palladium, the streets of the city through which Troilus passes, the gardens, the place of the 'parlement', and above all the palace rooms, the 'parlours' and 'closets' where the meetings, the dinners and the brilliant verbal skirmishes of Pandarus take place. And there is a private space, which reduces basically to the bed: here Troilus and Criseyde are free to think, to dream, to lament – but not, at first, to make love, because Pandarus is still there. This is one of the moments of greatest spatial concentration in *Troilus*: outdoors it is raining hard; indoors, in the room, Troilus is finally in bed with Criseyde; Pandarus moves away and puts the candle on the mantelpiece. Though it does not have the continued, pointed intensity of *Sir Gawain*, this is the most spatially mimetic moment of *Troilus*. Conversely, at the end of the poem, space opens out into an immense perspective: Troilus rises to the eighth sphere and contemplates from above 'this litel spot of erthe', while above him is the sky, that Heaven to which Chaucer directs all his readers.

We have now, in conclusion, to close the circle that we found open at the start: behind Chaucer the story, before him the book: 'go, litel bok'. But at the beginning and at the end there is God:

> And ek for me preieth to God so dere
> That I have myght to shewe, in som manere,
> Swich peyne and wo as Loves folk endure,
> In Troilus unsely aventure.
>
> (I, 32–5)

> Go, litel bok, go, litel myn tragedye,
> Ther God thi makere yet, er that he dye,
> So sende myght to make in som comedye!
> (v, 1786–8)

Evidently for this author–Narrator there is a relationship – close, even if not precisely defined – between God, inspiration and the poetic 'myght' to realise it; between God, the supreme Maker, and the 'makers' of tragedies and comedies. Just as there is a mysterious way in which God, through his minister Fortune, acts with prescience, but outside predestination, in the world and on Man.[49] Ultimately, God lies behind the *fictio*: the dichotomy between this story (the tragedy of an earthly love) and the truth (that of God who, 'right for *love* / Upon a crois...first starf') remains, but in the fourteenth century this was completely natural. Was it not Petrarch's eternal dilemma? And is it not at least curious that Chaucer prayed God to give him the strength to write a 'comedye', just at the moment when he was preparing to end his tragedy, with the solemn and heartfelt words that resound with the echo of that 'Comedy' which would later be called 'Divine'?

Chaucer could not rewrite that Comedy: he was prevented partly by 'the forme of olde clerkis speche / In poetrie' – the constraint of the story – and partly by the contradiction, which he evidently felt as lacerating, between that love which, in the 'yonge, fresshe folkes', grows with the flowering of the years, that love which is the 'lawe of kynde' instilled by God ('that after his ymage yow made'), and 'blynde lust'; between the vanity of the world, its fragility ('worldly vanite' and 'false worldes brotelnesse'), and, on the other hand, its flowering, festive but ephemeral beauty: 'and thynketh al nys but a faire / This world, that passeth soone as floures faire'.[50]

Thus, after demonstrating his 'myght' to produce the 'litel bok', after choosing the particular story to insert into history, after creating a Narrator and an audience; after exploiting the French and Italian lyric; after inventing the language of Pandarus, Troilus and Criseyde[51] – joining in one book, so to speak, 'verses of love and tales of romance', proverb and jest, interior monologue and social dialogue, comic invention, melodrama and philosophical meditation – after invoking God, Venus, the Muses, the Furies; after setting in motion the mechanisms of classical mythology and natural and astronomical images; after creating space and time to shape a wholly literary universe, which includes Narrator, audience, characters, story, 'historia' and meta-history – after doing all this, Chaucer could not fail to realise the profound ambiguity of his poem.[52] *Troilus* is a book such as no one had ever yet seen in England or in Europe: neither Chrétien nor Gottfried nor Wolfram nor Boccaccio had ever expanded the romance, horizontally and vertically, as far as Chaucer did with *Troilus*. Nor had the *Roman de la Rose* been so articulate, compact and alive as the work Chaucer constructed with so much care – a work that is, to all effects, impossible to catalogue among all the various forms of European narrative. Western literature was never again to see such a book, unless, *mutatis mutandis*, with Joyce's *Ulysses*: not with the *Faerie Queene*, which lacks several of Chaucer's comic registers, not with the bourgeois novel, which lacks the higher registers. Some Elizabethan dramas come near it – *Hamlet*, *King Lear*, certainly not *Troilus and Cressida* – but these are not verse narratives. Like *Sir Gawain*, but for completely different reasons, *Troilus* remains an isolated monument: Henryson felt the need to add to it; Shakespeare, apparently, ignored it; Dryden built on Shakespeare's ruins. Perhaps Chaucer's unconscious desire was to create a work that could stand as narrative parallel to the *Divine Comedy*, with all its many levels of style and meaning. But the *Divine Comedy* is not made of the story of Paolo and Francesca alone.

At this point, what could Chaucer do but pray to God that the public might understand his work (v, 1797–8)? He had made it both closed and open, on the one hand giving it 'fyn' and 'sentence' and on the other leaving it to the correction of those 'that felyng han in loves art'. While praying Venus to inspire his 'sentement', he had announced that he would write 'of no sentement'; he had shown his awareness of the language, its functioning and its passing. Now he ends the work by closing it on the one hand and leaving it open on the other. The 'litel bok' had to be 'subgit' to all poetry (v, 1790), paying obeisance to Virgil, Ovid, Homer, Lucan and Statius – in short, the humble 'sesto tra cotanto senno' ('sixth amid so much wisdom').[53] But, at the same time, the reader had to beware of the classics:

> Lo here, the forme of olde clerkis speche
> In poetrie, if ye hire bokes seche.
> (v, 1854–5)

In a thousand years a language changes (especially English). Meanwhile, the poet hopes no one will bastardise the text, which he evidently presumes will last a long time:

> And for there is so gret diversite
> In Englissh and in writyng of oure tonge,
> So prey I God that non myswrite the,
> Ne the mysmetre for defaute of tonge.
> (v, 1793–6)

Here, the text is closed in itself; the author, albeit through the expression of a modest and sensible realism, declares it complete. But he reopens it shortly afterwards: as he had entrusted his book to the servants of love, he now entrusts it to the correction and the *placet* of his poet friend Gower and his philosopher friend Strode (v, 1856–9).

The last fourteen stanzas of *Troilus* are a continual play between the

Narrator and his book. The polyphony, which in the poem involved all the characters as well as the Narrator, is now carried on within his voice alone. He often detaches himself from his book, always returns to it with love. He refers to 'historial' books, says he would like to write different books, prays to be able to write a comedy. But then he completes his story with Troilus's death and his final ascent. Yet again he detaches himself, speaking of Christian morality and Christian love, then immediately reveals his love for this work of his, entrusting it to the 'benignites and zeles goode' of his friends. Only in the last ten lines does Chaucer finally turn away from his book, to address himself to the Infinite; now, with the words of one who, in his poem, had contemplated God, he ends his fiction in truth: when one has found the beginning of everything, as Dante had said, there is nothing more to look for, and hence 'in ipso Deo terminatur tractatus'.[54]

3 The narrative collection

After examining Chaucer's dream poems, I moved into the field of romance; there, passing over the *Anelida*, I analysed the successful *Troilus*. Now I come to the type of narrative for which Chaucer is best known, the narrative collection. Chaucer's interest in the framed collection was quite natural: it suited his own inclinations, and this type of composition was very popular in England and in Europe during the fourteenth century. The three incomplete books of the *House of Fame* may or may not have been intended as a huge prologue-frame for a planned collection of stories, but in any case the 'tydynges' sought there by Geoffrey certainly cover a vast narrative range – marriages, journeys, love, death, animals, the whole natural and human universe. It is clear, in other words, that as early as the period of the *House of Fame* Chaucer felt the need to go beyond the love poem, even in narrative form – in other words, beyond the *Book of the Duchess*. With the *Parliament* and *Troilus*, Chaucer responded to the problems of narrative in different ways, accepting and at the same time transforming traditional structures and themes. But these solutions were temporary, and in any case unsatisfactory: dichotomy and ambiguity remain in these works as signs of a tentative approach, a continual experimentation, even though they were crowned with great poetic success.

Now, in the uncertain chronology of Chaucer's works, two things are certain: first, that the Prologue to the *Legend of Good Women* was written after the dream poems, after the translations of Boethius and the *Roman*, after *Troilus* and after the narratives that became the *Knight's Tale* and the *Second Nun's Tale*; secondly, while at least part of the *Canterbury Tales* was composed after the *Legend* as we have it, when Chaucer wrote the introduction to the *Man of Law's Tale*, he seemed still to be planning to continue the *Legend* itself.[1] Thus the two narrative collections seem to belong, in a sense, to one structural–narrative impulse, within the same period of time – just as the *Anelida*, the first version of the *Knight's Tale*, and *Troilus* seem to be linked – that is to say, they are all in the field of romance and all in some way dependent on Boccaccio's *Teseida*. Moreover, Gower's *Confessio Amantis* was probably composed shortly before the writing of at least one of the versions of the Prologue to the *Legend*.[2] Thus, without going into the intricate problem of the chronology of Chaucer and his contemporaries, it is evident that during the last fifteen years of the fourteenth century, two of the greatest English intellectuals and artists concentrated on the structure of the narrative collection. This has been already noted in the chapter on Gower; the point here is simply to recall the general context, so that Chaucer can be properly placed within it.

In the *Legend* and in the *Tales*, Chaucer gives two structurally different solutions to the problem of the framed composition: keeping Shklovsky's categories in mind,[3] we may say that, while in the *Legend* the device of the frame-tale is 'motivated', in the *Canterbury Tales* it is 'occasional'. That is to say, in the Prologue to the former, the task of narrating the legends is imposed on the narrator as a penance for having offended the God of Love; in the General Prologue to the latter, on the other hand, the only motive for telling the stories is to entertain the pilgrims as they travel to Canterbury. There is another, typological difference: the *Legend* combines the love dream (in the Prologue) with the narrative collection, whereas the General Prologue to the *Tales*, whatever else may be said about it, is meant to reproduce a real situation. Finally there is a difference in the mode of presentation: the stories of the *Legend* are told by a narrator who seems to be Chaucer himself. They are provided with a unifying thematic thread, but between them there are no 'dramatic' links based on the action. Moreover, one gets the distinct impression that these stories were conceived as 'written' from the very start. In the *Tales*, Chaucer appears as one of the pilgrim-narrators, and at the same time as a narrator–reporter, while most of the stories are purportedly narrated by the other pilgrims; the oral illusion and the written reality are intermingled; finally, there is a dramatic action – albeit sketchy and incomplete – which links each story to the next, at least within each section.

In the *Legend*, in fact, the Prologue opens the door to a series of chambers painted with scenes all centred on the same theme; the rooms have nothing in common except their contiguity, and the narration is therefore governed by a sort of structural metonymy.[4] In this sense, the body of the *Legend* – the nine legends – resembles the type elaborated by Boccaccio in his *De Claris Mulieribus*, just as the body of the *Monk's Tale* – the series of tragedies – is typologically related to Boccaccio's *De Casibus*. Structurally, the nine medallions of the legends are the most 'neoclassical' structure ever created by Chaucer, behind the utterly 'Gothic' façade of the Prologue.

Let us now examine the Prologue and the nine legends that make up this work. In the first place, the Prologue has reached us in two versions, now called 'F' and 'G', of which the second, slightly shorter than the first and extant in only one manuscript, is generally considered to be the later one. Between the two there are a few differences, some of them significant, but there is no reason not to consider them together, following the implicit suggestion of the editors who, from Skeat on, have printed them as parallel texts. The Prologue belongs to the structural stereotype of 'books–dreams–experience', which also includes the dream poems, and it is one of the most delicate, complex and brilliant inventions that Chaucer ever worked out. After opening with a typically Chaucerian discussion on the validity of 'experimental' and 'authorial' proofs – in other words proof from experience and from books (F 1–28: G 1–28), the Prologue then branches out into an apparently disorderly series of arabesques. The poet declares that he writes in honour of those who serve 'lef or flour'; then, recalling the initial stanzas of the *Filostrato*, in which Boccaccio dedicates his romance to 'Filomena', the lady-Muse, he reveals that he himself serves his flower, presumably the daisy.[5] And then the marvellous vision begins.

One night in May the poet has his bed made up in his small back garden, among the flowers. There he falls asleep and begins to dream.[6] In his dream he finds himself in the beautiful garden we recognise from the dream poems, here described with renewed vigour and marvellous freshness. The birds, like those in the *Parliament*, sing the praises of St Valentine, on whose day they choose their mates. Then a lark announces the arrival of the God of Love, who is accompanied by his queen, dressed all in green and crowned with white pearls, looking extraordinarily like a daisy. The two are followed by nineteen 'ladyes' and a great number of women, who all kneel before the queen, then rise and dance around her, singing a ballad 'in carole-wyse'.[7]

At the end of the song, the whole company sits down on the grass. The God of Love notices the poet and asks him what he, his mortal enemy, is doing there: has he not translated the *Roman de la Rose*, which is a heresy against the law of Love? Has he not written *Troilus*, in which a lady, Criseyde, is shown betraying a man? And yet he himself possesses at least sixty books, 'olde and newe', that speak well of women: is this not the case with Livy, Claudian, Ovid, St Jerome and Vincent of Beauvais?[8] Surely the poet must repent having written such things. A lady, however, defends the accused, saying that his offence was unintentional and recalling the works written by the poet in his youth, in praise of love. The lady pardons him in the name of the God of Love, and imposes a penance: he must write

> a glorious legende
> Of goode women, maydenes and wyves,
> That were trewe in lovynge al here lyves;
> And telle of false men that hem betrayen. (G 473–6)

On finishing the book, the poet is to present it to the queen, 'at Eltham or at Sheene'.[9] Love smiles, and reveals that the lady who has been speaking is in fact Alceste, the faithful queen who was transformed into a daisy, whom the poet had not recognised, and whom, above all, he had not celebrated in poetry. It is further decreed that the 'Legend' should begin with the story of Cleopatra, that it should speak of the other ladies seated on the grass,[10] and that it should tell of Alceste. Finally, the stories are to be short, treating only of the 'grete' part of the various women's lives.[11]

At these words, the poet takes up his books and begins to compose the *Legend*; in the G version, he awakens and begins writing. The Prologue ends, and the nine legends follow: Cleopatra, Thisbe, Dido, Hypsipyle and Medea, Lucrece, Ariadne, Philomela, Phyllis, Hypermestra. The last is incomplete; the story of Alceste announced in the Prologue is lacking, as are the other legends that Chaucer, at least up to a certain date, had intended to write.

Structurally, then, this Prologue clearly provides the motivation for the collection of stories. The mechanism is fairly simple in both versions: the poet has transgressed the laws of Love in the *Romaunt* and in *Troilus* and must atone with a series of narratives of a contrary tendency. This motif of transgression and penance, with the anti-woman/pro-woman antithesis, belongs to a tradition dating back to antiquity. However, it is equally clear that the Prologue actually contains many stratified motifs and motivations and that altogether it constitutes a very complex frame – or, more precisely, a frontispiece – for what follows.[12] In this context the differences between the F and G versions are significant but not of major importance.

At the centre of the Prologue, in both versions, stands the extraordinary figure of Alceste – the daisy, the queen, the narrator's 'heart's ease' – a model of *fin amors* and particularly of 'wifhod'. Towards the end of the Prologue, when the poet, instructed by the God of Love, finally recognises the lady,[13] he does so in revealing words, the same in both versions:

> And I answerde ayen, and seyde, 'Yis,
> Now knowe I hire. And is this goode Alceste,
> The dayesye, and myn owene hertes reste? . . .'
>
> (G 505–7)

> '. . . thow wost that calandier is she
> Of goodnesse, for she taughte of fyn lovynge,
> And namely of wifhod the lyvynge,
> And alle the boundes that she oughte kepe . . .'
>
> (G 533–6)

Thus the feminine figure at the centre of the Prologue is presented on different levels. In the first place, she is both inside and outside the dream

– in the dream experience and in the ritual of his daily life: the daisy is, in fact, an object of veneration for the poet every day of the spring, as he walks through the meadows in search of it. At the same time, it is the central image of his dream. Following a pattern typical of dreams, the poet finds in his dream what he looks for in waking life.

In the second place, the identification between Alceste and the lady of the poet's heart is, as we have seen, present in both versions. F, apparently the older version, is in this respect more complete than G: the latter lacks the passage derived from the initial stanzas of the *Filostrato*, as well as Alceste's command that the poet should deliver his finished book to the queen at Eltham or Shene. If F is really earlier than G, it seems obvious that Chaucer, who in *Troilus* had discarded those lines of Boccaccio's, was trying now, in the *Legend*, to construct a *senhal* modelled on that created by Boccaccio with the dedication to Filomena. The 'Lady' of F thus becomes a Muse who can inspire him in the manner of Laura and Fiammetta. Of course, this design does not have the coherence of the myths created by Boccaccio and Petrarch, and indeed Chaucer dropped it in the G version (if this is the later one), but it is enriched by an element that is perhaps even more precious – an implicit identity between Alceste – the daisy, the Muse, the queen of Love, the paragon of 'fyn lovynge' and 'wifhod' – and Anne of Bohemia, Richard II's queen, at the centre of the splendid English Court. The God of Love himself, 'god' and 'King', as both versions affirm (F 431; G 421), can in a way be seen as an allusion to Richard. Certainly in both versions the mention of the 'leef' and the 'flour' – that is, of the two chivalric orders into which Richard's Court was divided for the game of the *demandes d'amour* – is quite explicit. In this way, the Prologue to the *Legend*, especially in the F version, may be said to belong to that courtly and festive 'play' to which Gower's *Confessio Amantis* also belongs: the composition of the *Confessio*, the poet declared in the early version, had been ordered by King Richard, whom Gower met one day in a boat on the river. We are, then, in a courtly atmosphere, in the literal sense of the word. In fact the terms 'Ricardian' and 'Bohemian'[14] have been used, with regard to the *Legend*, to indicate the splendid fabric of the poem: the oriental pearl, the ritual, the decorations. It is an element that also belongs to the international Gothic and, for that matter, can be found in Boccaccio's celebrations of the Angevin Court at Naples. In a certain sense Chaucer seems, in the *Legend*, to return to the environment of the *Book of the Duchess* – the world of John of Gaunt and Blanche of Lancaster. At any rate there is an affinity between Alceste and the 'goode faire Whit' of the earlier work: both are supreme models of 'fyn lovynge', and *namely*, of 'wifhod' (and here we see once again

Chaucer's typical view of the relationship, not only compatibility but close connection, between courtly love and marriage).

However, the similarities between the two works end here; the *Legend* is much richer, more lyrically expansive and more varied, than the *Book of the Duchess*. The tradition of the 'marguerite-poems' was begun by the French – by Machaut, Froissart, Deschamps; Chaucer elaborated this, at least initially, with elements taken from Boccaccio and Petrarch. He set his dream in a framework of Ricardian ritual and classical myth, adding, as we shall see, a play on the daisy/pearl ambiguity. Indeed, he enriched classical tradition, in an ultra-Ovidian spirit, with the metamorphosis of Alceste into a daisy (F 512: G 500) and her eventual 'stellification' (F 525: G 513), and he identified the daisy, a symbol of perfect courtly love, with the pearl, a symbol of virginal purity and hence of divine love. What Chaucer does in the Prologue to the *Legend of Good Women*, then, is to construct a real 'legend' in today's sense of the word:[15] it is, as John Norton-Smith rightly says, a 'mythopoeic' operation.[16] Every means is used to this end: the description of the *locus amoenus*, perhaps the most dreamlike of those created by Chaucer; the birds' song to St Valentine, suggesting the themes of the *Parliament*; the ballad in honour of Alceste (or 'my lady' in F); the carol and the procession of ladies, the rite dedicated to the daisy. Chaucer boldly enters that world of faerie described in *Sir Orfeo* and *Sir Launfal*, and splendidly evoked by Gower in the story of Rosiphelee; he makes it his own by inventing for it several new meanings, containing all the most precious ideas offered to him by ancient and modern tradition.

All this, of course, could not have been meant simply as a rhetorical and structural device to embellish the text and broaden the motivations of the 'frontispiece'. It is true that the penance imposed by Alceste, the writing of the legends, is thus enriched with deeper motives – the pressure from the Court, perhaps from the queen herself, and the celebration of love. But it is also clear, on the one hand, that the Prologue is not devoted solely to these themes and on the other hand, that we are dealing with one more of Chaucer's numerous experiments in the art of poetic narrative. These two facts are connected. The underlying motives of the Prologue are the subject of a whole chapter in Robert Payne's book – all of which, as the title indicates, is inspired by ideas based on the Prologue. This Prologue is more concerned with poetry than any of Chaucer's other works; it examines the problems of poetry, first discursively, then in a figurative and symbolic manner. In the introduction (the first 195 lines in F: 88 in G)

The thematic pattern . . . is a movement back and forth between 'experience' and 'books', which might be roughly equated with pragmatic and traditionalist approaches to knowledge, and their respective attractions for the poet. At first this movement seems to be between wholly differentiated and apparently irreconcilable opposites, but in the epideictic apotheosis of the daisy, the pragmatic and the traditional become complementary, through the implication that tradition preserves at the level of generalised (universal) applicability the meanings or values of the facts of experience, so that the poet may identify them, may rightly order and direct his responses to them.[17]

In the Prologue's central passage, which Payne identifies in the ballad and the ladies' act of homage to Alceste, these conclusions are expressed figuratively and enriched by a further element:

The real daisy of the poet's own world becomes the ideal daisy of his visionary version of that world and then becomes, in turn, the Alceste who combines the natural [daisy] and the ideal [the daisy of the dream, the ideal of love] with the traditional past [classical myth]. Or perhaps the formula can be put another way: the ladies' recognition of Alceste is recognition of a possible identity of experience, vision and books.[18]

The solution to the problem that occupied Chaucer in the dream poems and in *Troilus* seems close at hand, if not actually achieved. But the God of Love, reproving the poet, 'throws the question back to fundamental matters of operation':

> Ek al the world of autours maystow here,
> Cristene and hethene, trete of swich matere;
> It nedeth nat al day thus for to endite.
> But yit, I seye, what eyleth the to wryte
> The draf of storyes, and forgete the corn?
> By Seynt Venus, of whom that I was born,
> Althogh thow reneyed hast my lay,
> As othere olde foles many a day,
> Thow shalt repente it, so that it shal be sene!
> (G 308–16)

'The poet', says Payne, 'must *know* truth, must himself know *how* to select the *right* traditional means, must manage to do actually what he intended ideally.'[19] By withdrawing into irony, failing to recognise Alceste despite all the signs, Chaucer stops on the brink of reaching a definite solution. He suggests, but does not really assert, that the paradise of love can become the Christian Paradise: Alceste is *margarita*, daisy and pearl. The poet of *Pearl* takes a definite direction, and his poem contains the vision of the Heavenly Jerusalem. But Chaucer stops here and remains ambiguous, as he did in the park of the *Parliament*. Alceste is a mythological character, the queen of Love, *and* the Virgin Mary: she is unlike Beatrice, who is neither of these and who brings Dante from the *Vita Nuova* to the beatific vision. Love rebukes Chaucer for choosing the 'draf' and forgetting the 'corn' of the stories – in other words, for making a superficial choice from the moral–aesthetic point of view. Furthermore, the poet has sinned against Love's law by translating the *Roman* and by writing *Troilus*. Chaucer replies that whatever his authors may have intended, he himself has tried, in his works, to uphold and celebrate 'trouthe in love'. In other words, Chaucer had failed to recognise the truth or at any rate had not managed to harmonise intention and effect. If the Prologue begins with the problem of human knowledge, in the end it returns to it without a solution. Yet again, as in the *House of Fame* one naturally thinks of Dante. In the Prologue Chaucer quotes from him and names him (F 359–60: G 335–6); it is perhaps significant that he opens his discussion by declaring with certainty that

> ... there ne is *non that dwelleth in this contre*,
> That eyther hath in helle or heven ybe,
> Ne may of it non other weyes witen,
> But as he hath herd seyd or founde it writen.
>
> (G 5–8)

In his role as protagonist of the *Divine Comedy*, Dante, the citizen of another country, had been to Hell and Paradise, and he knew their ways, as Chaucer was well aware;[20] but Dante the poet knew them precisely because he had found them written in the right books (Virgil, St Paul), and had learnt, using the 'key of remembrance', to make 'the shape accord with the intention of his art'.[21]

In the Prologue to the *Legend* Chaucer was trying to do something extremely delicate: he wished to invent the structural motivation, the device, of a narrative collection within an essentially lyrical dimension. This was one of the first times in European literature that two genres came together in a relationship not simply of superimposition but of symbiosis. The mythopoeic construction of Alceste was to provide the motivation for the narrative legends. Love lyric was to be the source of a love narrative. It was a bold attempt to combine the dream with the story collection. Despite the richness and complexity of the Prologue, however, this attempt could not but fail in Chaucer's hands. Only one poet of the Middle Ages had succeeded in setting a narrative into dream lyric: this was Guillaume de Lorris in the first part of the *Roman de la Rose*. There the narration allegorically describes an experience of the 'I', the narrator–protagonist. When the stories are detached from this 'I' and stand on their own as works of other authors, then the structure created by the lyrical 'frontispiece' is not solid enough to provide coherence.

Chaucer evidently had within him a lyric impulse, which emerged in his short poems and in *Troilus*. The idea of combining this with narrative was not new for him: he had taken the traditional French dream–love poem as his point of departure and given it an extraordinary narrative thrust, in his own dream poems, with the device of the quest. But in the Prologue to the *Legend*, the quest is in fact impeded by the lyrical, mythopoeic setting, in which Chaucer finds, sublimated in the dream, just what he wants when he is awake. The Geoffrey of the *House of Fame* looked for the 'tydynges', whether true or false, of pilgrims and pardoners; through these changeable, illusory, second-hand fragments, he had to try to reconstruct coherent stories, 'matters', and great poems. For that very reason, he had to broaden the narrative scope to include all of reality, real and imaginary, physical and metaphysical. But in the Prologue to the *Legend* the *Natureingang* never becomes a quest for nature, and the philosophical dimension is present only at the beginning. In such a rarefied atmosphere the reflection on poetry cannot provide a firm support for the narrative collection. And when Chaucer goes to choose his stories, it is from books that he draws the legends of heroines of antiquity, consecrated by the greatest authors, Virgil and Ovid. So it is a learned, 'neoclassical' choice as far as the body of the *Legend* is concerned, whereas the 'frontispiece' is distinctly Gothic. There is also a certain explanatory element, similar in part to that which Gower showed in the *Confessio*, an example of that tendency to 'translation' that was so typical, according to Duby,[22] of the fourteenth-century Courts. The medallions *de claris mulieribus* are mixtures of history and myth, composed not for scholars but for Queen Anne or the Countess of Altavilla (to whom Boccaccio dedicated his *De Claris Mulieribus*).

In the *Legend* Chaucer consistently exploits the classics, in particular Ovid. He modernises the stories by eliminating all the external elements and concentrating on the human interest of the action.[23] Each legend has its 'areas of special interest', as Norton-Smith has pointed out, and a fundamental structure that is repeated, with variations, in all of them: 'the general narration leads up by *ordo naturalis* to a passage of rhetorically elegant, pathetic utterance, thus showing an overall formulation similar to that of the narrative–amatory complaints such as *Mars*, *Anelida* and *Pity*'.[24] There are also what R. W. Frank has called 'the lessons learned': the art of brevity ('quick summary' and 'rapid brushstrokes'), the use of the heroic couplet, a first approach to the problem of characterisation, the pure and simple devotion to action, to the story.[25] But the precise aim of this work – standing between *Troilus* and the *Canterbury Tales* – which opens with a marvellous lyrical polyptych but then peters out in a series of decidedly minor narratives, remains for us a mystery. What did Chaucer mean to do with all this material when he left the work half-finished and began to write and organise the *Canterbury Tales*? And what flash of inspiration set him decisively on the road to Canterbury?

The story of the Canterbury stories is well known: with the flowering of spring, in April, people set off from all over England in pilgrimage towards Canterbury, where lie the mortal remains of the martyr Thomas Becket. A company of twenty-nine people meet one day at the Tabard Inn at Southwark, just across the Thames from the City of London. All of them are going to Canterbury. The cordial Host, Harry Bailly, invents the game that will entertain the pilgrims on their long ride to Canterbury and back: each of them is to tell two stories during each leg of the journey; on their return to the inn, the one who has told the most instructive and entertaining stories will be treated by the others to a dinner, which one imagines will be sumptuous. In other words, this is a sort of itinerant literary contest, based on oral narrative prowess, with a gastronomical reward. In fact things do not work out that way: the pilgrims never reach Canterbury, let alone return; the prize-dinner, alas, never takes place. About halfway through the third round, the Host guesses that none of the pilgrims is going to tell four stories; they will manage only one, or two at best (v, 696-7). On the threshold of the twenty-fourth story, the Host finally declares that only one story is now lacking to complete his plan (x, 15-19). This one is narrated (or rather preached) by the Parson, and in it the 'makere' of the book is surreptitiously introduced: he comes on the scene to take his leave, to repudiate the stories that have been told (or at least those that show sinful tendencies) together with all similar features of those other books of his which have been discussed here. He thanks God for the hagiographic, homiletic, moral and devotional works he has written and for the translation of Boethius; finally he prepares himself for the contrition, confession and regeneration which, he hopes, will guarantee his salvation on the Day of Judgement.

Thus the *Canterbury Tales* have an end, although it is different from the one at first foreseen and desired by the Host, who orchestrates the narrative action. Yet the *Tales* do not have a perfect architectural coherence: we read them, today, in ten unconnected fragments of varying length,[26] preceded by a General Prologue. One pilgrim, the Cook, fails to finish his tale, though there is no apparent external reason why he should not; in other cases the narration is interrupted by other pilgrims or by the Host. On the other hand, the itinerant company is joined at a certain point by a Canon and his Yeoman, of whom the latter not only tells a complete story but also narrates his own experiences as apprentice alchemist. Within those fragments which consist of more than one tale – that is to say, in all but the second, ninth and tenth – there are 'links' between one story and the next, which form part of the action as outlined in the General Prologue. However, there are some incongruities. At the end of the second Fragment, in the Epilogue to the *Man of Law's Tale*, the Shipman declares that he will tell a tale, but this comes only at the beginning of the seventh Fragment.[27] At the end of the seventh Fragment, in the Epilogue to the *Nun's Priest's Tale*, we are told that the Host is about to call on another person ('as ye shuln heere'), but he does not; the following Fragment begins *in medias res*, presumably with the voice of the Second Nun beginning her Prologue. The Shipman often seems to think he is a woman. Within the *Merchant's Tale*, a character in the story mentions the Wife of Bath, who does of course exist, but certainly 'outside [that] Tale on a different fictional level altogether'.[28]

The list of such inconsistencies could be continued, but even from the few cases mentioned here it is obvious that they affect not only the general structure of the work but also its internal mechanisms and the different levels of the narrative fiction. Philologists and critics have tried hard to find an explanation for these major and minor incongruities: haste because of the author's approaching death; his constitutional inability to finish a work; his participation in the Gothic aversion to organic structure. Others have tried to square the circle by reconstructing unities, defining models and describing techniques of construction. Thus, to cite a few significant examples, the frame of the *Tales* – the pilgrimage – is a dynamic entity, and the beginning and end of the work show a hidden allegorical meaning whereby the pilgrimage to Canterbury is also the pilgrimage of human life towards the Celestial Jerusalem, the City of God.[29] Others, developing earlier ideas, have found in the 'dramatic principle' the unifying form of the work: three stages of dramatic development (correspondence between tale and teller; external motivation; internal motivation) govern the performance of the various pilgrims.[30] Some have recognised the 'multiple unity' and the 'inorganic structure' of the *Canterbury Tales*,[31] some see them as 'modelled...on a biological metaphor partaking of the "*pèlerinage de la vie de l'homme*" and that of the *opus imperfectum*, achieved through a "natural" mode of construction'.[32] More recently, attempts have been made to grasp and describe the 'idea' of the *Tales*, the formal model of which is identified with the rose window of a church, while the structural model is found in the technique of 'interlace' and ultimately in the labyrinth, as conceived in the Middle Ages and as mentioned by Chaucer himself in the *House of Fame*.[33] All these attempts are very important, and I shall take due account of them – indeed, it would be impossible not to do so. I shall consider them, however, as approximations to the truth –

as paradigms. And working within these, I shall try to describe the 'phenomenon' of the *Canterbury Tales* as accurately as possible.

Perhaps the first necessary operation in the effort to comprehend this phenomenon is to identify the various fictions at work in it, which make it so complex. The first, and broadest, is the fiction whereby Geoffrey Chaucer presents himself as one of the many pilgrims travelling towards Canterbury: it is he who appears at the Tabard Inn, joins the group, listens to the words of the Host and sets off towards Becket's tomb.[34] As an anonymous pilgrim, when called upon by the Host he also tells his story, *Sir Thopas*; when this is interrupted he begins to narrate *Melibee*. Otherwise he does not appear in the action, except, presumably, as an observer – who, however, keeps his eyes on the ground. This pilgrim Chaucer is also the narrative 'I' of the whole action, the so-called frame: since the *Canterbury Tales* are not a diary, it must be presumed that the pilgrim Chaucer recreates from memory what he has seen and heard – that is, the physical appearance of the various pilgrims, their personalities, their conversations, their conflicts and finally their stories. It is significant that this narrative ambiguity (Chaucer the pilgrim and Narrator versus the pilgrim–narrators) is reflected at the end of the *Clerk's Tale*, where the Clerk, who has just told the story of Griselda, announces a 'song' of comment, which however is preceded by the rubric 'Lenvoy de Chaucer', and in which, therefore, it is not clear if the speaker is the Clerk himself or Chaucer the Narrator. This ambiguity is often noticeable in the *Tales*: for example, in the *Knight's Tale*, the narrating Knight comes out with a very revealing slip of the tongue when he says 'but of that storye list me nat to *write*'. In other words, the *persona* of the Narrator lies behind the stories purportedly narrated by the pilgrims. This is quite evident in the case of the Miller, who is presumably drunk when he undertakes to tell his 'cherles tale in his manere' but then narrates a well-rhymed story that is perfectly orchestrated. For that matter, the Narrator intervenes in person to justify the Miller's risqué tale with a claim of veracity, as he had done in the General Prologue (725–46). Here he again reveals his presence behind the scenes:

> What sholde I moore seyn, but this Millere
> He nolde his wordes for no man forbere,
> But told his cherles tale in his manere.
> M'athynketh that I shal reherce it heere.
> And therfore every gentil wight I preye,
> For Goddes love, demeth nat that I seye
> Of yvel entente, but for I moot reherce
> Hir tales alle, be they bettre or werse,
> Or elles falsen som of my mateere.

And therfore, whoso list it nat yheere,
Turne over the leef and chese another tale;
For he shal fynde ynowe, grete and smale,
Of storial thyng that toucheth gentillesse,
And eek moralitee and hoolynesse.
Blameth nat me if that ye chese amys.
The Millere is a cherl, ye knowe wel this;
So was the Reve eek and othere mo,
And harlotrie they tolden bothe two.
Avyseth yow, and put me out of blame;
And eek men shal nat maken ernest of game.
(I, 3167–86)

In short he presents himself as the reporter of stories narrated by others
and, at the same time, as the writer of a book: this was also the case in
Troilus, where the others were the 'auctours'. In this capacity he depicts
himself, as usual, as a man of no great intelligence (General Prologue 746),
and in his role of pilgrim–Narrator he seems to be incapable of better verse
than the undoubtedly exasperating rhymes of *Sir Thopas* (VII, 926–8).
Finally, there is a level at which the Narrator corresponds to Chaucer
himself. When the Man of Law is invited by the Host to tell a story, he
declares in his introduction that he certainly wants to conform to the
rules of the game but adds that at the moment he can tell no tale that
has not already been told by Chaucer:

But nathelees, certeyn,
I kan right now no thrifty tale seyn
That Chaucer, thogh he kan but lewedly
On metres and on rymyng craftily,
Hath seyd hem in swich Englissh as he kan
Of olde tyme, as knoweth many a man;
And if he have noght seyd hem, leve brother,
In o book, he hath seyd hem in another.
(II, 45–52)

The Man of Law then proceeds to list some of Chaucer's works (as I have
mentioned in connection with the *Legend*); he alludes, almost certainly,
to Gower's *Confessio Amantis* and concludes by saying that he does not
care 'a bene' if his simple language lags behind that of Chaucer. Let
Chaucer make rhymes – he will speak in prose (in fact he speaks in 'rhyme
royal').[35] It is clear, then, that the surviving text of the *Canterbury Tales*
contains, in rough outline, a literary game involving Chaucer the writer,
the 'real' Chaucer, the man and the poet, who is also present alongside
or above the fiction of the Narrator, the narrators and the pilgrim.
Chaucer's own voice returns with greater clarity at the end of the work
in the 'Retracciouns'. These are tacked onto the conclusion of the *Parson's*

Tale, preceded by the rubric: 'Heere Taketh the Makere of this Book his Leve'; they bring into the foreground a writer who rejects his own work 'of wordly vanitees'. A list is appended of some works to be saved and others to be condemned, followed by a prayer for the salvation of his soul. This writer in a sense nullifies his function as an artist in favour of the existential perspective of a wholly Christian man; he measures his work not by results but by intention, and this in turn is measured by the words of the Apostle:

Now preye I to hem alle that herkne this litel tretys or rede, that if ther be any thyng in it that liketh hem, that therof they thanken oure Lord Jhesu Crist, of whom procedeth al wit and al goodnesse. And if ther be any thyng that displese hem, I preye hem also that they arrette it to the defaute of myn unkonnynge, and nat to my wyl, that wolde ful fayn have seyd bettre if I hadde had konnynge. For oure book seith, 'Al that is writen is writen for oure doctrine,' and that is myn entente (x, 1081–3).

Thus the Narrator of the dream poems and *Troilus* is developed, his roles increased almost out of proportion: he is at the same time (if not consistently) extra- and intradiegetic, hetero- and homodiegetic.[36] He is a man who is writing this text, who has written other works, who is preparing to die and be judged as a man and a writer; he is the Narrator of other narrators; he is a fictive narrator among the other narrators.

Different authorial functions correspond to these fictions and realities: the man who makes his final examination of conscience uses moral discrimination; the Narrator who relates stories told by others uses memory; the pilgrim uses observation. All of them make use of words. But these functions are never clearly distinguished: the Chaucer of the 'Retracciouns' is also, for us, the 'I' who tells the story of the pilgrimage and the 'I' within it who narrates *Sir Thopas* and *Melibee*.

The first and largest fiction that dominates the *Canterbury Tales* in no way conceals the others: it includes them, defines them, points them out to the reader. As appears from some of the examples cited, there is a fiction, inherent in the text, regarding the ambiguity of its oral and written presentations: the Knight betrays it when he says 'but of that storye list me nat to write', and the Narrator declares it when he intervenes to justify his adherence to the words of his narrators, even inviting us to turn the page. And of course it is there for all to see in the text itself – even if the pilgrims were used to telling stories, as people were in the Middle Ages, how could they possibly do it in heroic couplets, in rhyme royal, in cadenced prose, using all the rhetorical devices and learned references? The *Canterbury Tales*, after all, are a book. But they were probably also read out one at a time in public, and this explains some of their characteristics –

even technical ones, such as repetition, accumulation, the use of formulae, direct questions to the audience, calls to attention, narrative transitions. The fiction within the work – the oral story told by a pilgrim to other pilgrims – reproduces a social and literary reality, the relation between the text and its author to their original public. In this context, the incongruities, inconsistencies and mis-matchings are much less obtrusive than they seem to the modern reader or even the medieval reader: to notice them at all one needs the manuscript; to catalogue them and use them to construct narrative theories one must have the printed page and must pass from the 'monde de l'à peu près' to the 'univers de la précision'.[37] Nor can we exclude the possibility that to a reader used to seeing incongruous grotesques and obscene drawings in the margins of the soberest manuscripts, it might not be too jarring to find the Wife of Bath mentioned by Justinus in the *Merchant's Tale*: the one is a joke of the copyist, the other of the author. The different levels of the narrative do not necessarily have to be parallel lines.

Certainly what strikes the modern reader most forcibly, even if he is accustomed to medieval narrative, is the dramatic fiction of the *Canterbury Tales*. This is, of course, present in Gower's *Confessio Amantis* and in the *Decameron*, as well as in the *Seven Sages* and the *Thousand and One Nights* – and even in the *Divine Comedy*. But Chaucer develops its mechanism and its gratuity with a vividness that had no precedents (and has had no successors). The action, as I have said, begins in the General Prologue, when the Host appears on the scene and presents his plan, and though the mechanism is set in motion by the luck of the draw, so that the Knight tells his story first, it is afterwards governed by a rather varied series of actions and reactions. Hostilities and arguments among the pilgrims lead them to tell stories aimed at each other: the best known case is that of the Miller, who tells the story of a cuckolded carpenter against the Reeve (who is also a carpenter), and the latter repays him with the story of a joke at the expense of a miller. The mechanism is referred to by the pilgrims themselves as 'quiting' – repayment, or giving as good as you get. In other cases it may be the Host himself who controls the narration, asking one or another of the pilgrims to come forward: this happens, for example, with the Clerk of Oxford, the Monk, the Prioress and Chaucer himself. Other voices are heard, especially at the beginning of each fragment, such as that of the Wife of Bath, the Second Nun and the Canon's Yeoman. Obviously these voices help to build the frame, but there is in them an element of gratuitousness, of autonomy, that goes beyond any teleology. The Miller is drunk; the Merchant has a wife, 'the worste that may be'; the Host gets angry at the Pardoner, and peace is restored through the good offices of the Knight; the Canon leaves the company shortly after it is formed because he is annoyed with his Yeoman, who is revealing his secrets; the Host calls the Parson a Lollard. On this level of dramatic fiction, the game of internal motivations and reciprocal relationships on the one hand, and of the narrative mechanism on the other, is so complex that the pilgrims are, artistically speaking, suspended between the roles of story-tellers and characters. The Narrator gives them a good deal of freedom, but this is conditional. He often diminishes or exaggerates them ironically: he makes Chaucer the pilgrim very small, magnifies the Wife of Bath, makes fun of the Monk. These are never allowed to become real characters, because the Narrator is never completely neutral in his attitude to them. Even the apparently 'ideal' characters, for example the Knight[38] and the Parson, are not autonomous, precisely because they have to serve as models of particular qualities.

In this state of suspension, characterisation cannot be organically integrated into the narrative fiction – nor, on the other hand, can it be extricated from it in any clear-cut way. Thus, on average, the correspondence between each tale and its teller is fairly rough-and-ready. In a few cases it is exact and even original: for example in the *Knight's Tale*, the *Parson's Tale*, the *Prioress's Tale* and the *Nun's Priest's Tale*. In the first two of these, the dynamic relationship between character and narrative is calibrated to order; in the third, the play between the worldly–religious character and her tale creates a subtle and significant contrast; in the fourth, where a rhetorically elaborate and complex tale is told by a practically unknown character, who has been mentioned only in the General Prologue together with two other priests, the reader is totally surprised. But in other cases the fit between character and narrative is much looser; for example, exactly what is the connection between the worldly Monk and his tragedies *de casibus virorum*; or between the Physician who made his fortune out of the plague and his story of violence, virginity and corrupt justice, or between the Manciple and his story of Phoebus and the raven, or between the Epicurean Franklin and his story full of humanity and idealism, ultimately concerned with the courtly problem of 'trouthe' and 'nobility'? The fiction is there, as a basic device, but now and then the machinery is exposed, or at least uncertain in its workings.

Finally, let us consider what might be called the ultimate fiction of the *Canterbury Tales*, the mimetic fiction. Bloomfield maintains that the authenticating device of the *Tales* is its frame,[39] which gives the whole work its realistic tone, and which has always given the impression that the *Canterbury Tales* are a portrait of English society in the late fourteenth century. This is quite true, but it raises various problems and needs to be worked out precisely. The frame is composed of the General Prologue and the links between the stories, in which the different pilgrims are described and in which they act. I shall begin with the Prologue, making considerable use of the conclusions of Jill Mann, one of the most subtle and perceptive of those who have studied the subject in recent years.[40] The form of the General Prologue is that of the 'estates satire' as it had developed in the Middle Ages. The characteristics of the pilgrims described in the Prologue are, on the whole, those traditionally associated with their estates or social conditions. Chaucer tends not to subvert these, but to emphasise some of their aspects, especially those having to do with professional skills or other specific abilities. As has often been observed, the pilgrims function both as types (based on the characteristics of their estates, immediately recognisable to a medieval reader) and as individuals. But what transforms them into individuals is a stylistic technique whereby Chaucer provokes in us a reaction similar to that produced by individuals in real life. To cite one of Jill Mann's examples, the portrait of the Monk in the General Prologue (165–207) suggests certain characteristics that form part of the traditional image of his estate: he loves to eat well, he dresses richly, he likes hunting and horses, he is lazy, he despises the monastic authorities, preferring to live outside the monastery. This information, however, is conveyed by Chaucer in an ambiguous and indirect way, so that the reader wonders, for example, if he is right to conclude that the Monk is a glutton because his appearance seems to suggest it and because the Narrator says he likes a roast swan better than any other meat. Moreover, Chaucer has the Monk defend his own way of life, and again the reader wonders if the defence is sincere or hypocritical. And then the Narrator himself shows enthusiasm for the Monk's clothes, horses and dogs. Thus the Monk, while he is a type, acquires the depth of a real individual through the reactions that Chaucer's presentation provokes in the reader. The key to Chaucer's mimesis is, in short, a fiction in which the mimetic function is shifted from the object of the description (the pilgrim) to the subject of its perception (the reader).

The individuality of the characters who thus take shape in the reader's mind serves to enhance the function of the frame, where they must act and speak in such a way as to make the world of the tales more credible. Their typical qualities, on the other hand, broaden the perspective by making us think of the pilgrims as representatives of the whole human race.

The General Prologue and the links set the form of the frame, that of the pilgrimage. It seems evident that the pilgrimage in the late fourteenth century had at least three different and complementary functions. In the

Chaucer

first place, it was part of religious practice, in which it occupied an important place: the pilgrim takes to the road for the salvation of his soul, or anyway for reasons of popular piety.[41] In this sense, every pilgrimage is a pilgrimage towards the Heavenly Jerusalem, like the one whose path is indicated by the Parson at the beginning of his tale. In the second place, the pilgrimage was a way of acquiring experience, knowledge of the world: *curiositas* dominated the man of the fourteenth century.[42] Late Gothic art reflects this need: 'The "travel landscape" is the most typical pictorial theme of the age and the pilgrim procession of the Ghent altar is to a certain extent the basic form of its world-view.'[43] Finally, the pilgrimage (and, more generally, the journey in company) is the ideal place for socialising and story-telling: in Italy, Sercambi used a journey as the frame for his *Novelle*.[44] In England, Langland declares:

> Pylgrimis and palmers ply3ten hem to-gederes,
> To seche seint Iame and seyntys of Rome,
> Wenten forth in hure way *with meny vn-wyse tales*,
> And hauen leue to lye al hure lyf-time.
> (*Piers Plowman*, c, 1, 47–50)

And Geoffrey himself, in the revolving House of Rumour, found sailors and pilgrims, pardoners and messengers, with sacks full of 'tydynges' and lies.

Thus in the *Canterbury Tales* Chaucer could consider the pilgrimage on various levels. One level is concerned with piety, ethics and salvation:

> ... The hooly blisful martir for to seke,
> That hem hath holpen whan that they were seeke.
> (General Prologue, 17–18)

> And Jhesu, for his grace, wit me sende
> To shewe yow the wey, in this viage,
> Of thilke parfit glorious pilgrymage
> That highte Jerusalem celestial.
> (x, 48–51)

There is an empirical–cognitive level:

> Thanne longen folk to goon on pilgrimages,
> And palmeres for to seken straunge strondes,   *countries*
> To ferne halwes, kowthe in sondry londes.   *distant shrines*
> (General Prologue, 12–14)

a social level:

> At nyght was come into that hostelrye
> Wel nyne and twenty in a compaignye,
> Of sondry folk, by aventure yfalle

244

> In felaweshipe, and pilgrimes were they alle,
> That toward Caunterbury wolden ryde.
> (General Prologue, 23–7)

and a level of artistic–literary entertainment:

> 'Ye goon to Caunterbury – God yow speede,
> The blisful martir quite yow youre meede!
> And wel I woot, as ye goon by the weye,
> Ye shapen yow to talen and to pleye;
> For trewely, confort ne myrthe is noon
> To ride by the weye doumb as a stoon . . .'
> (General Prologue, 769–74)

The mimetic fiction ought to contain these four dimensions, of which the foremost is of course the second, the search for experience and knowledge that we have already seen in the dream poems. Now if the frame of the *Tales* lays the mimetic foundation for the entire work, this frame should contain the basic realistic co-ordinates within which the empirical 'quest' can take place. We have already seen that the General Prologue, the first section of the frame, shifts the plane of mimesis from the pilgrims to the readers – or, to put it another way, mimesis becomes a question of technical approach. The treatment of space and time from the General Prologue through the links is, from a mimetic point of view, equally displaced. Donald Howard is absolutely right when he says that 'The pilgrimage progresses at a remove, as if displaced from geographical locations.'[45] The pilgrims meet in Southwark, not London: they see towns from afar or pass through their suburbs, and at the end of their journey they arrive 'at a thropes ende' (x, 12). There is no mention of overnight stops, meals, pauses for rest. Thus, as Howard puts it, the journey has a ghostly quality. This is reinforced by the fragmentary and contradictory nature of the time co-ordinates, which are anything but realistic, notwithstanding the complicated reconstructions carried out by scholars. Furthermore, everything is dominated by the imagined duration of an artificial day: the pilgrimage begins at dawn (General Prologue, 822–3) and ends at the end of the *Parson's Tale* (which begins at four in the afternoon and certainly goes on for a long time), around sunset. In the *Canterbury Tales*, as in *Troilus*, there is a double time-scheme, one fragmentarily mimetic and the other allusively symbolic.

The space and time of the frame are thus filled almost exclusively with the voices of the pilgrims. The search for experience and knowledge is shifted onto the artistic and literary plane. On the one hand, in fact, this search is carried forward during the autobiographical passages that constitute some of the prologues to the tales, such as those of the Canon's Yeoman, the Pardoner and the Wife of Bath. The last mentioned begins, significantly, with these words:

> Experience, though noon auctoritee
> Were in this world, is right ynogh for me
> To speke of wo that is in mariage.
>
> (III, 1–3)

In this way different fields are explored, such as alchemy, traffic in relics and indulgences, marriage; and, through these, vaster problems are probed: man's eternal desire to transform matter and get rich, the corruption of religious practice and the individual, relations between the sexes, or, again, the tricks and manoeuvres of intelligence, the creation of illusions, the recurrent problem of experience and authority. This experience of the real world, like those which emerge from shorter personal interventions by the pilgrims (the Host and the Merchant, for example), is doubly mediated: by the character as an individual and by the Narrator.

But the broadest search for experience and knowledge is accomplished within the tales themselves, where the artistic–literary system subsumes the others. The tales provide an experience of the world that is doubly re-invented (by each pilgrim and by the Narrator) – or, perhaps, an imitation of reality at least three times removed from the original. The 'real' in these tales is already filtered through myth, folk-lore, the *exemplum* and the authorial text; then it passes through the pilgrim's consciousness and finally through the memory and the stylistic organisation of the Narrator. The tales are, therefore, wholly literary models of reality.

I must now examine these models in the attempt to distinguish, at least in outline, what their nature is, where they lead, how they are constructed thematically and what formal mechanisms are at work within them. Derek Brewer has clearly shown how Chaucer, particularly in the *Canterbury Tales*, absorbed and recreated both the official and the unofficial culture of his age:[46] the ecclesiastical culture and that of the Courts, though both official, are often opposed to each other, and both come into conflict with unofficial culture, which they look down upon as something inferior. Thus, for example, the Parson condemns everything that does not serve the purpose of 'doctrine' – all 'solaas', including, presumably, the courtly and philosophical romance of the Knight. In this way the model of official culture – even in the artistic sense – is reflected only in the *Parson's Tale* itself (a homily on Penitence), the *Second Nun's Tale* (the legend of St Cecilia), the *Prioress's Tale* (the story of the child killed by the Jews), and perhaps *Melibee* (the allegorical story of prudence and wisdom, and ultimately of political ethics). But if the model of official culture is broadened to include the secular courtly element, then it undoubtedly takes in the *Knight's Tale*, the *Man of Law's Tale* and the *Clerk's Tale* (courtly elements are mixed with Boethian philosophy in the first and with typically Christian models in the other two),[47] as well as the *Franklin's Tale* and, on another plane, the *Monk's Tale*, with the *Physician's Tale* and the *Squire's Tale* in a marginal position. In the category of unofficial culture we find the tales of the Miller, the Reeve, the Wife of Bath, the Friar, the Summoner, the Shipman and the Manciple. In the *Pardoner's Tale* and the *Nun's Priest's Tale* the interaction between the two models is highly complex: in the former, for example, the Prologue deliberately and perversely overturns the schemes of official ecclesiastical culture (and conversely is implicitly condemned by it), while the story, though it is unofficial, points a moral that conforms to the Christian model.

The oppositions generated by these two models affect the 'interplay' not only among the different stories – and their narrators – but also among the characters, both those of the frame and those of the stories. One could, for example, set up a sort of scale from official to unofficial for the women of the *Canterbury Tales*: St Cecilia would stand at the top, followed by Custance and Griselda, Emily, Dorigen, Virginia, and the Wife of Bath, Alisoun, May and the various wives of the *fabliaux*. However, such a scheme cannot be considered absolute, for the anti-model corrects the model and cuts it down to size. If Alisoun is mocked for wanting to be a great lady in the romance style, it is also true that she scales down the ideal of the courtly-romance heroine. This is what Brewer calls 'two-way action'; it goes to produce the infinitely varied facets of Chaucer's world and its irony. In *Sir Thopas* the anti-model, this time an entirely literary one, parodies the popular romance and throws an ironic light also on the *Squire's Tale*, which starts out like a proper romance. And when all is said and done, the world of the Friar, the Summoner, the Pardoner and the Canon is a strong corrective to the austere and rigid world of the Parson; just as the world of Nicholas, the Oxford student in the *Miller's Tale*, is a comic antithesis to the world of the Clerk of Oxford, who tells the story of the infinitely patient Griselda. The Wife of Bath, her personal history and her *Tale*, are the living and literary answer to that of Griselda. May ridicules Dorigen. Arcite and Palamon, the two heroes of the *Knight's Tale* who, as they both love Emily and Emily alone, cannot escape from the feudal-courtly code that carries them inevitably to armed conflict, are set against John and Aleyn, the two Cambridge students who, in the *Reeve's Tale*, take their revenge against the Miller and in the process find purely sexual satisfaction with both his wife and his daughter. 'Quiting' is a general organising principle in the Tales, and it is the law of their world. Through it reality is constantly broken up and recomposed in a continual dialectic of high and low, positive and negative, which through the irony of the author's treatment sometimes change places.

The absolute paradigms of official secular culture are forced to a compromise, as in the *Knight's Tale*, where, after Arcite's death, Theseus restores order with the 'faire cheyne of love' and with political common sense, or else they are forced to leave the question open, as in the *Franklin's Tale*, which ends with this question, topical but not merely rhetorical:

> Lordynges, this questioun, thanne wol I aske yow,
> Which was the mooste fre, as thynketh yow?
>
> (v, 1621–2)

Or, lastly, they are forced to admit that the model itself is unreal and unrealisable, as, in the *Clerk's Tale*, that of Griselda:

> But o word, lordynges, herkneth er I go:
> It were ful hard to fynde now-a-dayes
> In al a toun Grisildis thre or two;
> For if that they were put to swiche assayes,
> The gold of hem hath now so badde alayes
> With bras, that thogh the coyne be fair at ye,
> It wolde rather breste a-two than plye.
>
> For which heere, for the Wyves love of Bathe –
> Whos lyf and al hire secte God mayntene
> In heigh maistrie, and elles were it scathe –
> I wol with lusty herte, fressh and grene,
> Seyn yow a song to glade yow, I wene;
> And lat us stynte of ernestful matere.
>
> (IV, 1163–75)

This concept comes in again in the immediately following 'Lenvoy de Chaucer', with even greater force:

> Grisilde is deed, and eek hire pacience,
> And bothe atones buryed in Ytaille;
> For which I crie in open audience,
> No wedded man so hardy be t'assaille
> His wyves pacience in trust to fynde
> Grisildis, for in certein he shal faille.
>
> (IV, 1177–82)

This game is abandoned only in the *Parson's Tale*, because it is the last one and because the official culture it represents and preaches is dominant, absolute and cannot be questioned. All the characters in the *Canterbury Tales* basically share it, apart from the three rascals of the *Pardoner's Tale*. All the others, in one way or another, more or less elastically, are *within* this culture and cannot escape it. Chaucer himself, of course, inevitably hastens to write his 'Retracciouns'. In this sense, the *Amen* with which the *Canterbury Tales* end *is* their 'unity', the unity to which, culturally, they cannot but belong.

The tension between official and unofficial is not merely a matter of social–ethical–cultural models. It is also an intellectual, literary and linguistic game. Most of the stories are based on popular material, on the folk-tale. Scanning the pages of the *Sources and Analogues*, one can connect almost all the *Tales* to motifs that cropped up all over medieval Europe, and not only in Europe. Even the story of Griselda, which Chaucer adapted from Petrarch's version of the last story in the *Decameron*, can be traced back ultimately to a popular motif. Certainly, in the *Canterbury Tales* there are stories of authorial derivation (the supreme example is the *Knight's Tale*, derived from Boccaccio's *Teseida*, or the *Clerk's Tale*, or the Monk's tragedies, or the *Melibee*), based on particular models in the sphere of official culture. And conversely, there are stories based on popular material re-elaborated by Chaucer, such as the *Miller's Tale* and the *Friar's Tale*, for which we can find parallels but not sources. This difference is in a way reflected in the thematic and stylistic differences between stories of different provenance and, more generally, in their diversity of registers. The *Knight's Tale*, which is adapted from a literary text, the *Teseida*, is full of noble themes – love, death, the order and disorder of the world, fortune and destiny – and its register is normally elevated, notwithstanding the fact that Chaucer has eliminated Boccaccio's epic posture and high-sounding language. In the *Miller's Tale*, the exact source of which has never been identified (though morphological and thematic prototypes certainly existed in oral and written form), Donaldson rightly sees the 'idiom of popular poetry', which, on the one hand, is characteristic of the Miller's cultural background and, on the other hand, is a device used by Chaucer to make fun of popular romance.[48] In this case, an openly comic–erotic theme is matched by a register that both harmonises with it and mocks it. In the *Reeve's Tale*, which has a parallel, if not a source, in the French *fabliau* 'Le Meunier et les II. Clers', Chaucer uses a register appropiate to the low theme, but he makes it extremely literary by using the northern dialect:[49] a historic event in English literature, the first use of dialect as a medium of irony and satire.

However, not even in this case can one generalise: the specific purport of the tales, as can be seen even from these three examples, vitiates any scheme for constructing an absolute harmony between their origin (cultured or popular), themes and stylistic register. The stories that come closest to such a harmony are some of those told by ecclesiastics (the Monk, the Prioress, the Second Nun and, of course, the Parson), where the official character of the material is reflected in the style; and, on the other hand, those in which a popular theme is treated without too many complications, such as the Friar's or Shipman's Tales; and lastly those, like the *Man of Law's Tale* and the *Clerk's Tale*, in which the thematic elements of the elevated source (Trevet and Petrarch) have not been drastically reorganised. Otherwise, the interrelationship between origin, theme and register varies from story to story according to no precise law except an aesthetic one. The *Franklin's Tale*, which has a parallel, if not a source, in an episode of Boccaccio's *Filocolo* and in one of the stories in the *Decameron*, can in no way be described on the basis of a clear separation between the three elements: its thematic direction ('gentillesse', 'trouthe', 'franchise') is as marked as it is consistently adhered to, personally and hence characteristically, by the narrator, the Franklin. The preferences of this narrator, the mere mention of the Breton lays, and the magic atmosphere evoked by places and circumstances, ultimately create an absolutely unique idiom. This phenomenon is repeated, though with a change in the first two variables (origin and theme), in the *Wife of Bath's Prologue* and *Tale*, and in the *Nun's Priest's Tale*: in all these, the freedom of invention and the specific aim of the narration go far beyond any limits imposed by the theme and even beyond verisimilitude. They are real literary *tours de force*, as precious and complicated as those of Rabelais and Joyce.

In this situation, for many of the Tales, there is clearly no hope of precise classification in terms of traditional genres. Such classifications have been attempted (in fact I have provided a summary one at the beginning of this chapter), but they are all inadequate, either because certain stories have to be left out, or because the categories adopted are so broad that they hardly mean anything. Robert Payne, for example, after dividing the Tales into the 'serious' and the 'humorous', identifies five formal genres in the first category (romances, saints' legends, miracles, sermons and fables) and two in the second (*fabliaux* and parodies). But he has to create a separate category for the 'anomalies' and even so still has to describe the *Friar's Tale* and the *Merchant's Tale* as unclassifiable.[50] Paul Ruggiers, emphasising the provisional and pragmatic character of his classification, lists eleven types (mainly-realistic tales, tales of chivalry, religious tales about saints, pious tales about saintly persons, moral treatises, fables with moral comments, confessions, preachers' *exempla*, Breton lays, tales of whatever sort with added didactic elements, tragedies).[51] Charles Muscatine, approaching the work from a stylistic point of view, limits his analysis to eight tales, which he divides into two 'versions of conventionalism', three 'versions of naturalism' and three of 'mixed style'.[52] Donald Howard deals with the Fragments: the first is said to contain stories 'of civil conduct'; the third, fourth and fifth, stories 'of domestic conduct'; the seventh, stories 'of private conduct'; there remain Fragments VIII and IX, which contain stories classified only as 'closing', Fragment VI, containing the *Physician's Tale* and the *Pardoner's Tale*, which for various reasons are described as 'floating', and Fragments II and X, apparently not included in any classification.[53] Derek Pearsall, who is more elastic and therefore perhaps wiser in his analysis, discusses the variations ('a series of forays into the borderland of the exemplary and the mimetic') on traditional narrative types and sees the tales essentially as explorations of 'the potentialities of narrative as a self-consistent and self-justifying literary form'.[54]

Certainly from the point of view of the traditional genres, one cannot but conclude that Chaucer carries out the same process of amplification, expansion, distortion and even reversal that he performed in the dream poems and *Troilus*. But when dealing with the individual tales, one naturally tries to fit them into established genres. It is a contradiction, but one to which we must resign ourselves. I prefer to approach the *Canterbury Tales* by two different paths – one indirect, by way of Boccaccio's *Decameron*, and the other involving structural and stylistic analysis of the text.

One of the best recent studies of Boccaccio's masterpiece, that of Mario Baratto,[55] begins with a very important chapter on 'Historicity and Invention in the *Decameron*', the main points of which I shall summarise here. Of the two essential nuclei of inspiration present in Boccaccio's work – 'the memory of a predominantly chivalric world that seems to be in decline', and 'the observation of a contemporary reality that is mainly urban' – the second 'asserts itself with unusual vigour'. Florence, the hub of the mercantile universe, is at the centre of the work, and merchants swarm from it towards Europe and the Mediterranean.[56] Boccaccio is 'a municipal–European writer: which means that the *Decameron* has a very precise *historicity*, as a document which is literary but which eloquently testifies to the conquests, the limits and the contradictions of the communal epoch, of which Florence was the typical model'.[57] This cultural and historical experience provides Boccaccio with the materials for his narration. On to these the author grafts his own 'invention', which moves between two fundamental poles:

on the one hand, the extraordinary, unforeseeable flux of 'temporal things', an inexhaustible source of events...on the other, the relationship between individuals...and the equally extraordinary and unforeseeable way in which the individual can reveal himself, in particular and decisive moments, in contact with others. In the stories the results are various and mutable: but they always offer the basic scheme of men's relationships with reality on the one hand, and relationships between individuals on the other...When observed in this way, measured against a more circumscribed everyday reality, empirical by definition, man begins to be valued according to the criteria which are inherent in that reality. In fact, in the *Decameron* all transcendental measures of value break down: man is defined, instinctively but with great sureness, as an earthly creature.[58]

The world of man is subjected to certain moral guidelines that are provisional but centred on the three basic concepts of Fortune, Nature and sociality, 'within the last of which the first two forces tend to create norms for the coexistence of men':

In his stories Boccaccio elaborates an ideal of social (or rather sociable) morality, which had its origin in a courtly ethos of feudal origin, but which is now being transformed into a code of good manners, of *savoir-vivre*, adopted by modern social and cultural groups that constitute an urban elite of *signori* and 'worthy citizens'.[59]

Finally, the *Decameron* is dominated by what Baratto calls 'narrative and stylistic pleasure':

Thanks to the narrative impulse that sustains it [the *Decameron*], the story for the first time becomes, organically and coherently, the *way* in which it is told.[60]

If we look at the *Canterbury Tales* in the light of this analysis, we can find very significant points of divergence and convergence. In the *Canterbury Tales*, on the whole, there is practically no 'historicity' in Baratto's sense. Not only is there nothing comparable to Boccaccio's description of the plague (a much more detailed and realistic passage than the description of the pilgrims in the General Prologue), but the historical and geographical localisation of the stories themselves is, in most cases, purely perfunctory. The point of setting the *Miller's Tale* in Oxford, or the *Reeve's Tale* in Trumpington, 'nat far fro Cantebrigge', is to indicate the contrast between the clerks and the non-clerks – an element commonly found in medieval comic stories. Oxford and Cambridge were the two university towns of England, which means they were full of clerics, and, given the traditional frictions between town and gown that marked them already in the fourteenth century, plus Chaucer's probable knowledge of the two places,[61] it is quite natural that the two *fabliaux* should be located there – without, however, any other scenic details, except that of 'Soler Halle', the great Cambridge college, and without any historical specification. The indications of place in the *Summoner's Tale* and the *Merchant's Tale* work in the same way. In the *Physician's Tale*, the *Friar's Tale*, *Melibee*, the *Nun's Priest's Tale*, the *Canon's Yeoman's Tale*, and the *Manciple's Tale*, there are no such indications at all. Chaucer comes a little nearer to a Boccaccian type of geography in the incomplete *Cook's Tale*, where London seems to acquire a certain substance, and in the *Shipman's Tale*, which significantly has at its centre a merchant who moves, like the Florentines, between St Denis, Paris and Bruges. Otherwise, the Flanders of the *Pardoner's Tale* and *Sir Thopas* remain vague and ridiculous, while the geography and history of the *Knight's Tale*, the *Squire's Tale*, the *Man of Law's Tale*, the *Wife of Bath's Tale*, the *Prioress's Tale*, and even the 'Roman' *Second Nun's Tale* and the 'Breton' *Franklin's Tale*, are entirely romantic and fabulous in nature.

On the other hand, it is interesting to note how 'historicity', in Baratto's sense, emerges in some of the stories that spring directly from an Italian source or are based on Italian models. This is the case in the *Clerk's Tale*, where the folk-tale, re-elaborated by Boccaccio, was passed on by Petrarch with a precise 'classical' geographical setting in Northern Italy. Chaucer's tale accordingly suggests a specific environment, although there is no attempt at historical collocation. In the Monk's tragedy of Ugolino, taken from Dante, both geographical and historical co-ordinates are indicated with precision.[62] This also occurs in the only 'historical' stories in the *Canterbury Tales*, the brief commemorations of the contemporary Pedro of Castille, Peter of Cyprus and Bernabò Visconti in the series of the *Monk's Tale*, inspired by Boccaccio's *De Casibus*.

In this sense, then, the *Canterbury Tales* do not have a historical, geographical, cultural and political centre like the Florence of the *Decameron*, and in them the international dimension has almost nothing to do with the contemporary world; it belongs to a trans-temporal and trans-spatial plane, the plane of stories, of *fabulae*, not that of *historia*. Chaucer's attitude in this respect is shown fairly clearly by his oscillating in the *Knight's Tale*: 'Ther is no newe gise that it nas old' and 'as was that time the gise';[63] there, however, there is a constant tendency to relegate everything, even the present, to the past – a past that is mythological, fabulistic, in a word, literary. If Dante is, in Auerbach's words, 'the poet of the secular world',[64] Chaucer, compared with the Florentines, is the 'poet of the literary world': he certainly deals with secular (or rather earthly) matters, but through the mediation of his fiction. This is why the Englishness of the *Canterbury Tales* is a subtle and refined game of allusion, rather than a substantial real background: it is Canterbury and the national saint, Thomas Becket; it is the 'shires' from which the pilgrims come; the few English places I have mentioned; Thomas Bradwardine, Jack Straw, and the term 'Lollard' with which the Host labels the Parson; it is, 'emblematically', the dialect of the *Reeve's Tale*, or the mockery of English popular romance in *Sir Thopas*, or the Parson's irony over the alliterative verses of the north. In the *Canterbury Tales* Englishness, like mimesis, is to be found in the details and in the literary technique: one breathes it everywhere, but cannot define it.

Chaucer's 'invention' is grafted onto this framework, but it moves on a different plane from that of Boccaccio. The fundamental scheme is, of course, the relationship between individuals, but not in a social context: it is based on problems, ideas and ideals, which in the end transcend even the relationship between men and reality. In the *Canterbury Tales* Chaucer carries on the discussion of the great themes that concerned him in the dream poems and in *Troilus*: love, fortune, predestination, the place of man in the universe. He does it, not through schemes organised according to a precise plan (as Boccaccio does, in Branca's view),[65] but in a continuous dialectic, and often with a complexity of motifs that cannot be described in general terms. In the *Knight's Tale*, for example, there is love, fortune, destiny, planetary influence and the 'faire cheyne of love' of the First Mover. Arcite, Palamon and Emily are the actors, not the agents of the affair. And the 'real' is the terrible and fascinating world of the figures that decorate the Temples of Mars and Venus, the 'dominion' of Saturn; or it is death and life, as in Arcite's words:

> What is this world? what asketh men to have?
> Now with his love, now in his colde grave
> Allone, withouten any compaignye.
>
> (I, 2777–9)

or in the words of Aegeus, who seems to be answering him from a distance:

> This world nys but a thurghfare ful of wo,
> And we been pilgrymes, passynge to and fro.
> Deeth is an ende of every worldly soore.
>
> (I, 2847–9)

or of Palamon, who much earlier had wondered:

> 'O crueel goddes that governe
> This world with byndyng of youre word eterne,
> And writen in the table of atthamaunt   *adamant*
> Youre parlement and youre eterne graunt,
> What is mankynde moore unto you holde
> Than is the sheep that rouketh in the folde?
> For slayn is man right as another beest,
> And dwelleth eek in prison and arreest,
> And hath siknesse and greet adversitee,
> And ofte tymes giltelees, pardee.
> What governance is in this prescience,
> That giltelees tormenteth innocence?
> And yet encresseth this al my penaunce,
> That man is bounden to his observaunce,

> For Goddes sake, to letten of his wille,   *refrain*
> Ther as a beest may al his lust fulfille.
> And whan a beest is deed he hath no payne;
> But man after his deeth moot wepe and pleyne,
> Though in this world he have care and wo;
> Withouten doute it may stonden so . . .'
>
>   (I, 1303–22)

This is an absolute reality: in philosophical terms existence is always set against being. And it will in fact be the great chain of being – a *principle* set forth in Theseus's last speech – that will restore order to the world torn by violence and death.

In the *Franklin's Tale* the basic scheme is not so much the relationship between one individual and another as the dilemma of ideals in conflict among themselves, of which the individuals are, again, actors: what is to prevail, 'trouthe' or 'franchise'? If the former, shall it be 'trouthe' to the husband or to the man to whom the promise was made, though in the belief that the conditions for keeping it would never come about? And if the latter, shall it be granted to the husband, the unwanted lover, or to the magician? The *Franklin's Tale* traditionally belongs to the so-called 'Marriage Group', in which Kittredge placed it together with the *Wife of Bath's Prologue* and *Tale*, the *Clerk's Tale* and the *Merchant's Tale*.[66] To these Patricia Kean has added the *Knight's Tale* and the *Man of Law's Tale*, maintaining in addition that the *Nun's Priest's Tale* 'provides a comic reversal of the picture [created in the three ideal tales of the Knight, the Man of Law and the Clerk] in which the married life of the cock and his hens contributes to his downfall and tends to disorder instead of order'.[67] If we consider these 'marriage' tales as a group, we realise that what is described in them is not the relationship between individuals, but the problem this relationship raises, measured against the ideal as delineated in the *Knight's Tale*, the *Man of Law's Tale* and the *Clerk's Tale*. All the stories of the series are 'exemplary' – they take a position with respect to the problem, but none of them solves it, because each is an extreme case. Even the *Wife of Bath's Prologue*, which is presented as an 'experience' of marriage, is, on the one hand, a learned discussion of the problem and, on the other, an experience that is credible but improbable. Even ignoring the exaggeration of *five* marriages, how could a woman deeply involved in such a complicated and difficult matrimonial life have managed to make three journeys to Jerusalem and one each to Rome, Cologne and Compostela (plus of course Canterbury), in an age when such journeys took months and years and were full of dangers?

Even those stories, both comic and serious, that are based on a structure involving a married couple and a third man (or men), such as the *Miller's Tale*, the *Reeve's Tale*, the *Shipman's Tale* and the *Manciple's Tale*, are basically extreme examples of marital relationships. The *Miller's Tale* and the *Reeve's Tale* are also comic reversals of the *Knight's Tale*; in the *Shipman's Tale* the merchant's wife goes to bed with the monk not only for mercenary reasons but also because she is deeply dissatisfied with the relationship she has with her husband (VII, 98–194). Thus in the *Canterbury Tales* the theme of marriage is developed through a series of approaches and oscillations between 'feminism' (the Wife of Bath) and 'male chauvinism'; they are like photographs of the same object taken from so many different angles. The method is therefore as circumlocutory as that of the dream poems.

The result of all this is that Man in the *Canterbury Tales* is not 'measured against a reality, empirical by definition', nor is he 'defined ...as an earthly creature'. The 'transcendental measures of value' remain, though they are accompanied by a morally neutral smile. The 'auctoritees', the Fathers, Boethius, Seneca, the ancient and contemporary philosophers, are continually called upon by the pilgrims and their characters. Man is in the power of forces that he cannot completely control; his wit can organise a joke, or a sexual conquest – but it may rebound against him, as in the *Pardoner's Tale* or, as in the *Canon's Yeoman's Tale*, it may be revealed in all its wretchedness and incapacity to deal even with matter. The *Canterbury Tales* begin, after all, with the *Knight's Tale*, and end with the *Parson's Tale*: with the First Mover who restores order to the world and with the Penitence that leads to the Celestial Jerusalem. The morality that dominates in these is not so much 'an ideal of social (or rather sociable) morality' as it is the morality of philosophers and Christians. With wonderful skill and comic verve, Chaucer shows how this morality can be set on its head, pulled by the leg and ignored by students, friars, monks, women and criminals; yet the transcendental judgement hangs over all and never misses its mark.

Finally, there is the question of narrative and stylistic zest. Chaucer never claims, like Boccaccio, to possess 'the best and sweetest tongue in the world', but there is no doubt that even in the *Canterbury Tales* the story becomes the *way* in which it is told. Indeed the structural and stylistic variety of the texts is wider and deeper than that of the *Decameron*: Pearsall is right in saying that the tales 'explore the potentialities of narrative as a self-consistent and self-justifying literary form',[68] even if the Parson's speech and the 'Retracciouns' bring the search to an abrupt end and negate the aesthetic function of the work.

Let us look briefly at some of the structural types used in the *Canterbury*

Tales. The *Squire's Tale*, in which what the Squire manages to tell is formally divided in three 'partes', seems to be a typical example of 'interlaced' narrative.[69] The Squire himself reveals this when, at the end of the 'secunda pars', he draws together all the threads of his story:

> First wol I telle yow of Cambyuskan,
> That in his tyme many a citee wan;
> And after wol I speke of Algarsif,
> How that he wan Theodora to his wif,
> For whom ful ofte in greet peril he was,
> Ne hadde he ben holpen by the steede of bras;
> And after wol I speke of Cambalo,
> That faught in lystes with the brethren two
> For Canacee er that he myghte hire wynne.
>
> (v, 661–9)

The *Franklin's Tale*, which follows it in the same Fragment, is referred to by its narrator as a Breton lay, but its construction is a good example of *ordo artificialis* that comes as close as possible to the *naturalis*, with a beginning, middle and end that would have pleased Aristotle. The *Man of Law's Tale* and the *Clerk's Tale* are models of what Shklovsky calls 'stringing' – that is, where 'one story-motif, complete in itself, is followed by another, and the whole is held together by the presence of a single protagonist'.[70] These are the tests to which Cunstance and Griselda are subjected – a motif repeated over and over again. Both these stories also fall into a formal *divisio* in *partes*. The same thing happens in the *Knight's Tale*, but there the division serves to determine and underline the symmetry of the construction and becomes a real structural principle, which organises with geometrical complexity what Shklovsky calls the device of the 'parallel'.[71]

Divisio recurs in two other Tales, the Canon's Yeoman's and Chaucer's *Sir Thopas*. In the former, however, it simply separates the Yeoman's personal history from his actual Tale, leaving the thematic unity intact. In the latter, the two 'fits', the second of which is interrupted by the Host, serve as parody: the 'romance' is dominated by a ridiculous caricature of stringing and of an interlace that is nothing but confusion. Chaucer then takes his revenge in *Melibee*, the construction of which is as precise and formal as that of a moral tract. The supreme example of this type is, of course, the *Parson's Tale*, with its theme of Penitence neatly and homiletically divided into three sections (Contrition, Confession and Satisfaction), plus the canonical treatise on the seven deadly sins.

The typically progressive and exemplary structure is determined *a priori* in stories like the *Prioress's Tale* and the *Second Nun's Tale*, where the denouement of the 'miracle' and the 'sacred legend' is fixed by tradition. The *Monk's Tale*, on the other hand, is a regular 'rosary of tales', a mechanical *accumulatio* of stories united by the same tragic theme, brought about by fortune: thus it amounts to a collection of *exempla* with variations on a preordained theme and without any precise chronological or historic plan.

An entirely linear construction is seen in the stories based on traditional motifs and on devices such as double meaning, word-play, role-playing, modifications of love triangles (or quadrangles): the *Miller's Tale*, the *Reeve's Tale*, the *Wife of Bath's Tale*, the *Merchant's Tale*, the *Friar's Tale*, the *Summoner's Tale*, the *Shipman's Tale*. Linearity does not, however, mean the absence of sudden and catalytic disparities. One thinks for example of the *Summoner's Tale*, where Thomas's trick on the friar is crowned with the splendid scientific–technical invention of the squire's method for dividing up the fart.

Here the carnival world of which Bakhtin speaks[72] is really the official world turned upside-down, with the fart taking the place of the offering; but the squire's speech (III, 2253–86) goes beyond even this, becoming pure play (and double disgrace for the friar), and comic–fantastic embroidery, in the vein followed later by Pulci and Rabelais. In fact the squire does not limit himself to giving general instructions, but prescribes a perfect set-up for experimental proof: the weather must be fine, 'withouten wynd or perturbynge of air' (this approximates the vacuum required for modern scientific experiments). The cartwheel with its twelve spokes is the geometric image of a convent, composed of at least twelve friars; at the same time it is the technical apparatus for verifying the hypothesis (III, 2257–9). Each friar is to place his nose at the end of a spoke, while the confessor (the friar–protagonist of the story) stands under the hub. Then the 'cherl' from above the wheel, is to release a fart:

> And ye shul seen, up peril of my lyf,
> By preeve which that is demonstratif,
> That equally the soun of it wol wende,
> And eke the stynk, unto the spokes ende,
> Save that this worthy man, youre confessour,
> By cause he is a man of greet honour,
> Shal have the firste fruyt, as resoun is.
>
> (III, 2271–7)

This plane of logic and 'preve by experience' is the same as that on which the Eagle in the *House of Fame* operated: but here the object of the experiment makes the whole operation ridiculous. Finally, the image is turned against the corruption of the mendicant orders: the confessor fully respects the customs according to which the more 'worthy' must be served first – which completely overturns the evangelical and Franciscan ideal of equality. At the end of the speech a last firework explodes: the confessor has entertained the faithful so well during the sermon, that certainly 'he hadde the first smel of fartes thre'. A marvellous inconsequentiality of logic and syntax, but in profound harmony with the 'resoun' of the Tale and its comic exaggeration.

Finally, there remain two structures that can only be called 'Chaucerian', in the particular sense that they depend largely on the oral–dramatic fiction of the Tales. These are found in the *Pardoner's Tale* and the *Nun's Priest's Tale*. The former begins with a long and fascinating Prologue–confession; the story itself, in contrast, has hardly begun when it is suddenly interrupted by a homiletic digression on the sins of gluttony, drunkenness, gambling and lying, seasoned with various *exempla* – that is, with short narrative digressions within the main narrative. The story is taken up again after about 200 lines, and from then on it follows a straight line, with a construction based on ambiguity. It ends with another short homiletic tract, which develops first into an offer of relics by the Pardoner and then into the quarrel between him and the Host, which is then settled by the Knight. The *Nun's Priest's Tale* is clearly divided into two parts. In the first, the cock Chauntecleer tells of his terrible dream; this is followed by the discussion between him and the hen Pertelote on the nature and significance of dreams, full of quotations and *exempla*, in this case real stories within the story. In the second part, the action begins with the appearance on the scene of Russell, the fox, who captures Chauntecleer by extravagantly praising his merits as a singer, but the cock frees himself with another vocal trick. In this second part the narrator – the Priest – abandons himself to an inexhaustible flow of invocations, comments, quotations, *exempla* and similes – building it all up into a real mock-heroic poem. In short, we are dealing with constructions just as deliberately artificial and digressive as those of *Tristram Shandy*: the narrative and the process of narration are inextricably mixed up, and the slightest hint from the plot is enough to set off the whole mechanism of imaginative and cultural associations. This play combines elements from the present text and a variety of others, and the whole is dominated by sheer verbal enjoyment.

This brings us to the last phase of this summary examination of the inner workings of the *Canterbury Tales* – that is, to the question of language and style. It is obviously impossible here to describe the stylistic system of the work as a whole, or to discover the constants (and variables) that inform it: that would require a whole book. Instead I shall begin, on the basis of what has been said so far and of the passages cited, with two observations that by now can be taken for granted: the polyphonic character[73] of the *Canterbury Tales* and the multiplicity of styles within the work. To illustrate these aspects I shall concentrate on two particular passages.

The first passage, from the *Pardoner's Tale*, is the famous appearance of the Old Man to the three criminals. The Pardoner's story is about three 'rioutoures' who have been drinking since dawn in a tavern; they hear a funeral bell and send a boy to ask who is dead. He reports that it is an old comrade of theirs, suddenly killed by a thief, commonly known as Death, who has claimed many victims during the plague. The three, who are drunk, decide to find Death and kill him. They set out towards the village where, according to the inkeeper, Death dwells. Along the way they meet the Old Man, who, when they threaten him, points out a certain oak tree under which Death cannot hide. The three proceed along the 'croked way' indicated by the Old Man and find, under the oak, a huge pile of golden florins. Then they draw lots to decide which of them must go to the village to buy food and wine, while they wait for night to carry off the treasure. The lot falls to the youngest, who sets off on his way. The other two decide to kill him on his return, so as to get his share of the florins. But the third rioter has a plan of his own: he buys poison and puts it in two of the wine bottles, keeping the third for himself. When he returns to the oak, his companions murder him; then, to celebrate, they drink the poisoned wine and die. Thus all three have found death. The story, which was widespread in various forms during the Middle Ages,[74] thus hinges on the ambiguity, death = person, and on the ambiguity of the old man's directions: treasure = death, because of the avarice of the three. It is certainly a powerful story.

In this tale, the three men's meeting with the Old Man occupies what in Aristotelian terms would be the 'middle' of the action; in itself it resolves nothing, but it sets in motion the process that will lead to the disastrous conclusion. The meeting takes place barely half a mile from the village where the three had gathered in the tavern and had decided to go out and kill Death. The Old Man is presented simply as old and poor, and he is first to speak. Meekly, he says: 'Now, lordes, God yow see!' But the 'proudeste' of the three insultingly asks him:

> 'Why artow all forwrapped save thy face?
> Why lyvestow so longe in so greet age?'
> (VI, 718–19)

The first of these questions indirectly provides another detail of the Old Man's appearance: his body is completely covered. Is he wrapped, perhaps, in a shroud, or against the cold, or because of illness (perhaps the plague, which is raging in the neighbourhood)? The form of the question suggests all three hypotheses: in just a few words, it begins, indirectly, to build up a chilling image. The second question makes no sense at all, except as a bit of insolence on the part of the criminal, in the same tone as that of the first question. The Old Man ('*this* olde man', which betrays the presence of a narrator, the Pardoner) looks into the face of the rioter and replies. What is the Old Man seeking in the gambler's face ('gan looke in his visage')? We are not told, but his scrutiny immediately suggests some knowledge and a wise superiority, perhaps mixed with fear. It is as if the Old Man were trying to discover, or to confirm, some sign on the rioter's face: his intentions, his true nature, his damnation? In any case the Old Man replies only to the second question:

> 'For I ne kan nat fynde
> A man, though that I walked into Ynde,
> Neither in citee ne in no village,
> That wolde chaunge his youthe for myn age;
> And therfore moot I han myn age stille,
> As longe tyme as it is Goddes wille.
> Ne Deeth, allas! ne wol nat han my lyf
> Thus walke I, lyk a restelees kaityf,
> And on the ground, which is my moodres gate,
> I knokke with my staf, bothe erly and late,
> And seye "Leeve mooder, leet me in!
> Lo how I vanysshe, flessh, and blood, and skyn!
> Allas! whan shul my bones been at reste?
> Mooder, with yow wolde I chaunge my cheste
> That in my chambre longe tyme hath be,
> Ye, for an heyre clowt to wrappe in me!"
> But yet to me she wol nat do that grace,
> For which ful pale and welked is my face.'
>
> (vi, 721–38)

This is the heart of the episode, and no reader can be unaware of its density. The Old Man's reply is divided into two or, perhaps, three parts: first, he has lived to such a great age because he can find no one in all the world who is ready to exchange youth for old age; second, Death does not want his life; third, he is a prisoner who knows no peace, who begs the earth to receive his body. Meanwhile, the speech indirectly reveals still more about the Old Man's appearance: his flesh, blood and skin are 'vanishing', his face is pale and dried up. The Old Man resembles Job struck by calamities and physically destroyed. Like Job, and like the old men of the Apocalypse, he hopefully awaits Death:

> Wherefore is light given to him that is in misery,
> And life unto the bitter in soul;
> Which long for death, but it cometh not;
> And dig for it more than for hid treasures;
> Which rejoice exceedingly,
> And are glad, when they can find the grave?
>
> (Job iii, 20–2)

And in those days shall men seek death, and shall not find it; and shall desire to die, and death shall flee from them.

> (Apocalypse, ix, 6)

Like Job, he still recognises the will of God ('as longe tyme as it is Goddes wille') and says he continually asks the earth for a 'grace' that has not *yet* been granted him. In reality the Old Man's whole answer is based on impossibilities: naturally it is impossible to find anyone willing to exchange his own youth for another person's old age, and it is impossible to hasten death and burial without doing violence to oneself. The Old Man's answer makes no sense at all in terms of logic; this corresponds very well with the senseless question that provoked it. We have overstepped the bounds of rationality, though not necessarily of nature. The Old Man is condemned to an indefinite suspension (but one that will end) between life and death: crystallised in old age, of which he has often been seen as the personification,[75] he is a prisoner without peace. But his body is still subject to the ravages of life and time: a sort of cancer is devouring him, flesh, blood and skin; his face gets ever nearer to the pallor and aridity of death; he disappears. The Old Man is not Death, as has often been said; if anything he is Dying, the gradual extinction of life, which has not yet reached final consummation. Perhaps this is why his body is completely covered, to avoid showing the signs of the truth, of mortal life that is also death:

> questo viver terreno,
> il patir nostro, il sospirar . . .
> . . . questo morir, questo supremo
> scolorar del sembiante,
> e perir dalla terra.[76]

('this earthly life, our suffering, our sighing; and this dying, this ultimate fading of our features, and perishing from the earth.')

In short, the Old Man is the life of all human beings in its journey towards death, represented here in one extreme figure, a combination of Job and the Wandering Jew, giving an apocalyptic atmosphere. The earth, on which the Old Man knocks with his staff,[77] is our common mother. The Old Man asks the earth to let him re-enter its bosom, calling it 'mother'

– a primeval invocation – and offering his chest with all his possessions in exchange for a haircloth shroud. Once again, the images are indirect: the Old Man does not invoke Death, but mother earth, which has given life and will receive it back again. Around the concept of death, which is mistakenly personified by the three gamblers and the boy, a broader perspective is gradually formed – by the stratification of images, by allusion, by scriptural implications. At first the Old Man speaks of Death as a person (727) who does not want his life, thus echoing the ambiguous notion of the criminals. He sets youth against age (724) and death against life. Then the image of the ground, the gate of mother earth, broadens and modifies the perspective: the indirect message that the Old Man addresses to the three rioters is truth. The earth is the mother of man, made of dust, and to it man will return at the will of God. The Old Man speaks of life while seeming to beg for death. Striking the ground with his staff he shows them the true path towards death and the impossibility of following it to the end without the grace of mother earth and the consent of God. This exhausted prisoner of an old age that dies every day, this weary and shrinking pilgrim so reminiscent of Langland's figures, has looked into the eyes of his questioner and seen there the boundless pride ('the proudeste'), the Lucifer-like arrogance, of one who wants to kill death – a privilege reserved to Christ. The figure of the Old Man emerges in all its greatness: he is neither an allegory of the *vetus homo* nor a personification of Death or Old Age, nor merely an old man,[78] but an image powerfully created through successive concretions, which in the end involves all of man and his destiny: 'I moot go thider as I *have* to go'.

The humility and generosity of the Old Man is still further deepened: he asks the rioters not to insult him, quoting a precept from Leviticus, then paraphrases Ecclesiastes and especially Matthew,[79] then, with an ironic reference to the fact that the three rascals may live to old age ('if that ye so longe abyde'), he takes leave of them: 'God be with yow, where ye go or ryde!' But the three understand nothing of all this, and threaten him:

'Nay, olde cherl, by God, thou shalt nat so,'
Seyde this oother hasardour anon;
'Thou partest nat so lightly, by Seint John!
Thou spak right now of thilke traytour Deeth,
That in this contree alle oure freendes sleeth.
Have heer my thouthe, as thou art his espye,
Telle where he is, or thou shalt it abye,
By God, and by the hooly sacrement!
For soothly thou art oon of his assent
To sleen us yonge folk, thou false theef!'
(VI, 750–9)

The Old Man then returns to the literal fiction: do you want Death? Death in person? Well, I've just left him under that great oak up there. Once again he tries to make them realise the truth: the path they must travel to reach Death is a 'croked way', the way of sin. That way they will indeed find Death – not the return to mother earth, not rest for their bones, but final, eternal death. The Old Man's farewell, which at first had been 'God yow see!' and then 'God be with yow', is now 'God *save* yow, that boghte agayn mankynde, and yow *amende*!' At the end of the road, the three will find the treasure that is to be their death, and 'No longer thanne after Deeth they soughte.' The Old Man has finished; he sets off again for his mysterious destination and with his last words disappears from the scene.

This episode with its simple and powerful image of a poor old man condemned to a life of dying, created by Chaucer through allusions, and without logical links, is a parable. That is the way the Old Man acts and speaks, 'because they seeing see not; and hearing they hear not, neither do they understand' (Matthew XIII, 14). So there is a parable within a parable.[80] Advice had been offered to the three men by the boy:

> 'Beth redy for to meete hym [Death] *everemoore*:
> Thus taughte me my dame ...'
> (VI, 683–4)

This warning had fallen on deaf ears, and the boy's mother ('my dame') is succeeded by the mother of all, the earth. The meeting reflects a total lack of comprehension between two cultures, that of the Old Man and that of the three gamblers. Communication between them is impossible: the three, tied to the earth, to their enemy's personification, cannot understand the profound meaning of the man's words and gestures. They seem to be completely outside Christian culture.

The poetry that shows us this truth, which proceeds through *impossibilia* and *aenigmata*, is the poetry of pathos, which dominates the whole episode, especially its culminating words:

> 'Thus walke I, lyk a restelees kaityf,
> And on the ground, which is my moodres gate,
> I knokke with my staf, bothe erly and late,
> And seye "Leeve mooder, leet me in!
> Lo how I vanysshe, flessh, and blood, and skyn!
> (VI, 728–32)

Yet in this one story Chaucer breaks through all the poetic and aesthetic schemes that we associate with his age: he has, in the words of Salvatore Battaglia, 'turned the parable into a myth of the imagination'.[81] For the first time in English literature he creates a figure such as we find in the three witches of *Macbeth*, in the 'fool' of *King Lear*, in the Phlebas of the *Waste Land*.

The second passage comes from the *Nun's Priest's Tale*, the plot of which has already been summarised. In the second part, after the long discussion of dreams, the real action begins. The narrator, the Priest, announces that now he will tell of Chauntecleer's 'aventure'. The overture is typically solemn:

> Whan that the month in which the world bigan,
> That highte March, whan God first maked man . . .
> (VII, 3187–8)

The chronological technique, learnt from the classics, Dante and Boccaccio, is further refined: we go right back to the time of Genesis. But then we at once take in the full absurdity of this procedure: what the Priest really wants to indicate is not March, but May, the topical month for the beginning of an adventure. Thus he adds:

> Was compleet, and passed were also,
> Syn March bigan, thritty dayes and two . . .
> (VII, 3189–90)

In other words it is the third day of May. To indicate this he has had to use two subordinate clauses of time ('whan that . . . and passed were also'), plus no less than three further dependent clauses, of which two are again temporal ('whan God', 'syn March', 'that highte'). This parody is brought off with a literary technique of rare refinement. But that is not all: at last comes the main clause, and with it the subject:

> Bifel that Chauntecleer in al his pryde,
> His seven wyves walkynge by his syde,
> Caste up his eyen to the brighte sonne . . .
> (VII, 3191–3)

Again the syntax is oblique; but the parody is finely balanced. The overture was the beginning of the world and the creation of man; now Chauntecleer, in all his sultan-like pride, raises his eyes to the sun. Chauntecleer is a barnyard cock, as we know, but here he behaves and feels like the lord of all creation, addressing himself to the sun, the primeval light; the sun, as the author specifies in another parenthesis:

> That in the signe of Taurus hadde yronne
> Twenty degrees and oon, and somewhat more . . .
> (VII, 3194–5)

This really carries the technique of astronomical timetelling a bit too far. But we at once return to Chauntecleer, now in his natural dress, as a 'commune astrologer', who

> ... knew by kynde, and by noon oother loore,
> That it was pryme ...
>
> (VII, 3196–7)

Chauntecleer, significantly, is more reliable 'than is a clokke or an abbey orlogge' (2854), and he knows by nature 'ech ascencioun of the equynoxial in thilke toun'; he crows infallibly when fifteen degrees are 'ascended' (2855–8). Step by step, a two-sided irony is constructed, aimed on the one hand at the cock that thinks it is lord of creation, and on the other hand at Man, who is called the lord of creation, but has to invent a complicated science ('loore') and sophisticated instruments ('orlogge') to work out what the cock knows naturally and infallibly:

> 'The sonne,' he seyde, 'is clombed up on hevene
> Fourty degrees and oon, and moore ywis ...'
>
> (VII, 3188–9)

Not even Chaucer could have done better with his astrolabe. For four lines the register and the sphere of reference remain the same, with the introduction of the new element, joy:

> 'Madame Pertelote, my worldes blis,
> Herkneth thise blisful briddes how they synge,
> And se the fresshe floures how they sprynge;
> Ful is myn herte of revel and solas!'
>
> (VII, 3200–3)

Chauntecleer, who refers to the other birds as '*thise* ... briddes', feels that he is definitely the lord and master, and that 'kynde' which inspires him to crow now fills him with the 'revel' and 'solas' of spring, the 'blis' of the *Parliament*. The paternalistic cock is still part of the animal and natural world.

At this point, by a process of association that can almost be called a 'stream of (narrative) consciousness', the Priest intervenes with his first comment:

> But sodeynly hym fil a sorweful cas,
> For evere the latter end of joye is wo.
> God woot that wordly joye is soone ago;
> And if a rethor koude faire endite,
> He in a cronycle saufly myghte it write
> As for a sovereyn notabilitee.
> Now every wys man, lat him herkne me;

This storie is also trewe, I undertake,
As is the book of Launcelot de Lake,
That wommen holde in ful greet reverence.
Now wol I torne agayn to my sentence.

(VII, 3204–14)

Here proverbial wisdom, similar to that of Aegeus in the *Knight's Tale*,
suddenly turns to literary allusion and makes fun of literature: a rhetorician
might write us a chronicle – that is, a noble *historia* in the high style – but
the Priest's tale is a true 'storie' like the story of Lancelot, which women
(witness Francesca da Rimini) esteem very highly. It is as true, in other
words, as a romance: completely fictitious, such that women can hold it
'in ful greet reverence'. In short, the Priest is playing with literature and
with his audience; later on he will find himself a rhetorician to make fun
of – no less a figure than Geoffrey of Vinsauf – and he will continue his
ironic remarks about women, who form the privileged audience of the
man of letters, as in *Troilus*. For the moment he restrains himself and
switches back to his 'sentence'; at last the fox appears:

A col-fox, ful of sly iniquitee,
That in the grove hadde woned yeres three,
By heigh ymaginacioun forncast,
The same nyght thurghout the hegges brast
Into the yerd ther Chauntecleer the faire
Was wont, and eek his wyves, to repaire;
And in a bed of wortes stille he lay,
Til it was passed undren of the day,
Waitynge his tyme on Chauntecleer to falle,
As gladly doon thise homycides alle
That in await liggen to mordre men.

(VII, 3215–25)

The narrator, however, cannot manage to stay outside his story: along with
the fox he introduces the subject of predestination ('by heigh ymaginacioun
forncast') and that of homicide, which has already been mentioned by
Chauntecleer himself in his speech on dreams (3050–7). The fox is full of
iniquity, like the worst sinners of the Bible, like the murderers. And again
the Priest cannot but let himself be carried away by his culture: he curses
Judas, Ganelon (who betrayed Roland in the *Chanson*) and Sinon (who
played a prominent part in the fall of Troy). Thus we find ourselves
between sacred and profane literature – in the latter case, the epic, the
chansons de geste and the romances. But now the narrator really comes
out into the open:

O Chauntecleer, acursed be that morwe
That thou into that yerd flaugh fro the bemes!

Thou were ful wel ywarned by thy dremes
That thilke day was perilous to thee;
But what that God forwoot moot nedes bee,
After the opinioun of certein clerkis.
Witnesse on hym that any parfit clerk is,
That in scole is greet altercacioun
In this mateere, and greet disputisoun,
And hath been of an hundred thousand men.
But I ne kan nat bulte it to the bren
As kan the hooly doctour Augustyn,
Or Boece, or the Bisshop Bradwardyn,
Wheither that Goddes worthy forwityng
Streyneth me nedely for to doon a thyng, –
'Nedely' clepe I symple necessitee;
Or elles, if free choys be graunted me
To do that same thyng, or do it noght,
Though God forwoot it er that was wroght;
Or if his wityng streyneth never a deel
But by necessitee condicioneel.

(VII, 3230–50)

This time it is the world of philosophy: the Priest, more briefly and more prosaically than Troilus, launches into a discussion on predestination, free will and necessity; unlike Troilus, he makes precise reference to the schools and the doctors, from Boethius to Augustine to the contemporary Bradwardine. Chauntecleer's imminent tragedy seems now to acquire a cosmic dimension and is placed on the level of universal destiny. But 'that is another story', as Sterne would say – the story of Troilus, or of Arcite and Palamon. Here,

I wol nat han to do of swich mateere;
My tale is of a cok, as ye may heere,
That tok his conseil of his wyf, with sorwe,
To walken in the yerd upon that morwe
That he hadde met that drem that I yow tolde.
Wommenes conseils been ful ofte colde;
Wommenes conseil broghte us first to wo,
And made Adam fro Paradys to go,
Ther as he was ful myrie and wel at ese.

(VII, 3251–9)

A stupendous, abrupt *reductio* ('my tale is of a cok'), but its purport is not really clear: is the Priest really talking about a cock, rather than about all mankind? This cock has taken the advice of his *wife*, not of the hen Pertelote, and this wife is immediately put on a par with all women, beginning with Eve. The irrepressible flux of words and mental associations takes us back once again to Genesis and the beginning of the world, marvellously and preposterously announced and misunderstood by Chauntecleer himself a hundred or more lines earlier:

> 'For al so siker as *In principio*,
> *Mulier est hominis confusio*, –
> Madame, the sentence of this Latyn is,
> "Womman is mannes joye and al his blis".'
>
> (VII, 3163–6)

Here the certainty of the affirmation hinges on the first words of Genesis (and the Gospel of St John). The affirmation itself, conforms in the original Latin to the real point of the story as understood by its narrator, the Priest, but is turned upside-down by Chauntecleer's macaronic translation. The Priest, however, does not admit to being a misogynist – indeed he hastens to modify his own interpretation:

> But for I noot to whom it myght displese,
> If I conseil of wommen wolde blame,
> Passe over, for I seyde it in my game.
>
> (VII, 3260–2)

So it was a joke. But was it really? The Priest (or at least one assumes it is still he who speaks) reverses this last affirmation with subtle malice, referring to the 'authors', and finally, for fear of his listeners (we think of the Wife of Bath) or the public (we think of the readers of *Troilus* and the *Legend*), he takes it all back, attributing his own words to the cock:

> Rede auctours, where they trete of swich mateere,
> And what they seyn of wommen ye may heere.
> Thise been the cokkes wordes, and nat myne;
> I kan noon harm of no womman divyne.
>
> (VII, 3263–6)

From this moment on the Tale is a succession of verbal fireworks and rapid changes of voice, from the characters to the narrator and vice versa. Texts and authors are invoked by all. The Priest manages to bring in the *Physiologus* (the Latin Bestiary), the *Aeneid* and the destruction of Troy, Hasdrubal and the sack of Carthage, Nero and the burning of Rome (3355–73). In this melodramatic, apocalyptic atmosphere, Chauntecleer's tragedy unfolds: in a mock-epic crescendo the men, women and animals of the farm rush to the scene. The style throws an ironic light on the protagonists of the action and, indirectly, on the protagonists of the Peasants' Revolt of 1381, who are reduced by assimilation, as in Gower's *Vox Clamantis*, to animal-like figures:

> So hydous was the noyse [of the animals], a, *benedicitee*!
> Certes, he Jakke Straw and his meynee

Ne made nevere shoutes half so shrille
Whan that they wolden any Flemyng kille,
As thilke day was maad upon the fox.
(vii, 3393–7)

At one point, beginning with an appeal to destiny, with a freely linked series of comic invocations, the Priest manages to harangue Friday, Venus and Geoffrey of Vinsauf, who lamented the killing of Richard the Lion Heart, which took place on a Friday. Nothing is spared – neither dreams, nor Venus, nor courtly love 'servyce', nor even natural love ('moore for delit than world to multiplye'):

O destinee, that mayst nat been eschewed!
Allas, that Chauntecleer fleigh fro the bemes!
Allas, his wyf ne roghte nat of dremes!
And on a Friday fil al this meschaunce.
O Venus, that art goddesse of plesaunce,
Syn that thy servant was this Chauntecleer,
And in thy service dide al his powveer,
Moore for delit than world to multiplye,
Why woldestow suffre hym on thy day to dye?
O Gaufred, deere maister soverayn,
That whan thy worthy kyng Richard was slayn
With shot, compleynedest his deeth so soore,
Why ne hadde I now thy sentence and thy loore,
The Friday for to chide, as diden ye?
(vii, 3338–51)

Meanwhile Chauntecleer, who once was Adam, the lord of creation, becomes Richard the Lion Heart, Priam, Hasdrubal, a Roman senator. Finally, when the cock has freed himself and the exchange between him and the duped fox is ended, the narrator concludes with another bit of dazzling profundity, a last literary reference, a flash of Scripture, where we might perhaps hear the voice of the Narrator, Chaucer:

But ye that holden this tale a folye,
As of a fox, or of a cok and hen,
Taketh the moralite, goode men.
For seint Paul seith that al that writen is,
To oure doctrine it is ywrite, ywis;
Taketh the fruyt, and lat the chaf be stille.
Now, goode God, if that it be thy wille,
As seith my lord, so make us alle goode men,
And brynge us to his heighe blisse! Amen.
(vii, 3438–46)

Are these the Priest's 'Retracciouns' (Chaucer repeats the quotation from

St Paul in his own 'Retracciouns')? Are we to believe all this? Do we have to take the 'moralite'? Are we really meant to take the 'fruyt' and let 'the chaf be stille'? Some have done so. But the whole point is not whether we do or not, it is that we *can*, if we wish to. The narrator implicitly shows us a way to discover 'doctrine' behind the 'folye'; he points to the possibility of a 'moral' interpretation. The whole point, in short, is that we are invited to ask ourselves these questions. In both the *Convivio* and the *Epistle to Cangrande* Dante imposes the fourfold interpretation on his readers. Chaucer, typically, is more reticent and – all things considered – more modern.[82]

The gap that separates the *Nun's Priest's Tale* from one of the first texts examined in this book, *The Fox and the Wolf*, is enormous. There we find the seeds of the narrative mechanism and of the middle style. Here we have the fruits of literary awareness: allusion, the construction of fields of reference (the beginning of the world, Genesis, the fall of cities); two-edged parody (the epic image at the start and the mock-heroic crescendo); the involvement and the travesty of literature (from the romance to the Bible to the *artes poeticae*), philosophy and morality; linguistic divertisse-ment (the cock's Latin and his translation), polyphony (characters, Priest-narrator, Narrator) and its ambiguity; and lastly the supreme control of the mechanism of affirmation–digression–narration, of the story as conversa-tion and flux of thought, images, culture. Here the *ordo artificialis* is fused with the *naturalis*: because the latter, for the first time in English literature, is an *ordo mentalis*, or as we would say today, a 'stream of consciousness'. Here the narration runs on its own track but also tends subtly to modify the position of the listeners (pilgrims and women) and looks further, to absolute ends – to mock and to warn: the Tale is not a 'folye'. Nothing with this sort of verve can be found again in English literature until Field-ing's mock-heroics, Sterne's digressions, and the broad mental and comic torrent of Joyce's prose.

The writer who can describe Absalon's kiss, invent the squire's speech, make Palamon talk as we have heard him do, create the figure of the Old Man, and write the *Nun's Priest's Tale*, can do anything he likes with his language and its mechanisms. He can be supremely lyrical, as when he shows up the 'bisy larke' greeting the 'morwe gray', the orient laughing with the dawn sun, the silver drops hanging on the leaves (I, 1491-6). He can be medically, almost cruelly, detached, realistic and tragic, as when he talks of dying Arcite, his 'clothered blood', his lungs swelling, 'every lacerte in his brest . . . shent with venym and corrupcioun' (I, 2743—54). He can have his Canon's Yeoman exhibit an extraordinary alchemical–linguistic virtuosity:

... As boole armonyak, verdegrees, boras,   *Armenian clay; borax*
And sondry vessels maad of erthe and glas,
Oure urynales and oure descensories,   *distilling vessels*
Violes, crosletz, and sublymatories,   *crucibles;*
Cucurbites and alambikes eek,   *gourds; alembics*
And othere swiche, deere ynough a leek.   *worthless*
Nat nedeth it for to reherce hem alle –
Watres rubifiyng, and boles galle,   *bowls*
Arsenyk, sal armonyak, and brymstoon ...

(VIII, 790–8)

and so on for thirty more lines, listing the materials of the 'elvysshe craft'. Ben Jonson's *Alchemist* was 200 years in the future. With the *Canterbury Tales*, and the other works of Chaucer that I have considered, Middle English narrative opens up vast new worlds ('God's plenty', as Dryden said), which only Elizabethan drama was able to explore again. In English literature no one but Chaucer has ever created such a multiform universe, such a Protean variety of language, except for Shakespeare. And no one has ever invented so many fictions, so many ambiguities and so many narrative personalities as Geoffrey Chaucer – administrator, diplomat, courtier, reader and, eventually, poet:

For what I drye, or what I thynke,
I wil myselven al hyt drynke,
Certeyn, for the more part,
As fer forth as I kan myn art.

Notes

1 The Religious Tradition

1 G. R. Owst, *Literature and Pulpit in Medieval England*, 2nd rev. ed. (Oxford, 1961), chapters 1–4.

2 S. Battaglia, 'L'esempio medievale', now in his *La coscienza letteraria del medioevo* (Naples, 1965), pp. 474, 480, 481.

3 *Pardoner's Prologue*, 435–8.

4 *Mirk's Festial*, ed. T. Erbe, E.E.T.S. E.S. no. 96 (London, 1905), pp. 186–91.

5 These were originally elaborated in the third-century (?) *Clementine Homilies* and *Clementine Recognitions*, apocryphal writings in Greek (the latter surviving only in the Latin adaptation by Rufinus) attributed to St Clement of Rome.

6 *Festial*, pp. 191–6.

7 Ed. W. O. Ross, E.E.T.S. O.S. no. 209 (London, 1940).

8 *Artes praedicandi*, ed. Th.-M. Charland (Paris and Ottawa, 1936).

9 Ed. R. Morris, E.E.T.S. O.S. nos. 57, 59, 62, 66, 68, 99, 101 (7 vols., London, 1874–93).

10 *Cursor Mundi*, 1–26, 232–56.

11 Quoted in R. Morris, *Cursor Mundi*, vol. VI, p. xix.

12 *Ibid.* 517–84.

13 *Ibid.* 9517–752.

14 *Ibid.* 9877–10122.

15 *Ibid.* 3555–94.

16 *Ibid.* 15961–998.

17 Bodley MS Eng. Poet. a 1, a vast collection of religious material in prose and verse, for a brief discussion of which see D. Pearsall, *Old English and Middle English Poetry* (London, 1977), pp. 140–3, and bibliography therein.

18 The text of *The Life of Adam and Eve* has been edited by N. F. Blake, *Middle English Religious Prose* (London, 1972), pp. 103–18. Quotation p. 103.

19 *The Northern Passion*, ed. F. A. Foster, E.E.T.S. O.S. nos. 145, 147, 183 (London, 1913, 1916, 1930).

20 *The Northern Passion*, 1601–46 in the *Camb.* Dd. 1. 1. version.

21 I have used the text of *Patience* as edited by J. J. Anderson (Manchester, 1969).

22 In the Vulgate, four brief chapters are dedicated to it, which correspond to two pages of a modern edition.

23 H. Melville, *Moby Dick*, chapter 9, 'The Sermon'.

24 See lines 35–6 and 528–9.

25 A. C. Spearing, *The Gawain-Poet: A Critical Study* (Cambridge, 1970), pp. 77–8.

26 See Owst, *Literature and Pulpit*, chapters 1 and 4.

27 E. Auerbach, *Mimesis*, Engl. trans. (Princeton, 1968 (1st ed., 1958)), p. 8.

28 I have used the text of *Cleanness* as edited by J. J. Anderson (Manchester, 1977).

29 Spearing, *The Gawain-Poet*, pp. 43–4.

30 *Ibid.* pp. 41–73.

31 N. Frye, *Anatomy of Criticism* (Princeton, 1957), pp. 316–17.

32 Genesis, xix, 24–5.

33 This expression was used by E. Auerbach to define the style of the Bible and to interpret Dante's style in the *Comedy*. See his 'Sacrae Scripturae sermo humilis', now in his *Studi su Dante*, It. trans., 3rd ed. (Milan, 1971), pp. 165–73.

34 *Seinte Marherete*, re-ed. F. M. Mack, E.E.T.S. O.S. no. 193 (London, 1934).

35 *The Early South English Legendary*, ed. C. Horstmann, E.E.T.S. O.S. no. 87 (London, 1887).

36 The best edition is printed in J. A. W. Bennett and G. V. Smithers (eds.), *Early Middle English Verse and Prose*, 2nd ed. (Oxford, 1968), pp. 96–107.

37 In *The Early South English Legendary*, pp. 106–77.

38 R. M. Wilson, *Early Middle English Literature*, 3rd ed. (London, 1968), p. 186.

39 In *The Early South English Legendary*, pp. 220–40.

40 A selection of passages from the 1438 version is available in Blake (ed.), *Middle English Religious Prose*, pp. 151–73. Caxton's *Golden Legend* has been edited by F. S. Ellis (London, 1892).

41 I have used the text of *St Erkenwald* as edited by C. Peterson (Philadelphia, 1977).

42 On these, see J. I. Wimsatt, *Allegory and Mirror* (New York, 1970).

43 *Robert of Brunne's Handlyng Synne*, re-ed. by F. J. Furnivall, E.E.T.S. O.S. nos. 119 and 123 (2 vols., London, 1901 and 1903), reprinted as one volume (Millwood, N.Y., 1975).

44 See D. W. Robertson, 'The Cultural Tradition of *Handlyng Synne*', *Speculum*, XXII (1947), 162–85.

45 The expression is Wimsatt's: *Allegory*, p. 150.

46 As he explicitly declares in lines 43–56 of his poem.

2 The Comic Tradition

1 In her *Antecedents of the English Novel, 1400–1600* (Warsaw–London, 1963), pp. 78–81.

2 Text in Bennett and Smithers (eds.), *Early Middle English Verse and Prose*, pp. 77–95.

3 Text in *ibid.* pp. 196–200.

4 *Ibid.* p. 96.

5 Text in *ibid.* pp. 65–76.

6 Text in *ibid.* pp. 136–44. Quotations p. 136.

7 Text in D. B. Sands (ed.), *Middle English Verse Romances* (New York–London, 1966), pp. 313–22.

8 *The History of Reynard the Fox*, ed. D. B. Sands (Cambridge, Mass., 1960).

9 Cf. above, note 1.

3 The World of Romance

1 D. Pearsall, 'The Development of Middle English Romance', *Medieval Studies*, xxvii (1965), 91–110.

2 The word *sen* is used, for example by Chrétien de Troyes, to indicate the general direction or significance of a romance. In a more strictly moral sense, *sen* would correspond to Chaucer's 'sentence'. On *sen*, see E. Vinaver, *The Rise of Romance* (Oxford, 1971), pp. 15–23, and all of chapter 2.

3 Pearsall, 'Development', p. 96.

4 The 'four-stress couplet' is a distich with four accents, e.g.:

> Hèrkneth to mè, gòde mèn,
> Wìves, maìdens, and àlle mèn.

The 'tail-rhyme stanza', in its typical form, is composed of twelve lines according to the scheme *aab ccb ddb eeb*. There are, however, many variations. The tradition of the 'tail-rhyme stanza', which at first developed mainly in the east–central part of the country, seems to have shifted northwards at the end of the fourteenth century. Cf. A. McI. Trounce, 'The English Tail-Rhyme Romances', *Medium Aevum*, i (1932), 87–108, 168–82; ii (1933), 34–57, 189–98; iii (1934), 30–50.

5 Pearsall, 'Development', p. 92.

6 The text used for *Brut* is the one edited by G. L. Brook and R. F. Leslie, E.E.T.S. nos. 250 and 277 (2 vols., London, 1963 and 1978), British Library MS Cotton Caligula A. ix.

7 Pearsall, *Old English and Middle English Poetry*, p. 112.

8 The text used for the *Morte Arthure* is that edited by V. Krishna (New York, 1976).

9 The edition is that prepared by W. W. Skeat for the E.E.T.S. (London, 1968), reprint.

10 Edition in Sands (ed.), *Middle English Verse Romances*, pp. 15–54.

11 Edition in *ibid.* pp. 55–129. See Wilson, *Early Middle English Literature*, pp. 221ff.

12 Edition in Sands (ed.), *Middle English Verse Romances*, pp. 279–309.

13 Edition in *Middle English Metrical Romances*, ed. W. H. French and C. B. Hale, vol. ii (New York, 1930), pp. 531–603.

14 The title of chapter 6 of Auerbach, *Mimesis*.

15 On the logic of adventure and of chance in the chivalrous romance, see M. Bakhtin, *Esthétique et théorie du roman*, French trans. (Paris, 1978), chapter 3; selections in English now in M. Bakhtin, *The Dialogic Imagination*, ed. M. Holquist (Austin, 1980).

16 Edition in *Fourteenth Century Verse and Prose*, ed. K. Sisam (Oxford, 1975, reprint), pp. 13–31.

17 Edition in Sands (ed.), *Middle English Verse Romances*, pp. 201–32.

18 Text: *The Romance of Sir Degrevant*, ed. L. F. Casson, E.E.T.S. O.S. no. 221 (London, 1949).

19 Edition in Sands (ed.), *Middle English Verse Romances*, pp. 249–78.

20 N. Frye, *The Secular Scripture: A Study of the Structure of Romance* (Cambridge, Mass., 1976).

21 These concepts, introduced by G. Genette (*Figures III* (Paris, 1972),

pp. 252–9) refer to the relationship between the narrator and his story, and between the narrator and the narrative level:

heterodiegetic – the story is told by the narrator himself (rather than one of the characters, for example)

homodiegetic – the story is told by one of the characters

In each of the above cases, the narrator may be either

extradiegetic – first-level narrator, e.g. Homer (heterodiegetic), and *Gil Blas* (homodiegetic),

or

intradiegetic – second-level narrator, e.g. Scheherazade (heterodiegetic), and Ulysses in cantos ix–xi of the *Odyssey* (homodiegetic).

And see now G. Genette, *Narrative Discourse*, Eng. trans. (Oxford, 1980), pp. 226–52 (245–8).

22 'Stringing': this term (in Russian, *nanizyvanie*) was introduced by the Russian critic V. Shklovsky in his *Theory of Prose* (*O Teorii Prozy* (Moscow–Leningrad, 1925), translated into Italian as *Una Teoria della Prosa* (Bari, 1966). No English translation of the whole book exists). It refers to the stringing-together of complete story motifs, linked by the presence of a single protagonist.

23 For these concepts cf. R. Jakobson and M. Halle, *Fundamentals of Language*, 2nd rev. ed. (The Hague–Paris, 1971), pp. 90–6.

24 This exploration has been carried further by Derek Brewer in his article ''The relationship of Chaucer to the English and European traditions', in D. S. Brewer (ed.), *Chaucer and Chaucerians* (London, 1966), pp. 1–16.

25 All the references to *Sir Gawain and the Green Knight*, and the quotations from it, are taken from *Sir Gawain and the Green Knight*, ed. by J. R. R. Tolkien and E. V. Gordon, 2nd ed. rev. by N. Davis (Oxford, 1967). In the following analysis of the poem, I am particularly indebted to J. A. Burrow, *A Reading of Sir Gawain and the Green Knight* (London, 1966) and especially to his conclusion.

26 Cf. *Sir Gawain and the Green Knight*, p. xiv.

27 But for the medieval public this was also historical: the legend of Troy and that of Brutus were seen as history from the time of Geoffrey of Monmouth.

28 D. R. Howard, 'Structure and Symmetry in "Sir Gawain"', now in D. R. Howard and C. Zacher (eds.), *Critical Studies of Sir Gawain and the Green Knight* (Notre Dame–London, 1968), p. 159.

29 *Ibid.* pp. 167–8.

30 'Silent, endless passing on of time': from the *Night Song of a Wandering Shepherd of Asia* by the Italian poet Giacomo Leopardi (1798–1837).

31 A. Renoir maintains that the basic descriptive technique in *Sir Gawain* is similar to that of the cinema. Cf. A. Renoir, 'Descriptive Techniques in Sir Gawain and the Green Knight', *Orbis Litterarum*, xiii, 126ff.

32 Guidoriccio da Fogliano is the knight shown in the famous fresco by Simone Martini (*c.* 1285–1344) in the Palazzo Pubblico at Siena. He is shown riding alone, gorgeously attired, through a bare, stylised landscape with fortified towns, against a deep blue sky.

33 Translation by John Gardner, *The Complete Works of the Gawain-Poet* (Carbondale, Ill., 1965), p. 254.

34 *Ibid.* p. 255.
35 An undoubtedly better example, though too long to lend itself to a detailed analysis, is that of the three hunts (cf. lines 1126–77 and 1319–71, 1412–67 and 1561–1622, 1690–1730 and 1894–1921). The three hunts are followed in minute detail, and each is different from the others.
36 J. Gardner's translation, *Complete Works*, p. 246.
37 *Ibid.* p. 227.

4 Dream and Vision

1 The text of *Piers Plowman* used in this chapter is that edited by G. Kane and E. T. Donaldson, B version, *Will's Visions of Piers Plowman, Do-Well, Do-Better, Do-Best* (London, 1975).
2 A view opposed to this division is expressed by A. V. C. Schmidt in the introduction to his edition of *Piers Plowman* (B version) (London, 1978), p. xx.
3 'The love that moves the sun and the other stars' (Dante, *Paradiso*, XXXIII, 145 (the last line of the *Divine Comedy*), trans. J. D. Sinclair).
4 See also G. Kane, 'The Vision of Piers Plowman', in his *Middle English Literature* (New York–London, 1951), p. 244.
5 Cf. J. Lawlor, 'The Imaginative Unity of *Piers Plowman*', now in E. Vasta (ed.), *Interpretations of Piers Plowman* (Notre Dame–London, 1968), pp. 278–97.
6 Cf. E. Salter, 'Medieval Poetry and the Figural View of Reality: Sir Israel Gollancz Memorial Lecture, British Academy, 1968', *Proceedings of the British Academy*, LIV (1968), 73–92.
7 For which see B. Smalley, *The Study of the Bible in the Middle Ages* (Oxford, 1952), chapter 1.
8 Cf. J. F. Goodridge, introduction to *Piers the Ploughman*, rev. ed. (Harmondsworth, 1966), p. 13.
9 T. P. Dunning, C.M., 'The Structure of the B Text of *Piers Plowman*', now in Vasta (ed.), *Interpretations of Piers Plowman*, p. 269.
10 The following analysis draws on N. K. Coghill, 'The Character of Piers Plowman Considered from the B Text', now in *Interpretations of Piers Plowman*, pp. 59–60.
11 This is my interpretation of the scene, but there have been many others. Cf. N. K. Coghill, 'The Pardon of Piers Plowman', *Proceedings of the British Academy*, XXX (1944), 303–57; J. Lawlor, '*Piers Plowman*: The Pardon Reconsidered', *Modern Language Review*, XLV (1950), 449–58; R. W. Frank, 'The Pardon Scene in Piers Plowman', *Speculum*, XXVI (1951), 317–31; R. Woolf, 'The Tearing of the Pardon', in S. S. Hussey (ed.), *Piers Plowman: Critical Approaches* (London, 1969), pp. 50–75.
12 H. W. Wells finds a three-part structure in both the *Visio* and the *Vita*. Cf. his 'The Construction of *Piers Plowman*', now in Vasta (ed.), *Interpretations of Piers Plowman*, pp. 6–7, 12–21. And H. W. Wells, 'The Philosophy of Piers Plowman', now in *Interpretations of Piers Plowman*, pp. 115–29. Here Wells maintains that Dowel, Dobet and Dobest 'are not vocational callings but mental states'.

Notes to pp. 79–92

13 Coghill, 'The Character of Piers Plowman', pp. 54–86. H. Meroney, 'The Life and Death of Longe Wille', *Journal of English Literary History*, XVII (1950), 8–15. Cf. T. P. Dunning, *Piers Plowman: An Interpretation of the A-Text* (London, 1937), pp. 173–4, 179, 182; E. T. Donaldson, *Piers Plowman: The C-Text and Its Poet* (New Haven, 1949), p. 159. D. W. Robertson, Jr and B. F. Huppé, *Piers Plowman and Scriptural Tradition* (Princeton, 1951), pp. 234–48.

14 S. S. Hussey, 'Langland, Hilton and the Three Lives', now in Vasta (ed.), *Interpretations of Piers Plowman*, especially pp. 254–8.

15 But see A. Middleton, 'Two Infinities: Grammatical Metaphor in *Piers Plowman*', *English Literary History*, XXXIX (1972), 169–88.

16 Cf. J. A. W. Bennett, *The Poetry of the Passion* (Oxford University Press, 1982).

17 See, however, Dante's doctrine on Trajan, *Paradiso*, XX, 89–117, and St Thomas, *Sum. Theol.* III, *Suppl.* 71, 5.

18 Kane, *Middle English Literature*, pp. 196–7. I am indebted to Kane for many of these observations.

19 Dante, *Paradiso*, XXII, 151.

20 Kane, *Middle English Literature*, p. 202.

21 K. Foster, O.P., 'The Mind in Love: Dante's Philosophy', in J. Freccero (ed.), *Dante* (Englewood Cliffs, N.J., 1965), pp. 43–60.

22 Cf. for example *Paradiso*, XVII, 106–42.

23 See C. Moeller, *Sagesse Grecque et Paradoxe Chrétien* (Paris–Tournai, 1947).

24 Cf. J. A. Burrow, 'The Audience of *Piers Plowman*', *Anglia*, LXXV (1957), 373–84.

25 Kane, *Middle English Literature*, p. 209: '*Piers Plowman* variously expresses and satisfies a religious and moral, a religious and emotional, a religious and intellectual impulse, and an artistic impulse.' M. W. Bloomfield, *Piers Plowman as a Fourteenth Century Apocalypse* (New Brunswick, N.J., 1962), pp. 3–43. Bloomfield distinguishes between three literary traditions (allegorical dream-narrative; dialogue, *consolatio* or debate; encyclopedic or Menippean satire) and three religious traditions (complaint or *contemptus*, commentary, sermon).

26 See B. Croce, *La poesia di Dante* (Bari, 1921), pp. 53–71.

27 Which the *Epistle to Cangrande* calls 'opus' or 'tractatus', but never 'poema'.

28 *Ep.* XIII, 27 and 40–1, 23–5, in *Le Opere di Dante* (Florence, 1921), pp. 438–40. Robertson and Huppé, *Piers Plowman and Scriptural Tradition*.

29 E. Salter, *Piers Plowman: An Introduction*, 2nd ed. (Oxford, 1969), pp. 65–105.

30 *Ibid.* pp. 102–3.

31 G. R. Owst, 'A Literary Echo of the Social Gospel', in his *Literature and Pulpit in Medieval England*, pp. 548–93; A. C. Spearing, 'The Art of Preaching and Piers Plowman', in his *Criticism and Medieval Poetry*, 2nd ed. (London, 1972), pp. 107–34.

32 G. Paparelli, under 'fictio', in *Enciclopedia dantesca*, vol. II (Rome, 1970), p. 855.

33 But consider, for example, the digression 'Ahi serva Italia' ('Ah, Italy enslaved') in *Purgatorio*, VI, 76–151, for an idea of how Dante uses this procedure.

34 In fact fourteenth-century England saw furious struggles between the Mendicants and the universities, and more generally between Mendicants and laymen. For Oxford, see M. McKisack, *The Fourteenth Century* (Oxford, 1959), pp. 503–4.

35 F. Tateo, under 'transumptio', in *Enciclopedia dantesca*, vol. v (Rome, 1976), p. 690.

36 Salter, *Piers Plowman: An Introduction*, p. 43.

37 For these concepts see Jakobson and Halle, *Fundamentals of Language*, pp. 90–6.

38 F. Tateo, under 'esempio', in *Enciclopedia dantesca*, vol. ii, p. 729.

39 Cf. E. Auerbach, 'Sacrae Scripturae sermo humilis', in his *Studi su Dante*, pp. 165–73.

40 Cf. Salter, *Piers Plowman: An Introduction*, pp. 37–43; cf. B. Huppé, '*Petrus id est Christus*: Word Play in *Piers Plowman*, the B text', *Journal of English Literary History*, xvii (1950), 163–90.

41 Cf. Salter, *Piers Plowman: An Introduction*, p. 35; J. Lawlor, *Piers Plowman: An Essay in Criticism* (London, 1962), p. 222, and, in general, pp. 189–236: 'In fact there remains for our judgement the view that Langland's distinctive achievement is to make poetry of speech, not by poeticising but rather, one would say, by *assembling* language – language considered not primarily for its diction or its capacity for adept manipulation, but language as phrase, and thus language in one way as unalterable as the fall of a phrase is unalterable.'

42 Dante, *Paradiso*, xxv, 2.

43 The text of *Pearl* used in the following pages is the one edited by E. V. Gordon (Oxford, 1953).

44 P. Gradon, *Form and Style in Early English Literature* (London, 1974), p. 98; cf. C. O. Chapman, 'Numerical Symbolism in Dante and the *Pearl*', *Modern Language Notes*, liv (1939), 256–9; and M. S. Rostvig, 'Numerical Composition in *Pearl*: A Theory', *English Studies*, xlviii (1967), 326–32; D. Everett, *Essays on Middle English Literature* (Oxford, 1955), p. 87.

45 Note the romance language: 'auenture' and 'meruayleȝ'.

46 Matthew xiii, 45–6: 'Again, the kingdom of heaven is like unto a merchant man, seeking goodly pearls, who, when he had found one pearl of great price, went and sold all that he had, and bought it.'

47 And see C. Nelson, '*Pearl*: The Circle as Figural Space', in his *The Incarnate Word, Literature as Verbal Space* (London, 1973), pp. 25–49.

48 François de Malherbe, 'Consolation à Monsieur Du Perrier', 15–16.

49 Gradon, *Form and Style*, p. 201. I acknowledge a particular debt to the pages that Pamela Gradon devotes, with great acuteness, to *Pearl* (pp. 194–211).

50 Cf. P. M. Kean, *The Pearl: An Interpretation* (London, 1967), p. 29; and Spearing, *The Gawain-Poet*, p. 111.

51 *De Genesi ad Litteram*, xii, 2, 3; 28, 56; *Sum. Theol.* ii, ii, q. 175, a. 3.

52 *De Genesi ad Litteram*, xii, 26, 54. Cf. E. Wilson, 'The "Gostly Drem" in *Pearl*', *Neuphilologische Mitteilungen*, lxix (1968), 90–101.

53 A. C. Spearing, now more clearly in his *Medieval Dream-Poetry* (Cambridge, 1976), pp. 117–18.

54 *Sum. Theol.* i, q. 12, a. 5.

55 Gradon, *Form and Style*, pp. 202–6, 205, 210.

56 *Ambrosii Theodosii Macrobii Commentarii in Somnivm Scipionis*, 1, 3, 10, ed. I. Willis (Leipzig, 1970), p. 10.

57 Cf. Spearing, *Medieval Dream-Poetry*, p. 116.

58 W. S. Johnson, 'The Imagery and Diction of *The Pearl*: Towards an Interpretation', now in J. Conley (ed.), *The Middle English Pearl* (Notre Dame–London, 1970), pp. 27–47.

59 Spearing, *The Gawain-Poet*, p. 143.

60 *S. Thomae Aquinatis In Librum Beati Dionysii De Divinis Nominibus Expositio*, 1, lectio III, 102–4 (27–8). See also P. Boitani, 'The Sibyl's Leaves: A Study of *Paradiso* xxxiii', *Dante Studies*, xcvi (1978), 83–126.

61 Cf. J. Conley, '*Pearl* and a Lost Tradition', now in Conley (ed.), *The Middle English Pearl*, pp. 50–72.

5 The Narrative Collections and Gower

1 Shklovsky, *O Teorii Prozy*, pp. 64–5; It. trans. *Una teoria della prosa*, pp. 91–2. See chapter 3, note 22.

2 S. Battaglia, 'Dall'esempio alla novella', now in his *La coscienza letteraria*, pp. 535–6.

3 G. R. Owst, *Literature and Pulpit in Medieval England*.

4 Battaglia, *La coscienza letteraria*, p. 485.

5 Text in *The Seven Sages of Rome* (Southern Version), E.E.T.S. O.S. no. 191, ed. K. Brunner (London, 1933).

6 G. Kane, 'The Middle English Metrical Romances' in his *Middle English Literature*, p. 60.

7 M. Detienne and J. P. Vernant, *Les ruses de l'intelligence* (Paris, 1974).

8 Here the word 'moral' can also mean 'philosophical'. Gower was so defined by Chaucer, with friendly objectivity; later critics continued to apply the label with some distaste.

9 The edition used for *Confessio Amantis* is that of *The English Works of John Gower*, E.E.T.S. E.S. nos. 81 and 82, ed. G. C. Macaulay (2 vols., London, 1900 and 1901). The passage cited is Book VIII, 2941–9*.

10 Text of both works in *The Complete Works of John Gower*, ed. G. C. Macaulay (4 vols., Oxford, 1899–1902). The French works are contained in vol. I, the Latin works in vol. IV.

11 *Confessio Amantis, English Works*, vol. II, pp. 479–80.

12 D. Pearsall, 'John Gower', in *Gower and Lydgate*, Writers and Their Work, no. 211 (London, 1969), p. 7.

13 Cf. G. Mathew, *The Court of Richard II* (London, 1968).

14 Here inspired also by Ovid, *Metamorphoses*, I, 85ff.

15 The first redaction had, in place of the last line, 'A bok for king Richardes sake, To whom belongeth my ligeance...' and referred to the occasion for the composition of the poem: Richard himself, meeting the poet in a boat on the Thames, had asked him to undertake it. The second redaction is dedicated to Henry of Lancaster.

16 J. A. W. Bennett, in the introduction to his edition of *Selections from John Gower* (Oxford, 1968), p. xi.

17 *Africa*, III, 90–262 (ed. N. Festa (Florence, 1926), pp. 54–62).

18 For these concepts see A. Gramsci, *Letteratura e vita nazionale* (Turin, 1966),

pp. 103–8; A. Gramsci, *Gli intellettuali e l'organizzazione della cultura* (Turin, 1966), pp. 21–38.

19 C. S. Lewis, *The Allegory of Love* (Oxford, 1970 reprint), p. 201.

20 Pearsall, *Gower and Lydgate*, p. 20.

21 E. Dorfman, *The Narreme in the Medieval Romance Epic* (Manchester, 1969). According to Dorfman,

'the structure of a narrative may ... be analysed in two ways: as a larger chain, containing all the incidents, central and marginal, that form the complete story; and as a much smaller chain of functionally central incidents, linked to each other in an organic relationship. By reason of their special function as core incidents in the structure of the narrative, these central units will be called *narremes*' (p. 5).

22 Lewis, *The Allegory of Love*, p. 206.

6 Chaucer

1 Chaucer's texts are quoted from F. N. Robinson's edition of *The Works of Geoffrey Chaucer*, 2nd ed. (London, 1966; Boston, 1957).

2 See also R. W. V. Elliott, *Chaucer's English* (London, 1974).

3 Cf. Charles Muscatine, *Chaucer and the French Tradition* (Berkeley and Los Angeles, 1957); D. S. Brewer, 'The Relationship of Chaucer to the English and European Traditions', in D. S. Brewer (ed.), *Chaucer and Chaucerians* (London, 1966), pp. 1–38.

4 Cf. Brewer, 'Relationship'; P. M. Kean, *Chaucer and the Making of English Poetry* (2 vols., London, 1972), vol. I, pp. 1–30; J. A. W. Bennett, 'Chaucer's Contemporary', in Hussey (ed.), *Piers Plowman: Critical Approaches*, pp. 310–24.

5 Cf. G. Kane, 'Chaucer and the Idea of a Poet', in *Geoffrey Chaucer*, Accademia Nazionale dei Lincei, Quaderno no. 234 (Rome, 1977), pp. 35–49.

6 Cf. J. Mann, *Chaucer and Medieval Estates Satire* (Cambridge, 1973).

7 See also M. Schlauch, 'Chaucer's Prose Rhythms', *PMLA*, LXV (1950), 568–89; and, also by Schlauch, 'The Art of Chaucer's Prose', in Brewer (ed.), *Chaucer and Chaucerians*, pp. 140–63.

1 The dream poem

1 Expression used by Paul Zumthor, *Essai de poétique médiévale* (Paris, 1972), p. 92.

2 On these, see E. R. Curtius, *European Literature and the Latin Middle Ages*, Engl. trans. (London, 1953).

3 On the *dits*, see Zumthor, *Essai*, pp. 406–20; on the French dream poems, Spearing, *Medieval Dream-Poetry*, pp. 41–7, to which this paragraph is heavily indebted.

4 Spearing, *Dream-Poetry*, p. 20.

5 V. Branca, introduction to the *Amorosa Visione*, in *Tutte le Opere di Giovanni Boccaccio*, vol. III (Milan, 1974), p. 8.

6 Petrarch in only one of the redactions of the *Triumphus Fame*, incomplete; Boccaccio in both versions of the *Amorosa Visione*, in the section devoted to Sapienza (Philosophy).

7 On this problem, cf. J. A. W. Bennett, *Chaucer's Book of Fame* (Oxford, 1969), *passim*, and the references therein.
8 R. O. Payne, *The Key of Remembrance* (New Haven, 1963), p. 117.
9 *Ibid.* pp. 119–21.
10 On 'fers' cf. Robinson, p. 776, note 653; and B. H. Bronson, '*The Book of the Duchess* Re-opened', now in E. Wagenknecht (ed.), *Chaucer* (Oxford, 1959), pp. 285–6.
11 Cf. for example W. Clemen, *Chaucer's Early Poetry*, Engl. trans. (London, 1968; 1st ed., 1963), pp. 24–37.
12 Bronson, '*The Book of the Duchess* Re-opened', p. 281.
13 J. Lawlor, 'The Pattern of Consolation in *The Book of the Duchess*', *Speculum*, XXXI (1956), 626–48.
14 Kean, *Chaucer and the Making of English Poetry*, vol. I, pp. 45–66.
15 For the references in this passage, see Robinson, p. 777, note 1162.
16 On this whole subject, see Payne, *The Key of Remembrance*, pp. 122–5.
17 See, for example, the scene of Juno's messenger in the cave of Morpheus (lines 178–91), and the protagonists' sceptical vow to the two gods (lines 221–69).
18 *Aeneid*, IV, 173–88; *House of Fame*, 1360–94.
19 *Metamorphoses*, XII, 39–63; *House of Fame*, 713–24 and 1920–2033.
20 *Paradiso*, I, 109–17. This canto was also used by Chaucer elsewhere in the *House of Fame*.
21 On the identity of this character, see Robinson, p. 787, note 1844.
22 *Purgatorio*, IX, 19–21 and 28–30; *Paradiso*, I, 61–3.
23 II Corinthians xii, 2; *House of Fame*, 981–2.
24 One is reminded too of Calumny's aria in the *Barber of Seville*, which is itself a form of fame.
25 Spearing, *Medieval Dream-Poetry*, pp. 73–89.
26 *House of Fame*, 588–9 and 981–2.
27 *Ibid.* 1383–5.
28 See P. Boitani, 'Chaucer's Temples of Venus', *Studi Inglesi*, II (1975), 17–21; also M. Twycross, *The Medieval Anadyomene* (Oxford, 1972).
29 C. S. Lewis, *English Literature in the Sixteenth Century* (Oxford, 1954), p. 27.
30 *Commentarii in Somnium Scipionis*, I, 3, 7, p. 10. Note that Macrobius has just quoted Virgil, and in particular a phrase of Dido (*Aeneid*, IV, 9), the heroine of Book I of the *House of Fame*.
31 Bennett, *Chaucer's Book of Fame*, p. 180.
32 Condemnation of the betrayal of Aeneas and other unfaithful lovers; collocation of the postulants of Fame in companies of the good, the lazy and the bad; consideration of the amorality of Venus and Fame.
33 D. Everett, 'Some Reflections on Chaucer's "Art-Poetical"', now in her *Essays on Middle English Literature* (Oxford, 1955), pp. 149–74.
34 A. S. Miskimin, *The Renaissance Chaucer* (New Haven and London, 1975), p. 85; also, for the *House of Fame*, pp. 67–80.
35 The phrase is that of Michel de Marbais, cit. in R. H. Robins, *A Short History of Linguistics*, 2nd ed. (London, 1979), p. 77 and note 22. See also G. L. Bursill-Hall, *Speculative Grammars of the Middle Ages* (The Hague–Paris, 1971); M. Heidegger, *Die Kategorien – und Bedeutungslehre des Duns*

Scotus (repr. Frankfurt a. M., 1972); E. Vance is completing a book on poetics and sign theory in the Middle Ages.

36 The passage has been analysed from the metrical and rhetorical point of view by H. S. Bennett, *Chaucer and the Fifteenth Century* (Oxford, 1947), pp. 89–90; and by D. Everett, 'Chaucer's "Art Poetical"', now in her *Essays on Middle English Literature*, pp. 153–4.

37 On this subject, see the introduction and notes by D. S. Brewer to his edition of *The Parlement of Foulys*, 2nd ed. (Manchester, 1972), especially pp. 3–13, 33–8.

38 A splendid step-by-step analysis of the interweaving of these traditions in the poem has been carried out by J. A. W. Bennett, *The Parlement of Foules* (Oxford, 1957). On the presence of the *Teseida*, see also my 'Chaucer's Temples of Venus', pp. 21–7.

39 See Payne, *The Key of Remembrance*, pp. 60–90.

40 This is, in a certain sense, the direction that J. A. W. Bennett has followed in his book on the *Parliament*, reconstructing the whole cultural–poetic universe of the work. It is not a matter of *Quellenforschung* pure and simple, but of rediscovering all the meanings with which Chaucer's own search is laden.

41 Those who find the blissful place after death are the 'rightful folk'; it is denied, at least initially, to the 'breakers of the lawe'.

42 See Brewer (ed.), *Parlement*, p. 102, note 47; also J. A. W. Bennett, *Parlement*, pp. 33–5.

43 See Bennett, *Parlement*, pp. 41–4.

44 On this subject, see my 'Chaucer's Temples of Venus', pp. 21–7; for an analysis of the Boccaccio passage, see my *Chaucer and Boccaccio* (Oxford, 1977), pp. 89–95.

45 See Bennett, *Parlement*, pp. 76–8.

46 See my 'Chaucer and Lists of Trees', *Reading Medieval Studies*, II (1976), 28–44.

47 Note also the contrast between this image, centred on the fish, and the image of aridity in the second inscription, which was also focussed on fish.

48 The procreating birds here anticipate those of the parliament to follow, each in search of its own mate.

49 See also Bennett, *Parlement*, pp. 140–8.

50 *Summa Contra Gentiles*, II, xlv, 4. Trans. English Dominican Fathers (London, 1923), p. 107.

51 See also A. O. Lovejoy, *The Great Chain of Being* (New York, 1960 reprint), pp. 24–98.

52 *Commentarii in Somnium Scipionis*, I, 14, and particularly I, 14, 15.

53 *Summa Contra Gentiles*, II, xlv, 6, p. 107.

54 Brewer (ed.), *Parlement*, p. 28.

55 *Summa Contra Gentiles*, III, cxxiii, 7. Trans. English Dominican Fathers (London, 1928), p. 116.

56 As will happen in the *Knight's Tale*, where Arcite and Palamon fight for Emily.

57 On the innate characteristics of the birds, partly derived from the Bestiaries, see Bennett, *Parlement*, pp. 148–52 and 166–74.

58 R. Scholes and R. Kellogg, *The Nature of Narrative* (New York, 1966), p. 4.

59 D. S. Brewer, 'Towards a Chaucerian Poetic', *Proceedings of The British Academy*, LX (1974), 8.

60 In the first line of this paragraph I am paraphrasing the German expression *Erwartungshorizont*, or 'horizon of expectations'. A work of art is inserted within a complex system of needs, expectations, tastes, readings and models of behaviour, which together constitute the audience's *Erwartungshorizont*. For these concepts see H. R. Jauss, *Literaturgeschichte als Provokation* (Frankfurt, a. M., 1970), pp. 171–89. 'Strangeness' approximately translates V. Shklovsky's *ostranenje*. See V. Shklovsky, 'Art as a Technique', in *Russian Formalist Criticism*, ed. and trans. L. T. Lemon and M. J. Reis (Lincoln, Nebraska, 1965), *passim*.

61 L. Spitzer, *Classical and Christian Ideas of World Harmony*, ed. A. G. Hatcher (Baltimore, 1963), chapters 3 and 4. See also *Parliament of Fowls*, lines 129, 191, 197, 203, 204.

62 See G. Duby, now in his *Le Temps des cathédrales* (Paris, 1976), pp. 317–25 (an English edition is now available: *The Age of the Cathedrals* (London, 1981)); A. D. Scaglione, *Nature and Love in the Late Middle Ages* (Berkeley and Los Angeles, 1963).

63 Duby, *Le Temps*, pp. 241–5.

64 See M. W. Bloomfield, 'Authenticating Realism and the Realism of Chaucer', *Thought*, XXXIX (1964), 335–58.

65 Duby, *Le Temps*, p. 253.

66 See also R. A. Peck, 'Chaucer and the Nominalist Questions', *Speculum*, LIII (1978), 745–60.

67 Cf. M. W. Stearns, 'Chaucer Mentions a Book', *Modern Language Notes*, LVII (1942), 28–31. Note how the book–dream parallel gradually becomes more complicated in the dream poems: in the *Book of the Duchess*, Chaucer reads a book, in which a dream occurs, and then dreams; in the *House of Fame*, Chaucer dreams, and dreams a book-temple; in the *Parliament*, Chaucer reads a dream-book, and dreams.

68 Brewer, 'Towards a Chaucerian Poetic', p. 32.

69 Genette, *Figures III*, pp. 252–9; and see chapter 3, note 21, above.

70 On these concepts, cf. M. Bakhtin, *Problems of Dostoevsky's Poetics*, Engl. trans. (Ardis, n.p., 1973), pp. 3–62.

71 See also Brewer, 'Towards a Chaucerian Poetic', p. 20.

72 See A. Hauser, *The Social History of Art*, vol. 1: 'From Prehistoric Times to the Middle Ages' (London, 1962), pp. 216–22; and D. S. Brewer, 'Gothic Chaucer', in D. S. Brewer (ed.), *Geoffrey Chaucer*, Writers and their Backgrounds (London, 1974).

73 *Bewegungsdrama*, as contraposed to *Einortsdrama* ('single-place drama'). The former is typical of the Middle Ages, with their passion for variety and change, the latter of Antiquity. And see Hauser, *The Social History of Art*, vol. 1, p. 217 and note 206.

74 The definition of the 'figures' in this and the following paragraphs is taken from H. Lausberg, *Elemente der literarischen Rhetorik*, 3rd ed. (Munich, 1967). See also R. Lanham, *A Handlist of Rhetorical Terms* (Berkeley and London, 1967).

75 The phenomenon is repeated again in line 287, and later in lines 365–6.

76 Again in line 1355 and lines 1179–80. In the *Book of the Duchess*.

praeteritio does not seem to occur; here, Chaucer fully describes everything that comes to his attention: the *locus amoenus*, the beauty of Blanche etc.

77 Here, and throughout this chapter on Chaucer, I use expressions such as 'multiplicity of styles', 'multiple register' etc. These are but an approximate translation of Gianfranco Contini's 'plurilinguismo', for which see his 'Preliminari sulla lingua del Petrarca', most recently reprinted in *Varianti e altra linguistica* (Turin, 1979), pp. 169–92. I prefer to avoid the term 'multilingualism'.

78 Brewer, 'Relationship', in Brewer (ed.), *Chaucer and Chaucerians*, pp. 1–15.

79 Bakhtin, *Dostoevsky*, pp. 87–113; and Frye, *Anatomy of Criticism*, pp. 308–12.

2 The romance

1 V. Branca, *Boccaccio Medievale*, 3rd ed. (Florence, 1970), pp. 191–249.

2 *Proemio*, 1. The texts referred to in the case of the *Filostrato* and the *Teseida* are those edited respectively by V. Branca and A. Limentani, in *Tutte le Opere di Giovanni Boccaccio*, vol. 1 (Milan, 1964).

3 See *Fil.* 1, 25; 1, 35, 8; 111, 1–2; 111, 33; 111, 94; VIII, 29–33; IX.

4 Chaucer adds Criseyde's dream (II, 925–31), which however has no function in the plot: it serves to sharpen the tension and to balance the dream of Troilus symmetrically. See also Spearing, *Criticism and Medieval Poetry*, pp. 139–47.

5 Payne, *The Key of Remembrance*, pp. 184–8.

6 A. Limentani in his introduction to the *Teseida*, in *Tutte le Opere di Giovanni Boccaccio*, vol. II, pp. 236 and 237. Limentani's remarks refer to all Boccaccio's early works.

7 C. S. Lewis, 'What Chaucer Really Did to *Il Filostrato*', most recently in his *Selected Literary Essays*, ed. W. Hooper (Cambridge, 1969), pp. 27–44.

8 *Dolce stil novo* is the name given by Dante (*Purgatorio*, XXIV, 57) to what later came to be considered the most important poetic movement of thirteenth-century Italy. See G. Petrocchi, 'Il Dolce stil novo', in E. Cecchi and N. Sapegno (eds.), *Storia della Letteratura Italiana*, vol. 1 (Milan, 1965), pp. 611–47.

9 Other cases (*TC* is an abbreviation for *Troilus and Criseyde*): *TC* I, 523–5: *Fil.* 1, 53, 7–8; *TC* III, 351–7: *Fil.* III, 12, 1–6; *TC* IV, 239–41: *Fil.* IV, 27, 1–4.

10 *TC* IV, 225ff: *Inferno*, III, 117ff; *TC* II, 764ff: *De Consolatione*, I, m. 3.

11 H. Schless, 'Transformations: Chaucer's Use of Italian', in Brewer (ed.), *Geoffrey Chaucer*, pp. 184–223, and particularly pp. 185–6; also H. Schless, 'Chaucer and Dante', in D. Bethurum (ed.), *Critical Approaches to Medieval Literature* (New York, 1960), pp. 136–7; and Boitani, *Chaucer and Boccaccio*, pp. 117–26. For *Troilus* and *Teseida* see R. A. Pratt, 'Chaucer's Use of the "Teseida"', *PMLA*, LXII (1947), 608–13.

12 D. C. Boughner, 'Elements of Epic Grandeur in the *Troilus*', now in R. J. Schoeck and J. Taylor (eds.), *Chaucer Criticism* (Notre Dame–London, 1961), vol. II, pp. 186–95, and in particular p. 193. However, as will appear later, I do not agree with Boughner's conclusions.

13 Here are two items chosen at random: *TC* II, 64–71: *Tes.* IV, 73; *TC* III, 1427–8: *Tes.* IV, 14.

14 *TC* v, 8–13: *Tes.* II, 1; *TC* v, 274–9: *Tes.* VII, 94.

15 *TC* III, 1–44: *Fil.* III, 74–9; *TC* III, 1807–13: *Tes.* I, 3, 3–6. Also compare *TC* IV, 22–8 and *Tes.* III, 1. The other invocations derive more directly from the *Thebaid*, one (*TC* III, 45–8) with an echo of Dante (*Purgatorio*, I, 7–9). Compare also *TC* II, 435 and *Tes.* I, 58, 1; Troilus's prayer to the gods before his nocturnal meeting with Criseyde (*TC* III, 712–35) could be an amalgam of various prayers of Arcite and Palamon: cf. *Tes.* IV, 43–8; VII, 24–5; VII, 43.

16 For which see my *Chaucer and Boccaccio*, pp. 16–20.

17 *TC* II, 100–8; v, 1464–1512, especially 1485–1510.

18 There is no need to tell the story of Thebes to demonstrate that the boar stands for Diomedes; it suffices to establish the genealogical tree of Meleager–Tydeus–Diomedes, as Cassandra in fact does in the course of her long speech.

19 Lewis, 'What Chaucer Really Did', pp. 59–60.

20 *Chaucer and Boccaccio*, pp. 148–54.

21 This has been splendidly and concisely carried out by D. S. Brewer, 'Troilus and Criseyde', in W. F. Bolton (ed.), *The Middle Ages* (London, 1970), pp. 195–228. See also G. T. Shepherd, 'Troilus and Criseyde', in Brewer (ed.), *Chaucer and Chaucerians*, pp. 65–87.

22 Whose names are recalled, among others, by D. Mehl in his important 'The Audience of Chaucer's *Troilus and Criseyde*', in B. Rowland (ed.), *Chaucer and Middle English Studies* (London, 1974), pp. 173–89.

23 For these terms see note 21 to chapter 3 of this volume.

24 On the problem of the Narrator see R. M. Jordan's fundamental essay, 'The Narrator in Chaucer's *Troilus*', *Journal of English Literary History*, xxv (1958), 237–57.

25 References to the 'author', to history and to the 'geste' are found in *TC* I, 392–9; II, 13–14, 49, 699–700; III, 90–1, 450, 575–6, 1325; v, 1037, 1044.

26 As, for the first, in *TC* II, 1751ff: 'But now to yow, ye loveres that ben here, / Was Troilus nought in a kankedort...?'; for the second, in *TC* I, 1086: 'Now lat us stynte of Troilus a stounde...'

27 See J. A. Burrow, *Ricardian Poetry* (London, 1971), pp. 68ff for a discussion of 'pointing' (*TC* III, 497) as a literary technique in Chaucer and other Ricardian poets.

28 Taken from Geoffrey of Vinsauf, *Poetria Nova*, 43–5.

29 In the *Filostrato* the hymn to Venus is sung by Troilus himself in one of his last songs in the poem (III, 74–9).

30 M. W. Bloomfield, 'Distance and Predestination in *Troilus and Criseyde*', now in Schoeck and Taylor (eds.), *Chaucer Criticism*, vol. II, pp. 196–210.

31 E. T. Donaldson, 'Criseide and her Narrator', now in his *Speaking of Chaucer* (London, 1970), p. 68 (pp. 63–83).

32 *Ibid.* p. 83. On the attitude of the Narrator to Criseyde see also Donaldson's 'The Masculine Narrator and Four Women of Style', in *Speaking of Chaucer*, pp. 53–9.

33 Muscatine, *Chaucer and the French Tradition*, p. 137. E. T. Donaldson, 'Chaucer and the Elusion of Clarity', *Essays and Studies*, n.s. xxv (1972), 33–4 (23–44).

34 On this problem see R. K. Root, *The Textual Tradition of Chaucer's Troilus* (London, 1916); C. A. Owen, Jr, 'The Significance of Chaucer's Revisions of *Troilus and Criseyde*', *Modern Philology*, LV (1957–8), 1–5.

35 On which see W. C. Curry, 'Destiny in *Troilus and Criseyde*', now in Schoeck and Taylor (eds.), *Chaucer Criticism*, vol. II, pp. 34–70; also H. R. Patch, 'Troilus on Determinism', in *Chaucer Criticism*, vol. II, pp. 71–85.

36 See G. Shepherd, 'Religion and Philosophy in Chaucer', in Brewer (ed.), *Geoffrey Chaucer*, pp. 212–99; G. Leff, *Bradwardine and the Pelagians* (Cambridge, 1957).

37 D. W. Robertson, 'Chaucerian Tragedy', now in Schoeck and Taylor (eds.), *Chaucer Criticism*, vol. II, pp. 86–121.

38 With whom he is associated in the *Parliament*, in lines 288–94, which contain all the names mentioned by Dante, *Inferno*, V, 58–66.

39 A. C. Spearing, *Chaucer: Troilus and Criseyde* (London, 1976), p. 61.

40 Robertson, 'Chaucerian Tragedy', takes these passages as his point of departure for a coherent and extreme interpretation of *Troilus*'s Christianity. For a very unusual interpretation of 'tragedy', see J. Norton-Smith, *Geoffrey Chaucer* (London, 1974), pp. 160–212.

41 Dante, *Inferno*, V, 103. Or, as Pandarus says (II, 392), love, which 'for love is skilful guerdonynge'.

42 Dante, *Inferno*, VII, 83–4.

43 Schlauch, *Antecedents of the English Novel, 1400–1600*, pp. 28–39 and all of chapter 2. On realistic tendencies in the 'romance', see R. Tuve, *Allegorical Imagery* (Princeton, 1966), pp. 336ff. See also A. C. Spearing, 'Chaucer as Novelist', in his *Criticism and Medieval Poetry*, pp. 135–56.

44 See also Peck, 'Chaucer and the Nominalist Questions', pp. 745–60; and U. Dotti, *Petrarca e la scoperta della coscienza moderna* (Milan, 1978).

45 Payne, *The Key of Remembrance*, p. 186.

46 H. W. Sams, 'The Dual Time-Scheme in Chaucer's *Troilus*', now in Schoeck and Taylor (eds.), *Chaucer Criticism*, vol. II, pp. 180–5.

47 As can be expected, this is not totally consistent. Pandarus tells Criseyde a 'tale of Wade', and Wade is the hero of an as-yet-unidentified medieval legend, certainly not a Greek mythological character.

48 See D. Pearsall, 'The Troilus Frontispiece and Chaucer's Audience', *The Yearbook of English Studies*, VII (1977), 68–74.

49 For a thorough analysis of the problem of God in *Troilus*, see T. P. Dunning, 'God and Man in *Troilus and Criseyde*', in N. Davis and C. L. Wrenn (eds.), *English and Medieval Studies Presented to J. R. R. Tolkien* (London, 1962), pp. 164–82.

50 On this subject see E. T. Donaldson, 'The Ending of *Troilus*', in his *Speaking of Chaucer*, pp. 84–101.

51 See also Muscatine, *Chaucer and the French Tradition*, pp. 132–65.

52 See also I. L. Gordon, *The Double Sorrow of Troilus* (Oxford, 1970). This analysis is based on W. Empson's observations in *Seven Types of Ambiguity* (London, 1947), pp. 58–68. See also L. W. Patterson, 'Ambiguity and Interpretation: A Fifteenth Century Reading of *Troilus and Criseyde*', *Speculum*, LIV (1979), 297–330.

53 Dante, *Inferno*, IV, 102.

54 'The work ends in God Himself' (*Epistole*, XIII, 90).

3 The narrative collection

1 All these works are in fact mentioned in the Prologue to the *Legend*, F 417–28: G 405–18; *Troilus* and the translation of the *Roman* in F 327–34: G 253–66. In the Introduction to the *Man of Law's Tale*, 57–76, the 'Seintes Legende of Cupide' is mentioned. For this citation and problems regarding the chronology of the *Legend* and the *Tales*, see W. W. Skeat, *The Complete Works of Geoffrey Chaucer* (7 vols., Oxford, 1894–7), vol. v, pp. 132–41, and Robinson, pp. 689–90, 839–41, 845, and bibliographical references indicated therein.

2 On this subject see D. D. Griffith, 'An Interpretation of Chaucer's *Legend of Good Women*', now in Wagenknecht (ed.), *Chaucer*, p. 403, and relevant notes.

3 Shklovsky, *O Teorii Prozy*, pp. 64–5; It. trans. *Una Teoria della Prosa*, pp. 91–2.

4 Metonymy, as Jakobson and Halle (*Fundamentals of Language*, pp. 90ff) maintain, refers to a discourse governed by contiguity rather than by similarity or contrast.

5 Only in F, 84–94.

6 Here the two versions differ. I have followed G. In F, the narrator is physically present in the meadow and observes the scene which in G appears to him in a dream; he hears the birds sing 'Welcome, somer' and at sunset returns home, has his bed made up in the garden, falls asleep and dreams. In both versions the dream begins before the arrival of the God of Love (F 210: G 104).

7 In the F version it is the poet himself who sings the ballad. Whereas the name of the daisy-queen is announced at once in G as Alceste, it is not mentioned in F.

8 The passage on the authors is absent in F.

9 Only in F.

10 Only in F.

11 Only in F, 570–7.

12 Strictly speaking, the Prologue by itself cannot be considered a frame, for it does not enclose the nine stories. Thus 'frontispiece' is a more precise metaphor.

13 In both versions there seems to be an incongruity on this point, more in G than in F. In G 179 the queen is identified as Alceste; in F 432 and G 422, Alceste herself mentions her own name. Of course the incongruity of the late recognition may be deliberate: only at the end of the episode is the poet able to comprehend the lady's identity.

14 By Burrow, *Ricardian Poetry*; and Norton-Smith, *Chaucer*, pp. 69–72, respectively.

15 See also R. W. Frank, 'The Legend of the *Legend of Good Women*', *Chaucer Review*, I (1966), 110–33; R. O. Payne, 'Making His Own Myth: The Prologue to Chaucer's *Legend of Good Women*', *Chaucer Review*, IX (1975), 197–211.

16 Norton-Smith, *Chaucer*, p. 63.

17 Payne, *The Key of Remembrance*, pp. 91–111, whose argument is here repeated, summarised and commented on.

18 *Ibid.* pp. 100–1.

19 *Ibid.* p. 105.
20 See also *House of Fame*, I, 450.
21 Cf. Dante, *Paradiso*, I, 128.
22 Duby, *Le Temps*, pp. 241–5.
23 See B. Harbert, 'Chaucer and the Latin Classics', in Brewer (ed.), *Geoffrey Chaucer*, especially pp. 149–53.
24 Norton-Smith, *Chaucer*, p. 73.
25 R. W. Frank, *Chaucer and the Legend of Good Women* (Cambridge, Mass., 1972), pp. 169–87.
26 I am using Robinson's division, without going into the question of the text of the *Canterbury Tales*, for which see the observations of Robinson himself, the bibliography given by him and the brief remarks of L. D. Benson, 'Chaucer: A Select Bibliography', in Brewer (ed.), *Geoffrey Chaucer*, p. 356.
27 In the division into 'groups' proposed by some critics (Skeat, for example), the *Shipman's Tale* in fact follows the *Man of Law's Tale* in Group B, or it is the first of Group B2, which includes the other stories of Fragment VII. But for various reasons this arrangement is not satisfactory either.
28 Brewer, 'Gothic Chaucer', in his *Geoffrey Chaucer*, p. 4; Brewer devotes pp. 3–6 of his essay to these incongruities.
29 R. Baldwin, *The Unity of the Canterbury Tales*, Anglistica 5 (Copenhagen, 1955). The exegetical line has since been emphasised by D. W. Robertson, *A Preface to Chaucer* (Princeton, 1962); and B. F. Huppé, *A Reading of the Canterbury Tales* (Albany, N.Y., 1964).
30 R. M. Lumiansky, *Of Sondry Folk* (Austin, Texas, 1955). Lumiansky develops and systematises the approach used by G. L. Kittredge, *Chaucer and his Poetry* (Cambridge, Mass., 1915).
31 R. M. Jordan, *Chaucer and the Shape of Creation* (Cambridge, Mass., 1967).
32 Norton-Smith, *Chaucer*, p. 86.
33 D. R. Howard, *The Idea of the Canterbury Tales* (Berkeley and Los Angeles, 1976).
34 See also E. T. Donaldson's fundamental essay, 'Chaucer the Pilgrim', now in his *Speaking of Chaucer*, pp. 1–12.
35 For 'prose' in the *Man of Law's Tale* standing for formal stanzas of equal length, see M. Stevens, 'The Royal Stanza in Early English Literature', *PMLA*, XCIV (1979), 62–76.
36 See chapter 3, note 21 of this volume.
37 See A. Koyre, 'Du monde de l' "à-peu-près" à l'univers de la précision' in his *Etudes d'histoire de la pensée philosophique* (Paris, 1961), pp. 311–29.
38 But see T. Jones, *Chaucer's Knight, the Portrait of a Medieval Mercenary* (London, 1980) for an opposite view – with which I do not agree – of the Knight.
39 Bloomfield, 'Authenticating Realism', p. 351.
40 Mann, *Chaucer and Medieval Estates Satire*, which I shall often paraphrase in the following lines.
41 On this last, see R. C. Finucane, *Miracles and Pilgrims* (London, 1977).
42 C. K. Zacher, *Curiosity and Pilgrimage* (Baltimore and London, 1976); on Chaucer, pp. 87–129.
43 Hauser, *The Social History of Art*, vol. I, p. 240.
44 On his relationship with Chaucer, see R. A. Pratt and K. Young, 'The

Literary Framework of the Canterbury Tales', in W. F. Bryan and G. Dempster (eds.), *Sources and Analogues of Chaucer's Canterbury Tales* (henceforth indicated as *SA*) (Chicago, 1941), pp. 1–81.

45 Howard, *The Idea of the Canterbury Tales*, p. 163, whose ideas are used throughout this paragraph.

46 Brewer, 'Gothic Chaucer', in his *Geoffrey Chaucer*, pp. 12–25.

47 Custance, the heroine of the *Man of Law's Tale*, is the Christian woman who supports and overcomes all adversities and the forces of evil. The story of Griselda in the *Clerk's Tale* is a parable of patience and humility. Both these stories are inserted into a context of romance and folk-tale.

48 E. T. Donaldson, 'Idiom of Popular Poetry in the Miller's Tale', now in his *Speaking of Chaucer*, pp. 13–29.

49 Cf. J. R. R. Tolkien, 'Chaucer as a Philologist: *The Reeve's Tale*', *Transactions of the Philological Society* (1934), 1–70.

50 Payne, *The Key of Remembrance*, pp. 157–8.

51 P. G. Ruggiers, *The Art of the Canterbury Tales* (Madison, Wisconsin, 1965), pp. 47–8.

52 Muscatine, *Chaucer and the French Tradition*, pp. 173–243.

53 Howard, *The Idea of the Canterbury Tales*, pp. 210–339.

54 D. A. Pearsall, 'The Canterbury Tales', in W. F. Bolton (ed.), *The Middle Ages* (London, 1970), pp. 163–93, especially p. 177.

55 M. Baratto, *Realtà e Stile nel Decameron*, 2nd ed. (Venice, 1974).

56 See also V. Branca, 'L'epopea dei mercatanti', in his *Boccaccio Medievale*, pp. 134–64.

57 Baratto, *Realtà e Stile*, p. 33.

58 *Ibid.* pp. 44–5 and 46.

59 *Ibid.* p. 62; see also all of chapter 2.

60 *Ibid.* p. 86.

61 Cf. J. A. W. Bennett, *Chaucer at Oxford and at Cambridge* (Oxford, 1974).

62 Cf. P. Boitani, '*The Monk's Tale*: Dante and Boccaccio', *Medium Aevum*, XLV (1976), 50–69.

63 See also Boitani, *Chaucer and Boccaccio*, pp. 148–54.

64 E. Auerbach, *Dante, Poet of the Secular World* (Chicago, 1961).

65 Branca describes the thematic construction of the *Decameron* in terms of the motifs of Fortune (days II and III), Love (days IV–V), Intelligence (days VI–VIII), and Virtue (day X), with days I and IX reserved for a free mixture of themes. See *Boccaccio Medievale*, pp. 16–17.

66 G. L. Kittredge, 'Chaucer's Discussion of Marriage', now in Wagenknecht (ed.), *Chaucer*, pp. 188–215.

67 Kean, *Chaucer and the Making of English Poetry*, vol. II, pp. 140 and, in general, pp. 139–64.

68 Pearsall, 'The Canterbury Tales', p. 177.

69 On which see E. Vinaver, *The Rise of Romance* (Oxford, 1971), pp. 68–98; also W. W. Ryding, *Structure in Medieval Narrative* (The Hague–Paris, 1971), pp. 139–54.

70 Shklovsky, *O Teorii Prozy*, p. 93; trans. *Una Teoria della Prosa*, p. 95.

71 Boitani, *Chaucer and Boccaccio*, pp. 127–34 and 76–8.

72 M. Bakhtin, *Rabelais and His World*, Engl. trans. (Cambridge, Mass., 1968).

73 On this subject see A. Brilli's illuminating lines in his introduction to *I racconti di Canterbury* (Milan, 1978), pp. 9–17, especially p. 17.

74 See also F. Tupper, 'The Pardoner's Tale', in *SA*, pp. 415–38.

75 For the various identifications of the Old Man see the summary bibliography in Robinson, p. 731, note 713.

76 Leopardi, *Canto notturno d'un pastore errante dell' Asia*, lines 63–7.

77 Imitated from Elegy 1 by Maximianus (cf. Skeat, vol. v, p. 287, note 727), but greatly intensified by Chaucer.

78 R. P. Miller, 'Chaucer's Pardoner, the Scriptural Eunuch, and the *Pardoner's Tale*', now in Schoeck and Taylor (eds.), *Chaucer Criticism*, vol. i, pp. 221–44; W. J. B. Owen, 'The Old Man in *The Pardoner's Tale*', now in Wagenknecht (ed.), *Chaucer*, pp. 159–65.

79 Lines 743–4 are a quotation from Leviticus xix, 32. Lines 745–7 recall Ecclesiastes viii, 6. Lines 745–7 also echo Matthew vii, 12.

80 For other interpretations of the episode, see A. C. Spearing, introduction to his edition of *The Pardoner's Prologue and Tale* (Cambridge, 1965), pp. 37–40; Howard, *The Idea of the Canterbury Tales*, pp. 358–63. For the *Pardoner's Tale* in general see D. R. Faulkner (ed.), *Twentieth-Century Interpretations of the Pardoner's Tale* (Englewood Cliffs, N.J., 1973). According to Salvatore Battaglia the whole *Pardoner's Tale* is a parable; see his 'Dall'esempio alla novella', now in *La coscienza letteraria*, pp. 536–47.

81 *Ibid.* p. 545.

82 B. F. Huppé and D. W. Robertson, *Fruyt and Chaf* (Princeton, 1963). For different interpretations of the *Nun's Priest's Tale*, cf. Robinson, pp. 751–2; Ruggiers, *The Art of the Canterbury Tales*, pp. 184–96, and references therein; Muscatine, *Chaucer and the French Tradition*, pp. 237–43.

Further Reading

1 The Religious Tradition

1 General

M. W. Bloomfield, *The Seven Deadly Sins* (East Lansing, Michigan, 1952).

D. C. Fowler, *The Bible in Early English Literature* (London, 1977).

J. A. Mosher, *The Exemplum in the Early Religious and Didactic Literature of England* (New York, 1911).

G. R. Owst, *Preaching in Medieval England* (Cambridge, 1926; repr. New York, 1965).

W. A. Pantin, *The English Church in the Fourteenth Century* (Cambridge, 1955).

J. D. Peter, *Complaint and Satire in Early English Literature* (Oxford, 1956).

E. M. C. Quinn, *The Quest of Seth for the Oil of Life* (Chicago, 1962).

B. Smalley, *English Friars and Antiquity in the Early Fourteenth Century* (Oxford, 1960), chapter 2.

R. M. Wilson, *The Lost Literature of Medieval England*, 2nd rev. ed. (London, 1970).

2 On *Patience, Cleanness, St Erkenwald*

N. Berlin, '*Patience*: A Study in Poetic Elaboration', *Studia Neophilologica*, XXXIII (1961), 80–5.

T. McAlindon, 'Hagiography into Art: A Study of *St Erkenwald*', *Studies in Philology*, LXVII (1970), 472–94.

V. Petronella, '*St Erkenwald*: Style as the Vehicle for Meaning', *Journal of English and Germanic Philology*, LXVI (1967), 532–40.

H. L. Savage, *The Gawain-Poet* (Chapel Hill, 1956).

E. Wilson, *The Gawain-Poet* (Leiden, 1976).

2 The Comic Tradition

R. Axton, *European Drama of The Early Middle Ages* (London, 1974).

M. Bakhtin, *Rabelais and His World*, Engl. trans. (Cambridge, Mass., 1968).

N. F. Blake, 'William Caxton's "Reynard the Fox" and his Dutch Original', *Bulletin of the John Rylands Library*, XLVI (1964), 298–325.

P. Camporesi, *Il Paese della Fame* (Bologna, 1978).

E. K. Chambers, *The Mediaeval Stage*, vol. 1 (London, 1903).

W. M. Hart, 'The Fabliau and Popular Literature', *PMLA*, XXIII (1908), 329–74.

W. Heuser, 'Das Interludium de Clerico et Puella und das Fabliau von Dame Siris', *Anglia*, XXX (1907), 306–19.

W. P. Ker, *English Literature: Medieval* (London, 1912), pp. 167–83.

P. Lehmann, *Die Parodie im Mittelalter* (Munich, 1963).
A. Nicoll, *Masks Mimes and Miracles* (London, 1931), pp. 171–5.
P. Nykrog, *Les Fabliaux*, 2nd ed. (Geneva, 1973).
H. R. Patch, *The Other World* (Cambridge, Mass., 1950).
E. Schroeder, 'Dame Sirith', *Nachrichten von der Gesellschaft der Wissenschaften zu Göttingen*, Phil.-hist. Klasse, IV, n.s. no. 8 1 (1936), 179–202.
H. Waddell, *The Wandering Scholars* (London, 1927).
G. F. Whieler, *The Goliard Poets* (New York, 1949).

3 The World of Romance

1 General

M. Bakhtin, *Esthétique et théorie du roman*, French trans. (Paris, 1978), chapters 3 and 4.
A. C. Gibbs (ed.), *Middle English Romances* (London, 1966), introduction.
D. H. Green, *Irony in the Medieval Romance* (Cambridge, 1979).
L. A. Hibbard, *Medieval Romance in England* (New York, 1960).
G. Kane, *Middle English Literature* (London, 1951), pp. 1–103.
W. P. Ker, *Epic and Romance* (Dover ed., New York, 1957).
E. Köhler, *Ideal und Wirklichkeit in der höfischen Epik* (Tübingen, 1956).
E. Köhler, *Trobadorlyrik und höfischer Roman* (Berlin, 1962).
R. S. Loomis (ed.), *Arthurian Literature in the Middle Ages* (London, 1959).
M. Lot-Borodine, *Le roman idyllique au moyen age* (Paris, 1913).
W. Matthews, *The Tragedy of Arthur* (Berkeley–Los Angeles, 1960).
D. Mehl, *The Middle English Romances of the Thirteenth and Fourteenth Centuries*, Engl. trans. (London, 1968).
D. Pearsall, 'The English Romance in the Fifteenth Century', *Essays and Studies*, n.s. XXIX (1976), 56–83.
C. E. Pickford, *L'Evolution du Roman Arthurien en Prose* (Paris, 1960).
W. W. Rydyng, *Structure in Medieval Narrative* (The Hague–Paris, 1971).
J. Stevens, *Medieval Romance* (London, 1973).
E. Vinaver, *The Rise of Romance* (Oxford, 1971).
H. L. D. Ward, *Catalogue of Romances in the Department of Manuscripts in the British Museum* (3 vols., London, 1893).
A. Wilson, *Traditional Romance and Tale* (Cambridge and Totowa, N.J., 1976).
S. Wittig, *Stylistic and Narrative Structures in the Middle English Romance* (Austin–London, 1978).

2 Specific

A. J. Bliss (ed.), *Sir Launfal* (London, 1960), introduction.
(ed.), *Sir Orfeo* (London, 1954), introduction.
A. C. L. Brown, 'The Grail and the English "Sir Perceval"', *Modern Philology*, XVI (1918–19), 553–68; XVII (1919–20), 361–82; XVIII (1920–1), 201–28, 661–73; XXII (1924–5), 79–96, 113–32.
L. F. Casson (ed.), *The Romance of Sir Degrevant*, E.E.T.S. O.S. no. 221 (London, 1949), introduction.
M. J. Donovan, *The Breton Lay: A Guide to Varieties* (Notre Dame–London, 1969).

D. Everett, *Essays on Middle English Literature* (Oxford, 1955), pp. 28–45 (Layamon).

J. Finlayson (ed.), *Morte Arthure* (London, 1967), introduction.

W. H. French, *Essays on King Horn* (Ithaca, 1940).

K. H. Göller (ed.), *The Alliterative Morte Arthure* (Cambridge, 1981).

D. M. Hill, 'An Interpretation of "King Horn" ', *Anglia*, LXXV (1957), 157–72.

J. P. Oakden, *Alliterative Poetry in Middle English* (2 vols., Manchester, 1930–5).

D. Pearsall, *Old and Middle English Poetry* (London, 1977), pp. 108–13 (Layamon).

G. V. Smithers, 'Story-Patterns in Some Breton Lays', *Medium Aevum*, XXII (1953), 61–92.

T. Turville-Petre, *The Alliterative Revival* (Cambridge and Totowa, 1977).

3 *Sir Gawain and the Green Knight*

Texts

ed. Sir I. Gollancz, E.E.T.S. O.S. no. 210 (London, 1940).

ed. A. C. Cawley and J. J. Anderson (London–New York, 1976).

ed. M. Andrew and R. Waldron (London, 1978).

Bibliography

A. M. Andrew, *An Annotated Bibliography of Writings on the Gawain-Poet* (New York, 1979).

Criticism

L. D. Benson, *Art and Tradition in Sir Gawain and the Green Knight* (New Brunswick, N.J., 1965).

R. J. Blanch (ed.), *Sir Gawain and Pearl: Critical Essays* (Bloomington–London, 1966).

M. Borroff, *Sir Gawain and the Green Knight: A Stylistic and Metrical Study* (New Haven, 1962).

J. A. Burrow, *A Reading of Sir Gawain and the Green Knight* (London, 1966).

W. A. Davenport, *The Art of the Gawain-Poet* (London, 1978).

D. R. Howard and C. Zacher (eds.), *Critical Studies of Sir Gawain and the Green Knight* (Notre Dame–London, 1968).

D. Pearsall, 'Rhetorical "Descriptio" in "Sir Gawain and the Green Knight" ', *Modern Language Review*, L (1955), 129–34.

A. C. Spearing, *The Gawain-Poet: A Critical Study* (Cambridge, 1970).

E. Wilson, *The Gawain-Poet* (Leiden, 1976).

For the University Library, Cambridge, J. A. W. Bennett has published four useful sets of *Supplementary Notes on Sir Gawain and the Green Knight* (1972–3).

4 Dream and Vision

1 On dream poetry, allegory and love poetry

Apart from A. C. Spearing's book quoted in the notes, the following are recommended:

V. Fleming, *The Roman de la Rose* (Princeton, 1969).

A. M. F. Gunn, *The Mirror of Love* (Lubbock, 1952).

C. B. Hieatt, *The Realism of Dream Visions* (The Hague–Paris, 1967).
C. S. Lewis, *The Allegory of Love* (Oxford, 1970; 1st ed. 1936).
P. Piehler, *The Visionary Landscape* (London, 1971).
R. Tuve, *Allegorical Imagery* (Princeton, 1966).

2 *Piers Plowman*

Texts
A version: T. A. Knott and D. C. Fowler (eds.) (Baltimore, 1952); G. Kane (ed.) (London, 1960).
B version: J. A. W. Bennett (ed.) (The Prologue and *Passus* i–vii) (Oxford, 1972); A. V. C. Schmidt (ed.) (London, 1978).
c version: D. Pearsall (ed.) (London, 1978).
A, B and c versions: W. W. Skeat (ed.) (London, 1886).

Bibliography
A. J. Colaianne (ed.), *Piers Plowman, An Annotated Bibliography, 1550–1977* (New York, 1978).

Criticism
Apart from the critical anthologies edited by E. Vasta and S. S. Hussey often quoted in the notes, the following are recommended:
D. Aers, *Piers Plowman and Christian Allegory* (London, 1975).
J. A. Alford, 'The Role of the Quotations in *Piers Plowman*', *Speculum*, LII (1977), 80–99.
J. H. Anderson, *The Growth of a Personal Voice* (New Haven–London, 1976).
R. J. Blanch (ed.), *Style and Symbolism in Piers Plowman* (Knoxville, 1969).
P. Calì, *Allegory and Vision in Dante and Langland* (Cork, 1971).
N. Coghill, 'God's Wenches and the Light that Spoke', in *English and Medieval Studies Presented to J. R. R. Tolkien*, ed. by N. Davis and C. L. Wrenn (London, 1962), pp. 200–18.
J. Coleman, *Piers Plowman and the Moderni* (Rome, 1981).
R. W. Frank, *Piers Plowman and the Scheme of Salvation* (New Haven, 1957).
E. D. Kirk, *The Dream Thought of Piers Plowman* (New Haven–London, 1972).
J. Mann, 'Eating and Drinking in "Piers Plowman"', *Essays and Studies*, n.s. xxxiii (1979), 26–43.
P. Martin, *Piers Plowman: The Field and the Tower* (London, 1979).
C. Muscatine, *Poetry and Crisis in the Age of Chaucer* (Notre Dame, 1972), pp. 71–109.
E. Salter, 'Langland and the Contexts of "Piers Plowman"', *Essays and Studies*, n.s. xxxii (1979), 19–25.
A. V. C. Schmidt, 'Langland and Scholastic Philosophy', *Medium Aevum*, xxxviii (1969), 134–56.

3 *Pearl*
A useful text is printed by A. C. Cawley and J. J. Anderson (eds.), *Pearl, Cleanness, Patience, Sir Gawain and the Green Knight* (London–New York, 1976). *The Poems of the Pearl Manuscript* have been most recently edited by M. Andrew and R. Waldron (London, 1978).

Bibliography

M. Andrew, *An Annotated Bibliography of Writings on the Gawain-Poet* (New York, 1979).

Criticism

Apart from the critical anthology edited by J. Conley, which is often quoted in the notes, the following are recommended:

W. R. J. Barron, 'Luf-daungere', in *A Medieval Miscellany Presented to Eugène Vinaver* (Manchester, 1965), pp. 1–18.

I. Bishop, *Pearl in its Setting* (Oxford, 1968).

R. J. Blanch (ed.), *Sir Gawain and Pearl: Critical Essays* (Bloomington–London, 1966).

W. A. Davenport, *The Art of the Gawain-Poet* (London, 1978).

D. Everett, *Essays on Middle English Literature* (Oxford, 1955), pp. 85–96.

M. P. Hamilton, 'The Meaning of the Middle English *Pearl*', now in E. Vasta (ed.), *Middle English Survey* (Notre Dame–London, 1965), pp. 117–45.

C. Hieatt, '*Pearl* and the Dream Vision Tradition', *Studia Neophilologica*, XXXVII (1965), 139–45.

M. Madeleva, *Pearl: A Study in Spiritual Dryness* (New York, 1925)

C. F. Moorman, *The Pearl Poet* (New York, 1968).

5 The Narrative Collections and Gower

J. A. W. Bennett, 'Gower's "Honeste Love"', in J. Lawlor (ed.), *Patterns of Love and Courtesy* (London, 1966), pp. 107–21.

J. Coleman, *Medieval Readers and Writers* (London, 1981), chapter 3, for the *Vox Clamantis* and other works by Gower.

A. E. Farnham, 'The Art of High Prosaic Seriousness: John Gower as Didactic Raconteur', in L. D. Benson (ed.), *The Learned and the Lewed* (Cambridge, Mass., 1974), pp. 161–73.

J. H. Fisher, *John Gower: Moral Philosopher and Friend of Chaucer* (New York, 1964).

P. J. Gallacher, *Love, the Word, and Mercury* (Albuquerque, 1975).

M. Ito, *John Gower, the Medieval Poet* (Tokyo, 1976).

J. Lawlor, 'On Romanticism in the "Confessio Amantis"', in *Patterns of Love and Courtesy*, pp. 122–40.

D. Pearsall, 'Gower's Narrative Art', *PMLA*, LXXXI (1966), 475–84.

B. Smalley, *English Friars and Antiquity in the Early Fourteenth Century* (Oxford, 1960).

E. W. Stockton, *The Major Latin Works of John Gower* (Seattle, 1962: English annotated translation and introduction).

M. Twycross, 'The Representation of the Major Classical Divinities in the Works of Chaucer, Gower, Lydgate and Henryson' (unpublished Oxford B.Litt. thesis, 1961).

M. Wickert, *Studien zu John Gower* (Cologne, 1953).

6 Chaucer

On Chaucer in general

On Chaucer's life: M. M. Crow and C. C. Olson (eds.), *Chaucer Life-Records* (Oxford, 1966).

On his world: G. G. Coulton, *Chaucer and his England*, with a new bibliography by T. W. Craik (London, 1963).

On his experiences: D. S. Brewer, *Chaucer in his Time*, 2nd ed. (London, 1973), *Chaucer*, 3rd ed. (London, 1973).

On his culture in general: T. R. Lounsbury, *Studies in Chaucer* (3 vols., London, 1892), especially chapter 5, 'The Learning of Chaucer'. On his scientific knowledge: W. C. Curry, *Chaucer and the Mediaeval Sciences* (New York, 1926).

As it is not possible here to cite all the studies dealing with particular aspects mentioned in this study, the following bibliographies are recommended:

E. P. Hammond, *Chaucer: A Bibliographical Manual*, repr. (New York, 1933).

D. D. Griffith, *Bibliography of Chaucer 1908–1953* (Seattle, 1955).

W. R. Crawford, *Bibliography of Chaucer 1954–63* (Seattle and London, 1967).

A. C. Baugh, *Chaucer* (New York, 1968).

L. Y. Baird, *A Bibliography of Chaucer, 1964–1973* (London, 1977).

A bibliography on Chaucer is published annually by the *Chaucer Review*.

Also recommended are the notes contained in the editions of the works edited by W. W. Skeat, *The Complete Works of Geoffrey Chaucer* (7 vols., Oxford, 1894–7); and F. N. Robinson, *The Works of Geoffrey Chaucer*, 2nd ed. (London, 1966; Boston, 1957).

On Chaucer's language

J. D. Burnley, *Chaucer's Language and the Philosophers' Tradition* (Cambridge–Totowa, N.J., 1979).

N. Davis, 'Chaucer and Fourteenth Century English', in D. S. Brewer (ed.), *Geoffrey Chaucer* (London, 1974).

R. W. V. Elliott, *Chaucer's English* (London, 1974).

J. Mersand, *Chaucer's Romance Vocabulary*, repr. (Port Washington, N.Y., 1968).

S. Wenzel, 'Chaucer and the Language of Contemporary Preaching', *Studies in Philology*, LXXIII (1976), 138–61.

On Latin influences

Useful summary in R. L. Hoffman, 'The Influence of the Classics on Chaucer', in B. Rowland (ed.), *Companion to Chaucer Studies* (Toronto–New York–London, 1979), pp. 185–201.

See in particular B. Harbert, 'Chaucer and the Latin Classics'; and P. Dronke and J. Mann, 'Chaucer and the Medieval Latin Poets', in D. S. Brewer (ed.), *Geoffrey Chaucer, Writers and their Backgrounds* (London, 1974), pp. 137–83.

On the French influence

Charles Muscatine, *Chaucer and the French Tradition* (Berkeley and Los Angeles, 1957). J. Wimsatt, *Chaucer and the French Love Poets* (Chapel Hill, 1968).

Further Reading

On the Italian influence

P. Boitani (ed.), *Chaucer and the Italian Trecento* (Cambridge, 1983).
M. Praz, 'Chaucer and the Great Italian Writers of the Trecento', in *The Flaming Heart* (Garden City, 1958), pp. 29–89.
H. Schless, 'Transformations: Chaucer's Use of Italian', in D. S. Brewer (ed.), *Geoffrey Chaucer* (London, 1974), pp. 184–223.

On Chaucer's prosody

Useful summary by R. F. Mustanoja, 'Chaucer's Prosody', in B. Rowland (ed.), *Companion*, pp. 65–94.
In particular: I. Robinson, *Chaucer's Prosody* (Cambridge, 1971).

On Chaucer's poetics, narrative and philosophy in general

B. H. Bronson, *In Search of Chaucer*, 2nd ed. (London, 1965).
R. B. Burlin, *Chaucerian Fiction* (Princeton, 1977).
J. A. Burrow, *Ricardian Poetry* (London, 1971).
D. R. Howard, *The Three Temptations* (Princeton, 1966).
B. F. Huppé and D. W. Robertson, *Fruyt and Chaf* (Princeton, 1963).
R. M. Jordan, *Chaucer and the Shape of Creation* (Cambridge, Mass., 1967).
P. M. Kean, *Chaucer and the Making of English Poetry* (2 vols., London, 1972).
D. Mehl, *Geoffrey Chaucer: Eine Einführung in seine erzählenden Dichtungen* (Berlin, 1973).
D. W. Robertson, *A Preface to Chaucer* (Princeton, 1962).
C. Schaar, *The Golden Mirror* (Lund, 1955).

6.1 The dream poem

On dream poetry, allegory and the Roman de la Rose

S. Battaglia, 'Il "Roman de la Rose" di Guillaume de Lorris', now in his *La coscienza letteraria del medioevo* (Naples, 1965), pp. 417–34.
V. Fleming, *The Roman de la Rose* (Princeton, 1969).
A. M. F. Gunn, *The Mirror of Love* (Lubbock, 1952).
C. B. Hieatt, *The Realism of Dream Visions* (The Hague–Paris, 1967).
H. R. Jauss, *Alterität und Modernität der mittelalterlichen Literatur* (Munich, 1977), pp. 153–307. (Now in English, trans. T. Bahti, 'The Alterity and Modernity of Medieval Literature', *New Literary History*, x, 2 (winter 1979), 181–231.)
C. S. Lewis, *The Allegory of Love* (Oxford, 1936).
R. Tuve, *Allegorical Imagery* (Princeton, 1966).
Paul Zumthor, *Essai de poétique médiévale* (Paris, 1972), pp. 370–8.

On the Book of the Duchess

J. N. Brown, 'Narrative Focus and Function in *The Book of the Duchess*', *Massachusetts Studies in English*, II (1970), 71–9.
M. D. Cherniss, 'The Boethian Dialogue in Chaucer's *Book of the Duchess*', *Journal of English and Germanic Philology*, LXVIII (1969), 655–65.
J. G. Ebel, 'Chaucer's *The Book of the Duchess*: A Study in Medieval Iconography and Literary Structure', *College English*, XXIX (1967), 197–206.

J. Gardner, 'Style as Meaning in the *Book of the Duchess*', *Language and Style*, II (1969), 143–71.

On the House of Fame
J. A. W. Bennett, *Chaucer's Book of Fame* (Oxford, 1969).
S. Delany, *Chaucer's House of Fame, The Poetics of Skeptical Fideism* (Chicago, 1972).
B. G. Koonce, *Chaucer and the Tradition of Fame* (Princeton, 1966).
J. Norton-Smith in his *Geoffrey Chaucer* (London, 1974), pp. 35–61.
P. G. Ruggiers, 'The Unity of Chaucer's *House of Fame*', now in E. Wagenknecht (ed.), *Chaucer* (London, 1959), pp. 295–308.
L. K. Shook, 'The House of Fame', in B. Rowland (ed.), *Companion*, pp. 414–27.
W. O. Sypherd, *Studies in Chaucer's House of Fame* (London, 1907).
W. S. Wilson, 'Scholastic Logic in Chaucer's *House of Fame*', *Chaucer Review*, I (1967), 181–4.
D. H. Zucker, 'The Detached and Judging Narrator in Chaucer's *House of Fame*', *Thoth*, VIII (1967), 3–22.

On the Parliament of Fowls
Apart from the works cited by Bennett and Brewer, the following studies are recommended:
W. Clemen (ed.), *Chaucer's Early Poetry* (London, 1968), pp. 122–69.
D. Everett, 'Chaucer's Love Visions, with Particular Reference to the *Parlement of Foules*', in her *Essays on Middle English Literature* (Oxford, 1955), pp. 97–114.
J. Lawlor, 'The Earlier Poems', in D. S. Brewer (ed.), *Chaucer and Chaucerians* (London, 1966), pp. 39–64.
R. M. Lumiansky, 'Chaucer's *Parlement of Foules*: A Philosophical Interpretation', *Review of English Studies*, XXIV (1948), 81–9.
C. O. McDonald, 'An Interpretation of Chaucer's *Parlement of Foules*', now in R. J. Schoeck and J. Taylor (eds.), *Chaucer Criticism* (Notre Dame–London, 1961), vol. II, pp. 275–93.
I. Robinson, *Chaucer and the English Tradition* (Cambridge, 1972), pp. 49–69.
J. Winny, *Chaucer's Dream-Poems* (London, 1973), pp. 113–43.

6.2 The romance

E. Carton, 'Complicity and Responsibility in Pandarus' Bed and Chaucer's Art', *PLMA*, XCIV (1979), 47–61.
H. M. Cummings, *The Indebtedness of Chaucer's Works to the Italian Works of Boccaccio* (Cincinnati, 1916; repr. New York, 1967).
P. Dronke, 'The Conclusion of *Troilus and Criseyde*', *Medium Aevum*, XXXIII (1964), 47–52.
N. E. Griffin and A. B. Myrick, *The Filostrato of Giovanni Boccaccio* (Philadelphia, 1929).
D. R. Howard, 'Experience, Language, and Consciousness: *Troilus and Criseyde*, II, 596–931', in J. Mandel and B. A. Rosenberg (eds.), *Medieval Literature and Folklore Studies* (New Brunswick, N.J., 1970), pp. 173–92.

D. R. Howard, 'Literature and Sexuality: Book III of Chaucer's *Troilus*', *Massachusetts Review*, VIII (1967), 442–56.

M. E. McAlpine, *The Genre of Troilus and Criseyde* (Ithaca–London, 1978).

C. Manlove, ' "Rooteles moot grene soone deye": The Helplessness of Chaucer's Troilus and Criseyde', *Essays and Studies*, n.s. XXXI (1978), 1–22.

S. B. Meech, *Design in Chaucer's Troilus* (Syracuse, 1959).

A. S. Miskimin, *The Renaissance Chaucer* (New Haven–London, 1975), pp. 156–225.

G. Morgan, 'The Significance of the Aubades in *Troilus and Criseyde*', *The Yearbook of English Studies*, IX (1979), 221–35.

C. A. Owen, 'Mimetic Form in the Central Love Scene of *Troilus and Criseyde*', *Modern Philology*, LXVII (1969), 125–32.

W. G. Provost, *The Structure of Chaucer's Troilus and Criseyde* (Copenhagen, 1974).

D. W. Rowe, *O Love, O Charite! Contraries Harmonised in Chaucer's Troilus* (Carbondale, Ill., 1976).

E. Salter, '*Troilus and Criseyde*: A Reconsideration', in J. Lawlor (ed.), *Patterns of Love and Courtesy* (London, 1966), pp. 86–106.

M. Salu, *Essays on Troilus and Criseyde* (Cambridge and Totowa, N.J., 1979).

A. C. Spearing, 'Chaucer as Novelist' in his *Criticism and Medieval Poetry*, 2nd ed. (London, 1972), pp. 135–56.

J. M. Steadman, *Disembodied Laughter: Troilus and the Apotheosis Tradition* (Berkeley–London, 1972).

E. Vance, 'Merveolous Signals: Poetics, Sign Theory and Politics in Chaucer's *Troilus*', *New Literary History*, X (1979), 293–337.

B. Windeatt, 'The "Paynted Proces": Italian to English in Chaucer's "Troilus" ', *English Miscellany*, XXVI–XXVII (1977–8), 79–103.

6.3 The narrative collection

Since I have discussed criticism on the *Legend* and the *Canterbury Tales* in the text and necessarily given the references in the notes, I refer the reader back to these.

ADDENDA (1984)

Romance

L. C. Ramsey, *Chivalric Romances: Popular Literature in Medieval England* (Bloomington, Indiana, 1983).

Piers Plowman

A. Baldwin, *The Theme of Government in Piers Plowman* (Cambridge-Totowa, N.J., 1981).

M. E. Goldsmith, *The Figure of Piers Plowman* (Cambridge-Totowa, N.J., 1981).

J. Norton-Smith, *William Langland* (Leiden, 1983).

Gower

P. G. Beidler, ed., *John Gower's Literary Transformations in the Confessio Amantis* (Washington, D.C., 1982).

A. J. Minnis, ed., *Gower's Confessio Amantis: Responses and Reassessments* (Cambridge, 1983).

M. Wickert, *Studies in John Gower*, trans. R. J. Meindl (Washington, D.C., 1982).

Chaucer

P. Boitani, *Chaucer and the Imaginary World of Fame* (Cambridge, 1984).

H. Cooper, *The Structure of the Canterbury Tales* (London, 1983).

J. O. Fichte, *Chaucer's 'Art Poetical'* (Tübingen, 1980).

V. A. Kolve, *Chaucer and the Imagery of Narrative* (London, 1984).

A. J. Minnis, *Chaucer and Pagan Antiquity* (Cambridge-Totowa, N.J., 1982).

A. F. Payne, *Chaucer and Menippean Satire* (Madison, Wisc., 1981).

D. M. Rose, ed., *New Perspectives in Chaucer Criticism* (Norman, Oklahoma, 1982).

W. Wetherbee, *Chaucer and the Poets: An Essay on 'Troilus and Criseyde'* (Ithaca and London, 1983).

New Chaucer Companions are due to be published in 1986 by the Cambridge (eds., P. Boitani and J. Mann) and Oxford (various authors) University Presses. Forthcoming is also D. Pearsall's volume on the *Canterbury Tales*.

Index

Index

Index